Policy and Law
in Heritage Conservation

Conservation of the European Built Heritage Series

Series editor: Robert Pickard

A series of books examining a wide range of issues in conservation of the built heritage, published in association with the Council of Europe

1 Policy and Law in Heritage Conservation
  Edited by Robert Pickard

2 Management of Historic Centres
  Edited by Robert Pickard

Forthcoming:

3 Financing the Preservation of the Architectural Heritage
  Edited by Robert Pickard

Policy and Law in Heritage Conservation

Edited by
Robert Pickard

London and New York

First published 2001
by Spon Press
11 New Fetter Lane, London EC4P 4EE

Simultaneously published in the USA and Canada
by Spon Press
29 West 35th Street, New York, NY 10001

Spon Press is an imprint of the Taylor & Francis Group

Typeset in Times New Roman by
Exe Valley Dataset Ltd, Exeter, Devon
Printed and bound in Great Britain by
Bell & Bain Ltd, Glasgow

British Library Cataloguing in Publication Data
A catalogue record for this book is available from the British Library

Library of Congress Cataloging in Publication Data
Policy and law in heritage conservation / edited by Robert Pickard.
    p.   cm – (Conservation of the European built heritage series: 1)
  Includes bibliographical references and index.
  1. Historic preservation – Law and legislation – Europe.   2. Cultural property –
Protecion – Law and legislation – Europe.   3. Historic preservation – Europe.
4. Cultural property – Protection – Europe.   I. Pickard, Robert.   II. Series.

KJC6405.P65 2000
344.4'094—dc21   00–044057

ISBN 0-419-23280-X

Contents

Contributors

Silvia Brüggemann read chemistry in Münster/Westf (1980–83) and history and history of art in Bochum (1984–92). In 1989 she was Magistra Artium of the College of Ruhr–University Bochum and in 1989/90 practised as an architect. In 1992/3 she worked for the Foundation of Weimar Classic. Since then she has carried out private research on building history and in 1995 she founded the 'Büro für Baugeschichte' (private research office on building history) (co-owned with Christoph Schwarzkopf since 1999). She has lectured on building history at Fachhochschule Erfurt between 1994 and 1997. She is the author of various articles on conservation issues.

Marina San Martín Calvo was awarded a Degree in Law from the University of País Vasco, Spain, in 1989 and undertook post-graduate research on European public law at the University of Burgos (1996–8). She has undertaken various professional studies in international law and other areas of law, and has held a number of positions in the field of law at the Common Office of Notification and Impounds of Alava (1990–91), at the Social Welfare Institute of Alava (1992), and as a practising lawyer in Vitoria (1994–97); she has held the position of Assistant Judge in the Court of Appeal of Vitoria in 1989, from 1992 to 1995 and currently. She is also working on a doctoral thesis concerning the international protection of the cultural heritage.

Thérèse Cortembos is an archaeologist and art historian. She is currently Première Attachée in the Directorate General l'Aménagement du Territoireet de Logement (Town and Country Planning and Housing), in the Ministry of theWalloon Region, Belgium.

Juris Dambis graduated from Riga Politechnical Institute, Department of Architecture in 1979 and completed a special course in restoration in 1980. From 1979 to 1989 he was Chief Architect at the Ministry of Culture of the Republic of Latvia. Since 1989 he has been the Head of the State Inspection for Heritage Protection. During this period he has developed the concept of cultural heritage preservation and has been responsible for drafting legislation in this field, subsequently approved by the Parliament of Latvia. He is a Deputy of the Council of the Latvian Institute and a member of the Architects Society Board of Latvia. From 1993 he has been actively involved in the work of the Cultural Heritage Committee of the Council of Europe and has chaired this committee since 1999. Other areas of work have included participation in international conferences, seminars, workshops in Europe and the implementation of several international projects regarding heritage protection in Latvia.

Anne-Mie Draye is a Doctor of Law and currently Course Leader in conservation studies at the Catholic University of Leuven/Louvain and the University of Limburgs Central, Belgium.

Giorgio Gianighian is a graduate in architecture from the Istituto Universitario di Architettura di Venezia, Italy (IUAV) (1970). Since 1973 he has held various teaching and research positions in conservation and restoration at the IUAV and has been Visiting Professor at various universities in Canada, Japan, Israel, and the United Kingdom. He has lectured and participated in many international conferences on conservation and urban restoration. In 1997 he became a Fellow of the Japan Society for the Promotion of Science in Japan. In 1998 he was responsible for the PVS-IUAV working unit for the survey of a historic area in Mostar (Bosnia Herzegovina), via the Aga Khan Trust for Culture and for the World Monuments Fund. He has an international publication record and runs a studio/practice in Venice.

Myriam Goblet is an archaeologist and art historian and is currently Attachée to the Service d'Etudes et Planification, Administration l'Aménagement du Territoireet de Logement (Town and Country Planning and Housing), in the Ministry of the Brussels-Capital Region, Belgium. She is also an expert member of the Council of Europe's Legislative Support Task Force in the field of cultural heritage.

Freddy Joris is a historian and is general administrator of the Walloon Heritage Institute, Belgium.

Seán Kirwan (archaeologist) and **Rachel MacRory** (architectural historian) have worked with the Heritage Policy and Legislation Division of the Department of Arts, Heritage, Gaeltacht and the Islands in Ireland since 1994. The multi-disciplinary Heritage Policy and Legislation Division is responsible for co-ordinating policy formulation and development in the physical heritage area. Their contribution to this book was made with the assistance of Gerry Browner.

Isabelle Longuet is Head of European and International Affairs in the Direction de l'architecture et du Patrimoine (Department of Architecture and Heritage Protection), Ministry of Culture and Communication, France.

Ulla Lunn graduated from the School of Architecture, Royal Academy of Fine Arts, Denmark in 1980. From 1980 to 1986 she was a Planning Officer in Køge Municipal Council. From 1986 to 1992 she was a consultant in the preservation and listing of buildings for the National Agency for Physical Planning and Project Manager for the Department of Physical Planning between 1992 and 1993. In 1993 she became Head of the Information Centre in the Ministry for the Environment and Energy. In 1995 she became Director of the Selsø Castle Museum and subsequently Director of Centre for the Preservation of Buildings, Raadvad Vestsjælland, from 1996 to 1999. From 1999 to 2000 she was Senior Consultant and Head of Section in the Department for Restoration of Listed Buildings in the National Forest and Nature Agency and is currently working in the field of urban renewal in the private sector.

Carsten Lund was awarded a Master of Law from Copenhagen University, Denmark, in 1973 and subsequently obtained post-graduate qualifications in Central Administration Policies (1974) and in Development and Social Planning (1989). Since 1973 he has worked for the Ministry of Environment (and Energy, as it became in 1997) in various agencies including, as Head of Section, the Cultural Heritage Division of the National Forest and Nature Agency between 1985 and 1997. From 1997 he has been a Special Adviser on International Relations in Cultural Heritage matters within the Ministry. He has also been a member of various international expert committees including drafting committees for international conventions in relation to architectural, archaeological and underwater heritage (under the auspices of the Council of Europe, ICOMOS and UNESCO). His international work also includes legislative and cultural heritage management assistance to the governments of Turkey, Hungary, Bulgaria and Slovakia, and membership of the Council of Europe's Legislative Support Task Force in the field of cultural heritage. He also has wide experience of teaching at Copenhagen and Aarhus Universities as well as being a Public Examiner in Law.

Anthony Pace read history and archaeology at the Universities of Malta and Cambridge. He is currently Director of the Museums Department which is responsible for national museums, the management of Malta's World Heritage and archaeological sites as well as providing superintendence services in heritage management. His research interests lie mainly in Mediterranean prehistory, museology and policy development in the heritage sector.

John Pendlebury is a lecturer in the Centre for Research on European Urban Environments, School of Architecture, Planning and Landscape at the University of Newcastle, United Kingdom and is Programme Director for the MA Urban Conservation. Previous experience includes working as Conservation Officer for Gateshead Metropolitan Borough Council and Liaison Officer for the Settle–Carlisle Railway Conservation Area Partnership. Research interests include conservation philosophy and policy and public engagement with conservation and the relationship between conservation and wider socio-political and economic processes.

Robert Pickard completed his first degree in surveying in 1979 and became a Professional Associate of the Royal Institution of Chartered Surveyors (RICS) in the United Kingdom in 1983. He was awarded a PhD in planning law and practice in 1990 and a post-graduate qualification in building conservation in 1992. In 1993 and 1998 he was granted research awards from the RICS Education Trust to investigate European Policy and Law in the field of conservation and to examine Methods of Funding the Preservation of the Architectural Heritage in Europe and North America respectively. Since 1994 he has been an expert consultant to the Council of Europe's Technical Co-operation and Consultancy Programme in the field of cultural heritage and in 1997 became a member of its Legislative Support Task Force (which he co-ordinated on secondment to the Council of Europe between 1998 and 2000). He was a member of the Education Committee of the Association of Conservation Officers between 1995 and 1998 (subsequently the Institute of Historic Building Conservation – Member since 1998). He has lectured on property investment, town and country planning and conservation issues; edited and authored books and articles and participated in several international conferences and events on conservation issues; and is external examiner to the MA in Historic Conservation at Oxford Brookes University/University of Oxford.

Jean-Pol Van Reybroeck is a civil engineer and architect, and is a University Professor at the Catholic University of Leuven/Louvain. He is also Deputy General Administrator of the Walloon Heritage Institute, Belgium.

Saskia Richel-Bottinga studied art history and English at the Universities of Utrecht and Amsterdam. Since 1975 she has worked for several museums and cultural organizations. In 1986 she became public relations officer for the Department for Conservation in The Netherlands, with law and regulations as her specializations. She has written articles on the subjects of art history and cultural heritage, as well as translating publications in this field.

Christoph Schwarzkopf was awarded a Diploma of the College of Architecture and Building in Weimar in 1989 and subsequently practised as an architect. From 1990 to 1994 he was Conservation Officer at the Thüringian Land Office for the Preservation of Historical Monuments. In 1994/5 he worked for the Foundation for Thüringian Palaces and Gardens. From 1995 to 1999 he was employed in the Büro für Baugeschichte (private research office on building history). Since 1999 he has been a self-employed architect and co-owner of the Büro für Baugeschichte, together with Silvia Brüggemann. He is a member of ICOMOS and since 1996 he has lectured on the Preservation of Monuments at the Bauhaus University in Weimar. He has written a number of articles on conservation issues.

Manana Simonishvili trained as a lawyer at Tbilisi State University, specializing in international law. She has worked with the Ministry of Culture as Head of the Legislative Service since 1992 and also with the Fund for the Preservation of Cultural Heritage of Georgia since 1997. She has been responsible for the co-ordination of Georgian activities for the reform of laws in the field of cultural heritage in relation to a programme of assistance organized by the Council of Europe and is a member of different commissions in the field of culture. In 1999 she undertook a period of probation in the law firm 'Nautas Dutilh' in The Netherlands.

Josef Štulc studied architecture and architectural history, following which he began work for the Czechoslovakian State Institute for the Care of Historic Monuments and Nature Conservancy in 1969, where he held various posts until being appointed head of the department for the care of the national heritage in 1982. In 1987 he was *de facto* suspended from his post because he refused to join the Communist Party and to work politically for them. During the November 1989 revolution he was elected as spokesman of the Civic Forum co-ordinating activities for a non-violent overthrow of the communist regime and the restoration of democracy in the country. After the revolution he initiated and co-authored manifestos for the preservation and care of the cultural heritage. He was appointed director of Státní ústav památkové péèe (the State Institute for the Preservation of Cultural Heritage in the Czech Republic) in 1990. He lectures and has written many articles on the care of historic buildings, and is co-author of the *ABC of Cultural Heritage in Czechoslovakia*, 1985. He is a member of the Club for Old Prague.

Peter Verhaegen is an architect and town planner. He is currently employed in the Land Management Department at the Ministry for the Brussels-Capital Region, Belgium.

Jean-Marie Vincent is Head of the Inspection Générale de l'Architecture et du Patrimoine (Department of the Inspection of Architecture Heritage Protection) in France.

Foreword

In fulfilment of its aims of achieving a greater unity within member states, in order to facilitate economic and social progress, the Council of Europe has for more than 25 years pursued a vigorous programme of cultural co-operation and celebration. During 1999–2000 this has been evidenced through the campaign 'Europe, A Common Heritage' to which this book makes an important contribution.

High-level political debate within the Council of Europe's Committee of Ministers and the European Conference of Ministers responsible for the cultural heritage has led to the adoption of a number of key texts and associated recommendations. These have been translated into practical programmes of technical consultancy, assistance, training, and raising of public awareness. Through its own experience and through being able to draw on an enormous resource of accumulated expertise within the member states, the Council of Europe is uniquely equipped to help national, regional, and local authorities to tackle complex issues of enhancing, managing and preserving the cultural heritage in an integrated way.

To move from questions of principle to issues of practical application, it is essential to act within the framework of agreed guidelines and standards that are allowed to evolve through changing circumstances. The *Granada* and *Malta Conventions* set out principles for the protection of the architectural and archaeological heritage respectively. These conventions provide an authoritative basis, achieved through consensus, upon which individual countries and organizations are able to move forward on the basis of commonly agreed assumptions and conclusions.

As the number of states that have acceded to the *European Cultural Convention* has grown to forty-seven it has become necessary not only to promote common values in the management and enhancement of the cultural heritage but also through cultural co-operation to develop the common mechanisms that allow us to preserve, celebrate and enrich the heritage for the benefit of those who follow. This study provides a reflection of the current progress within thirteen member states towards meeting the values embodied within the conventions and other recommendations for the protection of this common heritage.

JOSÉ MARÍA BALLESTER
Head of the Cultural Heritage Department
Directorate of Culture and Cultural Heritage
Council of Europe

Robert Pickard

Introduction

Context of the study

At the Second Summit of the Council of Europe, held in Strasbourg in October 1997, the Heads of State and Governments of the member states of the Council of Europe reaffirmed the importance attached to 'the protection of our European cultural and natural heritage and to the promotion of awareness of this heritage'. An Action Plan adopted by the summit decided on the need to launch a campaign on the theme *Europe, A Common Heritage* to be held 'respecting cultural diversity, based on existing or prospective partnerships between government, education and cultural institutions, and industry' (Fig. 1.1).

This campaign, which was launched in September 1999 and intended to last for one year, takes place 25 years after the European Architectural Heritage Year (1975). The 1975 campaign marked the start of the Council of Europe's activities that gave rise to the *European Charter of the Architectural Heritage* and subsequently the *Amsterdam Declaration* of the Congress on the European Architectural Heritage which introduced the concept of 'integrated heritage conservation'. This concept is now enshrined in the founding texts, the Convention for the Protection of the Architectural Heritage of Europe (1985) (the *Granada Convention*) and the European Convention on the Protection of the Archaeological Heritage (revised) (1992) (the *Malta Convention*).

The contracting parties to the Granda Convention have undertaken to make statutory measures to protect the architectural heritage which would satisfy certain minimum conditions laid down in the convention. These included the maintenance of inventories, the adoption of integrated conservation policies and the setting up machinery for consultation and co-operation in various stages of the decision-making process (including with cultural associations and the public), the provision of financial support and

Fig. 1.1 Europe – A Common Heritage: a Council of Europe Campaign 1999–2000 (Campaign Logo).

the fostering of sponsorship and of non-profit making associations, and the promotion of training in the various occupations and craft trades involved in the conservation of the architectural heritage. In addition, the convention endorsed the need for European co-ordination of conservation policies including the exchange of experiences.

The Malta Convention, replacing the earlier 1969 convention on the archaeological heritage, took note of the fact that the growth of major urban development projects made it necessary to find ways of protecting this heritage, including the provision of legal and financial machinery. The contracting parties to the 1992 revised convention have undertaken to devise supervision and protection measures and to promote an integrated policy, public awareness and co-operation between the parties and to facilitate the pooling of information.

It is within this context that this study has been developed in association with the Cultural Heritage Department of the Council of Europe. While the department's Technical Cooperation and Consultancy Programme has developed a programme of legislative and administrative assistance through its Legislative Support Task Force to support countries in meeting the objectives of the conventions, including the provision of *Guidance on the Development of Legislation and Administration Systems in the Field of Cultural Heritage* (Council of Europe, 2000), there has been little published evidence of the extent of implementation of the provisions contained in the

Granada and Malta Conventions or of the commonality of legal and policy provisions adopted by different countries in Europe.

The aim of this study, therefore, is to examine some key themes and objectives for the protection of the immovable heritage within a representative sample of European countries. Since 1993 the Council of Europe has increasingly focused its attention on assisting new member states, particularly the countries of central and eastern Europe. In light of this, a sample of thirteen countries has been chosen from different the regions of Europe. The sample includes countries of the west that have already made significant progress in developing systems for the protection of the immovable heritage and a smaller group to illustrate the situation in countries currently in the process of reforming their legislation and institutions in this field.

Undoubtedly, practice will vary between each country under consideration particularly as some of the countries are still in the process of developing laws and policies for the protection of the architectural and archaeological heritage. This can be reflected in Tables 1.1 and 1.2 which identify the countries and the position, as at the commencement of the year 2000, as to whether they have signed, ratified or brought into force the provisions of the Granada and Malta Conventions.

From Table 1.1 it can be seen that the representative sample of countries chosen for this study have largely signed, ratified and brought into force the provisions of the Granada Convention. It should be noted that Latvia and Georgia have been working to reform cultural heritage and associated legislation since 1996, with the assistance of the technical experts of the Legislative Support Task Force operated through the Cultural Heritage Department of the Council of Europe and the reform process for both countries is expected to be completed by 2001.

Table 1.1 The Granda Convention (European Treaty Series no. 121) – adoption of provisions by member states under study

Member state	Date of signature	Date of ratification	Date of entry into force
Belgium	21/10/1985	17/09/1992	01/01/1993
Czech Republic	24/06/1998		
Denmark	03/10/1985	23/07/1987	01/12/1987 T
France	03/10/1985	17/03/1987	01/12/1987 T
Georgia	17/09/1999		
Germany	03/10/1985	17/08/1987	01/12/1987
Ireland	03/10/1985	20/01/1997	01/05/1997 R
Italy	03/10/1985	31/05/1989	01/09/1989
Latvia			
Malta	20/06/1990	20/06/1990	01/10/1990
The Netherlands	03/10/1985	15/02/1994	01/06/1994 RT
Spain	03/10/1985	27/04/1989	01/08/1989
United Kingdom	03/10/1985	13/11/1987	01/03/1988 RT

R=reservations T=territorial declaration

Table 1.2 The Malta Convention (European Treaty Series no. 143) – adoption of provisions by member states under study

Member state	Date of signature	Date of ratification	Date of entry into force
Belgium			
Czech Republic	17/12/1998		
Denmark	16/01/1992		
France	16/01/1992	10/07/1995	11/01/1996
Georgia	17/09/1999		
Germany	16/01/1992		
Ireland	16/01/1992	18/03/1997	19/09/1997
Italy	16/01/1992		
Latvia			
Malta	16/01/1992	24/11/1994	20/05/1995
The Netherlands	16/01/1992		
Spain	16/01/1992		
United Kingdom	16/01/1992		

The situation regarding the Malta Convention is clearly not as advanced, as that of the Granada Convention due to the more recent date of the convention (Table 1.2). However, it should be emphasized that there has been progress on agreeing some common goals for the protection of archaeological heritage as indicated by the fact that Belgium, Denmark, France, Germany, Italy, Malta, Spain and the United Kingdom all signed, ratified and brought into force the provisions of the first European Convention on the Protection of the Archaeological Heritage dating from 1969.

Themes of the study

For the purposes of this study the authors of the individual country chapters were drawn towards a number of themes to reflect issues that may reveal the commonality, or otherwise, of approaches to the protection of the architectural and archaeological heritage. The campaign, *Europe, A Common Heritage*, provides the appropriate vehicle and timing for the study.

The issues which follow are examined in relation to these themes bearing in mind that the interpretation and relative importance of the individual issues will differ according to the different countries and the state of progress in adopting policy and legal approaches that have been advocated by the conventions. Moreover, it must be remembered that legal tools are not the only means to resolve issues and that there is a plethora of guidelines, recommendations and charters which have been developed in an international context.

Definition of the heritage

The objective under this heading is derived from article 1 of the Granada Convention and article 1 of the Malta Convention: to consider the broad definitions of monuments, buildings, and areas of the architectural and archaeological heritage that are selected for protection and preservation in each country, and the measures adopted to signify their particular importance or 'criteria for selection'.

The Granada Convention defines the architectural heritage according to three groups: monuments (buildings and structures), groups of buildings, and sites – those having conspicuous historical, architectural, archaeological, artistic, scientific, social or technological interest. In the Malta Convention it is specified that the archaeological heritage 'shall include structures, constructions, groups of buildings, developed sites, movable objects, monuments of other kinds as well as their context, whether situated on land or under water'. There is no specific 'interest' category except to say that this heritage should be regarded as 'a source of European collective memory and as an instrument for historical and scientific study'.

It is accepted that terms used in practice may vary from those used in the conventions, although they may still be within the spirit of the definitions contained therein.

Moreover, while the conventions do not specify an association (although it may be inferred) with the natural environment, where historic/cultural landscapes, parks or gardens are associated with the immovable heritage these may be relevant. In this context, the ICOMOS Florence Charter on Historic Gardens has considered such associations and such an association may be relevant to current laws and other policy statements that define these monuments.

In defining architectural assets to be protected, the full extent of the protection regime is a relevant consideration. This raises the question as to whether the protection regime applies, in the case of buildings, to the whole building or just to its external envelope, and whether other attached structures or other objects within the associated grounds or some other defined protection zone exists, and whether 'fixtures' or movable items within the building or monument are included within the protection regime. Moreover, the 'setting' or context of an architectural monument may have relevance. In relation to complexes, groups of buildings, or ensembles or sites different criteria for the scope of protection, as compared to single monuments, are likely to apply. Furthermore, other factors considered within the scope of protection may include items such as open spaces, parks, gardens, trees, ancient street patterns, other monuments and whether area-based forms of protection exist according topographically definable units such as historic quarters, reserves or other area-based protection mechanisms.

In relation to the archaeological heritage the Malta Convention considers the need for the protection of monuments and areas and the creation of archaeological reserves. The convention also considers the idea that sites defined for protection may include those where perceived remains, as well as known remains, exist. This then raises the question whether the mechanism for defining items to be protected covers the situation of the discovery of archaeological remains by chance (in other words, whether there is a system of mandatory reporting or mandatory protection).

For both the architectural and archaeological heritage the criteria for selecting monuments for protection, as well as the existence of any levels or categories of protection, may vary within law or policy statements.

Identification of the heritage

Article 2 of the Granada Convention and articles 2, 6, 7 and 8 of the Malta Convention suggest appropriate approaches and requirements for the use of inventories and recording methods for the immovable heritage. These have been further developed in the Core Data Index to Historic Buildings and Monuments of the Architectural Heritage (1995) (and further highlighted in Recommendation R (95) 3 of the Committee of Ministers of the Council of Europe on 'co-ordinating documentation methods and systems related to historic buildings of the architectural heritage) and the Core Data Standard for Archaeological Sites and Monuments (Council of Europe, 1999) or other methods for recording the immovable heritage.

The methods and procedures established and operated to identify and record the immovable heritage through schedules, lists, inventories or other records will vary according to the documentation and information that is included within the record, whether the record has a legislative basis, and as to how it is used in the protection and preservation process. The assembly of records may also be by different methods: by survey of towns or areas or by national survey.

For some countries the inventory may have been completed many years ago and the process will just require updating but for other countries the process of identifying the heritage may have only been partially completed. As knowledge about the heritage is not static there is likely to be a process by which records are updated.

The preservation and protection of the heritage

Articles 3, 4 and 5 of the Granada Convention highlight the need for statutory protection measures including appropriate supervision ansd authorization procedures to cover positive and negative aspects of preservation policy including repair, reuse, control over alteration or demolition of buildings and otherwise to prevent damage. The reuse of existing buidings is another consideration particularly in terms of how a new use may impact upon the historic integrity of an architectural asset. Moreover the idea of finding new uses for buildings is now widely accepted as a positive way of preserving the architectural heritage. This, however, will be dependent upon the flexibility of a structure to accept change without damage integrity and also on questions of financial viability.

In the case of ensembles, groups of buildings and sites the regulation of development that may have an impact upon the setting or character of such assets, articles 3, 4 and 6 of the Malta Convention consider the need for authorization and supervision of excavation and other archaeological activities including research work, the conservation and maintenance of the archaeological heritage (preferably *in situ*), rescue archaeology, and for the storage of remains which have been removed from their original location.

The movable nature of the archaeological heritage is further considered in articles 10 and 11 in terms of the need to control the illicit traffic of assets. The importance of this issue internationally is also reflected in the Council of Europe's *European Convention on Offences relating to Cultural Property* (1985a) (the 'Delphi Convention' has still not come into force for want of enough ratifications, despite being a highly comprehensive legal document), and the UNESCO (Paris) Convention (1970), European Community Directive of 1993 and the Unidroit Convention (1995).

The problems associated with the development of sites of potential or known archaeological remains is considerd in article 5 of the Malta Convention which deals with the integrated conservation of the archaeological heritage (see below).

Conservation philosophy

The foundation for an internationally accepted conservation philosophy is the ICOMOS *Venice Charter* of 1964 although the writings of John Ruskin and William Morris and others in the nineteenth century and the Athens Charter of 1931 have helped to devlop concepts and have influenced thinking in many different countries. Other charters and recommendations such as the ICOMOS AUSTRALIA *Burra Charter* and the ICOMOS *Nara Document* on 'Authenticity' have further helped to provide a basis for developing a philosophy of approach to conservation activity which conventions, through their legalistic nature, are less able to do. These have undoubtedly influenced the formulation of laws and, perhaps more appropriately, policies and attitudes. However, there remains considerable differences in terms of approach and also in the interpretation of terms such as 'conservation' and 'restoration' and therefore in the relative importance between conservative repair, maintenance and restoration, and furthermore, in the ethics of reconstruction as a perceived avenue for protection heritage policy.

Many countries have developed their own guiding principles and standards and this study will provide evidence of attitudes and interpretations of internationally accepted approaches in this context, reflecting in turn the traditions and cultural identity in the preservation formulae adopted by particular countries.

Sanctions and coercive measures

The use of legal provisions for enforcing preservation requirements and criminal sanctions are considered in article 9 of the Granada Convention and articles 3 and 10 of the Malta Convention.

In this context the present study examines the procedures that have been adopted to safeguard against the removal or dismantling of protected monuments including enforcement measures and powers to stop unauthorized work, obligations placed on owners to carry out work or powers to carry out work in the event of a failure to fulfil legal obligations. Other procedures may be utilized to ensure the restoration of damaged or removed items through unauthorized work, sanctions in the form of monetary fines or other criminal proceedings and other coercive measures such as powers of expropriation to safeguard the long-term preservation of monuments.

Integrated conservation

The need for integrated conservation policies for the protection of the architectural and archaeological heritage within the system of land-use planning, and the regulation of new buildings or other development within areas of cultural importance are considered in articles 7, 10, 11, 12 and 13 Granada Convention and article 5 of the Malta Convention. This integrated approach is now well developed in some countries but in others the process is just beginning. Nevertheless, the conventions advocate the necessity to manage this process and particularly to manage the capacity and acceptable limits of change within historic environments through authorization procedures.

Moreover, the concept of 'action' or specific preservation plans has been advocated not just for single monuments, but also for ensembles, groups of buildings or for larger historic areas or quarters including positive action to improve the physical environment surrounding buildings. This necessity extends to the treatment of roads, footpaths, ornamental features, and natural features including open spaces, historic parks, gardens or landscapes associated with the architectural heritage.

For the archaeological heritage it has become increasingly necessary in recent years to combat the increasing scale of development activity which can impact on both known and perceived remains. The idea of early consultation between archaeologists, town and regional planners and developers – whether they be public or private – is now being advocated. The need to ensure possibilities for the modification of development plan policies, the allocation of time and resources for appropriate scientific study of the impact of development proposals, and for the conservation *in situ* (wherever possible) of elements of the archaeological heritage found in the course of development activity are subjects of a proposed Code of Best Practice by the Council of Europe. This draft code is expected to be approved during the year 2000.

The planning system has an important role in promoting the restoration and maintenance of the architectural heritage and in safeguarding the archaeological heritage.

It may further include policies to assist in the regeneration of the historic built environment including sustainable strategies for long-term protection and rehabilitation strategies linked to historic buildings. In this respect, and as the Amsterdam Declaration made plain, state, regional or local authorities have an important role to play.

From a legal and policy point of view there may be a divergence between different countries as to whether the system of preservation derives from cultural heritage legislation or planning legislation. The study will reflect upon this and other relevant issues: the ultimate goal being to ensure that there are well-balanced strategies for protection, conservation and enhancement of assets of the immovable heritage. Co-ordination and communication between different authorities at all levels is important in this context.

Financial resources, funding mechanisms and the regeneration of historic environments

The need for financial resources in the form of grant aid (subsidies), loans, sympathetic taxation measures or other sources to assist in the preservation of the cultural built heritage, with particular reference to the reuse of buildings and the financing of archaeological research and conservation, are advocated by article 6 Granada Convention and article 6 Malta Convention. State, region, and municipal involvement or even 'joint venture' approaches may be necessary to create appropriate administrative measures. The implementation of strategies to discover the relative condition and use of monuments and to find solutions to problems of vacancy, disrepair or other threats to the immovable heritage is also of importance. Further consideration may be required of specific management policies to regenerate or preserve sites and areas through character appraisals, management/conservation plans and other management tools that may involve partnerships between private and public sectors.

A wide range of intervention measures have been utilized in different countries including the use of revolving funds, rehabilitation programmes, legal measures to ensure works, subsidized survey and maintenance programmes, measures to promote sponsorship and patronage, and the implementation of public and private sector partnerships.

The responsibility of owners and developers to pay for the necessary action may require the interaction of financial instruments with intervention and administrative measures. The effectiveness of such measures and their relative shortcomings will be judged in national, regional or local terms. Nevertheless one overriding factor tends to remain in all countries: there are never sufficient resources from the public purse to deal with all the heritage needs. This is increasingly so in the case of the new states of central and eastern Europe that are still in the process of moving towards establishing market-based economies. The private sector, foundations and other mechanisms are needed to provide funding and assist in developing strategies.

This co-ordinated form of approach was recommended in the Amsterdam Declaration and the ICOMOS Washington Charter for the Conservation of Historic Towns.

The role of agencies and specialist organizations

The role of state and other voluntary or private agencies involved in the promotion of conservation is highlighted in article 14 of the Granada Convention and article 9 of the Malta Convention.

In some countries, state institutions or agencies have been established to oversee legal and policy issues. In some instances this role is devolved to regional or local levels. The interaction of such agencies with the different the levels of authority responsible will provide an insight into the practical operation of integrated conservation and land-use policies.

Voluntary and charitable associations and other bodies connected with heritage preservation may also have a significant role in raising public consciousness, in educating and in identifying good practices. In some instances they may have a quasi-official role in the protection of the immovable heritage.

Education and training
The need for specialist training and the education of professionals or craft workers involved in conservation activities is advocated in articles 15 and 16 of the Granada Convention and article 12 of the Malta Convention. It has also been given a high degree of importance by ICOMOS and other international and non-governmental bodies.

In some countries there are clear standards for the professional qualifications which are required in order to work in the conservation field. In other countries requirements are less strict: it is the training of all professionals who may be associated with this field, and not just those from architectural or archaeological backgrounds, that is important.

The great debate about conservation philosophy in recent years perhaps presents the overriding consideration. This is particularly important in the context of craft trades and traditional techniques, many of which have been lost during the twentieth century due to the advent of modern materials and techniques and also for political reasons. The extent to which these techniques can be revived by legislative means is debateable. However, the pursuance of a public policy which encourages education and training is important. This is particularly relevant in the current climate when the world is moving towards ensuring sustainable policies. Moreover, in the case of architectural heritage it is generally accepted that building activity associated with the existing built environment predominates over new development work. The preservation and use of non-renewable resources, whether it be for cultural, economic or other functional reasons, is a sustainable action in itself, and is aided by the creation and safeguarding of employment for this purpose.

Summary
Through the themes outlined in this chapter, this study seeks to provide evidence of the different legal and policy mechanisms utilized for the protection of the immovable heritage within Europe. The Granada and Malta Conventions are important guiding principles for this purpose even if they are not specifically mentioned in national policy. The analysis of the individual countries and a final review of the sample will offer an assessment of how advanced current mechanisms are and what on-going problems remain to be managed in order to safeguard the 'common heritage'.

References
Council of Europe (1969): *European Convention on the Protection of the Archaeological Heritage* (6 May 1969) (ETS, No. 66).
Council of Europe (1975): *Amsterdam Declaration*: Congress on the European Architectural Heritage, 21–25 October 1975.

Council of Europe (1985): *Convention for the Protection of the Architectural Heritage of Europe* (3 October 1985) (ETS, No. 121) (Granada Convention)

Council of Europe (1985a): *European Convention on Offences relating to Cultural Property* (23 June 1985) (Delphi Convention).

Council of Europe (1992): *European Convention on the Protection of the Archaeological Heritage (revised)* (16 January 1992) (ETS, No. 143) (Malta Convention)

Council of Europe (1995): *Core Data Index to Historic Buildings and Monuments of the Architectural Heritage.*

Council of Europe (1999): *Core Data Standard for Archaeological Monuments and Sites.*

Council of Europe (2000): *Guidance on the Development of Legislation and Administration Systems in the Field of Cultural Heritage*, Legislative Support Task force, Technical Co-operation and Consultancy Programme, Cultural Heritage Department.

ICOMOS (1964): *International Charter for the Conservation and Restoration of Monuments and Sites* (Venice Charter).

UNESCO (1970): *Convention on the Means of Prohibiting and Preventing the Illicit Import, Export and Transfer of Ownership of Cultural Property* (Paris Convention)

Unidroit Convention (1995): Convention on Stolen or Illegally Exported Cultural Objects, 24 June 1995.

Myriam Goblet, Thérèse Cortembos,
Peter Verhaegen, Anne-Mie Draye,
Jeal-Pol Van Reybroeck and Freddy Joris

Belgium

Introduction

The legal framework for the conservation of the immovable heritage in Belgium has undergone major changes in the last two decades of the twentieth century.

Prerogatives in the cultural sphere shifted from the national level to the Communities (French and Flemish) in 1980, and powers and responsibilities as regards monuments and sites were entrusted to the regions by the special law on state institutional reforms of 8 August 1988. No federal competence remains, therefore, where the immovable heritage is concerned (see the section below on 'The role of public and specialized bodies').

The result has been that the Walloon, Flemish and Brussels-Capital Regions have inherited that responsibility within their respective Regional Spatial Planning and Housing authorities. Their task is to bring existing legal provisions into line with the new institutional situation and the characteristics of their heritage. The most recent international conventions, charters and recommendations also steer new legislation towards applying the main principles of 'integrated heritage conservation'.

At present, the three regions have legislation that is slightly different in terms of substance and completely autonomous in terms of its application.

In the *Walloon Region*, the Decree of 18 July 1991 on monuments, sites and excavations, amended by the Decrees of 1 July 1993 and 1 April 1999, is incorporated in the Walloon Spatial and Town Planning and Heritage Code (CWATUP), revised 6 May 1999. The first part of the decree gears the Walloon Code to regional competence for heritage. It supplements the provisions on planning permission and authorizations to sell, by lots, town planning certificates and sanctions. The second part lays down specific provisions for monuments, sites and excavations. It now constitutes Volume III of the CWATUP (Articles 185–237). In this way the Walloon Region

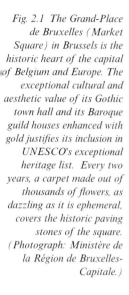

Fig. 2.1 The Grand-Place de Bruxelles (Market Square) in Brussels is the historic heart of the capital of Belgium and Europe. The exceptional cultural and aesthetic value of its Gothic town hall and its Baroque guild houses enhanced with gold justifies its inclusion in UNESCO's exceptional heritage list. Every two years, a carpet made out of thousands of flowers, as dazzling as it is ephemeral, covers the historic paving stones of the square. (Photograph: Ministère de la Région de Bruxelles-Capitale.)

has equipped itself with the legal machinery required, in principle, for optimal management of the architectural heritage in keeping with its built and natural environment.

In the *Brussels-Capital Region*, the architectural heritage is governed by the Ordinance (regional law) of 4 March 1993 on conservation of the immovable heritage (see Figs 2.1–2.6). Contrary to the Walloon Region, this ordinance is not pooled with legislation on spatial and urban planning within a single code. Consequently, its effects and obligations are applied concurrently with any other legislative texts applicable to the immovable heritage, and notably with the Ordinance of 29 August 1991 laying down principles for Spatial and Urban Planning.

This system also prevails in the *Flemish Region*. The key texts governing monuments and sites have not been blended into a whole as in the Walloon Region. The Law of 7 August 1931 on the conservation of monuments and sites, amended by the Decree of 14 July 1993, exists alongside the Decree of 3 March 1976 which regulates the protection of monuments and urban and rural sites, amended by the Decrees of 22 February 1995 and 8 December 1998, and also the Decree of 16 April 1996 on the protection of sites. There are also other more specific or technical regulatory texts such as the Order of 17 November 1993 laying down general requirements for the conservation and maintenance of monuments and urban and rural sites.

Since the first law (of 7 August 1931), governing immovable heritage conservation policy overall, a similar type of legal instrument has been adopted in Belgium. This is a general law (decree or ordinance) laying down the main thrusts of conservation policy on the one hand, and orders setting out provisions for the application of specific or technical aspects on the other hand. The advantage of this arrangement is its flexibility in a

Fig. 2.2 The Belgian Parliament (1778–1783) is part of the Royal quarter whose unified urban composition with its (neo)-classical emphasis is still appreciated today. The Parliament, which symbolically faces the Royal Palace, has ruled the destiny of the Belgian people ever since they won their independence in 1830. (Photograph: Robert Pickard.)

Fig. 2.3 The former department store 'Old England' in Brussels (1899). This echoes both the change in commercial practice in the capital, with the emergence of department stores, and the development in building techniques that enabled Art Nouveau architects to show their skills in the revolutionary treatment of large glass floors supported by delicate and intricate ironwork. (Photograph: Robert Pickard.)

changing situation: aspects likely to be modified on a regular basis are covered by orders which can be easily amended from a legal point of view, while the main principles set forth in the basic legal text enjoy greater stability.

Since there are three separate legislative provisions currently in existence – sometimes using the same term to describe different concepts (for example, 'protection list' means quite different things in Wallonia and in Brussels) – this section on Belgium will not systematically describe the existing situation in all three regions. Instead it will focus on some of the best practices in this or that region, depending on the themes studied. (The choice of this working method is the reason for resorting to several authors from the country's three regions.)

Definition of heritage

A considerable proportion of the texts constituting the three regional legislations on the immovable heritage is devoted to definitions and protection measures. Since there are fairly substantial differences between these acts, this section will be limited to the Walloon Region which has a protection system that is both effective and compliant with the European conventions.

Heritage categories

The Walloon Decree of 18 July 1991 lists the main heritage categories as defined in the conventions on the architectural heritage (Granada) and the archaeological heritage (Malta), while supplementing them to take account of specific regional heritage features.

Fig. 2.4 The St Michael and St Gudula Cathedral in Brussels, a masterpiece of thirteenth-century Gothic art, has just been returned to its former glory after long and thorough restoration work. This has been the setting, over the centuries, for the Royal family's great events such as the funeral of King Baudouin or, more recently, the wedding of the heir to the throne, Prince Philip of Belgium, to Princess Mathilde. (Photograph: Ministère de la Région de Bruxelles-Capitale.)

Four heritage categories are identified:

- monuments;
- groups of buildings;
- sites;
- archaeological sites.

The definition of 'monument' includes architectural and sculptural works. In practice it may also include historic parks and gardens containing important architectural elements, in line with the ICOMOS Florence Charter on Historic Gardens.

The Walloon Decree also elaborates on the Malta Convention, by defining 'archaeological sites' as 'any piece of land, rock formation, monument, group of buildings or site on which archaeological assets have been, are or are presumed to be present'. In this way it settles the question of overlapping between this category and the other three, as well as the question of the presence (past, present or presumed) of archaeological assets on an archaeological site. This latter distinction takes tangible form in the use of two different systems of identification and protection.

Selection criteria

Selection criteria establishing the heritage value of the assets to be conserved correspond to those laid down in the Granada Convention. These

Fig. 2.5 The Théâtre Royal de la Monnaie in Brussels (1819–1973) enjoys international renown for the quality of its operas. The building was completely renovated and raised by several metres in 1985 in response to the modern need of theatre production. The association of neo-classical with contemporary styles, both inside and out, is a gamble that has paid off. (Photograph: Ministère de la Région de Bruxelles-Capitale.)

are historical, archaeological, scientific, artistic, social and technical criteria. The criterion of *landscape* completes the list. Whichever heritage category is concerned, the selection criteria remain identical.

In practice, though, the criteria are still fairly difficult to apprehend. Since any edifice could meet one of them, it is necessary to consider the 'qualitative' or 'representative' aspects of the assets in question. Moreover, the styles in vogue and the subjective view resulting from the personality (training, taste) of the official responsible for this kind of study are bound to have some influence on selection and the weighting given to the different criteria. So if a heritage policy pursued by a region or a state is to be coherent, substantial ongoing collaboration is required between the different protagonists, so that divergences in interpretation can be ironed out.

Scope of protection

The current protection system can be applied on an *à la carte* basis to the different elements of the architectural heritage, according to their heritage value. It may be the whole of a building that is protected, or perhaps just the frontage or the roof, for example. In some cases, structural and/or decorative interior elements of a building will be protected without this necessarily entailing the protection of the exterior. Under the legislation it is possible to protect the installations and movable items associated with a building (as they are considered as statutory immovable items).

The land on which a legally protected monument stands is generally protected by the establishment of a *protection zone* around it. Protected groups of buildings, sites and archaeological sites may also benefit from protection zones preserving views of or from them. Any works modifying

Fig. 2.6 The Royal St Hubert Gallery in Brussels (1847) is the most remarkable covered arcade in Belgium and is among the largest in Europe (200 metres long and 15 metres high). Reproductions of paintings by the great Belgian surrealist, René Magritte, fall under the gaze of curious passers-by, alongside the Gallery's original windows and façades which have been restored down to the last detail. (Photograph: Ministère de la Région de Bruxelles-Capitale.)

those protection zones are now governed by special requirements as to integration and harmony with the protected asset. The scope of the protection zones is defined on a case by case basis (there are no fixed 50-metre zones around monuments); it is always identified with the protected asset on a map appended to the protection order.

Types of protection
There are three types of heritage protection: inventory, safeguard and listing.

The inventory
The *inventory* is used for all assets presenting heritage value from one or several standpoints. In Wallonia, during its preparation since 1966, the *Inventory of architectural heritage* has not been backed by orders published in the official journal, the *Moniteur belge*. Nevertheless, the wealth of information recorded makes it an important instrument for *ad hoc* protection and a benchmark for framing a planning-and-development-integrated conservation policy (see section below on 'Identifying and recording the heritage').

In parallel to this fundamental inventory, inventories organized by themes are used to guide choices in terms of classification/recording in a more detailed manner in order to avoid the pitfalls mentioned in relation to the 'Selection criteria' above.

The safeguard

The *safeguard* constitutes a legal means of temporary and emergency protection (valid for 1 year) for assets threatened with demolition or radical alteration. Although the procedure involved is a simple one, the impact of the safeguard is nevertheless very similar to the listing. This emergency protection measure can be extremely useful, especially in areas where the heritage is subject to pressure from property developers. It should be noted that the Walloon concept of a safeguard differs from that of the Brussels-Capital Region, where it forms an intermediate protection level between the inventory and the listing.

The listing

The listing concerns the most interesting and significant items of heritage having a regional and international value. Although procedurally it is the most restrictive and unwieldy legal means of definitive protection (see Figure 2.7 summarizing the procedure), it does give entitlement to grants and tax relief (see the section below on 'Financing resources and funding mechanisms'). This type of protection is identical in all three regions. Listed assets, furthermore, are identified by symbols on building frontages. The internationally recognized royal blue and white symbol is 'customized' according to the region: the Walloon cockerel, the Brussels *fleur-de-lis* and the Flemish lion.

Exceptional immovable heritage

It should be further noted that in the Walloon Region (only), 133 listed assets have been on a 'list of *exceptional immovable heritage* of the Region' since 1993. These assets benefit from special support measures and also upgraded regional grants covering up to 95 per cent of the total cost of restoration. The assets concerned are selected according to objective and specific criteria, largely drawn from the *Convention Concerning the Protection of the World Cultural and Natural Heritage* (UNESCO, 1972). Belgium's ratification of the convention in 1996 has resulted in the addition to the 'World Heritage List' of several exceptional assets in the three regions.

Identifying and recording the heritage

Essentially an inventory is a tool that may be used by local authorities for the management of heritage assets.

The first inventory of the immovable heritage in the Walloon Region has now been completed and published, as a series of 36 volumes. The aim at the outset (1966) was threefold: knowledge of the architectural heritage, protection, awareness-raising.

The first aim – knowledge of the architectural heritage – has been fulfilled to a large extent. The recording of some 30,000 buildings in Wallonia, identified via a systematic search of the region, is a work of capital importance. The other two aims, protection and awareness-raising, have been pursued over the years through a whole host of tools and convergent activities, and nothing has ever been completed in these areas.

*Figure 2.7 Classification
Procedures in the Walloon
Region*

Start of procedure

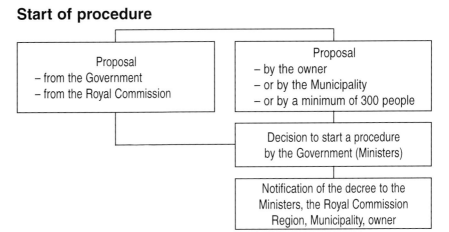

Final classification

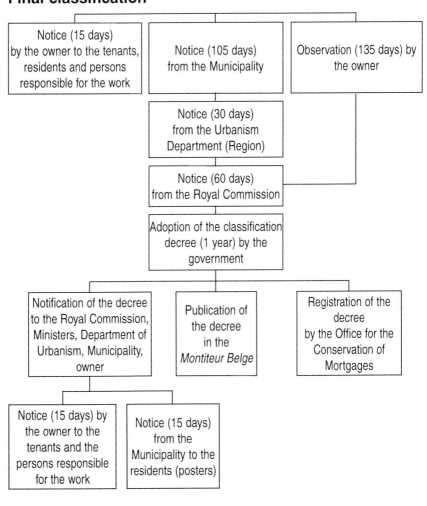

At the end of the 1980s, it became increasingly apparent that there was a need to update the series begun in 1966 although the whole of Wallonia had not been covered. But it was not until 1998 that the updating scheme could be put into practice, thanks to the commitment of ten additional art historians assigned solely to that task for the whole of Wallonia.

Reasons for updating the inventory

Following the incorporation of heritage affairs in the Directorate-General for Spatial Planning and Housing, and also in the wake of changing attitudes in this field, it became vital to update the heritage inventory devised 30 years ago so that it can be truly useful in improving our living environment.

The incorporation of heritage services in the Directorate-General for Spatial Planning and Housing in 1989–90 highlighted, in very practical terms, a whole series of problems concerning the management of the assets that had been recorded. Heritage legally recognized as such by decree but not benefiting from listing or a grant ought to be clearly identified in town planning applications, which are mandatory for any conversion or building work.

Furthermore, the concept of heritage has become considerably broader than it was 30 years ago: architecture of recent centuries and more technical typologies have been recognized; the value of groups of buildings has become apparent. Thus it is inconceivable today to devise a new inventory using a strictly *ad hoc* method, although this must remain the basis. Our heritage is made up of 'cultural landscapes' which we must seek to identify and above all publicize so that the general public can appreciate it to the full. This is a challenge which the Walloon Region wishes to take on, after covering its entire territory with a 'first inventory' of a more *ad hoc* nature.

Unfortunately, during the past 30 years, some assets have been modified or have sadly disappeared.

Finally, information technology has become an indispensable tool for managing our living environment.

Archiving architectural heritage data is obviously one of the important tasks facing a Heritage Service: knowledge of our heritage is a cornerstone of our thinking and thereby our judgement and action. Indeed the relevant Order stipulates that the 'Executive authorities shall prepare, *update* and publish an inventory of the architectural heritage'. Updating the inventory is therefore an obligation.

At the same time, a more pragmatic management tool must be devised to cater for the everyday practices of the policy-makers and administrators responsible for heritage. But over and above these *ad hoc* demands, it is proving increasingly necessary to work upstream of any project.

With the gradual decentralization of the Communes, a number of planning tools have had to be introduced. The *communal development plan*, providing guidelines, and the town planning regulations have a direct effect on cultural landscapes and on the built heritage in particular. For the Communes, which are still centralized, the communal development plan, regulatory in its effect, governs the future evolution of sometimes very sizeable areas. Similarly, sector plans, which define land-use on a regional scale, are decisive in the evolution of an area's landscape. Other decisions affecting spatial development are taken by bodies responsible for managing the environment, transport or agriculture for example. Finally, in operational terms, there are a number of financial incentives to encourage communes and private owners to undertake projects and works directly affecting the built landscape.

The new inventory cannot ignore all these aspects if it is to reflect the real situation and not remain a 'parallel system'. It must therefore pursue the objective of identifying the specific heritage features of a Commune, taking a global, forward-looking view, so that these may be taken into account in the thinking process and the preparation of documents that will govern our built landscapes. It must provide a heritage 'situation report', a point of view on a given area, which may serve as a point of reference for all actions touching on the living environment.

The new inventory
What does this new inventory entail?

Scope
The new inventory it remains first and foremost a field inventory. The first areas reviewed are naturally enough those explored the first time round, i.e. from 1966 to 1976. Present work is organized in sections, dealing with each individual Commune, from prospecting to publication. It covers a far more diverse range of heritage, the chronological limits having been substantially shifted if not all but abolished. However, it is still selective, as it does not record all the buildings in the 1,425 ancient communes of Wallonia. Therefore, it is not neutral since it evaluates with a view to selection.

The inventory also establishes a hierarchy between heritage assets. It pinpoints four categories of asset: assets listed as having exceptional heritage value; assets simply listed; assets worth protecting; and finally – the largest category – assets mentioned in the inventory. The use of the word 'asset' is quite deliberate here, in that the approach is not limited to individual buildings but also covers groups of buildings, the built heritage that makes up the essential part of our towns and villages.

Form
In the new inventory, *all of the assets* will be covered by a European-standard computerized data-sheet, giving exact topographical references as per the land register for built-up centres and the 1/10,000-scale map elsewhere. Obviously, this will make it possible to have selective lists for each Commune and each category of assets and, later, to situate assets on a digitized land register. The aim is to be able to cross-reference all these 'sensitive layers' relating to the living environment.

Aims

The gradual introduction of these instruments is clearly aimed at more integrated and effective management of the built and natural heritage of the Walloon Region, benefiting from fuller knowledge of all the issues. While these technical tools are truly indispensable, they alone will not be enough to attain all the goals set. That is why, for the new inventory, there is provision for a strategy of communication and awareness-raising aimed at the general public in each local authority area. This strategy will principally be developed according to three methods: establishing contact prior to and during inventory work; holding a conference/debate on the Commune's heritage once the field work is complete; issuing a well illustrated publication on the Commune's heritage.

It is certain that, if the exercise is not to be dragged out over 20 years, 'sacrifices' must be made. The inventory's content must be geared, therefore, to the needs and objectives of planning. This obliges us to take greater account of the inter-play between the landscape, economic and social history and morphology of the territory inventoried, so that its strong points are emphasized. This 'reading' of human geography focuses attention on the importance of the whole, as much as it does on the different heritage typologies whose significance often stretches beyond architectural interest alone.

The inventory is intended to be more than a tool for enhancing knowledge and management; it is a link in a chain designed to move across partitions by all possible means, to be a bridge between objects and people, in the context of a given territory. The aim is also to forge informal contact between local communities and decision-makers, serving to channel and develop a flow of ideas promoting a 'living environment' heritage.

The preservation and protection of the heritage

There are numerous initiatives and legal provisions linked to the conservation and use of the immovable heritage in *all three regions*. In this context, the most important issues concern the procedures for granting permission for work on listed assets together with a few special support measures positively influencing heritage conservation.

Granting of permission

Work to maintain and restore legally protected monuments is subject to particularly strict and complex regulations in all three regions. With the exception of works which do not in any way alter the external or internal appearance of the asset or the materials or characteristics giving rise to its protected status, all operations require permission.

In the Flemish and Brussels Regions, two separate authorizations are required: planning permission from the Commune or the Regional Spatial Planning Department and a Government order authorizing the work, prepared and served by the Monuments and Sites Service.

In the Walloon Region, a single building permit is required, subject to the opinion of the Heritage Division of the Regional Spatial Planning

Department and of the Royal Commission on Monuments and Sites. This single-track procedure is the most successful in terms of the application of the principle of 'integrated conservation' (see Figure 2.8 summarizing the planning permission).

Technical support

Few property owners are consummate restoration experts. Many are enthusiastic enough but feel out of their depth or take the wrong course of action out of ignorance. In all three regions, many efforts are made to actively assist owners, in particular by producing specialized information booklets.

A fundamental body, in terms of architectural heritage maintenance policy, has existed in the Flemish Region for several years: *Monumentenwacht Vlaanderen* (Monument Watch in Flanders) is an association whose membership is open to all owners of monuments, protected or not (Binst and Hoflack, 1996). At the owner's request, the association produces a complete, detailed situation report of the monument (state of conservation, work to be carried out, etc.). The members also receive regular updates on monuments policy, together with specialist publications concerning heritage maintenance. The association emphasizes monument maintenance as an alternative to more radical and above all more costly restoration. The information is structured so as to give owners an important and judicious instrument for planning the work necessary to maintain their property.

In contrast to private owners, the assistance required by the associations active in the heritage field is primarily of an administrative nature. The *Vlaamse Contactcommissie Monumentenzorg* (Flemish contact committee for monument maintenance) was created to serve as a forum for these associations. It co-ordinates the interests and also the problems of local groups taking an interest in monuments. Its functional structure permits substantial, rapid exchanges of information between the member associations. It is their common partner in dialogue with the different levels of authority.

Administrative support

There are limits to the functional possibilities of a monument and they are essentially determined by the monument itself. The possible uses to which a monument may be put can sometimes be completely at odds with the planning requirements of the surrounding area. In the Brussels-Capital Region, the problem has been overcome by not imposing any *a priori* functional requirements for protected buildings. Unlike other buildings strictly assigned to a function, monuments may have another function on the condition that the characteristics giving rise to its protected status are maintained (see also the section below on 'Integrated conservation').

Only in exceptional circumstances do the authorities responsible for the heritage take steps to restore a monument instead of the owner. It is only in cases where the owner takes no action whatsoever for the maintenance of his or her monument that the Brussels authorities can take action. This can

Prior notice (heritage)

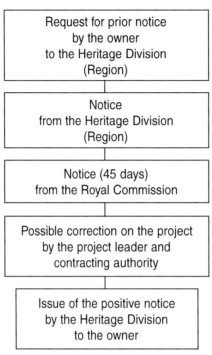

Fig. 2.8 Authorization procedures for work done on classified goods in the Walloon Region

Construction permit (urbanism)   and then . . .

be either by carrying out maintenance work or by expropriation regardless of whether the owner is a private body or a public body (depending on the legal point of view) (see also the section below on 'Sanctions and coercive measures').

Financial assistance

The financial consequences of restoration are still a source of dissatisfaction for many owners. Under the system of public funding for conservation it is nevertheless possible to recover 50 per cent of expenditure on average, for both private and public owners. This system is an incentive for maintaining buildings and, only secondly for restoring them. The underlying idea is that the right kind of maintenance work at the right time obviates the need for far more costly restoration. The system comprises both direct support through cash allowances and indirect funding through tax relief (see 'Financial resources and funding mechanisms', below).

The financial resources available will doubtless always be too small. That is why it is fundamental that optimal use be made of the funds at hand. For this reason, it is disappointing to see that urgent maintenance work carried out by one public authority must sometimes be interrupted pending the payment of road taxes levied by another public authority. It is obvious that the different bodies concerned must collaborate fully so that all monies invested in restoration can actually be used for the intended purpose.

Information

These different measures can be successful only if they match the existing needs and if they are widely known. Providing information on legislation and support measures, to architects and designers as well as owners, is therefore a basic priority. Various historic cities have long understood this and have their own heritage departments. These departments can provide detailed information both to the authorities and to citizens.

It is a pity that this trend is not universal. In many small towns of great heritage value, there is a total lack of knowledge and policy in the heritage sphere. The monuments in these places, being fewer in number, are more vulnerable than in the larger cities. The function of the Deputy Burgomaster responsible for monuments often seems more ceremonial than anything else. In such cases, heritage maintenance hinges on the motivation of the building's owner alone. For this reason, an adequate heritage policy should be drawn up and at least one official should be responsible for restoration problems.

Conservation philosophy

In *all three regions*, the owner and/or occupier of a protected monument or of property located within a protected group of buildings has an obligation to maintain it *through necessary conservation or maintenance work*. This positive obligation is in addition to restrictions forbidding any disfigurement of, damage to, or destruction of, the protected asset. Obligations of maintenance and restrictions are equally valid whether protection is provisional or definitive.

In the Flemish Region, the obligation of maintenance is set forth in an 'implementing order' of 17 November 1993. This contains a whole series of obligations relating to the exterior of a monument/property located within a protected group, to the interior of a protected monument and also to the conservation of the ground and vegetation within the perimeter of a protected group. There are also specific requirements governing certain categories of protected assets, such as organs, chimes, church bells and clocks, assets significant for industrial archaeology and funereal monuments.

In the Brussels-Capital and Walloon Regions, no general orders concerning the obligation of maintenance have been approved; only 'special conservation requirements' may be noted in the actual protection orders, an option which also exists in the Flemish Region but which is rarely used, given the existence of the general Government order. Special conservation requirements relate to the maximum level of maintenance of the features giving rise to protected status and are therefore quite case specific.

In the Walloon Region, the relevant authorities are responsible for running checks on the obligation of active 'maintenance of one's property through conservation work'; if they find that work must be carried out to this end, the authorities notify the owner. The owner must apply for planning permission for the necessary conservation work within ninety days of receiving such notification. He or she may also apply for a government grant for the work. An owner not having begun the necessary work in the year when planning permission was given or in the year of notification of a promise of grant, should this be subsequently received, is deemed not to have fulfilled his obligation of maintenance.

In all three regions, the obligation of maintenance is linked to the possibility of obtaining *grant aid*. This possibility exists only for listed monuments and not for property located within a listed group – a situation often regarded as unfair. In the Flemish Region, a distinction is drawn between the maintenance allowance and the restoration allowance. In the other two regions, maintenance and restoration are covered by the same system of grants (see 'Financial resources and funding mechanisms', below). Nevertheless, in all three regions the authorities prefer a policy of *preventive protection*. Maintenance is regarded as a basic condition of building protection and is preferred to restoration – which is a very onerous step with major (and indeed excessive) consequences for a monument.

In practice it is rare for all conservation work to be carried out on the basis of a cash allowance or grant: in every case there is a choice to be made, taking account of the value of the monument, its state and the resources available. The state of the monument may prompt a decision to restore the elements of value still present or to replace them, choosing modern materials where appropriate. Such decisions are taken on a case-by-case basis by heritage service architects and town planning service directors who have substantial powers in this area. However, missing elements of value may be replaced only when certain conditions are fulfilled, as expressly set out in the ICOMOS Venice Charter (1964).

In parallel to grants, there is provision for *partial tax relief* for work carried out on monuments, sites or property located within definitively protected groups (discussed in the section 'Financial resources and funding mechanisms', below).

For the first time in Belgium and since 1 November 1993, the 're-siting of a protected monument' has been formally enshrined in a provision in the 'ordinance' (regional law) on conservation of the architectural heritage in force in the Brussels-Capital Region. Re-siting is prohibited without prior, written authorization from the Government or its representative. Even in the absence of a formal text, the same conditions are applied in the other two regions, via planning permission which is subject to the duly formulated opinion of the official responsible for heritage matters.

Sanctions and coercive measures

In the respective acts in force in Belgium's three regions, sanctions may be imposed on owners and other parties, such as officials who draw up formal documents, architects and entrepreneurs. The main thrusts of the system for ensuring that buildings are maintained in the three regions are as follows.

Monuments and groups of buildings

Administrative sanctions

First, the owners of monuments and buildings forming part of a protected group, and any third parties concerned, are liable to *administrative sanctions*. These apply to work begun before the necessary permit has been obtained or carried out contrary to the conditions stipulated in a permit. Such work may be stopped by several authorities, such as the Ministries responsible for heritage, Burgomasters, certain criminal investigation department officers and also officials empowered by the Minister.

From the heritage point of view, a 'preventive' sanction of this kind is far preferable to the 'reparation' measures described below. However, it does imply regular checking, covering all monuments and protected groups, which is not always possible for the officials assigned by the Ministries responsible for heritage. In practice, the other authorities having the power to stop illegal works almost never use them.

Criminal sanctions

Besides administrative sanctions, there are also *criminal sanctions*. Those persons that, through their acts, by carrying out work or by some other means, infringe the legal provisions set forth in the decrees in force, are liable to a prison sentence or fine. In practice, criminal sanctions are limited to fines, which may be for:

• failing to comply with the regulations on maintaining and conserving provisionally or definitively protected assets;

- carrying out work on a monument or property located within a pro-visionally or definitively protected group without a permit or not in accordance with the conditions stipulated in the permit;
- modifying the use of their (provisionally or definitively) protected property without the necessary prior authorization (not applicable in the Flemish Region where there are no regulations governing modification of use);
- failing to notify their tenants or the users of their property of potential or definitive protection measures.

Sanctions (fines again in such cases) may be imposed on the officials responsible for drawing up formal documents. In most cases this applies to notaries who, during the transfer of a monument or of property located within a provisionally or definitively protected urban or rural site, fail to request a town planning certificate or to indicate in the deed of transfer that the monument or property in question enjoys provisional or definitive protection. In two of the three Belgian regions, more severe sanctions are provided for, not only for notaries who fail to fulfil their obligations but also for any individual dealing with heritage in the course of his profession who commits a punishable offence.

Additionally, any criminal sentence handed down will order that the *assets in question be restored to their previous state*, at the offender's cost, without prejudice to damages and interest. Upon expiry of the deadline for restoration set in the judgment, the Minister or his appointed representative may have the work carried out at the expense of the owner. If the asset can no longer be restored to its previous state, alteration work may also be ordered.

Previously the courts tended to be indulgent towards owners and third parties breaching heritage regulations. Complaints from the relevant authorities were often filed with no further action being taken. If proceedings were instituted, minimal sanctions were imposed, often in the form of a conditional sentence. Fortunately, there has been a clampdown towards the end of the 1990s, at both first instance and appeal levels.

It should be noted that in the Flemish and Brussels-Capital Regions, where heritage legislation is not incorporated in the regional and town planning code, a breach of heritage legislation often implies a breach of town planning legislation. This means that the authorities responsible for town planning may also institute proceedings.

Archaeological assets
In the Flemish Region there is a specific decree governing the protection of archaeological assets. It also sets out sanctions and other coercive measures comparable to the measures described above. *Work* carried out contrary to protection regulations, without prior permission or not in accordance with the conditions stipulated therein, *may be stopped* by criminal investigation officers, the governor of the province, the burgo-master and officials appointed by the Government.

There is provision in the decree, without prejudice to the application of the criminal code or other punishments established by other laws or decrees, for *prison sentences and fines* for numerous offences, including:

- carrying out excavations or earthworks with a view to researching or examining archaeological monuments without or in breach of an authorization;
- opposing an order permitting the temporary occupation of land with a view to carrying out excavations of recognized public interest;
- failure to take the necessary conservation and protection measures on the part of the owner or the user of the asset.

An official drawing up the formal documents who fails to record the asset concerned in a deed benefits from protection under the decree on protection of the archaeological heritage.

Any sentence will furthermore entail *the restoration of the protected assets or of their external appearance* at the expense of the offender, without prejudice to any compensation payable. Upon expiry of the deadline set in the judgment, the minister or his appointed representative may have the work carried out at the expense of the offender.

In the Brussels-Capital Region, specific legislation on protection of the archaeological heritage has not yet been established. Such protection is possible, though, via the ordinance on conservation of the immovable heritage. In the Walloon Region, protection of archaeological assets, like the protection of monuments and groups of buildings, comes under the Walloon Spatial and Town Planning and Heritage Code (CWATUP). In both these regions, the sanctions described in the sub-section above on 'Monuments and groups of buildings', also apply to archaeological assets.

Integrated conservation
Since its formulation some 25 years ago, the idea of 'integrated heritage conservation' has slowly found its way into mentalities and behaviour. At the time, the trans-sectoral and multi-disciplinary nature of integrated conservation did not sit at all well with the working habits of the different protagonists involved or the new division of powers and responsibilities resulting from the first institutional reforms of the state. For this reason, its application was – and still is – a source of considerable debate. Even so, the main principles of integrated conservation have now been largely accepted and transposed into the regulatory texts of the three regions.

This section will focus on the Brussels-Capital Region since the architectural heritage and spatial and town planning are strongly interlinked. In the area of spatial planning, the Brussels-Capital Region has four types of plan: the Regional Development Plan, the Regional Land Use Plan, Communal Development Plans and Specific Land Use Plans.

The development plans serve a strategic and informational purpose (non-binding); their aims are (re-)defined with every change of government. The land-use plans are based on the aims of the development plans; they are binding and applicable for as long as they remain unchanged.

Development plans

The *Regional Development Plan* – which deals with the different development sectors from a spatial viewpoint – attaches importance to heritage conservation. Its main thrusts confirm the determination of the public-service decision-makers in Brussels to pursue a major policy aimed at protecting the heritage, living environment and landscapes as well as embellishing the city. This policy is seen as vital to successfully achieving the economic, social and cultural objectives of urban development.

Of the ten strategic thrusts of the Plan's 'city project', two directly concern the architectural heritage in the broad sense of the term:

- reinforcing the metropolitan centre (historic heart of Brussels) and the old centres (the region's nineteen communes) which are bearers of local identity;
- strengthening the identity of the city by emphasizing urban landscape elements (existing or to be created) which contribute to the city's beauty.

For this purpose, the Plan maps a number of elements making up the urban fabric which are to be respected, so that the region's living environment can regain an overall composition. These elements include: structural areas (historic routes and roadways, major urban and landscape axes, major park areas, canal axis), the points of entry into the city, the exceptional architectural heritage and the 'Perimeters offering cultural, historic, aesthetic interest or embellishment'.

In terms of 'implementation', three priorities are laid down:

- the redevelopment of structural areas and the development of the points of entry into the city;
- increased protection and enhancement of the archaeological and architectural heritage;
- protection of green areas and the creation of a 'green network' throughout the territory.

These priorities are transposed and focused on a local scale in the *Communal Development Plans* of the nineteen communes making up the Brussels-Capital Region. These identify the heritage in precise terms and set out the enhancement measures to be taken.

Land-use plans

The *Regional Land-Use Plan* (a new plan was submitted to public inquiry in 1999) transposes in principle the main options set out in the Regional Development Plan. Provisions concerning the architectural heritage appear in written and mapped form alongside provisions concerning the allocation of the region's different zones. The objective of maintaining a 'functional mix' throughout the Brussels territory, advocated by the Regional Land-Use Plan, must not run counter to heritage conservation aims.

A general provision applicable to all the zones listed in the plan is designed to avoid damage to the architectural heritage arising from its disuse. For any building listed as safeguarded (in its entirety or in respect of its main elements) it is possible to derogate from the use provided for in the plan, as long as the impossibility of maintaining its original use without modifying its architectural design is proven.

In addition, there is a specific provision aimed at preserving the value of certain remarkable groups of buildings, mapped as 'Perimeters offering cultural, historic, aesthetic interest or embellishment'. Within these peri-meters, any changes to the dimensions or appearance of frontages visible from public areas are subject to special requirements arising from the need to protect or enhance the cultural, historical or aesthetic value of those perimeters and foster their embellishment, including through the quality of the architecture and any installations to be mounted.

A similar determination to preserve and improve the quality of the urban landscape is manifested in structural areas.

Finally, several specific provisions concerning green belt zones are aimed at protecting the natural environment and species as well as the aesthetic and landscape qualities of these zones. They extend to the prohibition of any construction not directly necessary to the use of such zones.

The provisions of the Regional Land-Use Plan are supplemented at a local level by *Specific Land-Use Plans*. These set out provisions concerning the heritage in one or several districts of the communal territory. Some of these provisions (like those concerning the 'Perimeters offering cultural, historic, aesthetic interest or embellishment') were already present in the 'Sector Plan' which in the 1970s established land-use in Brussels, and this testifies to a certain tradition of collaboration between heritage conserv-ationists and developers.

Town planning regulations

Like spatial planning, town planning plays a fairly important role in architectural heritage protection policy.

Some provisions of the *Regional Town Planning Regulations* concern the heritage directly. The aim of these regulations, established 3 June 1999, is to ensure *inter alia* the salubrity, conservation, solidity and beauty of buildings, thoroughfares and their adjacent surroundings, as well as their safety, notably against fire and flooding. For this reason, all works on existing or future buildings must comply with the regulations as regards siting, dimensions and work carried out on ground floors, frontages and the surrounding land. These provisions can have a very real impact on the quality of public areas and groups of buildings which do not enjoy legal protection, as well as major urban perspectives.

The *Zone-specific Communal Town Planning Regulations* also contribute to the protection of groups of buildings which have heritage value. At present, there are three sets of zone-specific regulations supplementing the Regional Regulations since 'guarantees should be afforded for protection of the architectural and urban heritage, in order to preserve the desired state of spatial planning and the aesthetics of buildings and groups of buildings visible from public areas'.

Having established the boundaries of its application and its general aims, each set of zone-specific regulations indicates:

- the overall characteristics to be preserved (dimensions, frontages, roofing, materials);
- specific elements to be supervised (openings, projecting items, decorative items, etc.);
- provisions for the protection of buildings of great architectural quality (whether listed or not).

Planning procedures

Planning procedures also apply the principles of integrated conservation in that they use trans-sectoral advisory committees. The *Ordinance of 29 August 1991 laying down principles for Spatial and Urban Planning* established advisory committees at regional and communal level.

At the communal level, *joint advisory committees* comprise representatives (i) of the communal authorities and the regional planning authorities, (ii) of monuments and sites and (iii) from the spheres of environmental and regional development.

These multi-disciplinary committees are tasked with issuing opinions prior to the granting of permission and the adoption of communal plans or regulations. For example, the representative of the monuments and sites section must therefore give his or her opinion on any planning application concerning new or existing edifices. To lend greater weight to this opinion, he or she may request an opinion from the Royal Commission on Monuments and Sites, as this can be highly influential with the decision-makers in Brussels.

This right of inspection is exercised at the regional level by the *Regional Development Committee*. A representative of the Royal Commission on Monuments and Sites sits on this committee, together with representatives from the different regional advisory bodies, and gives his or her opinion on the various regional plans and regulations.

In conclusion, it may be said that spatial and urban planning procedures back up and even add to the existing provisions in the Ordinance of 4 March 1993 on conservation of the immovable heritage. Some monuments and sites not (yet) enjoying legal protection in heritage terms can be protected as a result of the planning and administration tools available to regional planners. However, there must be a genuine desire for co-operation between heritage conservationists and planners if these regulatory provisions are to be truly effective.

Financial resources and funding mechanisms

There are two main means of heritage financing in Belgium: direct financing in the form of grants and indirect financing in the form of tax relief.

Grants for classified heritage

Each region has specific orders defining the levels of grants available and the criteria on which they are awarded. Given the noteworthiness of the policies in each of the three regions, the current trends for all three regions will be described.

At present, only listed architectural heritage may benefit from regional grants when they are maintained and restored. This means that inventoried and safeguarded assets are not eligible. Similarly, grants may not be awarded for listed groups of buildings, sites and archaeological sites, with the exception of privately owned listed groups of buildings in the Brussels-Capital Region and listed sites in the Flemish Region.

The type of *maintenance and restoration works* usually eligible for grants are generally those aimed at:

* protecting the monument against damage caused by the elements (weather, fire, etc.) or by man (vandalism, theft);
* maintaining and repairing the different structural elements vital to the conservation of the monument (paintwork, coatings, joints, beams, doors, windows, etc.);
* restoring elements justifying the protection and enhancement of the monument (lighting, etc.);
* maintaining, repairing or installing equipment governing access to the monument (security systems, etc.) and replacing elements damaged beyond repair;
* installing certain equipment which will aid the conservation of the asset and its distinctive elements (central heating, electricity, air conditioning).

In order to make the reassigning of a listed monument to another use economically competitive with new construction, the Walloon Region also subsidises the adaptation of the main fabric to a new use. All the preliminary studies, measurements, investigations and installations necessary to compiling the work specifications are also subsidised. The grant is therefore calculated in relation to the total approved expenditure (preliminary studies, works and architect's fee).

The regions, provinces and communes on the territory where the asset is located contribute to such grants. Contributions from the provinces and communes are mandatory in the Flemish Region whereas, in the Walloon and Brussels Regions, contributions are 'desirable' but relatively rare.

The *levels and criteria* for grants vary greatly from one region to another. They can be summarized as follows.

* In the *Walloon Region*, the rate of subsidy depends on the 'quality' of the asset. It is often 60 per cent and can reach 95 per cent if the asset is

on the list of exceptional architectural heritage of the region. In the latter case, works can be spread over several years and benefit from 'framework agreements' guaranteeing the continuity of grants. The region pays its share of the grant directly to the entrepreneur as and when the work progresses.

- In the *Brussels-Capital Region*, grants depend on the kind of work, the category of owner and the income of private owners. The rates of subsidy reach 25 per cent for preliminary studies and restoration work, 40 per cent for maintenance work and 40 per cent for restoration work on property where the owners have a low income or form a non-profit association active in heritage conservation.
- In the *Flemish Region*, the awarding of grants for restoration varies according to the category of owner (private, public, religious, association or educational), the revenue generated by the property and the extent of public access. The region's share varies from 25 per cent to 60 per cent, the province's share from 7.5 per cent to 30 per cent and the commune's share from 7.5 per cent to 15 per cent. If contributions are forthcoming from region, province and commune, the total subsidy will cover between 40 per cent and 90 per cent of the total restoration cost.

The maintenance of listed monuments and sites is also encouraged in the Flemish Region by the payment of incentives calculated using a coefficient on a sliding scale from 40 per cent to 25 per cent for works costing under 30,000 euros. The incentives paid therefore range between 1,250 and 10,000 euros. The advantage of this system is that the planning permission procedure is made far easier, which encourages owners to opt for regular maintenance rather than onerous and costly restoration work.

Tax relief for listed heritage

At present there are various means of tax relief – federal and regional – designed to assist private owners in conserving their heritage and also to incite taxpayers in general to participate in heritage programmes.

Tax relief for owners of listed property
Deduction of certain conservation charges (Article 104 sub-paragraph 1.8 of the Income Tax Code).

The owners of listed property which is accessible to the public and not rented out may deduct from their taxable net income half of the maintenance and restoration costs not covered by subsidies, up to a ceiling of 25,000 euros. They must have applied for the necessary permission from the regional department responsible for heritage affairs and have carried out the works in accordance with established practice. This fiscal measure, first applied in 1986 and broadened in 1997, is by far the most efficient as regards Belgium's listed immovable heritage.

Exemption from the advance on income tax payable on immovable property ('précompte immobilier') (Article 39 of the Ordinance of 4 March 1993 on conservation of the immovable heritage of the Brussels-Capital Region).

Cadastral income from listed property not rented out or commercially exploited (within the meaning of Article 20 paragraph 1 of the Income Tax Code) is exempt from the advance on income tax payable on immovable property (an annual tax levied on all real estate property in Belgium). Obviously, this measure applies solely to the listed monuments and sites in the Brussels-Capital Region.

Tax relief for taxpayers participating in heritage projects
Inclusion of sponsorship costs as deductible advertising costs (Article 49 of the Income Tax Code).

Subject to certain conditions, patronage or sponsorship costs are considered as advertising costs fiscally deductible as business expenses.

Deduction of cash donations (Article 104 sub-paragraph 1.3 of the Income Tax Code).

Cash donations of at least 250 euros and at most 500,000 euros in the year are deductible from the taxable income of companies or private individuals if the beneficiary is an institution cited in law or authorized by Royal Order.

Deduction of donations of works of art (Article 104 sub-paragraph 1.5 of the Income Tax Code).

Donations of works of art to museums (owned by the state, communities, regions, provinces and communes) are deductible from the net income of private individuals. The amount of donations may not exceed 250,000 euros in the year.

Surrendering a work of art by way of payment of inheritance tax (Article 83 paragraph 3 of the Inheritance Tax Code).

Any beneficiary, legatee or donee may ask to pay inheritance tax in whole or part by surrendering works of art left to them by the deceased by way of payment. The conditions governing this arrangement are identical to those applying to donations of works of art.

Exemption from inheritance tax for legacies (Article 40 of the Ordinance of 4 March 1993 on conservation of the immovable heritage).

Listed property bequeathed to the Brussels-Capital Region or foundations with the legal statute of an established public utility is exempt from inheritance tax and succession duty on condition that it is located in the region. The property bequeathed is inalienable and cannot be assigned.

It should be noted that these different fiscal measures have achieved varying degrees of success and some, such as the last one, have never been applied. The presence of fairly well organised and active structures providing assistance are the key – often more so than tax provisions themselves – to the true effectiveness of tax incentives applicable on Belgian territory.

The role of public and specialized bodies
In the heritage sphere, as elsewhere, the public authorities have constantly striven to combine continuity with change. A consistent approach to

heritage, pursued since the creation of the state in 1830, has been accompanied by an ongoing process of institutional development. With the adoption of the Royal Order of 7 January 1835 the young Kingdom of Belgium set up a Royal Commission on Monuments, one of whose roles was to issue opinions regulating the construction of the numerous public edifices being built in the new state.

In another area, the first 'blots on the landscape' caused by galloping industrialization prompted the Belgian Parliament to pass the law of 12 August 1911 (on the conservation of landscapes), which, subsequently, has been utilized by certain environmental protection associations to have a number of particularly 'scarred' natural sites restored.

It was not until the law of 7 August 1931 on the conservation of monuments and sites that action was first taken on a grand scale as regards the protection of immovable heritage and conservation policy. Some 40 years later, the country at last had its first heritage authorities: at the time, state involvement generally went no further than subsidizing more or less endangered architectural assets.

The state then went on to confirm its role as purchaser or administrator of major heritage assets such as the gothic abbeys of Villers-la-Ville and Orval, the fortresses of Bouillon and La Roche-en-Ardenne, the Abbey Palace of Saint-Hubert and the Lion's Mound at Waterloo, where the former battlefield is also protected by a special law. While they have not been particularly affected by institutional change in the country, these major heritage assets still remain under the aegis of the Federal State Buildings Authority.

The biggest change towards the end of the twentieth century has undeniably been the establishment and division of responsibility within the state. The special law on institutional reform of 8 August 1980 transferred the sovereign exercise of responsibility for the heritage to the communities, integrating it with culture to form part of the political responsibilities assigned to individuals and not to the territory in question. The way was thus opened for heritage – public authority involvement, bringing together community, province and commune although still restricted to the realms of grants dependent on the interest and attitude shown by owners.

When the second special law on institutional reform was passed on 8 August 1988, responsibility for the immovable heritage was taken away from the communities and entrusted to the regions, essentially giving them authority for the management of the territory.

The political conditions were at last in place, albeit over 10 years late, to take up the theme of the European Architectural Heritage Year of 1975, 'a future for our past', for which the Head of State, King Baudouin, had clearly set the tone in his speech of 19 February 1975:

The public authorities have a duty to do their utmost to pursue a conservation policy, which is an integral part of a social progress strategy. For this they require a better legislative tool and budgets matching their goals as soon as possible. I also believe it essential to closely involve the Belgian people in the decisions concerning the planning of our environment and living space in particular. It is, after all, they who are the first affected.

In the efforts to safeguard our architectural heritage, man must remain the central consideration. The rehabilitation of groups of buildings must be accompanied by social provisions. It is not only a question of conserving our architectural heritage or finding new uses for old districts but also and above all of maintaining or perhaps restoring a socially balanced population in the places in question.

It is a matter of improving the living conditions of man in urban and rural areas
.

The legislative and budgetary follow-up was not slow in coming: the Parliament of the Walloon Region passed the decree of 18 July 1991 concerning monuments, sites and excavations. This guaranteed both a consideration and the enhancement of the immovable heritage (monuments, groups of buildings, sites and archaeological heritage) in all decisions regarding spatial and town planning. Subsequently, the Walloon Parliament approved budgetary decrees, which, from year on year, increased the funding earmarked for the region's conservation policy tenfold. The latest development at the time of writing is the decree of 1 April 1999, which supplements the provisions of 1991, in particular by setting up the *Walloon Heritage Institute.*

The efforts, undertaken for so many years by the *Fondation Roi Baudouin*, to encourage any private or public initiative which entails not simply subsidising but actually taking in hand the future of endangered heritage have been highly successful. The wishes expressed by the Foundation in a 'Whiter Paper on the heritage in the Walloon Region' (Fondation Roi Baudouin, 1993) have now been realized. From its very inception the Heritage Institute was entrusted with the task not only of exploiting listed assets belonging to the Walloon Region but also and, above all, of taking the necessary steps with regard to several dozen heritage assets which were no longer guaranteed a future worthy of their history or a use worthy of their quality, owing to their state or size or to their owners' limited resources.

For these threatened assets, the job of the Walloon Heritage Institute is first to establish, together with the owner, the state of health of the monument and decide what conservation measures are initially required. This vital first step goes hand in hand with a consideration of the potential for assigning the asset to another use and of the technical and financial solutions necessary to its possible acquisition, restoration, reassignment and finally to leasing or renting it out.

In this respect the Walloon Heritage Institute is a dynamic property developer, capable of devising projects, forging partnerships, mobilizing funds with great flexibility and speed and seeking the necessary administrative permission to execute delicate operations. Its role can be extended, where necessary, to that of a contracting authority acting on behalf of the owner.

In conclusion, in a context of transformation and adaptation to modern needs in terms of built and non-built space, the Walloon Heritage Institute has a duty to step into a breach left open for too long by the public authorities. Its role is that of a fully-fledged public property developer, with the aim not of guaranteeing immediate profitability but of ensuring, in tangible form, 'a future for the past' for the heritage which it aims to protect.

Education and training

The Belgian special law on institutional reforms of 8 August 1988 put the regions in charge of exercising prerogatives over the protection and conservation of the immovable heritage.

This enabled, for example, the Walloon Region, keen to ensure a future for the vestiges of the rich and varied past that characterizes Wallonia, to effecively capitalize on its initial efforts to promote the vernacular heritage. Its increased legitimacy in terms of raising awareness sphere was particularly reflected in a very powerful increase in budget allocation, which rose steadily from BEF 180 million in 1989 to over BEF 2 billion in 1999.

However, this expansion, once translated into restoration projects ran into a cruel lack of skilled labour. Aware of this blight on any fresh budget increase, the Walloon Region initially entrusted the Meuse Foundation for Art, Architecture and Crafts with the task of exploring how a training centre for developing heritage skills might be set up.

Picking up on the earlier initiatives of the *Fondation Roi Baudouin*, the Euro-regional Centre for Heritage Crafts now provides further training grants for experienced craftsmen wishing to perfect their skills in another country. But the Centre's most important activity is organizing training courses on the restoration site of the old Paix-Dieu abbey at Amay (Liège province). This highly specialized 'educational' project was planned back in 1992 and set up by the Walloon Government in April 1995. Several types of course have been successfully piloted in recent years (training for company employees working on the site, classes raising awareness of heritage crafts, and further training courses run on certain themes) and these will form the backbone of the Centre's activities from 2000 onwards.

Since 1999, the Paix-Dieu centre has been managed by the Walloon Heritage Institute. At the Institute's prompting, in early 2000, the Paix-Dieu centre organized eighteen further training courses, in addition to its awareness-raising classes, covering topics such as analytical methods, composite or decorated frontages, stucco, moulded plasterwork and coatings, gilding, cob walls and paving techniques.

The organization of the Centre's courses is intended to reflect the real situation 'on the ground', while catering for individuals as diverse as:

- craftsmen keen to improve their skills in the interests of lasting employment and personal achievement;
- project authors and managers keen to commission high-quality work and to play their part, with due compliance and efficiency, in integrated heritage conservation;
- researchers and scientists who further our knowledge of the heritage in historical, architectural or technical terms.

The themes, *ad hoc* or recurrent, are identified through research carried out in the sphere of the restoration and rehabilitation of ancient monuments:

- increased scarcity or poor knowledge of certain materials or techniques;
- the emergence of certain problems in heritage conservation;
- requests for training or further training from professional associations.

Each course comprises three modules:

- general theory, designed to 'set the scene', define what is meant by heritage and identify what is at stake in conservation and restoration;
- specific theory, designed to develop the specific aspects of the theme chosen (characteristics of materials, techniques, alteration factors, etc.);
- application on a site (ongoing site project) or in a workshop, designed to perfect knowledge (of practice and procedure).

To maintain a high standard in the training provided on these courses by experienced craftsmen or specialists on the materials in question, the number of participants is limited.

While in no way competing with the very large range of building craft training courses, the Paix-Dieu Centre also seeks to serve as an extension to programmes geared to apprenticeship, youth opportunities or return to work.

Conclusion

This chapter was not intended to provide an exhaustive inventory of the legal and regulatory provisions currently applicable in the three regions of Belgium considered, but rather to highlight certain 'best practices', and to suggest new directions for ideas and initiatives of benefit to the heritage.

We have, therefore, discussed examples such as the integrated heritage conservation policy in the Brussels-Capital Region; recent developments in inventory work and heritage craft training in the Walloon Region; assistance provided to the owners of protected assets and incentives for heritage maintenance in the Flemish Region; and, the diverse and complementary policies of grants and tax relief pursued by all three regions and the Belgian federal authorities.

However, there is always a certain gap between the spirit and the letter, between legal provisions and their actual interpretation. For that reason, it is thought important to conclude by stressing the importance of communication between the 'theoreticians' of conservation, the legislators, the protagonists on the ground (owners, entrepreneurs, architects and officials responsible for the heritage) and the general public.

Note

This chapter was authored by Myriam Goblet except for the following sections:

- Identifying and recording the heritage: Thérèse Cortembos
- The preservation and protection of the heritage: Peter Verhaegen

- Conservation philosophy/sanctions and coercive measures: Anne-Mie Draye
- Role of public and specialized bodies: Jeal-Pol Van Reybroeck
- Education and training: Freddy Joris

References

UNESCO (1972): *Convention Concerning the Protection of the World Cultural and Natural Heritage /Convention relative à la protection du patrimoine culturel et naturel.*

Binst, S. and Hoflach, M. (1996): *Monumentenwacht Vlaanderen: Vijf Jaar.*

Draye, A.M. (1997): *La protection du patrimoine immobilier,* in *Répertoire notarial (pour toute la Belgique).*

Koning Baudewijn Stichting (1992): *Dossier 2, monumenten en fiscale aspecten van de monumentenzorg.*

Fondation Roi Baudouin (1993): *Livre blanc du patrimoine en Région wallonne.*

Fondation Roi Baudouin (1997): *Mieux restaurer le patrimoine architectural? Plaidoyer, des professionnels, un marché, des réglementations, des exigences, des savoir-faire, des perfectionnements.*

Josef Štulc

Czech Republic

Introduction

The cultural heritage of the Czech Republic is multifarious. The location of the historical lands of the Crown of Bohemia in the very centre of Europe and the multinational character of their inhabitants' culture has contributed to this. From the thirteenth century, together with the Czechs, the German settlers participated in the cultivation, and the economic and cultural development of the country and from the early Middle Ages, the economic contribution of the Jewish diaspora, quite considerable until recent times, cannot be ignored. During the Renaissance and the seventeenth and eighteenth centuries, artistic activities were influenced strikingly by Italian architects and craftsmen naturalized in the country. In the typologically oldest sphere of building activities, namely vernacular architecture (Fig. 3.1), the varied character of the individual regions of Czech lands is manifested by the presence of all existing types of European houses: earthen, timbered, half-timbered and stone or brick construction.

During its evolution over more than one thousand years, the monumental architecture of the country has attained the European apex in several periods. Petr Parléř and the fourteenth-century Gothic buildings, the Borromini and Guarini-inspired Czech Baroque architecture of the first third of the eighteenth century, the very original Czech architectural cubism and the magnificent works of the functionalist trend in the Modern Movement of the twentieth century, are all worthy of mention (Fig. 3.2).

The preservation and integrity of our material cultural heritage has been considerably aided by the fact that the country was not noticeably damaged during either World War I or II. Unlike neighbouring countries, the Czech Republic did not experience the post-war reconstruction and economic boom that proved to be so destructive for the built heritage elsewhere. In spite of a lack of maintenance and bad management during the 40 years of the socialist era, the richness of architectural monuments has been

Fig. 3.1 Dolní Vidim in central Bohemia, a characteristic example of a wooden vernacular farmhouse. The Czech Republic is very rich in vernacular architecture that survived largely thanks to the vogue for using such buildings for weekend recreation.

preserved in this country to an astonishing extent and, in particular, with an extraordinary measure of authenticity.

The idea of protecting and preserving historically and artistically important buildings has a long-standing tradition in our country. The beginnings of this tradition go back to the late eighteenth century. The more or less amateurish investigative and collective activities of the Society of the Patriotic Friends of Art, founded at that time, were followed by the scientifically based archaeological, ethnographic and art-historical research of architectural monuments, carried out by the National Museum in Prague (founded in 1818). From 1854, its Archaeological Department published *Památky Archeologické a Místopisné* (*Archaeological and Topographical Monuments*), the very first specialized review of its kind in the whole of Central Europe. A dense network of Czech and Moravian regional conservators and reporters made important contributions to the work of Imperial and Royal Central Commission for the Exploration and Preservation of Artistic Monuments, founded in Vienna in 1850.

The advanced state of the Czech approach to preservation of the cultural heritage within the multinational Austro-Hungarian monarchy is illustrated by the fact that the first scientifically conceived inventories of the monuments of art in individual districts, documented by detailed photographs and measurements, were published in the Czech lands from 1897, i.e. 10 years sooner than in Austria. A great Czech historian of art, Max Dvořák, participated in this work. Subsequently, he played a role that was of basic importance for the whole of Central Europe: as the General Conservator for the Austrian part of the monarchy, he put the new revolutionary ideas of his great teacher, the Viennese Professor Alois Riegl, into the practice of

'g. 3.2 Kutná Hora, former Royal town, in the Middle Ages important for its silver-mining, has preserved a number of strikingly monumental Gothic churches, which form a most dramatic skyline to the city.

the preservation of monuments. This meant, in the first place, the categorical refusal of the previous purist attempt to renew the monuments in their 'pure' form with a uniform style. In the new conception of the Viennese art-historian school, a monument is understood and conserved as an artistic individuality generated by evolution, that is to say that due respect is paid to the traces of its age (Riegl's *Alterswert*). Riegl's and Dvořák's reform of conservation philosophy soon spread from Vienna throughout Central Europe. At the same time, Prague also became an important centre of innovative ideas. These ideas concerned the protection of entire historic urban wholes. From 1900, the passionate criticism of the brutal clearance of some historical Prague districts led the Prague artists, historians and architects – associated with the Club for Old Prague – to the opinion that an entire historical city quarter, as well as individual buildings, may have the character of a rare work of art. Therefore, as early as 1893, they advanced the proposal, subsequently repeated several times, for the protection of the historic core of Prague by law (Fig. 3.3).

After the constitution of independent Czechoslovakia in 1918, the adoption of Riegl's conservation philosophy was convincingly demonstrated in the establishment of institutions such as the State Archaeological Institute, the State Photomeasuring Institute and the two Public Offices for the Preservation of Monuments, one in Prague and the other in Brno. This philosophy was accompanied by the consistent modernism (also derived from Riegl's ideas), of all the annexes to, and modifications of, the monuments and of all new buildings being put in historic settings. Alas, the liberalism and novelty-hunting of the economic, political and spiritual climate of the inter-war period barred the adoption of the Monument Preservation Act despite the draft law being repeatedly submitted to the

Fig. 3.3 Prague, a panoramic view of the Prague Castle and the Lesser Quarter. A freely-evolved but extremely harmonious composition of dominant city buildings and roof-scapes resembles an intentionally created work of art.

Parliament. In the 1930s and 1940s, the philosophy and the practical methods of the preservation of cultural heritage were polarized by a sharp controversy between the followers of Riegl, based on an analytical-modern-istic approach, and the new, 'synthesized' method of the renovation of monuments (Fig. 3.4). This new method again recognized the legitimacy of the reconstruction, or the replication, of missing or damaged historical forms and details in order to respect the wholeness and artistic integrity of monuments.

In its approach to cultural heritage, the period after World War II, and especially after the communist coup in 1948, was characterized by sharp contrasts. The expropriation of Sudeten Germans (1945) and, soon after-wards, of all well-to-do citizens (1948) deprived the country of the cultivated collectors, sponsors and house-owners and led to immense cultural losses. The impact of the expropriation of, and the ideologically hostile attitude of the communist regime towards the churches and religious orders were no less destructive. On the other hand, as early as 1950, before any other European country, communist Czechoslovakia declared thirty historic cores of towns to be conservation sites. At the same time, the state carried out costly repairs to and the restoration of 150 selected confiscated castles and chateaux and opened them to the public. The Cultural Heritage Act, one of the best in Europe, was finally adopted in 1958, after being called for many times. At a time of oppression, when excellent scientists and architects had to leave universities during political purges, the state made it possible to explore and document monuments and entire historic towns systematically through generous grants. Still more generous grants were given to the extensive archaeological exploration of both prehistoric and early medieval sites, carried out systematically by the Archaeological Institute of the Academy of Science. This activity was unique in Europe at that time in terms of its extent and scientific thoroughness.

The communist era was typified by a gradually increasing difference between the high level of theoretical thought, research and studies on town planning and architecture on the one hand and rapidly deteriorating

Fig. 3.4 Nové Město nad Metují, restored and largely reconstructed northern front of the main square in the style of the Venetian Renaissance. The restoration is a typical result of the so-called 'synthetic method' of conservation frequently used in the 1950s.

practice on the other. In particular, during the so-called 'normalization' period after the Soviet occupation in 1968, architecture and town planning degenerated to the artistically sterile mass-production of prefabricated housing estates and industrial complexes. Historic settlements had to make way for these and were largely torn down (for example, the ancient towns of Most, Horní Slavkov and Aš among others). The economic maintenance of existing buildings almost stopped. The inheritance of buildings of value began to disappear at an increasingly rapid pace while new ones were not being brought into being.

Despite the still high level of its theoretical thought, the state preservation of the cultural heritage was unable to prevent the spontaneous collapse, or the demolition, of hundreds of protected items of cultural heritage including even larger numbers of still unrecognized items of cultural heritage and of archaeological sites. The losses in the 1970s and 1980s are estimated at some 3,000 historical buildings, i.e. a full 10 per cent of the then registered immovable cultural heritage. Adopted in 1987, the admirable Cultural Heritage State Preservation Act, the second of its kind, showed itself to be an insufficient instrument of protection against economic incapability, wastefulness and a lack of political concern.

The present situation of the Czech preservation of cultural heritage and its problems during the period following the revolution in November 1989 will be discussed more specifically in the following sections. As is the case after each radical social convulsion, the 10 years of the 1990s was a period of sharp contrasts. The renewal of the rights and duties of private ownership and the release of social and creative energy, the much sought-after individualized architectural creation not excepted, comprise a great contribution. However, as regards cultural heritage, these assets are diminished by individual egotism, speculation, an enormously increased crime rate and bad taste. Proceeding only slowly and not always successfully, the state authorities are building up their new position not as instruments of oppression any more, but as guarantors and protectors of public interest.

In a situation characterized by dramatic social changes, it is important for the Czech cultural heritage that the specialist institutions for its preservation maintain – irrespective of the extent of their direct competence – the continuity of their research, theoretical thought and a high level of technical expertise and become closely involved in European collaboration. It is only this sort of approach which will enable the Czech preservation of cultural heritage to honour the excellent and still inspiring tradition which has resulted from its centuries of remarkable development.

Definition of the heritage

The exploration of historical buildings and the sporadic archaeological excavations in the nineteenth century had already seen the importance of protecting the most precious explored objects. Due to further development, the originally narrow interest in the Czech artistic and archaeological cultural heritage was widening, resulting in the very broad definition in article 2 of law no. 20/1987 concerning the state preservation of cultural heritage.

Individual objects and sets of objects

Article 2 of the 1987 law provides the following definition:

> 1. As cultural heritage according to this Act, the Ministry of Culture of the Czech Republic declares the immovable and movable objects or, as the case may be, their sets a) which are outstanding documents of the historical development, lifestyle and milieu of society from the oldest time to the present as manifestations of man's creative capacities and work in the most varied spheres of his activity, because of their revolutionary, historic, artistic, scientific and technological values, b) which are in direct relationship with important personalities and historic events.
> 2. Sets of objects according to Art. 1 are declared to be cultural heritage even if some things in them are not cultural heritage.

This general definition is not in contradiction with the Granada Convention or the Malta Convention. The definitions of heritage, which are contained in these conventions, may also be considered valid in the conditions existing in the Czech Republic.

The selection of the items of cultural heritage covered by state protection is not defined by any other technical criteria or guidelines specified in greater detail. According to the first Czech Cultural Heritage Preservation Act, adopted in 1958, all the objects that conformed with the above-quoted definition were protected. This was changed by the law adopted in 1987. This law broadened the range of items which can be considered cultural objects and from this range the Ministry of Culture declares assets to be cultural heritage. The objects are under the protection of the state, and their owners' ensuing rights as well as limiting duties apply to them. At present, 38,700 immovable cultural properties are protected in this way.

Proposals for the declaration of objects to be cultural heritage are usually submitted to the Ministry of Culture by local councils, civic associations, technical institutions and, exceptionally, owners or individual citizens. Movable and immovable archaeological finds are declared to be cultural heritage by the Ministry of Culture at the proposal of the Academy of Science of the Czech Republic. The territorially competent regional Institute for the Preservation of Cultural Heritage is always one of bodies that gives an opinion on a proposal. The proposals put forward are co-ordinated technically by the central State Institute for the Preservation of Cultural Heritage. This Institute organizes and assists the work of an evaluating commission, specially set up for this purpose by the Ministry of Culture. The commission consists of eminent Czech art historians, archaeologists, architects and other specialists. This process provides the greatest possible measure of scientific objectivity and national representation.

In conclusion it may be said that the identification of items of cultural heritage in the Czech Republic is not based on officially codified criteria which are specified in detail, but on the qualified judgement of reputed experts. This differs from the situation in the communist past, in that political and ideological viewpoints are no longer reflected in the selection of cultural heritage items. In this respect, on the contrary, the list of cultural monuments has become more objective during the last 10 years of the twentieth century due to the strenuous work of the evaluating commission. After careful reflection, numerous objects documenting the history of the Communist Party have been deleted from the list while some 4,000 buildings previously unprotected for ideological reasons (especially churches and buildings associated with Catholicism and Judaism) have been declared to be part of the cultural heritage.

The Ministry of Culture always declares an object to be part of the cultural heritage *as a whole*, i.e. not only its outer walls, but also its inner architectural composition, its interiors and the artistic decoration connected with the object. The designation of a cultural monument also includes plots of land, courtyards, gardens, boundary walls, annexes and structures, although some of them may not have cultural heritage value in themselves. The protection of the precincts of a building does not ensue automatically from the declaration of an object as a cultural heritage item. However, if necessary, an individually defined protective zone may be fixed not by the Ministry of Culture, but by the District Office. It may be said that such zones have already been set for practically all the Czech Republic's important monumental buildings.

The specification of the regulations governing the protection of a given item of cultural heritage may be part of such a declaration, but usually is not. The law lays down the principle that all changes and modifications may be carried out only with the consent of the respective state authority. Carried out during the communist regime, but actually harmful in practice, the classification of the cultural heritage items into three categories according to their value, was abolished after 1989. Only the highly selective category of 'National Cultural Monuments' has been preserved. This category consists of the 134 most valuable objects declared to be of national importance by the government of the Czech Republic. Their increased level of protection and the specialist aspect of their preservation is the direct responsibility of the Ministry of Culture itself and the central State Institute for the Preservation of Cultural Heritage.

Movable objects
Movable objects (55,440 items at present) are a special category of the protected cultural heritage. In this respect, the Ministry of Culture is again responsible for declaring them to be protected items of cultural heritage. Their number is greatly increasing, because objects which were previously part of collections in state museums and galleries and which were then returned as part of the so-called restitution to their original owners are subsequently being declared to be cultural heritage in order to prevent their undesirable export from the country. Art collections, historic furniture and other valuable elements of the movable furnishings of state castles and chateaux open to the public (767,470 items of which have been recorded on an inventory) have been declared *en masse* to be cultural heritage. Conversely, the collections kept in state museums are not cultural heritage by law, because a special law (no. 54/1959, concerning museums and galleries) sets down the regulations governing their protection.

Urban ensembles
The Czech Republic has a time-honoured tradition, and a comprehensive system for the protection of urban ensembles – historic towns, villages and selected zones of cultural landscape. This will be dealt with in the section entitled 'The protection of historic settlements and cultural landscapes' below.

Identification of the heritage
The history of the inventories of cultural heritage items in the Czech lands exceeds one hundred years. The first *Inventory of Historic and Artistic Monuments in the Kingdom of Bohemia from Primeval Times to the Beginning of the 19th Century* was published in 1897 by the Archaeological Commission of the Czech Academy of Science, Literature and Art. This contained a descriptive inventory of monuments in the district Kolín nad Labem. Gradually, such an inventory was compiled in the Czech language, with a translation into German, for each district. In Bohemia, as many as 27 such volumes were published before 1907, when, at the instigation of the Central Commission for Artistic and Historic Monuments in Austria-Hungary, the first volume of the Austrian Topography was issued as an example of scientific inventory. Work on the Inventory continued in Czechoslovakia after 1918. As many as 51 volumes were published there until 1934. However, World War II led to the discontinuance of this series. In 1957, the Czechoslovak Academy of Science published *Umělecké Památky Republiky Československé* (*Artistic Cultural Heritage of the*

Czechoslovak Republic) in one volume. In 1977, a team of authors working
in the Institute of the Theory and History of Art, Czechoslovak Academy
of Science, began to publish the inventory *Umělecké Památky Čech* (*Artistic
Cultural Heritage of Bohemia*: volumes 1 to 4), *Umělecké Památky Prahy*
(*Artistic Cultural Heritage of Prague*: 2 volumes to date) and *Umělecké
Památky Moravy a Slezska* (*Artistic Cultural Heritage of Moravia and
Silesia*: 2 volumes to date).

The State List
The law no. 22/1958 Sb., concerning the cultural heritage, set up a new
registration system using inventories – the *State List of Cultural Heritage*.
The State List consisted of an index of cultural heritage (movable or
immovable) and authorized uniform record cards, containing basic information for identification, description and complementary information.
Changes reported in a given cultural heritage were written on such a card.
This card also included an informative photograph – 6 by 6 centimetres. In
the descriptive part, the names of the authors of the cultural heritage were
given (if known) together with the respective dates of its creation, a
definition of its style, a technical description (dimensions and material in
the case of movable cultural heritage), use and, again for movable cultural
heritage, its location. The 'decree', i.e. a written document about the
decision to record a given cultural heritage on the State List or about the
annulment of the record, formed another part of the State List.

The Central List
At the instigation of the Warsaw Conference of ICOMOS, held in 1977, the
methodological preparation of the *Central List of Cultural Heritage* was
undertaken by the State Institute for the Preservation of Cultural Heritage
and Protection of Nature. This institute was set up according to article 19
of the 1958 law as the supreme specialist and methodological organization
for the state preservation of the cultural heritage.

   This methodological preparation consisted of the creation of uniform
names for the items of cultural heritage (classifiers), a more exact specification, and completion of the shape of the record cards, the elaboration of
the methodology of the description of the items of cultural heritage, and
the creation of a uniform system for the recording of documentation
material (plans, photographic documentation, etc.) In fact, as a higher
degree of registration using inventories, the Central List of Cultural
Heritage was established by the new law no. 20/1987 Sb., concerned with the
state preservation of cultural heritage. The Central List consists of an
index, record cards with complementary sheets and the territorial identification of an immovable cultural heritage, or a territory protected as cultural
heritage or a protective zone, on a duplicate of the cadastral map. The
Central List of Cultural Heritage is maintained by the State Institute for the
Preservation of Cultural Heritage. Objects are included in the Central List as
a result of the Ministry of Culture declaring items to be cultural heritage.
Cultural heritage items included in the former State Lists in individual

regions are considered as cultural heritage according to the new law as well. Gradually, they are also being recorded in the Central List. Under the new law, protection is not given to objects that have not been declared as cultural heritage. If such an object bears recognizable marks of value as cultural heritage, it has to be proposed for declaration as such. In order to maintain the continuity of this form of registration, a relatively complicated index numbering method has been created for the Central List, the second part of which consists of a number indicating the regional State List and the serial number in this list (nnnnn/x-yyyy). In the case of the newly declared items of cultural heritage, the series of numbers in former regions continue in a way which follows the State List. The Central List is divided into:

- the list of immovable cultural heritage;
- the list of movable cultural heritage;
- the list of territories protected as cultural heritage (conservation sites and conservation zones).

The declaration of an object as a National Cultural Monument is marked in the Central List, and the same is true of the declaration of a protective zone for individual items of the immovable cultural heritage, a conservation site and a conservation zone. Inventories of the fittings and art collections of castles, chateaux, monasteries and palaces form a special, separate part of the record files with a specific methodology for their classification. In these cases, the whole set is registered under a single index number in the Central List of Cultural Heritage, with the number of items given and a reference to the basic registration of furniture of a given immovable property.

Revision of the Central List
After the social changes in 1989, a number of problems in the records of the cultural heritage have gradually appeared. Extensive changes of ownership due to restitution, redress for wrongs, and the unauthorized use of private property have greatly altered even the basic data concerning the cultural heritage. During the massive process of these changes, the requirement to register the new owners has not always been complied with. Changes in the ownership of land have often led to the integration of separate plots of land or, on the contrary, their division. Under the condi-tions of state ownership, prevailing until 1989, a detailed and unequivocal definition of the extent of the individual items of cultural heritage and the exact location of the boundaries of the territories protected as cultural heritage (and protective zones, etc.), were not necessary. Since then they have become necessary for the owners' legal safeguard on the one hand and, for the correct apportionment of grants from the budgets of the state and public entities on the other. According to law no. 20/1987 Sb., these grants can be given only and without exception to the objects declared to be cultural heritage. This was one of the reasons why the Ministry of Culture submitted the 'Conception of a More Efficient Preservation of Cultural

Heritage in the Czech Republic until 2005' to the government, which approved it in the spring of 1998. One of the basic purposes of this Conception is the renewed identification of the immovable cultural heritage and of the territories protected as cultural heritage. During this renewed identification all the shortcomings identified above should be remedied and the basic data concerning all the items of immovable properties in the Central List of Cultural Heritage updated, made more precise and complete. Of course the cognition of cultural heritage and the completion of the Central List by the declaration of other objects to be cultural heritage will continue unhampered at the same time.

Special consideration for the movable heritage
The social changes also brought a number of negative phenomena such as theft, especially from churches, but also from collections in addition to thefts of works of art, antiquities and other objects of cultural value. Subsequently, these items appear on the antiquity market and a strong pressure to export then is brought to bear. Therefore, the special law no. 70 Sb., concerning the export of objects of cultural value, was adopted in 1994. Under this law, Parliament adopted the Integrated System for the Protection of Movable Heritage, in which video documentation supports the inventory of these threatened sets of objects.

Special consideration of the archaeological heritage
The new wave of building and development activity in the Czech Republic has shown that a better definition and procedure is needed for the protection of the archaeological heritage. Improvements were sought in the definition of the sphere in which archaeological heritage has to be preserved and to the organization of 'saving' archaeological research endangered by building orders. In 1993 and 1995, on an archaeologists' recommendation, the Ministry of Culture, after reaching an agreement with the Academy of Science of the Czech Republic, set up four specialized Institutes for the Preservation of Archaeological Heritage to carry out archaeological rescue research. In 1993 and 1994 specialists came to an agreement over establishing a national information system for archaeological sites. In the Central Institute for the Preservation of Cultural Heritage, a department for the preservation of archaeological heritage was set up in 1996 and has been devising an information and documentation basis for carrying out the preservation of archaeological heritage. Since 1995, in collaboration with the archaeological institutions and the executive bodies of the state administration (District Offices), this department has been working on the research project 'The Official List of Archaeological Sites' (OLAS) in the Czech Republic. The aim of this project is to draw up a map of archaeological sites throughout the country. Automated data processing and assessment in an environment given by geographical information systems (GIS) is an integral part of this project. The project represents a system for providing information about territories where archaeological finds have been made. The use of continuously updated data and outputs being available at the level of

regional archaeological branches greatly improves the quality of the decisions made by authorities about the use of land, especially in the procedure for issuing building permits and in land-use planning. Forty-one per cent of the territory of the Czech Republic has been processed up to the time of writing. The 'Archaeology 1.1' applications for interactive work with project data in the GIS ArcView environment and T-Map Viewer are used by twelve bodies of the state administration (three more bodies use data in the GIS environment itself) and eleven technical organizations. The OLAS 'CR 1' applications for the collection of, and work with, data in the Windows 9x(NT) environment are used, in addition to units of the State Institute for the Preservation of Cultural Heritage, by thirty-eight collaborating organizations, which also make use of the data to solve the technical problems in the regions. Continuously being introduced into practice, this technical solution corresponds to the generally recommended European Union standard, and it is in accordance with the principles of the 1992 European Convention on the protection of Archaeological Heritage (revised) (the Malta Convention) – to which the Czech Republic is now acceding.

The protection of historic settlements and cultural landscapes

An outstanding feature of the Czech preservation of cultural heritage after World War II was the fact that, in addition to the protection and upgrading of individual cultural-heritage buildings, it focused on the identification, protection and integrated conservation (regeneration) of the environment of the settlements. This concerned, in the first place, the historic cores of towns; followed by historic villages (from the 1970s) and selected parts of cultural landscape (from the 1980s).

Conservation sites and zones

As early as 1950, the government included thirty urban conservation sites in Bohemia and Moravia (and ten such sites in what is now Slovakia) in the programme of the restoration of selected cultural heritage. This programme aimed in particular to prevent the dilapidation of selected historical centres of towns and to provide for the repair of the mantles of buildings (roofs and façades) and the restoration of some important public and culturally significant buildings.

The notation of 'conservation site' was used for the most precious historic cores of towns and was laid down in law 22/1958, concerning cultural heritage, this being the first such law of its kind. In the course of time, thirty-five urban conservation sites have been selected in the Czech Republic and declared as being protected. A conservation site has always included the integrated territory of a historic town – usually defined by the line of its historic fortification – and not just selected parts of a square or of streets. The 1958 law also made it possible to declare a protective zone round a conservation site, this zone being a wider territory where the regime is regulated in a way that does not threatening the basic urban values of the conservation site. A synthesized view of the evolution of towns and their comprehensive protection has been applied here.

Law no. 20/1987, concerning the state preservation of the cultural heritage, introduced another category of protection – the conservation zone, in addition to the conservation site. These two concepts are defined by the law in the following manner.

- According to article 5, the government of the Czech Republic may, by its decree, declare a terrritory – the character and environment of which are defined by a set of items of immovable cultural heritage or, as the case may be, according to archaeological finds – to be a conservation site as a whole and lay down the conditions for its protection.
- According to article 6, the Ministry of Culture may declare the territory of a settlement or of its part where the share of the cultural heritage is smaller, the historic environment or part of a landscape showing important cultural value, to be a conservation zone and lay down the conditions of its protection.
- According to article 17, if an immovable item of cultural heritage, an item of the National Cultural Heritage, a conservation site or a conservation zone require protection of their environment the respective District Office delimits a protective zone round them, where it may limit or prohibit certain activities or apply other suitable measures.

The legal protection of selected parts of settlements (towns and villages) and cultural landscape is the basic prerequisite for their preservation and artistic, technological and social rehabilitation.

It has been obvious since the early 1970s that the whole structure of the settlements in the country has to be investigated and an inventory gradually made of all settlements in their entirety. The Czech Republic has some 15,000 settlement units, i.e. towns, villages, hamlets and lonely houses, of which there are some 1,000 historic urban settlements (municipalities that had town rights). Between 1972 and 1973, a register and categorization of all historical towns founded up to 1850, comprising 924 items, was drawn up by the State Institute for the Preservation of Cultural Heritage. In 1985, this register was updated and enlarged to comprise the towns founded up to 1985. It included 1,200 historic towns in all. The main effort was directed at the transition to a broader and more differentiated conception of the protection of historic towns. In 1984, the Ministry of Culture approved the 'Conception of the Protection of Historic Towns', which proposed:

- to increase the number of thirty-five urban conservation sites by five other towns (with a strict regime of protection);
- to protect the most important parts of another 160 historic towns as conservation zones (with a more moderate, differentiated regime of protection);
- to adequately protect the cultural values of other historic towns by means of layout (space) plans.

From 1987 to 1995, this conception was put quickly into effect and the number of conservation zones exceeded, by far, that originally intended.

Similarly, from the early 1970s, the State Institute for the Preservation of Cultural Heritage worked on a 'Conception of the protection of village settlements'. The first set of village conservation sites and conservation zones was selected and declared during the 1990s. The work on an overall inventory of the villages will be completed in the early years of the twenty-first century and will be the basis for an increase in the number of protected villages.

The systematic evaluation of selected parts of cultural landscape was started in the 1980s and the first seventeen landscape conservation zones were declared in the 1990s. This process is far from being complete, because the conception foresees the protection of seventy-two landscape ensembles. The selection of landscape zones is based mainly on the criteria concerning their cultural, not natural values. This is in contrast to the completely independent network of national parks, wildlife reserves and protected wildlife areas, which has been established according to the special law concerning the state protection of nature.

The present conception of the protection of settlements and landscapes is already fully representative of the country (Fig. 3.5). It contains all the important elements of settlements and landscapes in the Czech Republic, namely:

• 40 urban conservation sites and 209 urban conservation zones;
• 61 village conservation sites and 164 village conservation zones;
• 1 landscape conservation site and 17 landscape conservation zones;
• 12 archaeological conservation sites.

(There are 125 conservation sites and 389 conservation areas in total). The ensemble consisting of protected settlements and selected parts of the landscape contains 515 items.

Other sites
The archaeological sphere is being charted independently in an extensive long-term national research project for the identification of the areas where archaeological finds are located in the GIS environment: 'The Official List of Archaeological Sites in the Czech Republic'. The UNESCO List of World Cultural Heritage already contains four urban conservation sites – Prague, Český Krumlov (Fig. 3.6), Telč and Kutná Hora– the Holašovice village conservation site, the Lednice–Valtice landscape conservation zone and the Kroměříž gardens with the castle.

The preservation and protection of heritage
As the first of its kind, the Czech law no. 22/1958, concerning the protection of the cultural heritage, was a very modern document at the time. It created a highly efficient instrument for the preservation of the cultural heritage, although in the then existing social conditions its provisions were sometimes overridden by the ideological and political interests of the decision-making bodies. Regarding the choice of cultural heritage items to

Fig 3.5 Map of the Czech Republic showing the dense net of historic towns and cities protected as conservation reserves and zones.

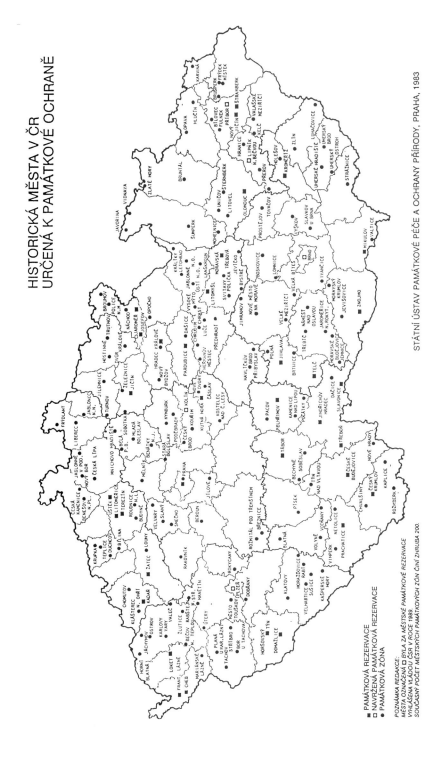

Fig. 3.6 Český Krumlov, a characteristic middle-sized town of medieval South Bohemian origin, its historical urban structure and tissue preserved nearly untouched, including very impressive links with the surrounding picturesque landscape.

be recorded, and the implementation of real preservation work, some categories of the cultural heritage (notably ecclesiastical) were discriminated against while others (e.g. the monuments of the labour movement) were overemphasized. However, a serious drawback appeared in practice, as neither the law nor the implementing regulations that were issued were sufficiently detailed and resulted in some lawsuits. Therefore, the preparation of a new law began, but lasted almost 20 years. The new law, no. 20/1987 Sb., 'Concerning the State preservation of cultural heritage', which remains in force, did away with the said drawback. It also substantially changed the philosophy of the protection of the cultural heritage.

Conditions applied to items declared for protection
The fundamental change is the fact that *only an item that the Ministry of Culture declares to be cultural heritage is protected heritage*. The process of declaration is not an administrative ruling according to general regulations. Legal remedies against this decision do not exist. The declaration may be annulled only by the Ministry of Culture in particularly well-founded cases and at the owner's instigation or on the basis of a proven legal interest. *Thus, protection has become a selective matter dependent on the administrative ruling, not on the presence itself of the values of an item.* The law authorizes the government to declare the most important cultural heritage items to be National Cultural Monuments and lays down the conditions of their protection. Alas, given the present extreme interpretation of the Charter of Fundamental Rights and Liberties, these conditions are not laid down. The reason given for this is that it would be an inadmissible limitation of the owners' rights. Similarly, the limiting conditions are lacking in the decrees concerning the conservation sites declared by the government and the conservation zones, which are now within the authority of the Ministry of Culture. The owner of a cultural heritage item has a basic duty to preserve it. The owner is also charged with keeping records, as each

change of ownership, location or use and any threat or damage must be reported to the relevant authority. Citizens, communities and organizations have a duty not to cause unfavourable changes to items of the cultural heritage and their environment and not to threaten them; otherwise their activity may be limited or prohibited.

In deciding, the authorities have to proceed in agreement with the specialist bodies for the preservation of cultural heritage. *A direct link between land-use planning and the preservation of the cultural heritage does not ensue from the law, but the bodies deciding on the territorial and building procedure have to do this in accordance with the opinion, binding for them, of the body for the preservation of cultural heritage.* This opinion is given at the request of the owner, who has to seek it for any intended change and for each renovation project of an item of the cultural heritage. The same duty is imposed on owners of immovable properties that are not declared cultural heritage, but which are on the area of a conservation site or zone or which are in the protective zone. As extreme means for the protection of cultural heritage, the right of pre-emption by the state has been provided for cases of the continuous non-fulfilment of the owner's duties, even to the extent of the expropriation of the respective item of cultural heritage. The owner is obliged to allow the survey and scientific examination of his or her property by authorized persons. A decision made by the authorities for the preservation of cultural heritage is also needed before moving a cultural heritage item.

Movement of objects of cultural value
Based on a permission granted by the Ministry of Culture or, as the case may be, the government, the export of National Cultural Monuments from the country is possible only for a limited period of time for the purpose of its exhibition, etc. – permanent export is not possible. On the other hand, objects of cultural value may be imported from abroad only with the permission and consent of the respective authority of the country from which such objects are to be imported. However, the law concerning the export and sale of objects with a cultural value, which limits the possibility of movement out of the country and sets the conditions for such activity, was only adopted in 1994. Now objects with a cultural value may be exported from the Czech Republic only with a certificate issued according to the quoted law.

The protection of the archaeological heritage
The protection of archaeological cultural heritage has been strengthened substantially by imposing an owners' duty to report every intended inter-vention on the terrain where archaeological finds may be expected. In such cases, the District Office may decide to carry out archaeological rescue research at the developers' cost, with the exception of activities subsidised or set up by the state. In the latter case exploration is paid for by the specialist organizations carrying out the activity. The bodies authorized to carry out archaeological rescue research are the Archaeological Institute of the Academy of Science of the Czech Republic and any organization authorized by the Ministry of Culture to do this.

Authorizations

Special authorization to restore listed works of visual arts and the objects of arts and crafts is given by the Ministry of Culture to individual persons, according to their education and practice. As to the organization of the state preservation of cultural heritage, the contemporary law has confirmed the status of the state authorities and specialist organizations, and of their associated bodies which gradually came into being during the period of the previous law concerning cultural heritage. The central body for the preservation of cultural heritage is the Ministry of Culture, which set up the specialist organizations for the preservation of the cultural heritage, the State Institute for the Preservation of Cultural Heritage and the regional Institutes for the Preservation of Cultural Heritage.

The Ministry of Culture declares items to be cultural heritage, and may annul such a declaration. It also provides funds for research and development in the preservation of cultural heritage and creates the conceptions and strategies of state care for the heritage. The Ministry of Culture also makes decisions about National Cultural Monuments and authorizes selected activities concerning the preservation of the cultural heritage. The basic executive bodies are the District Offices. Specialist position papers for the activity of these bodies and their decision making are given by the regional Institutes for the Preservation of Cultural Heritage and the specialist working papers for the Ministry of Culture are given by the State Institute for the Preservation of Cultural Heritage. The Inspection of the Preservation of Cultural Heritage, as a part of the Ministry of Culture, is the controlling authority in this area. The state bodies for the preservation of cultural heritage may make financial contributions to the owners of cultural heritage. Tax regulations entitle them to certain allowances or exemption (see 'Financial resources in the form of grants, loans and tax measures', below). Conversely, the failure to perform the duties resulting from the law may lead to the imposition of fines (see 'Sanctions and coercive measures', below).

Review of legal provisions

The 1987 law concerning the state preservation of the cultural heritage is a good instrument for the protection of the cultural heritage. However, the social conditions developed since 1989 cause many problems not foreseen by the law. Therefore, at present, *a readjustment of the protection of items of cultural heritage and territories protected as cultural heritage by law is being prepared*, which will allow for more efficient preservation of the cultural heritage while at the same time improving owners' motivation and simplifying the decision-making processes. However, not even an improved legal machine will affect the current main problem in the protection of cultural heritage, namely the attitude of a large proportion of society towards the cultural heritage. In theory, most people are happy to acknowledge that this heritage is of value, but in practice economic pressures clearly prevail and territories and objects are utilized to their maximum economic capacity irrespective of their character, age, cultural value or the protection provided by law. Perhaps this problem may by solved by improving the quality of education and instruction, but this will certainly be a long-term process.

Conservation philosophy

Specialist opinion and philosophies on the optimum means of preserving the Czech cultural heritage have been characterized by great intellectual originality since the beginning of the twentieth century. However, the evolution of conservation philosophy in this country has never led to the codification of a specifically Czech conservation charter. During the entire twentieth century, Max Dvořák's *Katechismus der Denkmalpflege (Compendium of the Preservation of Monuments)*, published in 1916, has been much respected although not always consistently observed. Mentioned in the introduction, the passionate controversy unleashed in the mid-1930s between the protagonists of the analytical-modernistic conception of the conservation of historic buildings and those favouring a more synthesising-reconstructing approach has never been definitively decided. However, its high theoretical level and the weight of the arguments adduced by both parties have had a permanent positive impact: they freed the Czech preservation of cultural heritage from one-sidedness, from a mechanical application of ready-made methods and uncritical doctrinaire attitudes. What is characteristic of the evolution of the Czech preservation of cultural heritage from the end of World War II practically to the present day, is its flexibility and lack of dogmatism. Based on the individual character of a monument or historic settlement, a quite individual methodological approach and means of rehabilitation are sought.

The permanently valid Rieglian respect for the original material substance of a given historical building or work of art remains the common basis of present Czech conservation philosophy and practice. The maximum preservation of all historical constructions, surfaces and details is always the prefered principle. However, it is realized at the same time that the preservation of historical works of art and architecture cannot be conditioned by the existence of their transient material substance only. This would lead to scepticism and resignation. Therefore, efforts are made to rehabilitate cultural heritage just as much as integral works of art. Whether this can be achieved by reconstructing the missing parts of a given building according to attainable historical knowledge or whether, and to what extent, it is more appropriate to emphasize, in a sort of counterpoint, the present creative contribution, depends on the infinitely variable circumstances of each case. These circumstances, among which the historical and artistic value of a given object, identified as precisely as possible, always plays the decisive role, and also determines the acceptable level of compromise between the owners' and users' demands will vary from case to case. It is quite logical that these demands should follow from the careful process of the functional transformation and re-animation of historic buildings and settlements, this process being seen by the Czech preservation of cultural heritage as the only real instrument for permanent preservation. The principle of the indivisible protection of the exterior and the internal composition, constructions and interior of historical buildings is firmly anchored in the Czech tradition of the preservation of monuments. Consequently, Czech conservation theory unequivocally rejects the so-called façadism, which began to spread into this country after 1989.

The philosophy briefly sketched above came into being independently, but certainly does not contradict in any way the ICOMOS Venice Charter, adopted in 1964. It has been confirmed by the national specialist conference organized by the ICOMOS Czech National Committee in 1994 that the Venice Charter continues to be a valid document. In the conditions existing in the Czech preservation of cultural heritage, this charter does not need fundamental revision in any of its points. However, the acknowledgement of the Venice Charter does not mean that there is no further development in theoretical thought. This development partly stimulates and partly reflects the movement that appears in conservation practice. In architectural conservation, the present generation of experts engaged in preservation adopts, in some respects, a critical attitude towards the results of the care of cultural heritage in the 1970s and 1980s. This generation rejects especially the costly comprehensive reconstruction of historic buildings, then extorted by the strong lobby of large socialist building contractors. The present system of providing state grants, and the efforts of the specialist institutes for the preservation of cultural heritage, unequivocally gives preference to timely repairs, limited in their extent, and to continuous maintenance. Increasing reservations about reconstructions and replicas are evident. Unfortunately, this trend in conservation philosophy is not always fully understood and accepted by the public. The majority of the owners of cultural heritage continue to prefer substantial renovation and do not appreciate the difference between the value of an original with a noble patina and a present-day duplicate. Thus, the present boom in building activities poses a serious risk for the authenticity of cultural heritage, in spite of the efforts of the specialist staff.

Due to its fairly strict requirements, the preservation of cultural heritage is taking a lead in preserving or reviving traditional building crafts and techniques and the use of traditional building materials. In this respect, the preservation of the cultural heritage is alone in opposing the – unfortunately massive – influx of different west European products – synthetic coating compositions for façades, artificial roofs, windows made of plastic, etc. – which is pernicious for the authenticity of historic buildings. It may be said that these materials are excluded from the renovation of listed buildings.

The dialogue between representatives of the preservation of the cultural heritage and present-day architects as well as the collaboration between these representatives and artists restoring historical works of plastic arts and their mutual influence are important for the evolution of heritage conservation philosophy. The attitude towards present-day architecture is still negatively influenced by the tragic experiences of the 1950s, when the socialist realism of the Soviet provenance was forcibly introduced into this country and into architecture. This socialist realism resulted in the distinctively decorative neo-Renaissance and neo-classical styles – and produced insurmountable repugnance in more than one generation of architects to any form of historicism. An indirect consequence was an aversion to the preservation of the cultural heritage, still unjustly considered by a number of architects as a brake being put on, and undesirable competition with, present architectural creation.

Unlike the still problematic relationship, often full of conflict, between the preservationists and contemporary architects, the artist–restorers' involvement in the evolution of conservation philosophy is very positive and inspiring. The restoration of works of art has a long tradition and excellent reputation for quality in the Czech Republic. This is favoured by a system of restorer licences (see above). To maintain the high level of their work, the artist–restorers founded their own professional association in 1990 and published *The Restorer's Ethical Code* in 1991. In addition to the strict demands placed on the investigation and documentation of the work of art being restored, this publication regards meticulous consideration for the original material substance of the object and the present-day restorers' absolute servitude to the original artist as the main principles of the restorers' work. It is very gratifying that a substantial part of this philosophy is beginning to pass into the approach to the conservation of historic buildings (Fig. 3.7).

To increase the quality of practical techniques and procedures used in the preservation of the cultural heritage, and in order to avoid the most frequent errors made in this process, the State Institute for the Preservation of Cultural Heritage began to publish thematic methodological handbooks in 1996, of which *The Preservation of Roofs of Historical Buildings, Standard*

Fig. 3.7 Prague, St Nicolaus Church in the Lesser Quarter. The recently cleaned and restored spire demonstrates the new orientation in the philosophy of conservation. The goal is to make the restoration nearly invisible, in spite of the large amount of work undertaken on the building.

Non-Destructive Historical and Archaeological Survey of Historical Buildings, The Preservation of Stone-Made Sculpture and Buildings and *The Maintenance and Building Adaptations of Castle Ruins*, have been published so far. The issue of *The Protection and Conservation of Wooden Structures, The Colours of Historical Façades and the Preservation of Historical Plasters, The Exploration and Protection of Village Settlements* and other handbooks are being prepared.

These slender pamphlets do not seek to produce new theory or codify the general principles of conservation. Their aim is purely practical. They generalize positive experience and well-tried methods and specify interventions, techniques, technologies and materials the use of which is unequivocally unsuitable in the preservation of cultural heritage.

The evolution of the preservation of cultural heritage as a specialist discipline, its philosophy, scientific research and its practical results are reflected in the specialist review *Zprávy Památkové Péče* (*News of Cultural Heritage Preservation:* 10 issues a year), published since 1937. Besides this, the review *Průzkumy Památek* (*Investigation of Historical Buildings*) has been published since 1994, focusing, as its title shows, on the publication of the results of research in archives, archaeology and art history carried out wduring the preparation and progress of the conservation of historic buildings. The results of extensive archaeological research are being published in monographs and papers in the reviews *Památky Archeologické* (*Archaeological Heritage*), *Archeologické Rozhledy* (*Archaeological Review*), *Archeologické Výzkumy v Jižních Čechách* (*Archaeological Research in South Bohemia*), *Archeologie ve Středních Čechách* (*Archaeology in Central Bohemia*) and information on the results of archaeological research is given in numerous omnibus volumes issued by regional museums.

Sanctions and coercive measures

Law no. 20/1987 very fittingly and aptly specifies the duties of the owners with respect to the protection and use of cultural heritage items. At the same times, the law also states the measures and sanctions that the authorities may apply if these duties are not fulfilled. The law also allows the prohibition of activities conducted by owner's that threaten a protected cultural heritage item (article 11), and of carrying out the necessary measures to protect the cultural heritage even against the owner's will, but at his or her cost. Expropriation of the cultural heritage if no corrective action is undertaken (article 15) is one of the most stringent measures that can be taken.

Sanctions against both natural and juridical persons not respecting the law are specified in articles 35 to 39 of the law. They range from 10,000 to 500,0000 Kč, which are ridiculously low fines in view of the present-day prices of immovable properties and construction work. Apart from that, punishment under special regulations is possible. According to the present version of law no. 50/1976 Sb., concerning land-use planning and the con-struction code, substantially higher fines may be imposed on both natural and juridical persons for the infringement of this law if their illicit acts concern buildings or areas which are covered by the state preservation of cultural heritage.

Similarly, illicit acts affecting parks, gardens and other natural growth protected as cultural heritage according to law no. 114/1992 Sb., which concerns the protection of nature and landscape, may also be punished.

In some cases, the acts punishable according to the above-mentioned regulations may also constitute the facts of a case relating to an offence consisting of damaging someone else's property, protected by special regulations according to article 257 of the penal code. In such circumstances the punishment is detention of up to 1 year. This procedure is worth considering especially in the case of the destruction of, or damage done to, movable archaeological finds, which by law are considered national property. Besides, damage to the cultural heritage is punishable as misuse of property according to the provision of article 258 of the penal code by a prison sentence lasting up to 2 years.

In summary, it may be said that, except for the low level of the fines which may be imposed, the law theoretically goes a long way in influencing owners' rights and gives a wide number of instruments for protecting public interest in the cultural heritage. However, in practice, the respective authorities institute proceedings only sporadically and the full range of penalties are infrequently imposed. The fact is that legal proceedings progress so sluggishly that the one-year preclusive period, during which any breach of the law may be dealt with, finishes before a legally binding decision is reached. Criminal prosecutions are conducted only very rarely, due to the fact that the bodies for the preservation of cultural heritage usually do not inform the authorities active in criminal proceedings, even in justified cases.

Integrated conservation

The development of towns during the nineteenth century and the effort to organize that development led, especially from the 1890s, to the establishment of a special branch, namely land-planning. In the inter-war period, the Czech town-planners applied the principles expressed in the 1933 Athens Charter while preferring the functional organization of the territory. After World War II, during the period of the totalitarian political system and central planning (1948–89), economic policy was directed to the extensive development of towns following the growth in industry and then to the building of housing estates round their perimeters. The historical centres became dilapidated, but paradoxically preserved the authenticity of the built-up area and this subsequently allowed their regeneration. The specialized State Institute for the Reconstruction of Historical Towns and Properties was drawing up layout plans for the historic cores of towns for a period of 35 years. Although this was a monopoly, a qualified professional angle was guaranteed in the recognition of historical ensembles and in the approach to their regeneration. The legal basis for the town-planners' activity was law no. 84/1958, concerning land-use planning, and the subsequent law no. 50/1976, concerning land-use planning and the construction code, amended between 1990 and 1998.

As a broader organizational and social system, land-use planning deals with the functional use of the territory, its organization and the co-ordination of any development. It also creates prerequisites for ensuring permanent harmony between all natural, cultural and civil values on a given territory with regard to the care of the environment, including the heritage preservation.

Three types of land-use planning documentation are required for the development of a territory and the protection and regeneration of its historically important parts:

- the layout plan of a large commune, dealing with the territory of several local councils or districts;
- the layout plan of a commune, dealing with the territory of the whole commune;
- the regulatory plan, dealing with part of the territory of a commune, in most cases that of its centre.

For the protection of the cultural heritage and protected territories (conservation sites and conservation zones), the executive bodies of the state preservation of cultural heritage give their binding opinions when land-use planning working papers are being drawn up and when land-use planning documentation is being drawn up and approved. The regime, including the limits and regulatory conditions, is an important final output. If the demands concerning the elements of the cultural heritage are reflected in these documents, the protection of the cultural-historical elements is duly provided for. However, in practice, different situations may arise. The interests of the state preservation of cultural heritage are taken into account sometimes to a larger extent and sometimes to a lesser extent and some compromises are made.

There are no specific regulations for the planning of new house building in towns. The law concerning land-use planning and that concerning the state preservation of cultural heritage are in force and allow the definition, in the assignment, of the principles and conditions of new development in a territory.

During the last 10 years of the twentieth century, a still greater decentralization of the powers of the land-use planning bodies has been carried out than that laid down by the law no. 50/1976.

Land-use planning has the following bodies:

- the Communes, which order and approve their layout plans and regulation plans;
- the District Offices, which have the competence of the superior land-planning body for the communes;
- the Ministry of Local Development, which draws up and approves the layout plans of large territorial wholes (these layout plans were approved previously by the government).

The assessment of the layout plan and regulation plan of a commune is ensured by a democratic process with the participation of all the citizens who are owners and of the respective bodies of public administration.

The town and parish councils formulate their development policy usually for the time of their election period. Within the meaning of the governmental ruling no. 209/1992, the towns with protected historical cores have drawn up their own Programmes of the Regeneration of Urban Conservation Sites or Urban Conservation Zones. These programmes are linked to the organization of the grant policy of the state.

The owners of cultural heritage items are responsible for their preservation. The communes, which supervise the state of the buildings, are responsible for the preservation of conservation sites and conservation zones. The communes are responsible for the preservation and development of the settlements and have their own revenues and powers to do this. The communes draw up and approve the land plans and issue generally binding by-laws defining the regime of activities on the respective territory.

Since 1989, after the political and economic life of the state had been liberalized, the urgent problem of the regulation of the spontaneity of investment in the town centres and the channelling of the owners' interests has arisen (Fig 3.8). Therefore, the regulating measures for land development and the regeneration of individual buildings need to be made more thorough. In land-use planning this means the effective application of the requirements of the state preservation of cultural heritage in conceiving the individual layout plans of towns. 'Plans for the principles of the protection of territories in view of their cultural heritage' have been applied of late, which specify the values of buildings and other elements in the territory and the possibilities of the adaptability of individual buildings and their wider environment.

Consisting of the representatives of 176 towns, the Association of the Historical Settlements in Bohemia, Moravia and Silesia plays an important

Fig. 3.8 Prague, the building lot of the future Four Seasons Hotel. The picture shows the brutality with which the present-day powerful developers try to penetrate the very core of the historic city with their new buildings.

role in the active policy of the preservation of historical towns and promotes a positive relationship towards the cultural heritage.

Financial resources in the form of grants, loans and tax measures

According to law no. 20/1987 Sb., concerning the state preservation of cultural heritage, owners have a duty to preserve their cultural heritage at their own cost. For the renovation of the cultural heritage, the state may give them a grant, usually equivalent to 50 per cent of the cost and, in the case of the restoration of artistic elements of listed buildings, 100 per cent of the cost. For economic reasons, the state cannot give these grants automatically to all owners. Gradually, the Ministry of Culture has initiated several saving and stimulation programmes so that the limited resources may be utilized to maximum effect.

Programmes of support

Grant assistance for repair, renovation and regenerative action

Since the early 1990s, the Ministry of Culture has had relatively small funds available for grants to be used for the salvation of threatened items cultural heritage. These funds form the 'Programme for the Removal of Breakdowns and Repairs of Roofs', amounting to a maximum of 50 million Kč annually. Contributions to the renovation of cultural heritage may also be given by District Offices in the form of grants or repayable accommodations from their budgets. Extensive research into the amount of funds needed for the preservation of the cultural heritage was carried out in 1993. This research revealed then an alarming 40,000 million Kč would be needed for the renovation of neglected and threatened immovable cultural heritage, of which a substantial part was the ecclesiastical cultural heritage. It was found that at least 6,500 million Kč would be needed every year simply to prevent the further deterioration of the cultural heritage. The biggest part of this amount is the cost of remedying the consequences of neglected maintenance or environmental pollution during the period of the totalitarian regime. At that time, 90 per cent of all cultural heritage items were owned by the state, which, however, did not maintain them. After 1989, ownership relations changed fundamentally, as the largest part of the cultural heritage was returned to its original owners, privatized or transferred to the communes, which are privatizing them in their turn. Together with the cultural heritage, its new owners have 'inherited' the debts arising from the past lack of maintenance and, in most cases, are unable to pay off these debts. The research mentioned above was used as background material and to build an argument for using funds from the state budget for the preservation of the cultural heritage in 1994 and 1995, and also for the 'Programme for the Removal of Breakdowns and Repairs of Roofs' as well as the new 'Programme for the Regeneration of Urban Conservation Sites and Urban Conservation Areas in the Czech Republic' which was drawn up in 1992. The overall sum of the grants included in this programme and paid from the state budget amounts to 300 million Kč a year on average while the requests for grants from this Programme have amounted annually to 2,000 million Kč.

In 1996, the cost of the implemented programme was 845 million Kč, of which 350 million Kč was provided from state grants, 390 million Kč by a contribution from the communes, including the grants given to other owners and the shares in the renovation of the cultural heritage owned by them, and the owners' share made up the remainder of 105 million Kč. For the renovation of the cultural heritage the state grants represented some 30 per cent of cost, but for the comprehensive regeneration of territorial conservation sites or conservation zones initiated by the programme, these state grants represented only 10 per cent.

The principles set by the Ministry of Culture for the use of grants from the 1996 programme introduced a points system according to the fulfilment of three criteria: the town should have an up-to-date layout plan, a functional working group and a topical Municipal Programme of Regeneration. The quantum of the percentage of the approved need for a grant was a result of this score. Thus, an element of competitiveness has been introduced into the calculation. The principles have also introduced the possibility of financing the renewal of the cultural heritage being drawn from several sources: they also limited the state grant to a maximum of 50 per cent or, in the case of the churches, to a maximum of 70 per cent, and laid down the duty of financial participation by municipalities from their own budgets, amounting to a minimum of 10 per cent in the case of the private owners of cultural heritage and a minimum of 20 per cent in the case of churches. The shares of the small towns were subsequently lowered and the criterion for payment to be drawn from the taxes of a given territory has been added. At the same time the responsibility of the towns to participate in the decisions about renovation of cultural heritage has been increased.

Action for the countryside
A similar programme has been the 'Programme for the Renewal of the Countryside', implemented in 1998 and administered by the Ministry of Local Development. The programme is comprehensive, focusing on the lifestyle in the countryside, the partnership between the countryside and the towns, on micro-regions, the development of economy, the preservation and renewal of the aspect of the villages, including their cultural heritage, a better arrangement of public open spaces, the improvement of community facilities and technological equipment, the protection of the environment, transport and the preservation and renewal of the landscape. The funds forming part of this programme vary from 200 to 500 million Kč per year. They may also be used for building schemes and layout plans and take the form of direct grants amounting to up to 60 per cent of the cost of the renovation of the cultural heritage, up to 50 per cent in the case of other properties, and up to 30 per cent of the cost of the arrangement of public open spaces. The grants may also be used to make credits and loans more advantageous by using these grants for the payment of interest of up to10 per cent and up to 1 million Kč.

In 1997, the Ministry of Culture added to this the small 'Programme for the Preservation of Village Conservation Sites and Zones and Landscape

Conservation Zones', focusing on the renovation of the cultural heritage in these territories. Relatively small funds have been made available for the implementation of this programme: in 1997 and 1998, 15 million Kč in each year and, in 1999 and 2000, 20 million Kč each year.

Support for the threatened architectural heritage
Since 1995, the introduction of a new programme directed at the salvation of architectural heritage has meant an important strengthening of the support given to the owners of cultural heritage items. An exploration of threatened large items of the architectural heritage was carried out towards the end of 1994 and its results provided a long list including castles, chateaux, monasteries, churches, palaces and towns houses. The estimated sums needed for the overall renovation of individual premises often amounted to some 300 million Kč. Grants of between 300 and 400 million Kč are now given annually from the 'Programme for the Salvation of the Architectural Cultural Heritage' while the need, according to the applications submitted, exceeds 2,000 million Kč annually.

The grant funds from this programme have been graded according to:

- the cultural value of the individual item of the cultural heritage;
- its impact on its environment;
- the degree to which it is threatened, the character of its renovation;
- its efficiency and life-span;
- the time needed for the renovation;
- the character of, and the interest in, its use, the use of the surface areas;
- the owners' shares, the shares represented by the grants, the share of its own receipts and the share of grants in the future;
- the need and efficiency of the renovation and the quality of the projects.

Other support
In addition to the grants specified above, the Ministry of Culture now has the opportunity to support the restoration of works of art and archaeological rescue explorations, but these funds are very small. The financing of archaeological research is borne mainly by archaeological organizations. In the case of archaeological rescue explorations made necessary by business activities on a given territory, these explorations are paid by the physical or juridical persons whose entrepreneurial activities threaten to damage or destroy the archaeological value of the area. The explorations on the terrain, scientific reports on the finds and their deposition or safeguarding may be included in the calculation of the costs.

Privileged loans can be given by the state to small and medium-sized businesses through the Ministry of Local Development. This plays a role complementary to the programmes mentioned above. Furthermore, due to an archaeologists' proposal, the Ministry of Culture established, in 1994, a fund for the subsidization of archaeological rescue research. It was not until 1999 that this fund was given the sum of 11 million Kč to be distributed by technical commissions of the Ministry of Culture. Such funds are directed towards cases where the provision of financial resources for carrying out research is problematic.

Since 1993, the tax system has taken into account the need for the preservation and renovation of the cultural heritage and for public access to it. At present, cultural-heritage immovable properties are exempt from the payment of the real estate tax for eight years after the issue of the building permit for the renovation of the respective property. Moreover, on the basis of an agreement concluded with the Ministry of Culture, that part of the cultural-heritage immovable property which is open to the public is fully exempt from the payment of the real estate tax for the whole period of opening. Used for the calculation of the real estate tax base, the accelerated depreciation of investments due to the shortening of their period from 45 to 15 years in the case of cultural-heritage immovable properties is a privilege. The importance of this is reflected in the shortening of the renewal cycle and the increases gained through the growth of revenues.

Through the comprehensive programmes of support and the tax allowances, the state provides funds for the salvation of cultural heritage in a manner previously unparalleled. All these programmes are intended to promote growth, but for the time being it has been impossible to get rid of the debt accumulated during the decades of insufficient maintenance and this will remain the case for the foreseeable future.

The role of agencies and specialist organizations
To avoid losses in the cultural value of the heritage during the process of its maintenance or renewal, the state applies the following means:

1 the regulation, with legal backup, of all building or other alterations to the state of the cultural heritage;
2 a specialist consulting service provided free of charge;
3 grants that may or may not be given.

The activities concerning points (1) and (3) are carried out by state authorities – in the first case by the District Offices and in the second by the Ministry of Culture. The activities concerning point (2) are pursued in the regions by nine specialist Institutes for the Preservation of Cultural Heritage, established for this purpose, and by the State Institute for the Preservation of Cultural Heritage, which is superior to them in terms of specialization but not organization. All these institutes have been founded and are financed by the Ministry of Culture. They have staffs consisting of qualified historians, art historians, architects, archaeologists and technologists (about 350 specialists in total), archives with plentiful geometric and photographic documentation of the cultural heritage and relatively large technical libraries. The main purpose of these regional institutes is to give advice on the everyday practical preservation of the cultural heritage in the field. The role of the State Institute of the Preservation of Cultural Monuments is concerned with scientific research, the philosophy and methodology of the preservation of the cultural heritage, the compilation of its inventories, the keeping of the Central List of Cultural Heritage and the education of G.C.E. holders in the conservation of the cultural heritage. Moreover, most institutes directly administer and preserve selected state castles, chateaux and other monuments open to the public. Their qualified administration and the high level of the services supplied to their visitors are very important. The cultural heritage open to the public includes 100 items owned by the state and 40 owned by private persons to whom they were returned by restitution. Public accessibility is the most efficient means of popularizing the heritage and of encouraging the public to undertake its protection (castles and chateaux open to the public were visited by more than 6 million tourists in 1998).

Archaeological rescue research is overseen by three Institutes for the Preservation of Archaeological Heritage, regional museums, two Archaeological Institutes of the Academy of Science of the Czech Republic and, from the mid-1990s, two civil associations that have been authorized to carry out archaeological research. These civil associations operate in particular in the regions where the technical organizations do not have enough archaeologists. Apart from that, most archaeological organizations are working on tasks concerning research and development in the field of cultural heritage within the programmes formulated by the Ministry of Culture.

According to article 14 of the Cultural Heritage State Preservation Act, in the case of an intervention which requires a building permit and is to be carried out on a protected cultural heritage item, its owner has to see the binding opinion of the District Office. This District Office has to ask the respective regional Institute for the Preservation of Cultural Heritage for its specialist opinion. In these proceedings, only the owner of a cultural heritage item may appeal to the Ministry of Culture. Both making a decision, this Ministry asks the State Institute for the Preservation of Cultural Heritage for its opinion. In the most important cases, the third and final resort is a decision reached by the Minister of Culture after discussion in a commission of appeal set up by him or her. In what is called the extra-appellate procedure, i.e. which does not suspend the usual proceedings, other participants, such as specialist organizations, civil associations or individuals, may also enter into the process of approval.

The system described here, with the executive function separated from the specialist function, although seemingly rather complicated and inflexible, works relatively well in practice, allowing for controversial cases to be comprehensively weighed several times. The system offers independence to the participating specialist institutes and does not oblige them to consider the matter with the inclusion of other than purely specialist viewpoints.

The role of the voluntary civil societies and associations has been increasing greatly since the fall of the totalitarian regime in 1989. Founded in 1900, the Club for Old Prague has the most important tradition. Eminent historians, architects and town-planners are its members today giving it great authority. Neither the state authorities nor the local councils can make light of its initiatives. In parallel, an association called Pražské Gremium (the Prague Society) operates in the capital and has a wider sphere of interest: besides the protection of historic values, it makes efforts to improve the culture, increase the level of new development, sensitively limit increasing car traffic, protect and increase green areas and so on.

After 1989, associations with similar objectives have been set up or activated in a whole number of other historic towns. They represent a large moral and technical resource and can be an important ally, or sometimes even an opponent, of the state authorities and specialist institutes. Being highly flexible, they set up pressure groups and lead campaigns against insensitive interventions into the historical structures of their towns, especially if they feel that the state protection of cultural heritage is failing. The most important voluntary organization is the Association of Historic Settlements in Bohemia, Moravia and Silesia, whose members are the mayors, town-clerks and elected representatives of more than 170 historic towns. The Association has become an important political force, lobbying in particular for the consideration of the protection of the towns and the preservation of architectural heritage as national priorities by the parliament and the government and for the non-annulment and non-curtailment, even in economically unfavourable years, of the state grants for the preservation of the cultural heritage. In addition, the Association aims to spread its message as widely as possible and influence the public. Every year, on the occasion of the International Day of Monuments and Sites, the Association awards prize and gives a special grant to the most active town. Working with the Ministry of Culture, the Association has organized the inauguration of European Heritage Days and opened items of cultural heritage in its towns to the public free of charge.

Education and training

The system of education in the preservation of cultural heritage is very well developed in the Czech Republic although not all disciplines are covered to the same extent. The following list provides an indication of educational provision in cultural heritage at university level.

*   The students at the Arts Faculties of the universities in Prague, Brno and Olomouc may, after graduating as BA in the history of art, specialize in cultural heritage preservation which emphasizes the knowledge of historical evolution, the philosophy of conservation and develops the ability to analyse and interpret historical works of architecture and plastic arts.
*   The conservation and reconstruction of historical buildings, including drawing up the respective building schemes and projects as a prerequisite of graduation, are an optional subject taught to the students at the Faculties of Architecture at the technological universities in Prague and Brno.
*   At the Academy of Arts in Prague, there are two studios which specialize in the restoration of paintings and sculptures.
*   At the Chemical-Technological University in Prague, a degree course is offered in the technology of the conservation and restoration of cultural heritage.

- At the School of Economics in Prague, the preservation of cultural heritage is an obligatory subject in the Tourist Trade Department.
- Prehistory, archaeology and classical archaeology may be read for MA degrees at the Arts Faculties of the universities in Prague, Brno and Plzeň. In Opava, Olomouc and Ústí nad Labem, archaeology is taught as part of the study of humanities for a BA degree. Most students of archaeology also graduate in history, ethnology, ethnography and similar subjects.

In addition to the courses listed the above, a specialized two-year post-graduate study of the preservation of cultural heritage is available at all the above-mentioned Faculties of Arts and the Faculty of Architecture in Prague. Although more of a marginal subject, the preservation of the cultural heritage is taught together with museum science at five other regional universities.

The lecturers of these courses are mainly university professors or experts working in the practice of the protection of cultural heritage. The students tend to be people working in widely different spheres of life: public servants, artists-restorers, managers, or members of the staff of building enterprises, persons working in the tourist trade and members of the Police of the Czech Republic.

Although the extent of coverage varies, the preservation of cultural heritage is taught at almost thirty technical secondary schools, especially arts-and-craft schools, building-industry technical schools, but also economic and teaching schools.

This brief resumé of courses available in the Czech Republic illustrates the great possibilities offered to anyone interested in learning about the preservation of the cultural heritage. In the university studies in particular there is generally a high level of specialism. The fact that the exploration of historic buildings or the building schemes of their renovation are themes of the students' work drawn up for credits or degrees is also important. However, the lack of information about cultural heritage and its preservation, existing in the curricula of the primary schools and the secondary schools for general education, has to be considered a serious weak spot in the Czech educational system. The lack of teaching on the preservation of cultural heritage at theological faculties also has negative consequences. At these institutions not even the history of art was taught during the whole of the communist era and this has had a calamitous effect on the attitude of many priests' to the value of the cultural heritage administered by them. At the Catholic theological faculties in Prague nad Olomouc, the history of art at least has been reintroduced into the curriculum. Another area where improvement is desperately needed is the better education of apprentices in traditional building crafts and especially acquainting them practically with historical manual techniques, technologies and materials for finishing the surfaces of buildings. At all these educational levels, it is proving difficult to restore the continuity, almost torn asunder, of the technological knowledge and the craftsmen's skills required to maintain the Czech cultural heritage.

Ulla Lunn and Carsten Lund

Denmark

Introduction

The traveller in Denmark immediately becomes aware of a rich and well-preserved building culture. This is characterized by numerous ancient monuments and ruins and more recent building structures. As a trading and maritime nation, Denmark, throughout history, has had close contacts with the rest of Scandinavia, the countries of central Europe, and the British Isles. These contacts have left a distinctive imprint on Denmark's landscape, urban environment and building culture. For example Danish coastal towns share a clear structural affinity with the commercial centres of Denmark's historical maritime trading partners. The country's architecture also reflects foreign influences, mainly from Germany, Holland and Italy, but at the same time it has its own unmistakably Danish character (Figs 4.1 and 4.2).

Denmark also has a strong agricultural tradition, and farm buildings are another element of the nation's architectural heritage. The country's orderly rural landscape is home to a building culture that is rich in tradition and ranges from magnificent country estates to a network of villages and isolated farms (Fig. 4.3). Each district has its own characteristics and local traditions in building customs that depend on the materials available, local topography, etc.

Denmark's heritage of ancient monuments is represented by numerous ruins from the Bronze Age and the late Stone Age, large ruins from the Middle Ages, usually defensive structures, and more recently, coastal forts and the well-preserved defence system around Copenhagen dating from the end of the nineteenth century.

Denmark has managed to retain its tradition for buildings of high architectural merit after the industrial revolution. This is particularly evident in the case of public buildings such as railway stations, town halls,

Fig. 4.1 Tersløsegård (1737), the summer residence of the author Ludvig Holberg (exterior). An example of a Danish manor house from the enlightenment era. Built on the ideas of the baroque, but with significant Scandinavian features: the use of daylight, and the best materials and craftsmanship available. (Copyright: Henriette Bjarne Hansen.)

Fig. 4.2 Tersløsegård (interior). (Copyright: Henriette Bjarne Hansen.)

Fig. 4.3 The country estate of Klintholm on Sealand. A large part of the built heritage of great value comprises several hundred manors and estates; they are of central importance in the preservation of the landscape and the cultural environment. (Copyright: National Forest and Nature Agency.)

courthouses, schools and hospitals. Buildings of such quality are common to most major towns in the nation. This has been a result of the Danish tradition for relatively decentralized administration.

During the twentieth century, Denmark has won international acclaim for high quality in architecture and building. The urban development and individual buildings may have drawn some inspiration from external sources, especially German modernism and British planning ideals, but in modern architecture too the characteristic Danish hallmarks persist in design, materials and construction.

Definition of the heritage
The built heritage

The definition of the heritage to be protected has tended to broaden over the last century. When the idea of protecting buildings was first introduced, approximately one hundred years ago, it was very old historic buildings, monuments and buildings of great and classical architectural value that were identified for society to protect. The Preservation of Buildings Act was introduced in 1918 (Fig. 4.4). This law recognized that it was the right and duty of society to protect the most valuable architectural treasures and also that this was an area in which society's interest should be seen as more important than those of the individual owner. A list of 1,258 buildings protected by this legislation, both privately and publicly owned, was drawn up. By the middle of the twentieth century the scope of this protection had changed so that a greater number of buildings were listed, specifically to protect the façades of a street, a square or a village.

Originally the effort to protect the built heritage through the Preservation of Buildings Act had specialized in particularly vulnerable and precious

Fig. 4.4 Rosenborg, the summer residence of Christian IV. The king created the layout himself in 1606. The Castle was listed when the Preservation of Buildings Act first came into function in 1918.

buildings, both privately and publicly owned. In recognition of the twentieth century's large monuments from the modern school, the newly altered law changed the age criterion for inclusion from 100 years to 50 years allowing even younger buildings to be listed if necessary.

The current legislation is the Consolidated Act no. 845 of 13 November 1997 (*Lovbekendgørelse nr. 845 af 13 november 1997*): the Listed Buildings and Preservation of Buildings and Urban Environment Act (*Lov om bygningsfredning og bevaring af bygninger og bymiljøer*) (hereafter known as the Preservation of Buildings Act 1997). Section 1 states that the object of the Act is 'to safeguard older buildings of special architectural, cultural-historical or environmental value, including buildings which illustrate building, working, and other production conditions and other significant characteristics of social development' (Fig. 4.5). Section 3 paragraph 2 of the Act further identifies that a preservation order may include 'the immediate surroundings of a building in the form of courtyards, squares, pavements, gardens, parks, and similar, to the extent that they form part of a whole which is to be protected'.

For the last 20 years other ways of protection have emerged. In this context Section 17 of the Preservation of Buildings Act 1997 identifies the concept of 'Buildings worthy of preservation'. Local preservation plans and urban renewal schemes have taken over the protection of the buildings worthy of preservation in a broader sense of the word.

Ancient monuments and archaeological interests

Protection of ancient monuments is fully integrated in nature protection in the Danish Protection of Nature Act, Act No. 9 of 3 January 1992. The legislation provides for the protection of both monuments and their

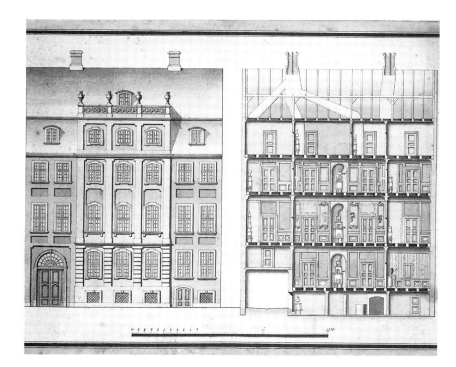

Fig. 4.5 Cross-section of Amaliegade 7, Copenhagen (privately owned). This drawing from around 1750 shows the structure of a magnificent bourgeois urban dwelling. In a listed building all structural parts of the building and all interior features are protected.

surroundings. Furthermore the legislation provides for the protection of landscapes with cultural as well as natural features.

The monuments covered by this provision are described in an annex to the Act. The annex divides the monuments into three categories:

1   Traditional ancient monuments easy to recognize, such as barrows, megalith monuments, ruins, etc. These are automatically protected whether they have been registered or not, apart from ruins totally covered by earth.
2   Other ancient monuments more difficult to recognize, such as dams and dikes, holy wells, bridges and road constructions, etc. These are protected only if the landowner has received notification of their existence from the Ministry of Environment and Energy.
3   More recent monuments and monuments connected with popular beliefs, historical tradition or folklore. These monuments are protected only if the landowner has received notification of their existence.

The difference between monuments in groups (2) and (3) is that for those within group (2) a protection zone of 100 metres around the monument is applied, while this is not so for monuments in group (3).

Underwater monuments and historic shipwrecks are protected under Section 14 of the Protection of Nature Act. It provides for the protection of all archaeological structures and shipwrecks wrecked more than 100 years ago in the territorial waters and on the continental shelf in a zone of 24 nautical miles from the coast or from the base-lines used to delimit the territorial waters.

While the protection of shipwrecks depends of their age as wrecks there is no statutory age limit for ancient monuments but it is assumed in the explanation to Section 12 of the Act that a monument should be at least 100 years old, although parts of it might be younger.

Identification of the heritage
Architectural assets
The process of identifying architectural assets to be *listed for protection* was originally undertaken by the National Museum. Surveys were carried out on rural building traditions, provincial town houses and large estates all over the country. This was the basis used in first decades when buildings were listed for protection. The tradition was developed and continued through the 1960s, 1970s and 1980s, when most major towns were subject to surveillance. Likewise there have been inventories made of typical buildings such as railway stations or the work of specific architects. These thematic surveys have resulted in a few buildings being highlighted in each category.

Lately thematic surveys have developed into larger projects in co-operation either with groups of specialists or with the network of local museums. For example the thematic listing of early industrial monuments was based on a major investigation carried out by a group of specialists. The thematic listing of early school buildings was based upon research of old school buildings that the local museums held records of (Ministry for the Environment and Energy/National Forest and Nature Agency) (MEE/NFNA, 1999).

The wide interest that has surrounded urban conservation and the preservation of buildings in Denmark in the 1990s prompted the Danish parliament to press for increased priority to be given to the activities in this field. To comply with this request, *Skov- og Naturrstyrelsen* (the National Forest and Nature Agency) developed a quick and simple system – SAVE – for the survey and registration of items of architectural value in the environment and of *buildings worthy of preservation*. These surveys are conducted on a municipal basis in co-operation with the Agency.

The purpose of the survey is first of all to identify which buildings and urban environments require protection in municipal planning and in the local administration of building applications. The second purpose is to establish a platform for evaluating ways in which new buildings can be fitted into existing urban environments. Rarely a survey leads to the listing of buildings under the auspices of the National Forest and Nature Agency (MEE/NFNA, 1995).

Proposals for buildings to be considered for preservation (listing) under the 1997 Act may also be submitted by local authorities or by the National Society for the Protection of Buildings and Landscapes, or by individuals. Proposals are brought before the Historic Building Council, which is an advisory board whose expert members represent relevant organizations and institutions.

Once the advisory board has approved a proposal an elaborate procedure commences. The procedure ensures that the opinions of the owner, the local authorities and any organizations involved are all heard. Often the future of the building must be discussed and enlightened thoroughly in connection to this procedure. The National Forest and Nature Agency is then responsible for taking the final decision on whether to list the building or not. An appeal can be made against this decision to the Minister of the Environment and Energy.

There is no compensation implied in the listing of a building. The basic idea is that the building is listed as it is, and special demands are only meant to deal with future alterations. But to make up for the higher costs of good craftsmanship and high quality materials there are different fiscal compensations available to the owners (see the section, 'Financial support for listed buildings and buildings worthy of preservation', below). The basic demands to the owner are that the building should, as a minimum, be structurally safe, i.e. roofing, façades and windows must be in good repair. Also the owner must apply to the National Forest and Nature Agency for permission to do all works on the building that go beyond regular maintenance of both the exterior and interior.

By the turn of the millennium 9,200 buildings had been protected through the listing process. Public buildings, for example town halls, schools and railway stations, account for 12 per cent of the total number of listed buildings. Another 12.5 per cent are manor houses and buildings in their surroundings, 13 per cent are other rural buildings, 58 per cent are urban buildings, and the remaining 4.5 per cent comprise a group of different types of buildings such as windmills, factories, etc.

Ancient monuments and archaeological sites

The National Museum has also been responsible for the registration of ancient monuments defined by the Protection of Nature Act. More than 30,000 ancient monuments have been registered in data banks as protected monuments under this legislation. The National Museum has also registered over 100,000 sites where archaeological remains or finds have been made which are temporarily protected through the Act on Museums (see the subsection, 'Ancient monuments and archaeological interests', below).

There are a further 3,000 registered underwater monuments, mainly ancient settlement sites, and a similar number of historic shipwrecks registered, but the estimated number of monuments and shipwrecks in the protection zone of 24 nautical miles is far higher.

The preservation and protection of the heritage
The built heritage
Authorities responsible for the preservation of buildings
The Minister for the Environment and Energy has delegated the administration of the Preservation of Buildings Act 1997 to the National Forest and Nature Agency. The expertise of protection of the built heritage in these premises exists as a parallel to two other major institutions in this field.

Buildings belonging to the Danish Evangelical Lutheran Church are protected by legislation administered by the Ministry of Ecclesiastical Affairs (Fig. 4.6). These buildings are subject to regular supervision – maintenance works being funded by parish councils in co-operation with the National Museum. Churches that are listed buildings owned by other religious denominations are protected under the Preservation and Buildings Act.

Government ministries and agencies in Denmark are themselves responsible for the buildings they occupy. However, the Palaces and Properties Agency of the Ministry of Housing and Urban Affairs has prepared a classification scheme for these buildings which sets out the extent to which plans for alterations and repairs must be submitted to the Palace and Properties Agency. The Agency also has responsibility for the upkeep of Royal palaces and gardens.

As one might expect, the listed buildings in public ownership are in the top classification (Fig. 4.7). Plans for such buildings must be submitted to the National Forest and Nature Agency as the authority for the preservation of buildings. The supervision of public buildings, including churches, are performed by six architects appointed as Royal Building Inspectors.

Co-operation with the authorities
The object and scope of the Preservation of Buildings Act 1997 is two-fold: under Section 1 of the Act the *object* is to protect the country's older buildings according different values and other criterion (see above). The

Fig. 4.6 A medieval church with its wall and barn, a typical and original feature of the Danish architectural heritage and significant landmarks of the rural landscape. The churches are protected by the ecclesiastical legislation as long as they serve as churches of the Danish Evangelical Lutheran Church. (Copyright: National Forest and Nature Agency.)

section further identifies in para. 2 that the 'administration of the Act shall emphasise that safegarded buildings are given a function which is appropriate to the special character of such buildings and which serves their long-term upkeep'.

Accordingly, it is essential, once the procedure of listing has established that the building is protected under the Preservation of Buildings Act 1997, that the Agency fosters an atmosphere of co-operation with the owners and caretakers of the buildings.

We are currently observing a very keen and increasing interest in historical buildings. The beauty, atmosphere, and heritage of the buildings make them attractive, and owners of such properties often have a special love for them. This means a positive and creative approach to the task of preserving and restoration of the building from most owners and caretakers.

An appropriate function does not mean that it should be possible to remodel the house to fulfil all conceivable functions. A building originally constructed as a residence is still most appropriately used as a residence. Even though it is technically possible to use it for other purposes, for example as office space. Such alterations may entail a danger of many changes that would damage the particular preservation values of that building.

Listed buildings in Denmark often command a high price (the listing usually has a positive effect on market value). Thus, it is likely that owners will wish to make full use of their buildings. Utilizing attics is an example of this. The use of this space leads to windows being inserted in a roof that otherwise may have constituted a beautiful, uninterrupted surface in the urban landscape. But at the same time, dealing with more than 9,000 buildings, there will frequently be differing interests in the demands of protecting historical or architectural values versus the demands of intensive use.

Ancient monuments and archaeological interests

Under section 12 of the Protection of Nature Act it states that: 'It is prohibited to alter the state of ancient monuments. Parcelling out, land registration and transfer of ownership of land whereby new boundaries are established through ancient monuments are also prohibited'.

The protection is a prohibition on any change of state. This applies to the monument as such and to a 2-metre zone around it. There is no prohibition against the cutting of trees and exploitation of the natural vegetation on the monuments. On the other hand any change to a monument without the consent of the Ministry of Environment and Energy is assumed in law to have been made by the landowner or user. This means that he or she will have to pay for its restoration to its former state if it cannot be proved that another person made the change.

As with listed buildings, the protection of ancient monuments is administered by the National Forest and Nature Agency. It requires special circumstances for the agency to grant exemptions from the general prohibition on altering the state of a monument. Such exemptions are hardly ever granted apart from situations where a building situated on a protected, moated site is in need of restoration or modernization. Also archaeological investigation of a monument requires exemption but less than twenty are granted per year.

Supervision of the compliance of the prohibition on altering the state of ancient monuments is carried out by the fourteen county councils which also have the right to carry out maintenance works – not restoration works – on the monuments. They can alter the vegetation on the monuments for reasons of making the monuments visible in the landscape or to create stable conditions for vegetation in order to avoid erosion.

The county councils also administer the protection zone around the monuments. Ancient monuments, mentioned in chapters 1 and 2 of the annex to the Protection of Nature Act, have a protection zone of 100 metres around the monument. Section 18 of the Act prohibits any change of state in this zone. The county council grants exemptions from Section 18 in special circumstances. About 200 such exemptions are granted each year.

Restoration of ancient monuments is also the responsibility of the National Forest and Nature Agency. During the last decade a restoration campaign covering roughly 200 medieval ruins has been undertaken. Also a number of the most visited megalith monuments such as passage graves and dolmens have been restored.

For the 100,000 or so other registered archaeological sites and remains, Section 26 of the Act on Museums provides temporary protection against damage being incurred by potentially damaging activities. Archaeological remains found during construction works or other activities implying removal or tilling of the soil have to be reported to the State Antiquarian.

The administration of this provision has been transferred to the local cultural history museums which have academically trained archaeologists in their permanent staff.

After having received reports of such encounters of archaeological remains the museum has one year to excavate the remains. However, in practice, most of the archaeological excavations are carried out as part of the design phase of construction works because archaeological evaluations are part of the planning process. This also means that mitigation of the projects occurs and excavation can be avoided.

The 'disturber' pays the costs of archaeological excavations if it is a public authority that carries out the construction work. The State Antiquarian pays for excavations caused by private 'disturbers'.

Maintenance, conservation and restoration

Of course, the less that is changed about a listed building, the better. Listing a building for preservation means that the structure and parts of the building must not be tampered with so far as this is not necessary for its long-term preservation. The basic premise of preservation work is to strive to maintain as much as possible of the original building for as long as possible.

Recurrent and thorough maintenance is vitally important to the upkeep of preservation values. An annual check-up of the building's components is a good tool for preventing substantial damage from developing. Follow-up in the form of regular maintenance, such as applying putty to window frames, whitewashing façades, cleaning gutters, new ridges, and new flashing, etc., can postpone major construction work for decades. If regular maintenance is not carried out, the need for such work mounts. Such a backlog of a lack of maintenance will eventually lead to a need for repairs. Larger repairs tend to involve replacing parts of the building, and in this way authentic parts of the building disappear.

If substantial repair work is required, it is necessary to carry out a very critical assessment of what measures need to be taken to restore the standard of the building and which authentic or high-quality parts of the building should remain untouched. The National Forest and Nature Agency recommend that the advice of an architect with special knowledge of restoration should be sought in order to establish what maintenance should be carried out and what more substantial work should be planned. A schedule for regular maintenance work should be carefully planned, so that work is carried out in the right order. And it must be borne in mind that a permit is required for all work that does not qualify as regular maintenance.

The individual parts of the building testify to building techniques, craftsmen's skills, building use, the changing aesthetic views over the periods, and much more. These are all sources for understanding the building and of the life and lives it has witnessed for both our current and future generations. Changes to historical buildings should always be carried out in accordance with the 'less is more' principle.

Great demands are placed on the quality of maintenance and restoration work, quite simply because such work needs to last. These requirements address the quality of both the design and function, as well as the materials and craftsmanship used. Maintaining a high level of quality within work on listed buildings, also helps to ensure that a demand still remains for craftsmen who are skilled in traditional methods. By so doing, quality requirements help to maintain craft skill levels in Denmark. Maintenance work can often be carried out by an individual owner or by occupiers, but even a skilled person will need to seek the advice of a craftsman before starting work. In connection with larger tasks it is necessary to seek the advice of an architect with special knowledge about conservation. It may also be necessary to inspect professional project materials in order to have the restoration process elucidated and see exact information on the work to be performed before granting a permit.

Making use of buildings such as former industrial plants for new purposes often requires extensive conversion work. In these cases it is necessary to have a greater architectural approach to the task. Owners of listed buildings should prepare an overall plan for their buildings, incorporating both the use, or change of use, of the building and elements which testify to the history of the building.

The National Forest and Nature Agency deals every year with numerous applications for restoration projects on listed buildings. All buildings are considered individually. The more authentic the building is the less one should plan for changes. But apart from the general demand on traditional craft methods and materials there are no general rules that are relevant for all listed buildings. That is because the circumstances of historic and architectural values, the state of repair, the plans for the future functions and the economic conditions vary from case to case. Most importantly, it is a good idea to enter into co-operation with the National Forest and Nature Agency when considering the issue of use of buildings.

Sanction and coercive measures

Owners of listed buildings must at the very least keep their buildings in good repair. 'Good repair' in this respect is usually defined as sealed roofs, windows and bays, i.e. the building must be sealed off against the elements. However, it is not enough that the house has doors, windows and a roof. It must also be in a condition where individual building parts are not in disrepair or in a condition so bad as to pose a danger of long-term damage to the building. For example, windows must be joined and painted to prevent the wood from deteriorating. Drains must not be clogged so that water runs down the façade. Roofs and flashing must be sealed to prevent the danger of dry rot, etc.

The public often takes an interest in the condition of listed buildings. If a listed house is gradually decaying, at some point someone will take exception to this, and both the media and the authorities will be notified. The National Forest and Nature Agency will also make a direct approach to the owner if it becomes aware that a listed building is in dire need of remedial action.

Local authorities are under the obligation of the Building Act to take action if the condition of buildings poses a threat to users or passers-by, but local authorities must also report cases where they become aware of illegal work or mistreatment of a listed building.

When offences are registered, the Agency will seek to have them set right by having the owner remedy the state of affairs, or by making this a prerequisite for future approvals or subsidies. It is also possible to grant a subsequent permit if the work in question has in actual fact been carried out properly.

However, where offences are deliberate and repeated, the National Forest and Nature Agency will quickly take legal steps to make sure that the condition is put right. In practice, however, it is very rare for cases not to be solved in co-operation with the Agency. Using a combination of counselling and subsidies or loans, it is usually possible to remedy the situation.

If a case is not resolved by means of normal negotiations, the Agency may issue a juridical order, stipulating that repairs must be made. The Agency also have the opportunity of entering properties and carrying out work as necessary to ensure building safety, such as spreading tarpaulins and boarding up windows against vandalism. Such work may be carried out at the owner's expense. A juridical order will not, however, be issued without previous notice and negotiations; but once an enforcement case commences, the owner will be reported to the police and prosecutions and fines may follow.

If owners of listed buildings carry out work on their properties without a permit, they have sole responsibility. Thus where an owner claims that he or she thought only the exterior of the house was protected, not the interior, this is not a legal remedy. Similarly, where an owner has asked for a permit at the local authorities, and no mention was made of the fact that it was also necessary to apply to the National Forest and Nature Agency, a failure to apply to the Agency cannot be circumnavigated.

It may also happen that illegal changes are not discovered until long after a new owner has taken over the property. Such new owners may be ordered to remedy the illegal changes. Depending on the nature of the case, the Agency may stipulate that new approvals will only be granted on the condition that previous illegal changes are redressed. As an owner, one has the duty to know the law oneself. Consequently, owners may be ordered to remedy their illegal changes.

Prosecutions where owners are ordered to rectify illegal changes are very rare. As was mentioned above, a practicable solution or settlement is almost always found. However, the Agency is currently seeking to render both supervision and enforcement more rigorous, which means that more juridical orders are being issued.

Financial support for listed buildings and buildings worthy of preservation

Financial support for listed buildings

Support may be granted for work on listed buildings in the form of subsidies or loans. The annual budget is about DKK 40–45 million, of which approximately DKK 10 million are earmarked for manor houses.

Thus, the National Forest and Nature Agency can to some extent assign special priority to certain types of buildings, and set aside funds for such purposes. The Agency does not grant support for publicly owned buildings – only to buildings owned by private individuals or by private foundations.

Loans are only granted for more substantial building work. The loan is granted on easy terms, and may amount to up to 100 per cent of the property value. The interest is comparatively low. This also applies to repayments. In 1999, repayments were set at 2 per cent per year until expiry; however, repayment must be made in full in the event of transfer of ownership.

The work carried out on listed buildings is required to be of a high quality, and consequently it is possible to apply for subsidies to cover some of the extra cost involved. It is up to individual owners of listed buildings to maintain their condition. Generally speaking, the condition of listed buildings is satisfactory: approximately 58 per cent of listed buildings are in good condition, 40 per cent are in reasonable condition, and only 2 per cent are in poor condition.

Support can only be granted for repairs on listed buildings, and only for work which ensures the preservation values of buildings. Such work could be facade work, roof work, repairs of windows and doors, indoor work on significant parts of the interior, or combinations of the above. No support is granted for modernization/renovation work, such as bathrooms, central heating, plumbing, etc.

Each project is individually assessed, and support is calculated as a proportion of the expenses that qualify for support. This proportion depends on the nature of the work, the opportunities for receiving other direct or indirect support, etc. Thus, complicated conservation work on, for example, wall coverings or sandstone carvings, would typically receive relatively greater support than work to replace a tiled roof. Moreover, support can be granted in the form of materials from the Agency's stores of reusable materials.

Applications for support must be prepared on the basis of a project and a rough estimate of the costs and should be directed to the Agency's Division of Conservation of Buildings. The average case processing time has been three months. Restoration projects are often very complex, and for this reason it would ease the case process if owners would involve an architect with specialist knowledge of restoration as a consultant from the outset. The Agency may also demand that the project is prepared by an architect with specialist knowledge of conservation techniques if it is found that the task cannot be expediently solved by owners and craftsmen alone.

Subsidies are paid when work has been completed and the completed accounts with receipted bills have been submitted to the Agency. Payment is made on the condition that it is possible to approve the work that has been carried out. The Agency must also be able to approve the accounts, and if other requirements have been stipulated for the subsidies, these too must be met.

Private funding and sponsorships are often found to support the larger building tasks or new schemes for historic buildings. The authorities have no regulation and make no demands in this direction but the owner must inform the authorities of private funding if grants are applied for from the State.

Owners of listed buildings are granted indirect support through the 'Annual Decay' scheme. The objective of the annual decay scheme is to ensure the condition of listed buildings in the best possible way. Owners of listed buildings have an annual tax allowance which is calculated on the basis of the repairs which are found to be required to avoid decay. This annual decay amount is calculated by *Bygnings Frednings Foreningen* (BYFO) (the Association of Owners of Historic Houses) for each separate part of buildings. Thus, the annual decay amount is the amount which owners may spend on repairs and deduct from their taxes. On the basis of receipted bills, it is possible to deduct costs for annual maintenance. And if in any given year these expenses do not add up to the 'annual decay' amount, it is possible to transfer the rest of this amount to the next fiscal year, thus making it possible to 'save' it for more substantial work. However, if an owner does not make full use of the annual decay amount, it cannot be transferred to any new owner.

Owners of listed buildings are exempt from paying property taxes or land taxes if a preservation declaration has been registered on the property in question. Exemption from property tax applies to the area where the listed building is situated. If the surrounding areas are also included in the listing, these are also exempt from land tax.

Other funding sources

The Minister of Housing and Urban Affairs (*By – og Boligministeriet*) also has a large budget available to support urban renewal action in all Danish towns. Until recently the use of such funds was limited to houses within towns. However, following the revision of legislation through the Preservation of Buildings Act 1997 and the Town Renewal Act 1998 and through an agreement between the Housing and Environment Ministries, it has become possible to support houses in rural areas, including in villages and the open countryside.

Out of the funding for urban renewal, funds have been set aside to support repairs to ensure architectural values in villages, rural districts, and listed (house) buildings and other buildings worthy of preservation. This support is administered by local authorities by setting up building improvement councils, and is a voluntary scheme. Funding comes from local authorities, the state, as well as private donors. Moreover, a number of local authorities have preservation funds, which were established before this scheme commenced.

While the building improvement scheme will support listed houses, it is principally directed towards buildings *worthy of preservation* and in this context may be developed in connection with the SAVE system (see the subsection, 'Architectural assets', above). In principle the SAVE system covers the whole municipal area but it tends to concentrate on an agglomeration of buildings such as the main town and the groups of villages within a municipality. There are 267 municipal areas in Denmark and about 60 of these areas have been surveyed for the purpose of the SAVE system so far. However, financial support from the Ministry of Housing and Urban Affairs may now speed up this process. Moreover, if the municipality has carried out a survey under the SAVE system there is a special funding for the top graded buildings worthy of preservation.

Financial support can also be derived from other schemes such as when there is high unemployment. Special schemes may be set up to create work, such as improving and maintaining housing, i.e. special housing grants which can indirectly help listed buildings and buildings worthy of preservation.

Integrated conservation

The protection of the built heritage derives from the cultural heritage legislation. The protection of the prehistoric monuments and ruins and other features of heritage in the landscape are protected by the legislation governing the conservation of nature and countryside. The local and regional museums have a responsibility to safeguard areas of certain interest for medieval and prehistoric interest. These areas have been recognized in the general plans carried out by the local or regional authorities.

The fourteen county councils of Denmark have a responsibility to form a regional plan for the development of the rural areas. The different interests of conservation, nature preservation, environmental and other sector interests are considered. The National Forest and Nature Agency take an active part in these considerations being the owner of the state's vast forests and nature areas, and furthermore being the provider of the funding for major natural rehabilitation projects.

The urban landscape and the features of towns, including buildings worthy of preservation, are protected by local plan policies at the municipal level. A local plan for protection may be in operation for 20 years, but if the local authorities wish it, they may change the aim and scope of policies. Local planning is subject to an elaborate procedure of informing the public and allowing time and the possibility to object and discuss the matter. Often local plans are changed because of strong local engagement in the matters concerning protection of the heritage. This is solely the responsibility of the local community.

As mentioned earlier, the National Forest and Nature Agency work in co-operation with the local municipalities to survey architectural values through the SAVE system. This survey work is the basis of many local preservation plans.

In Denmark, however, private organizations have an important role to play in matters of conservation and protection of the heritage. Councils have been set up in fourteen counties to supervise and give advice to local authorities on matters concerning the protection and development of the cultural environment. In all legislation concerning the protection of heritage these organizations have a right to comment on the decisions made. There is an elaborate procedure for informing the public and allowing sufficient time to respond to decisions.

Education and training

The upkeep of traditional craft skills is essential to the building preservation sector in Denmark. The building preservation authorities and the Palace and Property Agency demand traditional methods and materials be used in all projects involving listed buildings. This demand has kept the traditional crafts alive through periods where the industrialization of the building sector has given little or no priority to traditional craft skills.

Since 1987 The Raadvad Centre has been the main centre of knowledge for gathering and distributing knowledge and information on traditional crafts. Through courses, training and projects they offer information and further education to different groups within the restoration sector. For example a course in special forging techniques for blacksmiths, or a course in gilding techniques for painters and conservationists. The Raadvad Centre also offers courses in general maintenance to owners of listed buildings, or seminars for architects and conservationists on the ethics of restoration and conservation. Furthermore the Raadvad Centre has established a 6-month educational programme for craftsmen with an interest in highly specialized craft skills. This is a supplement to the formal educational system for craftsmen.

Apart from skilled craftsmen, architects play an important role in the restoration process. Danish architects are educated either at the Royal Academy of Fine Arts, School of Architecture, or the School of Architecture in Aarhus. The artistic approach forms the basis for the education of architects within the field of restoration and care for architectural and cultural sites in the cultural environment.

This educational approach focuses on the relation between the old and the new, conservation and creation of new features in connection with sites of historic and architectural monuments, sites and towns. The basic approach is that architectural values and historic features should always be taken into consideration along with the functional and economic factors when steps are taken to change the built environment.

The preservation and upkeep of the cultural environment is closely connected to an understanding and awareness of the historical and architectural conditions and is a prerequisite for historic continuity. Preservation of the cultural environment is regarded as a basic condition for the human self-awareness and the human ability to understand both the present and the past. The common memory is an important factor when the architect creates and plans the future. Any built environment is regarded as a source of history that fixes the common memory. The educational aim is to give the student skills and methods to:

- make an architectural, historical and technical investigation and evaluation of the existing built environment;
- make an analysis of the importance of the specific features of the site from a local, national (and international) perspective;
- put up an idiom for the restoration project;

- create an architectural and technical project for the restoration and conservation of a building;
- create an urban project considering, architectural, structural and spatial features.

'Care of the townscape' is an important discipline in the education of architects. Studies are divided into three phases:

- Phase 1: method;
- Phase 2: mapping;
- Phase 3: project.

The three phases are significant for the subject 'care of the townscape' and reflects the basic idea of the schools of architecture, which is to develop a realistic method fixed to the location, i.e. to offer an education that is oriented towards the solving of problems and the creation of projects. During the method phase the emphasis is put on drawing/sketching and written analysis. During the mapping phase, the emphasis is put on examination and studying the location and to gathering information as preliminary conditions for the project.

The project phase consist of at least three project levels on different scales:

- the landscape in relation to the town;
- the town in relation to the neighbourhood;
- the neighbourhood in relation to smaller areas and sites.

'Care of the monument' is another important discipline in the education of restoration architects. This reflects upon a building's life through a historic process where the common ageing and various alterations leave their marks and traces on the monument. During the restoration and conservation of a monument it is important not to wipe out these traces as this would result in the destruction of the narrative value of the building.

'Care of the monument' as a subject for education will put forward methods and disciplines as preliminary conditions for understanding and documentating historic traces. The basis of this study is the archaeological investigation of buildings, i.e. the study of the existing architecture by measuring and watching. On top of that it includes analyses of the materials and the colour scheme. The aim is to make the students extract the experience of materials used and construction principles put into the building throughout history. Also the effects of the architectural features like form, light/shadow, ornamentation, and so on are subjects for study, along with the written sources.

Measuring a building is one special method available to an architect to study an old building. However, both the manual and the electronic methods have a systematic problem: they tend to be objective. Any measurement must be interpreted into the whole of an image and a drawing.

The specialist skills of a restoration architect are often demanded by the building preservation authorities, as being necessary to a competent handling of historic buildings.

Conclusions

Denmark is a small country but with a long architectural tradition and a legacy of relics from the ancient past. No major disasters or wars have jeopardized this heritage for approximately 150 years. With such a background, the preservation and conservation tasks in Denmark are of a reasonable size for society to handle.

There is a relative high, and still growing, awareness of the need to preserve the national heritage. The imposition of preservation orders is therefore generally regarded by the public as being a necessary requirement. The public might even want a more strict preservation policy than the authorities can implement regarding the needs for new building schemes and development of the towns and rural landscape.

Denmark has taken steps to make the broader preservation tasks and the care for the local built heritage to be the responsibility of the local community. The dialogue in the local community between the public and the authorities on preservation matters is lively and involves all kinds of professionals and organizations engaged in preservation. With central institutions as a back-up function this decentralized policy appears to work well.

Note

The majority of this chapter was written by Ulla Lunn with additional sections on the archaeological heritage by Carsten Lund

References

Ministry for the Environment and Energy/National Forest and Nature Agency (MEE/NFNA) (1995): *InterSAVE, international survey of Architectural Values*. Skov- og Naturstyrelsen, Miljø og Energiministeriet.

Ministry for the Environment and Energy/National Forest and Nature Agency (MEE/NFNA) (1999): *Listed Buildings in Denmark*. Skov- og Naturstyrelsen, Miljø og Energiministeriet.

Other sources of information

The Association of Owners of Listed Buildings (BYFO), homepage: *www.byfo.dk*

National Forest and Nature Agency, homepage: *www.sns.dk/byer-byg/bygloveng.htm*

The National Society for Protection of Buildings and Landscapes, homepage: *www.byogland.dk*

The Raadvad Centre, homepage: *www.raadvad.dk*

Isabelle Longuet and Jean-Marie Vincent

France

Introduction

In France, for institutional and historical reasons, heritage conservation has predominantly been the task of central government, which, as part of the decentralization process that has taken place over the past 20 years, has gradually transferred some of its responsibilities to local and regional authorities.

The French Revolution resulted in a heightened awareness of the French people's common heritage, which it is the state's duty to preserve in the public interest. However, it was the July Monarchy that, in 1830, established the first historic monuments department responsible for protecting and managing that heritage. Over the course of the nineteenth and twentieth centuries the state authorities gradually developed a range of legal instruments designed to safeguard public and private monuments, and subsequently their surroundings, individual landscapes and – lastly – entire urban areas. This went hand in hand with a diversification of the government agencies responsible for heritage identification, protection and conservation.

In recent decades considerable changes have taken place, given the general public's rapidly developing interest in the heritage in all its forms. The concept itself is becoming ever broader and now ranges from 'monuments' as such, recognized for their historical, artistic or symbolic worth, to a multitude of material or immaterial reminders of earlier ways of life, testifying to how past generations worked and organized their societies. Central government alone can no longer satisfy the growing demand for heritage conservation, especially as the Decentralisation Acts of 1983 transferred responsibility for town planning to local and regional authorities, which in turn led to the introduction of contractual instruments for heritage conservation and management, passed between the state and the local authorities, mainly municipalities.

However, although the protection systems function fairly well, they can cover only a small part of the heritage. The search is therefore under way for more flexible solutions, supplementing the existing arrangements, which would be part and parcel of spatial planning policy or would take a contractual form. These efforts reflect a will to treat the entire heritage field as a continuum, combining respect for a site's history with contemporary art and design.

The definition of the heritage

Solely as regards the immovable, man-made heritage, in modern-day France protection extends to archaeological remains; individual monuments or groups of buildings; developed sites, whether built upon or not, such as parks and gardens; and entire areas of cities, towns and villages.

The *loi du 31 décembre 1913 sur les monuments historiques* (Historic Monuments Act 1913), which has been amended on a number of occasions, laid the foundations of the protection system still in force today. This law provides for the protection and conservation of buildings or parts thereof ('statutory immovables') and of movable objects. It establishes two levels of protection: 'classification' and 'inclusion in the supplementary inventory of historic monuments'.

Initially, protection applied to properties which it was in the public interest to conserve for historical or artistic reasons. Then it was gradually extended to objects of technical, scientific or ethnological interest. The selection criteria applied today may encompass aesthetic quality, rarity, representative examples of a given style or production technique, or historical significance. Account is also taken of a property's physical state of repair and hence whether it lends itself to successful conservation.

No restrictions are imposed by law concerning either the types of buildings that may be protected or their date period. As a result, an extremely broad range of properties, in terms of both their nature and their age, is covered: prehistoric caves, archaeological sites, churches, castles, public buildings, private dwellings, whether rural or urban, farm buildings, factories, leisure facilities, parks and gardens, and so on (Figs 5.1–5.3). Some protected monuments were built as recently as the 1970s. The façades and roofs of the *Bételgueuse* building and the *le Flaine* hotel, built in 1966 in the ski resort of the same name to a design by the architect Marcel Breuer, were included in the supplementary inventory of historic monuments in 1991. The two most recently protected buildings are works by Jean Dubuffet: the *Closerie Falbala* in Périgny-sur-Yerres, built from 1971 to 1973 and classified in 1998, and the *Tour aux Figures*, built on the Ile Saint-Germain at Issy-les-Moulineaux in 1985 and included in the supplementary inventory in 1992.

France now has a total of 40,000 buildings protected under the legislation on historic monuments, 15,000 of which are classified and 25,000 included in the supplementary inventory. About half of these are publicly owned (mainly owned by local communities), and half belong to private owners. The number of protected buildings increases by about 700 a year.

Fig. 5.1 Hôtel d'Assezat in Toulouse, classified as a historic monument in 1914. (Photograph : G. Soula, Inventaire Général Centre.)

Fig. 5.2 Mining site in Oignies, Pas-de-Calais Department, classified as a historic monument in 1994.

Fig. 5.3 Villa Cavroix, in the Nord Department, built by Mallet-Stevens, classifie as a historic monument in 1996.

This number may seem small compared with other countries. It should none the less be noted that, first, under the French system protection confers entitlement to public subsidies and tax deductions, and an effort is therefore made to keep its expansion under control. Second, several tens of thousands of other buildings are located in protected urban or rural areas and are therefore covered by the specific protection and enhancement measures applicable in such cases.

A classification of historic monuments by type shows that religious buildings are in the majority (35 per cent of the total). This high percentage can be ascribed, in particular, to the Act of 1905 separating Church and State. That Act deprived municipal-owned parish churches of the funding provided by the former Ministry of Religions, which it abolished. The protection system established under the Act of 1913 offered a substitute source of funds, wherever justified by a building's interest. The many civil residential buildings covered by protective measures come next (25 per cent), followed by castles and manor houses (15 per cent). These three categories together account for three-quarters of all protected properties, since few buildings used for economic activities (farming, trade, craft or industry) are protected as yet (only 3 per cent of the total).

As regards the age of the buildings protected under the French legislation on historic monuments: a large majority were built in the Middle Ages (40 per cent), followed by the sixteenth century (16 per cent). It can be noted that twentieth century buildings are very under-represented (1,000 in all), as is industrial architecture (again 1,000). These disparities can be explained by the way in which the concept of heritage has evolved over time. Influenced by the Romantic movement, the authorities in charge of heritage conservation first focused on medieval buildings, before gradually transferring their attention to increasingly recent periods. It was not until the 1970s that they began to show an interest in ninetenth and twentieth century buildings and the industrial heritage.

In France the focus of conservation efforts only very gradually progressed from individual monuments to entire landscapes or urban areas. An Act of 2 May 1930 did broaden the scope of protection from 'natural monuments' to sites and landscapes. However, it was not until the Act of 25 February 1943, which systematically extended protective measures to the surroundings of monuments listed (within a 500-metre radius) or included items in the supplementary inventory, that it became possible to take a wider view of heritage conservation. This enabled the preservation of a monument to be linked to the management of the entire urban area or landscape of which it is part. From the 1960s this trend led to the adoption of a more comprehensive approach entailing the protection of entire sites, including groups of buildings and public areas, delimited by a legal instrument. An Act of 4 August 1962 provided for the establishment of *secteurs sauvegardés* (conservation areas). This idea was a reaction to the sweeping renovation projects of the time, which consisted in 'cleaning up' the historic centres of France's towns and cities by razing all the old buildings, in line with the then prevailing preference for all things modern. The *plan de sauvegarde et de mise en valeur* (preservation and enhancement plan) applicable to a *secteur sauvegardé* is a town planning document which *de facto* extends the scope of protective measures to encompass urban infrastructure, the quality of public areas and landscape aspects.

There are now 92 *secteurs sauvegardés* in France, covering a total of 5,694 hectares which are home to 800,000 people. This procedure mainly concerns towns and cities with historic centres, sometimes showing a decline in their population, characterized by a high concentration of old buildings. Typical examples are the Marais and Faubourg Saint-Germain districts in Paris, the historic part of Lyon, the centres of Bayonne (Fig. 5.4), Lille and Bordeaux, but also parts of much smaller towns such as Saintes and Cluny, the walled town of Montpazier, or the small seaside resort of Mers-les-Bains.

This broadening of the concept, from individual monuments to whole areas, led to the creation, under the Decentralisation Act of 7 January 1983, supplemented by an Act of 8 January 1993, of *zones de protection du patrimoine architectural, urbain et paysager* (ZPPAUPs) (architectural, urban and landscape heritage protection zones). The purpose of the ZPPAUPs is to enable the protection and management of the urban and rural heritage, of built areas and landscapes, on a contractual basis, allocating the responsibilities between central government and local authorities – the mayor and the municipality. This form of protective measure, now becoming increasingly popular following an initial trial period, has already been adopted in some 300 municipalities, generally villages or small towns.

The French concept of heritage, as reflected in the conservation measures now in force, is therefore consistent with the definitions found in the European conventions. It should merely be said that the term 'site', used in those conventions, encompasses two complementary ideas in France:

- the first, older concept (which dates back to the Act of 2 May 1930) entails strict conservation of outstanding landscapes in an unaltered state and applies to exceptional sites whether formed by both man and nature or being entirely natural (examples are the Pointe du Raz and the Cirque at Gavarnie);

Fig. 5.4 The centre of Bayonne, a secteur sauvegardé, in the Pyrénées Atlantiques Department. (Photograph: A. Mélissinos.)

- the second, more recent concept is linked to the efforts to master the development of places of historical interest in intensive use today; conservation areas and ZPPAUPs offer appropriate solutions for the management of this category of 'site'.

Identification of the heritage

Activities to identify the heritage can be divided into two main categories: systematic inventories applying research principles and studies relating to protection and restoration.

Systematic inventories applying research principles

The *Inventaire général des monuments et des richesses artistiques de la France* (General Inventory of the Monuments and Art Treasures of France) was set up in 1964. It is a specialist department of the Ministry of Culture, which, through agencies established in each region, conducts a systematic survey of the heritage, based on a strict methodology. This takes the form of a topographical inventory of all categories of buildings, whether protected or not, whatever their period, provided they are pre-1940. This topographical inventory, which has so far covered about 25 per cent of French territory, is supplemented by thematic inventories necessitating more specialized knowledge (stained-glass windows, maritime and fluvial heritage, industrial heritage, scientific and technical heritage, twentieth-century heritage, etc.).

To be meaningful, inventory compilation must not be a finite process. This work is therefore entirely separate from the protection procedures. However, the results of the inventory process increasingly serve as a basis for new protection decisions, whether relating to individual monuments or whole urban areas (*secteurs sauvegardés* and ZPPAUPs).

The information gathered by the General Inventory is entered in two main databases, the Mérimée database for architecture and the Palissy database for movable objects, which can be consulted on the French Ministry of Culture's Internet site. The database records are cross-referenced to files containing information on the location and history of each item, a description of it, document archive references, plans and photographs; general synoptic files are also accessible. The databases are organized along the lines of the Council of Europe Core Data Index, which was devised with the help of the General Inventory. To achieve maximum efficiency, the department is currently developing electronic archives, again using the structure of the core data index, which will permit considerable savings of both time and resources.

To fulfil its role in the fields of information and training, the General Inventory distributes the results of its work in a variety of widely available publications,[1] in hard-copy format and also increasingly on CD-ROM. Lastly, it is becoming increasingly common for local authorities to commission the General Inventory to compile precise inventories of their heritage, with a view to its conservation and enhancement.

Another systematic, computerized topographical inventory relates to archaeological sites. Known as the *carte archéologique de la France* (archaeological map of France), it includes information gleaned from archives, archaeological prospection and the findings of other types of field work using many different techniques. This map does not only have the function of reviewing archaeological discoveries, it especially serves as a document advising on archaeological potentialities for purposes of land management. It is managed by the regional archaeological services of the Ministry of Culture and Communication.

The Ministry is currently studying the possibility of making these various items of information systematically available, in particular to decision-makers and local authorities, in the form of an *atlas du patrimoine* (heritage atlas). This would be based on a common geographical information system and would combine all of the heritage data available in a given region – currently split among a number of different databases – allowing their simultaneous consultation in a consolidated form.

As regards the immaterial heritage, a *mission du patrimoine ethnographique* (ethnographic heritage task force) is conducting a series of additional surveys which, without aiming to achieve the same systematic coverage of French territory, make it possible to identify traditional skills and to analyse social behaviour patterns from the heritage viewpoint.

Studies relating to protection and restoration
Other studies are undertaken on a more *ad hoc* basis prior to the adoption of protective measures, with a view to both making preparations for implementing the protection procedure and providing the documentation needed for future management activities. These studies are conducted:

- by the documentation departments of the regional historic monuments conservation authorities in the case of protection of monuments, where the study relates to an individual building or a series of buildings in the same category;
- by specialist freelance architects/town planners in the case of protection of entire areas (conservation areas and architectural, urban and landscape heritage protection zones), where the study covers all of the historical and development aspects of an urban or rural site and entails compiling an index of the buildings to be found there.

Mention must also be made of the studies conducted prior to restoration of historic monuments. Before restoring any classified building, it has become routine practice to commission a study with a view to gathering historical, technical and scientific information intended to be used for decision-making purposes during the restoration process. These studies are led by the chief architects for historic monuments.

Studies are also led more widely on the technical knowledge of buildings or on restoration problems. Depending on the circumstances, such studies are commissioned from two bodies reporting to the central historic monuments

Fig.5.5 The Notre Dame Cathedral in Paris, façade of the central portal – testing laser cleaning. (Photograph: B. Fonquernie.)

department. These are: the *Centre de recherche sur les monuments historiques* (Historic Monuments Research Centre), which collates and registers documentary information on building finishes, fixtures and fittings, and the *Laboratoire de recherche sur les monuments historiques* (Historic Monuments Research Laboratory) in Champs-sur-Marne, which conducts scientific and technical research into conservation techniques (such as analysis on the alteration of stone and means to remedy this situation, restoration of reinforced concrete, etc.) (Fig. 5.5).

Heritage conservation and protection in France
Historic monuments

French legislation on historic monuments (the Act of 1913) provides for two protection procedures: classification and inclusion in the supplementary inventory. Protection proposals are examined by boards made up of professionals, researchers, public officials and elected representatives:

- decisions to include buildings in the supplementary inventory of historic monuments are taken by a regional board chaired by the Prefect; the measure is ordered by the Prefect after consulting the owner, although the owner's consent is not mandatory;
- decisions to classify a building are taken by a national board, chaired by the Minister for Culture; the measure is ordered by the minister where the owner has consented thereto, or by the *Conseil d'Etat* where the owner has opposed it.

All work on protected buildings is subject to approval by the relevant departments of the Ministry of Culture, on the basis of a preliminary project.

In most cases, applications are examined by administratively decentralized agencies at regional level (the regional cultural affairs directorates) under the scientific supervision of the general inspectorate for historic monuments. The Minister for Culture may refer the most complex cases to the above-mentioned national historic monuments commission for an opinion.

Work on buildings included in the supplementary inventory of historic monuments is governed by the general rules on building permits. Work on classified buildings, apart from actual restoration of the monument, involves public safety constraints. The creation of new floor areas or a change in use of the premises, departing from their initial purpose, also necessitates a building permit, in addition to the authorizations required under the legislation on historic monuments.

Archaeology

Permission is required for any archaeological excavation, and applications are examined in the light of the project's scientific merits and the applicant's competence (Act of 27 September 1941). Along the same lines, permission must be sought before using metal detectors 'for the purpose of seeking monuments and objects of potential prehistoric, historic, artistic or archaeological relevance' (Act of 18 December 1989). Furthermore, any archaeological find, whether made by chance in the course of site work or any other activity or the result of an authorized archaeological excavation, must be reported immediately. It is then for the competent state authorities to decide what measures should be taken: preservation of the remains *in situ*, excavation prior to the site's destruction, etc. The state authorities are, moreover, empowered to carry out excavations *ex officio*, where necessary availing themselves of the procedures permitting the classification of a site as being of public interest and its temporary occupation, subject to the payment of appropriate compensation.

Protected areas

All projects in the surroundings of historic monuments (within a radius of 500 metres), in architectural, urban and landscape heritage protection zones (ZPPAUPs) or in *secteurs sauvegardés*, which are likely to alter the state of land or buildings in the protected area, require the express approval of the official architect (*architecte des bâtiments de France*) assigned to the government agency with jurisdiction for the area concerned which is known as the local architecture and heritage department (*service départemental de l'architecture et du patrimoine* – SDAP). Authorities issuing permits must abide by official architects' views on projects located in the surroundings of historic monuments, where the site concerned is visible along with the monument. The official architect's opinion is also binding for projects in ZPPAUPs, under the rules specific to each of these zones, and in *secteurs sauvegardés*, under the provisions of the relevant preservation and enhancement plan (*plan de sauvegarde et de mise en valeur* – PSMV), which cover not only the buildings' external appearance (Fig. 5.6) but also their internal lay-out and decoration.

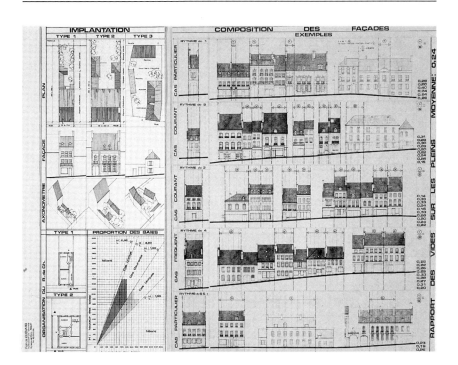

Fig. 5.6 The secteur sauvegardé in Autun – analytical elements.

Principles of heritage conservation

In France heritage restoration policy long bore the imprint of the thinking of the architects and historians who worked in the heritage conservation field during its early days in the nineteenth century and devised the first theories on the subject. Among them, Eugène Viollet-Le-Duc had had a determining influence both through the decisive progress he had led in reasoned knowledge of medieval architecture and through the method of intervention he had recommended which tended towards restituting the monument to its ideal original state. His restoration work on the Vezelay basilica, the Cité de Carcassonne (Fig. 5.7) or the Castle of Pierrefonds demonstrates his approach, considered today as a historical stratum in conservation. In the first half of the twentieth century, the approach to restoration work was influenced by the two major campaigns undertaken in the wake of the 1914–18 and 1939–45 wars as part of the wider efforts to rebuild the country. This context has favoured a practice mainly geared towards restoring deteriorated monuments identically to their original state, calling, however, on modern techniques and materials in some cases.

In 1960–1970, restoration escaped the pressure of emergency actions and safeguard to come within the framework of the ICOMOS Venice Charter in which the French specialists had actively participated. The constant evolution and circulation of scientific knowledge, together with the introduction of advanced technologies, are now making the concept of restoration evolve towards conservation of the entire building and its authenticity while respecting the strata of its history which leads to limiting

Fig. 5.7 Gateway to t
town of Carcassonn
drawing by Viollet-le-Du
1853; watercolour of t.
restoration project, includi
the reconstruction of a pa
of the buildir.
(Photograph : Archives a
monuments historique.

curettage and restitution to a maximum. This is made possible by an extension of the circle of those involved in restoration projects to include architects, historians, archaeologists and landscape designers, and also specialists in a range of scientific disciplines.

Today, another evolution influences the attitude towards historical monuments: the increasing awareness of the link tying the monument to its environment, especially in urban areas, which leads to treating it as an essential part of a living entity and to conceive its restoration in such a manner as to contribute to the overall value of this entity. This brings about a constantly developing reflection on the compatibility between the initial use of the monument, which has granted it its symbol, and the use which today's society would like to convert it to in order to reappropriate it.

Sanctions and coercive measures

The Historic Monuments Act 1913 provides for a number of procedures that can be implemented in cases where owners fail to fulfil their obligations in respect of protected buildings:

- where the conservation of a classified building is seriously jeopardized and notice to carry out the necessary work has been served on the owner to no avail, the state authorities may have the work done of their own motion and require the owner to reimburse half the cost;
- where a building that is classified or included in the supplementary inventory has been unlawfully broken up or dismantled, the relevant Minister may order a search for any missing parts of the building and have it reassembled under the supervision of the relevant ministerial departments, at the expense of the offending sellers and buyers.

The historic monuments department may seek the assistance of the police to have unauthorized work stopped. Moreover, any failure to comply with the obligations laid down by law, in particular carrying out unauthorized work, carries a criminal penalty. However, the scale of penalties has not been reviewed for many years and has become obsolete. The penalties are in fact rarely applied. A bill to update the legislation, in line with the provisions of a new Criminal Code that came into force in 1994, is currently before Parliament. This will result in far stiffer penalties, which should make the legislation on heritage offences more dissuasive and contribute to more effective law enforcement in this field.

With regard to archaeological remains, penalties exist for failing to report a find or to obtain consent for excavation work. Penalties also exist for breaching the general or specific rules governing protected areas.

Integrated conservation
Archaeology
Consideration of archaeological factors in town planning and development schemes is a more recent phenomenon than the protection of remains or supervision of excavations. In town planning matters, the main mechanism relied on is involvement of the authorities responsible for archaeology (the government agencies at regional level) in the preparation of land-use plans. Although their participation is not mandatory, these authorities are systematically involved in the planning process in historic towns and cities. These government agencies provide municipal authorities with information on any sectors of archaeological interest which – as permitted by the Town-Planning Code – should, depending on the circumstances, be designated either as areas to be protected on archaeological grounds or areas where any permits issued will be made subject to conditions aimed at preserving remains. Where such proposals concern sites or remains safeguarded under the legislation on historic monuments or protected areas they are binding, and the restrictions concerning such areas must figure in the land-use plan at the local level (*Plan d'Occupation des Sols* – POS). In all other cases the municipal authorities may exercise discretion, but their decisions are subject to review by the administrative courts, which may cancel a land-use plan which fails to take account of the need to protect the archaeological heritage on the ground that there has been a manifest error of judgement or a breach of the law.

As regards spatial development schemes and work not subject to the Town Planning Code, the main mechanisms used to take archaeological interests into account are impact studies and joint inquiries, which may overlap in scope. A joint inquiry, where all the Ministries concerned are asked for their views on a project, enables the Ministry of Culture, which is responsible for archaeology at national level, to intervene. For example, this may involve the re-routing of a proposed road or railway so as to safeguard a major archaeological site, or to have the necessary archaeological investigations included in a work programme.

Environmental impact studies, which were introduced in France under the nature conservation law of 1976, were extended to the archaeological field only in 1993. This change was specifically aimed at enabling the French authorities to honour their commitments under the Malta Convention, and thus, is potentially of considerable importance to the conservation of the archaeological heritage. However, these impact studies are only really effective where the authorities in charge of archaeology are closely involved in their implementation. This is not always the case, as such studies are the responsibility of the developer, who bears the cost. However, the findings are vetted at the administrative approval stage, and a project may then be made subject to specific requirements.

The situation in France regarding preventative archaeology is less satisfactory from the viewpoint of compliance with the Malta Convention. The practice of having developers finance archaeological digs before building or development work begins has become widespread, but poses a number of problems. The government has therefore tabled a bill establishing a code governing such archaeological activities, which should be passed in 2000. The two main measures proposed are the foundation of a public body with authority for field archaeology and related studies throughout French territory and the creation of a tax to fund preventive archaeological digs. The bill also extends the state's powers to supervise work, which possibly may result in damage to the archaeological heritage. To reinforce the protection mechanisms, the state will be empowered to take protective measures of its own motion (where the work does not require a permit) or to impose their implementation (where a permit is required) – whether physical conservation measures or digs carried out for study purposes.

The architectural heritage and protected areas

The legal provisions on heritage conservation are part and parcel of the Town Planning Code. In particular, the legislation on protection of the surroundings of monuments makes it possible to preserve a monument's environment (objects within a radius of 500 metres of a monument or visible along with it). The heritage features of a monument's surroundings, the boundaries of the area concerned and the rules governing its management may also be stipulated by establishing a ZPPAUP, instead of applying the 500 metres rule. This takes the form of an annex to the land-use plan (POS), and its requirements are binding on all concerned, under the official architect's supervision.

Secteurs sauvegardés are managed in a similar way. Development work is strictly regulated under the preservation and enhancement plan, which qualifies as a town planning document, and by a system of permits and controls.

Apart from these regulatory instruments in the heritage field, a recent practice helps to further the efforts to preserve old buildings in towns and cities. This does not involve any specific legal mechanism but consists in improving the ordinary town-planning rules, as set forth in the land-use plan (POS), so that they take into account the heritage features of a district on the basis of historical studies (an example is the Faubourg Saint-Antoine district in Paris, shaped by the centuries-old presence of the capital's woodworkers and furniture-makers). Particular mention should be made of the increasing tendency to take archaeological factors into consideration when drawing up land-use plans (POS). Areas of archaeological interest may be designated after consulting archaeological experts.

Spatial development schemes can also include a number of measures to safeguard the unprotected heritage. Mention might first be made of the regional *parcs naturels* (nature parks), where, as part of a comprehensive spatial management approach, economic development is geared to the conservation of traditional buildings, the specific characteristics of local landscapes, and natural resources and the environment. Along the same lines, the government recently established a procedure for designating heritage-based economic growth areas, rural areas where cultural and natural heritage resources can be used to underpin an economic revival.

Financial resources, funding arrangements and the revitalization of historic areas

Public funding

Apart from state-owned historic monuments, which are financed entirely out of public funds, the French system offers considerable financial assistance to owners of historic properties, whether public (more often than not local authorities) or private.

Under the budget of the Ministry of Culture and Communication, and through legislation provided in 1994, funding of conservation actions is provided for heritage items protected under the Historic Monuments Act 1913 and for the archaeological, ethnological, industrial, rural and horticultural heritage. In 1994 a guaranteed level of investment was established for the next five years amounting to a total figure of FF 7.849 billion. This programme provided FF 1.63 billion in 1998 and in this year further funding was guaranteed, amounting to an increase of nearly 40 per cent in 1999.

On average, grants cover between 30–50 per cent of the cost of work on classified buildings, and between 15–25 per cent of that on properties included in the supplementary inventory, subject to a 40 per cent limit. Local government authorities (municipalities and *départements*) devote considerable sums to restoration work. Expenses incurred by private owners are deductible for personal income tax purposes; the rules vary according to whether the property is open to the public.

Under a budget administered by Architecture and Heritage Directorate of the Ministry of Culture and Communication, formerly administered by the Ministry of Infrastructure until 1996, managed funds have been provided for studies and work in connection with the policy and enhancement of *secteurs sauvegardés*, ZPPAUPs and sites and surroundings of historic monuments. Grants for these areas amounted to FF 12.1 million in 1998.

As state funding is at a much lower level in *secteurs sauvegardés* and ZPPAUPs, owners must generally cover the cost themselves. On the other hand, generous tax incentives apply, under certain conditions, to landlords who undertake restoration work on residential properties intended for renting. Many municipalities also provide grants for restoration work on buildings located in their historic districts, which are additional to the state funding for residential property improvements.

The rehabilitation of old parts of towns is supported through *Opérations programmées pour l'amélioration de l'habitat* (OPAH) (Planned Housing Improvement Operations). Since 1977, when the OPAH programme was introduced, over 3,000 improvement operations have been carried out, resulting in the rehabilitation of over 600,000 dwellings (mostly in old quarters and historic centres). The main body for grant provision is the *Agence nationale pour l'amélioration de l'habitat* (ANAH) (National Housing Improvement Agency) whose role is to subsidize work undertaken by private landlords. ANAH has an annual budget of approximately FF 2.2 billion. It mostly supports OPAHs but the national agency may offer small grants for one-off cases. The rules of the agency also allow for the possibility of additional funding for buildings of architectural interest located in *secteurs sauvegardés*, ZPPAUPs and OPAHs with a heritage component.

In the field of preventative archaeology, the routine practice, so far unwritten, is that developers provide the necessary funding. Legislation currently in the pipeline will introduce a tax to fund such activities.

Private funding and sponsors

Private cultural initiatives are governed by legislation dating from 1987 on the development of sponsorships. This allows firms to deduct from their taxable profit any unconditional paid sponsorship to projects and bodies of general public interest. Of particular significance to the heritage are the provisions that allow firms to deduct from their net profits the charges they bear on account from operations arising out of the purchase or leasing and maintenance of stately homes that are classified or included in the supplementary inventory of historic monuments.

Furthermore, to encourage commercial and industrial firms to sponsor culture, particularly the heritage, a legal framework known as the *fondation d'entreprise* (enterprise foundation) was implemented in 1991. Such a foundation is a legal entity set up for carrying out, for profit, work in the public interest that cannot be funded through donations, bequests or public appeals. Permission to set up an enterprise is granted by the *Prefect* of the *département* in which the foundation is based.

The encouragement of firms wishing develop their sponsorship policy subsequently led to a choice of four types of foundation:

1 public-interest foundations;
2 enterprise foundations;
3 foundations created under the aegis of the *Fondation de France* (set up in 1969 to assist individuals, businesses and carrying out general interest projects of a philanthropic, cultural or scientific nature and non-profit making);

4   The *Fondation du Patrimoine* (Heritage Foundation) (a non-profit-making private-law corporation, set up in 1996, to promote the understanding, preservation and enhancement of the national heritage).

The role of public and specialized bodies

State-owned historic monuments, coming under the aegis of the Ministry of Culture and Communication, are managed by a public body, the '*Caisse nationale des monuments historiques et des sites*' (NFHMS) (National Fund for Historic Monuments and Sites). The NFHMS manages about a hundred monuments such as the castles of Chambord and Azay-le-Rideau, the Pantheon, the Glanum or Carnac sites. This institution is responsible for opening these monuments to the public, providing information on them and promoting their cultural enhancement. It also retains the entry fees paid by visitors, which enables it to balance its monuments management budget, since the revenues generated by the most popular monuments offset the shortfall on those less frequently visited.

The owners of other monuments – the vast majority – whether public, in particular municipalities (two-thirds of the total), or private (the remaining third), cover the costs of conservation and any opening to the public (not mandatory under French law) with the specific financial aids described above.

Apart from the official bodies for funding mechanisms (see above) and professional associations (see the next subsection) there is also a long-established tradition of voluntary associations working in support of the architectural heritage of France. Some bring together scholars or amateurs of history and heritage conservation, organize volunteer restoration sites, others gather owners of monuments. In the past few years new associations geared more towards the protection of heritage have developed. Among these are:

*   *La Demeure Historique* – a professional association of private owners of historic monuments which aims to establish establish a fiscal, legal and economic framework to assist such owners in protecting and conserving their property;
*   *Les Vieilles Maisons Françaises* – an association with 16,000 members that represents owners of private historic monuments;
*   *Maisons paysannes de France* – a locally-based national association for the protection of rural houses and their surroundings;
*   *La Ligue urbaine et rurale* – founded in 1945 by personalities of the literary world to create an upsurge in opinion in favour of heritage during the country's reconstruction period;
*   FNASSEM, *Fédération nationale de Sauvegarde des Sites et Ensembles Monumentaux* – set up to raise public awareness of the cultural heritage that is endangered.

Education and training

Training

Training of conservators

The *Ecole Nationale du Patrimoine* (National Heritage School), which was established in 1990, is a public body, coming under the Ministry of Culture, that provides practical initial training for heritage conservators who are accepted following a competition preceded by an initial training in a university or specialized school. The course combines in-school activities with training periods spent in government offices and cultural establishments. Before graduating, students must complete a one-month assignment in a foreign heritage institution corresponding to their chosen specialization. The school also provides further vocational training, in the form of seminars and one-day study sessions, for conservation and other heritage staff already in post.

Training of architects

Initial training of architects is provided by twenty schools of architecture coming under the Ministry of Culture, located in various French cities, which award a government-recognized diploma, the DPLG. Two other institutions are also authorized to issue diplomas: the *Ecole Spéciale d'Architecture* (ESA) (Special School of Architecture), a private establishment based in Paris, and an engineering college in Strasbourg, *Ecole Nationale Supérieure d'Art et d'Industrie* (ENSAI) (Higher National School of Art and Industry).

To meet with the evolving housing/building market in France where, in the past 10 years, construction work on existing buildings has been catching up with the construction of new buildings, more and more schools of architecture offer specific training in the rehabilitation of existing buildings. This is, in differing forms, the case for the schools of architecture of Brittany (Rennes), Languedoc-Rousillon (Montpellier), Lyon, Normandy (Rouen-Darnetal), Paris-Val de Marne, Paris-La Villette and Versailles.

However, the only real specialist training for architects wishing to work on the architectural and urban heritage is dispensed by the *Centre des Hautes Etudes de Chaillot* (CHEC), known as the Chaillot School. This school dates from 1887, when Anatole de Baudot, a disciple of Viollet-le-Duc, was appointed to the newly created French chair of architecture. The school trains qualified architects to specialize in heritage work, some of whom will become, following a competition, chief architects for historic monuments or state architects/town-planners. The course lasts 2 years and prepares architects for work on heritage and its monument, architectural and urban dimension. In co-operation with the Ecole Nationale des Ponts et Chaussées (National Civil Engineering School), the CHEC trains newly appointed state architects/town planners, who follow one of the two courses on offer: development or heritage studies. The CHEC specifically monitors the training of these professionals in heritage conservation, the majority of whom will become official architects. The 'traditional' Chaillot course, which has made the school's international reputation, is aimed at qualified architects.

Training of landscape designers to work on historic parks and gardens and protected landscapes

Initial training of landscape designers, leading to the award of a government recognized diploma, is offered by two establishments. These are the

Ecole Nationale du Paysage (National Landscape School) in Versailles, which comes under the Ministry of Agriculture, and the Bordeaux school of architecture, under the Ministry of Culture, which runs a specialist master's course. Specialist training in the conservation, management and enhancement of historic parks and gardens and in work on protected sites (in rural areas or in urban and suburban planted areas) is offered by the Versailles school of architecture in partnership with the National Landscape School, the Chaillot school and Paris I University.

Training of restorers of works of art
A Master's course in the science and techniques of conservation and restoration of cultural assets, was established at the Paris I University (Panthéon Sorbonne) in 1973. This is the only course of its kind available at the university level.

The *Institut de formation des restaurateurs d'oeuvres d'art* (IFROA) (Training Institute for restorers of works of art), established in 1978, offers a course in restoration techniques. It has been part of the National Heritage School since 1996. The Tours School of Fine Art offers a course on the conservation and restoration of sculptures and the Avignon School of Art provides a course in the conservation and restoration of paintings.

Training of trade guild members and craftworkers
Traditionally, heritage restoration specialists acquire their skills over a number of years through hands-on experience of working with older practitioners of a particular craft. This is still the rule in most firms specializing in the restoration of historic monuments.

People entering the specialist heritage professions have usually obtained an initial occupational qualification in the building trades or the applied arts, either by following a course at a vocational or technical training college or by undergoing an apprenticeship. There are some specialist qualifications relating to the architectural heritage, such as the vocational training certificate (*brevet*) in stonecarving on historic monuments, or the supplementary certificate in restoration of the structural fabric of ancient buildings.

In the field of further training, one has to mention the Avignon school, a centre specializing in training in the rehabilitation of the architectural heritage, was established in 1983, the *Confédération de l'artisanat et des petites entreprises du bâtiment* (CAPEB) (Confederation of Craftworkers and Small Building Firms) and the trade guilds. In 1998 the CAPEB introduced a professional identity certificate, the 'heritage CIP', with the aim of enabling craftspeople with experience of working on old buildings to make themselves better known. The *Fédération Compagnonnique des Métiers du Bâtiment* (Federation of Building Trade Guilds) has a number of training centres where it runs refresher courses leading to the award of qualifications or diplomas. The *Association Ouvrière des Compagnons du Devoir du Tour de France* has made similar arrangements. In particular, its *Institut supérieur de Recherche et de Formation aux Métiers de la Pierre* (Higher Institute for Research and Training in the Stone Trades), located in

Rodez (Aveyron), aims to bring technological developments within the reach of smaller firms.

Training in heritage mediation and enhancement
Several universities have set up courses to train people in cultural management or cultural mediation methods and practices. Some of these have a heritage emphasis.

Heritage restoration firms

The French building industry includes about 284,000 firms, over 90 per cent of which have less than fifty employees and which together achieve a turnover in the region of FF 600 billion. A very small number of these firms specialize in restoration of the architectural heritage. Every year about 1,200 firms, with a total of 9,000 employees, work on historic monuments under one of the 4,800 restoration or 3,500 maintenance projects subsidized or financed directly by the Ministry of Culture.

Quality approval certificates relevant to historic monuments and old buildings
In France QUALIBAT, a professional certification organization having the form of an association, is entrusted with the task of approving, classifying and certifying building firms. In 1994 it adopted a classification which includes eleven quality approval standards expressly linked to heritage restoration activities, whether concerning old buildings or historic monuments.

Professional organizations

Architects
The *L'Ordre des architects* is the institutional organization of architects in France to which all liberal professionals must belong in order to practise their trade.

Architects working in the field of heritage do not have another specific organization. However, they have gathered in varying associations which provide them and their work with a framework of assistance and promotion. This is specifically the case for:

- the *Association des architectes du patrimoine* bringing together alumni from the *Centre des Hautes Etudes de Chaillot* (CHEC);
- the *Compagnie des architectes en chef des monuments historiques* (Chief architects for historical monuments);
- The *Association nationale des architectes des bâtiments de France* (National association of architects for the buildings of France).

Firms
In the same spirit firms have also created differing types of association:

- the *Groupement national des entreprises de restauration des monuments historiques* (GNERMH) (National association of historical monument restoration enterprises) which federates 153 enterprises;

- the *Confédération de l'artisanat et des petites entreprises du bâtiment* (CAPEB) (Confederation for the craft industry and small building enterprises) which looks out for the interests of 289,000 small enterprises through its 105 departmental trade unions and its 8 national crafts unions.

Trade guilds

The *Institution du compagnonnage* (Institution of trade guilds) is still very important in heritage trades. The guild is the extension of a technical and philosophical teaching method stemming from an ancient tradition founded on the experience of sites which the journeyman acquires touring France after his apprenticeship. The journeymen are gathered within two main federations: the *Association ouvrière des compagnons* (Craftsmen association of the journeymen) has available 105 houses in France and abroad to house young people touring France, and the *Fédération compagnonnique des métiers du bâtiment* (Guild association of building trades) which has twenty-four training and specialization centres in metropolitan France.

Restorers of works of art

The *Fédération française des conservateurs-restaurateurs* (FFCR) (French federation of conservators and restorers) was founded in 1992 through the merger of seven professional associations subscribing to a shared code of ethics and training guidelines adopted in 1993–94 by the European Confederation of Conservator-Restorers' Organizations (ECCO). Its aim is to secure recognition of the profession of conservator-restorer and defend and promote its interests, on the basis of a text published in 1984 by ICCROM.

Notes

1 Editées aux Editions du Patrimoine.

The authors wish to acknowledge the participation of François Goven (Deputy Director of Historic Monuments), Sabine Didelot (Head of the Office for the Protection of Immovable Heritage) and Vesna Berrnard (Head of Archaeology Sub-Division, Department of Architecture and Heritage Protection) in writing this chapter.

References

On the notion of heritage protection and problems concerning conservation and management:
Chastel, A. and Babelon, J.- P.(1995) : *La notion de patrimoine*, Liana Levi.
Choay, F. (1992): *L'allégorie du patrimoine*, Le Seuil.
Mémoire et Projet – Les conditions de l'intervention architecturale dans les espaces protégés, Synthèse des travaux du groupe de réflexion animé par Joseph Belmont de janvier à juillet 1997, Direction de l'architecture et du patrimoine, 1998.
Patrimoine culturel, Patrimoine naturel, Actes du colloque de l'Ecole nationale du patrimoine, La Documentation française, 1995.

On French legislation and regulations:

Bady, J.-P. (1985): *Les monuments historiques,* « Que sais-je ? », P.U.F.

Frier, P.-L. (1997): *Droit du patrimoine culturel,* P.U.F.

ICOMOS de DIJON (ed. S.T.U.) (1988): *Les secteurs sauvegardés ont trente ans,* Actes du colloque.Sire, M.-A. (1996): *La France du patrimoine,* Gallimard.

Ministère de la culture et de la communication (ed.) (2000) : Chantal Ausseur-Dolléans, *Les secteurs sauvegardés,*

Protection du patrimoine historique et esthétique de la France – Textes législatifs et réglementaires. Editions du Journal officiel de la République française no. 1345, 1997.

Sire, M.-A. (1996): *La France du patrimoine,* Gallimard.

Further source

Further information on the French system of heritage conservation can be found in the European information network on cultural heritage policies: http://www.european-heritage.net

Manana Simonishvili

Georgia

Introduction

Georgia is a country of old legislative traditions. Justice is an indispensable part of the spiritual culture of the people of Georgia. It is a characteristic feature of a Georgian man, which is well reflected in many proverbs and sayings: 'A hand fairly cut from me won't hurt me' or 'Strike me, if I deserve', etc. The law of Georgia has been developing for centuries, becoming more and more elaborated thanks to the nature, character, culture, history, customs and ancient traditions of Georgia.

The first book of law dates back to the ninth century. Probably, books of this content existed even before the ninth century. This assumption is made on the basis of the level of the fragment of the Book of Law of the Georgian King, Bagrat Kurapalat (a ninth-century fragment contains 61 articles) which is very elaborate in terms of the legislative and codification aspects. There are only a few representatives of the modern civilized world that have books of this level and age.

Examples of the law of Georgia are as follows: 'Legislation' compiled by King Giorgi Brtskinvale (containing 46 articles) and the Book of Law of Beka-Aghbugha uniting two law books. The first one written by Beka, Governor of the Southern Georgia, dates back to end of the thirteenth and beginning of the fourteenth centuries, while the second was written in the fourteenth century by his grandson Aghbugha. Fragments of old books of law are also incorporated in this book. This Book of Law, containing 175 articles, provides a picture of a political structure, forms of separate crimes, concepts of obligations, norms of family laws, etc. of Southern Georgia (part of the territory which at present belongs to Turkey) of that period. Another important book is *State Regulations* containing 39 paragraphs, dating from the fourteenth century. There were very few states having such a legislative document of this kind at this time. Its significance lies in the fact that it gives us a clear picture of the state of the economic, historical and cultural fabric of Georgia in that period.

The *Book of Law of Vakhtang VI* containing 270 articles, dates back to the early eighteenth century and includes criminal as well as civil law norms. It considers laws of obligation and inheritance, forms of separate crimes, obligations of judges, court evidences, etc. A Book entitled *Dasturlamali* (guidelines, regulations) dating back to the eighteenth century was written under the leadership of King Vakhtang VI. It represents a state law and basically considers the authority of the king, the functions of the state and local bodies in the late feudal period. Books of Church Law also existed in Georgia, namely, *Minor Canon* (Canon Law) and *Major Canon* (Fig. 6.1). On the basis of the latter Regulations of the Ruis-Urbnisi Meeting of 1103 were created. According to the scholars, neither Byzantine nor the Christian East had such elaborated books in this field. The above-listed books evidence the high level development of the legislative culture of Georgia.

The development reached its highest stage at the end of eighteenth century, when the draft laws *Law of Davit Batonishvili, Sjuldeba* by John Bagrationi as well as other books of unknown authors were written by Georgian specialists. Unfortunately, abolition of the Georgian statehood by the Russian Empire affected their adoption. It was owing to this that many other laws also lost validity.

Georgia was a member of the Soviet Union for 70 years and this has affected legislative development in Georgia. During this period all the Soviet Republics had very similar laws. After the collapse of the Soviet Union, Georgia needs a new, strong legislative basis to retain its independent statehood. The restoration of the old legislative culture has been commenced. Legislative activities are now being carried out in all spheres through the assistance of different international structures. Approximately

Fig. 6.1 Canon Law: Book of Church Law (1031). Institute of Manuscripts, Tbilisi, Georgia.

600 laws and thousands of subordinate legislative acts have been adopted since independence and there are many still to be drafted in all the spheres including the cultural heritage.

State policy is now directed towards the integration of Georgia into European processes, evidence for which is provided by the accession of Georgia to the European conventions and charters. On 16 April 1997 Georgia signed the Cultural Convention of Europe, formulated under the auspices of the Council of Europe. Georgia became a full member of the Council of Europe in April 1999. Although this is a great achievement in itself, at the same time it is associated with huge responsibilities related to the supremacy of law and the protection of human rights. Included within this is the aim to move towards accepted criteria for the protection of the cultural heritage as expressed in the Granada and Malta Conventions. Moreover, within the context of the campaign, 'Europe, A Common Heritage', led by the Council of Europe, Georgia is hoping to will play its part by hosting a conference on this subject.

'Let us save the culture and the culture will save the nation' – declared President Shevardnadze at the UN General Assembly Session (1999). This attitude revealed by the President gives us hope that the protection of cultural heritage will be considered on the same level as protection of human rights. Cultural wealth will be saved for the future generations through the supremacy of law, which is so important for mankind.

Definition of the cultural heritage
The law *On Cultural Heritage Protection* was adopted by the Georgian Parliament on 25 June 1999. This law provides a system of legal protection for immovable and movable monuments of culture, movable fragments of an immovable monument (a constituent part, that is separated because of some reason or condition and is acknowledged) and items with heritage significance within the 'protection zone' of an immovable monument. Protection is afforded whatever the status of ownership.

Classification of immovable monuments
The classification of immovable monuments is based on typology, function, chronology or other features as well as their historical, artistic, scientific, aesthetic or spiritual significance. The following types of immovable monuments are included in the law:

- archaeological monument (ancient town and village settlements);
- historical monuments (places connected with historical processes, events or people);
- urban parks and landscape art monuments (historical settlements and their complexes), engineering or other systems, architectural complexes, ensembles or their parts, gardens, parks, etc.);
- architectural monuments (civic, cult, fortification, industrial and other buildings or their parts or fragments, among them samples of modern construction);

- monumental fine art monuments (frescoes, reliefs, statues, menchires, stone-crosses, steles, grave stones, etc.)
- monuments associated with the development of science, technology and industry.

They are categorized according to their relative artistic, historical, scientific, aesthetic or spiritual values as follows:

- immovable monuments that have entered UNESCO's *World Heritage List.*
- immovable monuments of national significance;
- immovable monuments of local significance.

The law generally protects all the monuments of all categories. Unfortunately, the law does not determine different levels of protection for separate categories. The category of a monument is taken into consideration only in the case of concluding an agreement on protection between the state and owner regarding the implementation of state policy for the protection of cultural heritage. Criminal law provides a relatively strict punishment for crimes committed against a protected monument.

Protection zones
Protection is facilitated by defining a 'protection zone' (functionally occupied by and historically related to the monument). The zone is approved under the established rule whereby a special exploitation regime is applied. Its purpose and function is to protect the immovable monument as an object incorporating recognized values and a cultural layer (layers of earth, as well as water covered areas (beds) containing the traces of human habitation and activity).

Protection zones cover archaeological sites and architectural monuments and include the regulation of the wider built environment and protection of natural landscapes. The zone mechanism is used to preserve individual monuments, monument complexes and ensembles, and associated natural and artificial environments. Within the boundaries of the protection zone, activities that are likely to cause damage or destruction or worsen the visibility of cultural layers are generally prohibited. Activities conducted within the protection zone that may endanger an immovable monument (explosion, vibrations, exhaust fumes and the like) can be specifically restricted or prohibited by the Ministry of Culture. Such activities carried on outside the zone but which may still endanger a monument can be similarly regulated through the Ministry of Culture submitting a proposal to the President of Georgia.

Issues specific to the archaeological heritage
A wider consideration is specifically required for the archaeological heritage which includes remnants, objects and traces of mankind's history (structures, buildings, architectural ensembles, arranged lands, objects, other

monuments and their environment either on land or in water). The study of this heritage enables the ascertainment of knowledge of the development of mankind and its relationship with the natural environment. Revealed archaeological monuments are protected under the law On Cultural Heritage Protection which identifies the concept of 'archaeological zones' and 'reserves'. The form of their protection is no different to that of the other immovable monuments. Bodies for archaeological investigation, research, excavations and other kinds of archaeological activities are defined in the law. At present there is no concrete legislative basis to control activities in this sphere except Presidential Decrees and orders issued for separate cases. Charters and instructions of international conventions have not yet been accessed. A draft law *On Archaeology*, intended to regulate the issues related to the archaeological heritage, will be formulated during 2000.

Identification of the heritage
The cultural heritage is identified according to a process of recording relevant information in an inventory. Corresponding documentation has been drawn up and a legal framework for protection has been created in accordance with the law. The Department for Georgia's Monument Protection is the national body that has responsibility for overseeing protection matters including the registration and classification of objects of cultural value. The current situation is relatively better in cases of the architectural heritage as its protection has a legislative basis through the law On Cultural Heritage Protection. This law determines the concept of an architectural monument, its categories, possibilities for use, and identifies the official authorities for monument protection and their responsibilities and obligations.

The law also protects monuments of the archaeological heritage. However, at the present time, protection is carried out by established practice due to the fact that specific procedural details have not yet been clarified. This is not only insufficient, but at the same time causes certain misunderstandings regarding the archaeological heritage. This emphasizes the necessity to adopt a further proposed law 'On Archaeology' (a draft of which will be developed during 2000).

Identification of the architectural heritage
Before the law On Cultural Heritage Protection came into effect, matters in relation to cultural heritage protection were regulated by the Soviet law of 1977 'On Protection and Application of Historical and Cultural Monuments'. Through this former law an inventory of architectural monuments was developed according to three specific forms:

1 an 'identity card' for buildings (which provided brief details);
2 an extensive 'passport' for each building;
3 a 'passport' for each architectural ensemble.

The identity card contained the following data: the title of the monument (identity), location (address), type, date, the character of its use, category. Each card was completed on hard copy in accordance with a specific format.

A new inventory of architectural monuments has been prepared in compliance with preliminary elaborated plans for regions and includes structures granted with a status of 'historical, architectural and artistic monument'. The purpose of this activity has been to fulfil the requirements of articles 2.2 of the Granada Convention.

A new form of 'identity card' was adopted for this purpose in 1997 within the state programme for cultural heritage protection. This follows the ideas contained in the Council of Europe's Core Data Index system for developing inventories (Council of Europe, 1995). Items 1–11 of the 'registration card' are based on a variant of the Core Data Index (revising and verifying existing records by reference to local districts) while items 12–24 are new. The new system was developed by Georgian experts on the basis of the recommendations proposed by the Council of Europe.

Compared to an old 'identity card', the new 'identity card' is more extensive and includes data on the infrastructure as well as sociological information. The format also differs – the information is broken into several items and sub-items. This information is then recorded on a computer database that has been specifically created to improve the inventory system. Furthermore, the old 'identity card' was drawn up only for a building granted with the status of a 'monument' whereas the new 'registration card' has been compiled for all buildings located in selected areas – disregarding their artistic and historical significance and status. Thus, the new system provides more extensive information. The process of recording in wide areas has also been much easier, partially because of the fact that a measurement or drawing of the building to be registered is no longer required while this was mandatory in case of the former card.

Thematic maps have also been created on the basis of the materials obtained in Zemo Kala (Upper Kala), part of old Tbilisi, reflecting the physical state, artistic significance, ownership of separate buildings, building materials, chronology, etc., with documentary precision (Pickard, 2001).

This identification and recording work is of paramount importance for an elaboration of a cultural heritage conservation policy. A 'Framework Document', developed by the *Fund for the Preservation of Cultural Heritage of Georgia* (1999) with the technical and financial assistance of the Council of Europe includes proposals for a partial conservation plan for Zemo Kala. The inventory work serves as a basis for this document. In future, it may be used to determine the trends of old area development.

Based on the experience obtained, the works were commenced in Kvemo Kala (Lower Kala) – another area of old Tbilisi. The new form of 'identity card' will be applied there. It is likely that the same form of recording will be applied in other cities/towns of Georgia. Eventually the new system of recording information will become mandatory.

Identification of the archaeological heritage

Archaeological monuments were registered in the same way as architectural monuments but the system has not yet been updated. In the best case, the 'identity card' for a monument exists and a protection zone is defined. Unfortunately, a unified list of archaeological monuments does not exist. But information on the archaeological heritage can be found in the reports of archaeological expeditions, details of which have been published in special collections.

The archaeological heritage has been studied and recorded according to a traditional-standard scheme. This implies carrying out excavations under a special permit, registration of the material obtained in all expeditions, creation of monument protection zones (disregarding whether they are visible or invisible). Where necessary, archaeological expertise can be provided for monuments existing under water.

There are several protected archaeological monuments in Georgia, which have a protection zone or represent a 'reserve'. Monument classification and the granting of the status of a reserve, as well as the provision of an annual permit on conducting excavations and other activities, are exercised by the Archaeological Commission of the Academy of Sciences of Georgia – consisting of leading archaeologists. The commission is a non-state body acting on a voluntary basis, which, in turn, limits its possibilities. Considering the importance of the problems to be solved by the Commission, it will be necessary to create a strong state body with the relevant rights and responsibilities.

A permit ('certificate') to conduct archaeological excavations is issued only to an expert having the relevant qualifications and on the recommendations of two archaeologists who have considerable experience in this field. The permit should identify:

- the person to whom it is issued;
- the place of excavations;
- the research methodology (excavations, prospecting through small excavation works and superficial prospecting).

Permission to conduct archaeological research includes a requirement to submit a report on the works executed to the Archaeological Commission (covering the place and period of working; what has been revealed; what is the character of the monument; and the sources used to finance the works). Certification concerning the protection and preservation of the materials obtained must also be provided. Formal documentation must be submitted by April of the following year. The Archaeological Commission has the right (in accordance with its charter) to verify the progress of research activities (methods of research and rules for the protection of safety).

Excavations are mainly conducted by the Archaeological Research Centre of the Academy of Sciences of Georgia, the State and Art Museums of Georgia, as well as archaeological expeditions of Tbilisi State University and the Scientific-Research Institutions of the Autonomous Republics. The

Archaeological Research Centre co-ordinates the preservation of archaeological monuments in construction zones.

In order to ensure the physical protection of archaeological monuments,
monuments of paramount importance are defined as 'archaeological
reserves' (Mtskheta, Vani); a protection zone is created around the monument; conservation works are conducted on the architectural monuments
that have been revealed.

Unfortunately, at the present time there is little interest in researching the
archaeological heritage. This is largely due to the fact that available funds
from the state budget are scarce and salaries are very low. The state is
responsible for financing as far as it is the only owner of archaeological
monuments (and for the greater portion of movable monuments associated
with them). There is an opinion that other owners – natural persons –
would take better care of monuments in their ownership. Consideration has
been given to the idea of passing ownership over to private citizens but no
such precedent has been established yet. Moreover, the situation may now
change due to the law On Cultural Heritage Protection which specifically
states that a natural person can be the owner of a monument.

Conservation of movable monuments found through archaeological
investigation is exercised at laboratories (Fig. 6.2). Objects transformed
from the place of their location are kept at museum depositories, in
exhibitions, or in special temporary bases owned by expeditions until
relevant studies and documentation have been completed. But not all the
expeditions have their own bases and museums prefer to receive the finds,
which can be exhibited. Proceeding from the situation mentioned above,
many objects of scientific significance may be 'left' outside depositories.
This situation endangers newly discovered objects, many of which will merit
protection as monuments of the archaeological heritage.

*Fig. 6.2 Mtskheta:
Armazis-Khevi, Chalice,
second millennium BC.
Metalwork: gold, garnets,
agates, filigree, granulation.
Georgian State Museum,
Tbilisi.*

The preservation and protection of the heritage
General procedures

Protection, repair, new use, alteration or demolition of cultural heritage monuments is regulated under the law On Cultural Heritage Protection. 'Protection' is provided separately from the other components mentioned above and implies legal and institutional protection through various activities: recording, scientific analysis, technological, practical, controlling, educational and other forms of activity. As for repair, new uses, alterations and dismantling, these are regarded as 'maintenance' activities through preservation, conservation, restoration, regeneration actions and the adaptation of the monument. 'New use' is defined as an 'eligible use of the monument', i.e. the use of the monument which does not result in negative or irreparable changes. Regulation of the above-mentioned procedural stages is reserved for state bodies, local self-governmental and governmental bodies (local authorities), legal persons within the limits of their competence, and also natural persons. All of these subjects make one whole system for cultural heritage protection.

There are complicated (but easily comprehensible) procedures applied for the implementation of the above-mentioned activities. The Ministry of Culture of Georgia, the Academy of Sciences, State Archive Department, also other state and non-state bodies, if delegated with the authority to protect cultural heritage by the Ministry of Culture through the legislation, protect cultural heritage in the name of the Ministry of Culture. The principle of delegation laid down in this law is very useful since it prevents the scattering of the protection function among different institutions (though this function is exercised by the above-mentioned institutions but under the leadership of the Ministry of Culture). Otherwise, it would be difficult to control the implementation of the obligations for protecting cultural heritage. All this would consequently complicate the definition and distribution of responsibilities. Thus, it is the Ministry of Culture that co-ordinates all the components in the sphere of cultural heritage.

All the issues regarding cultural heritage protection are to be resolved by the President of Georgia since the Ministry will confirm an annual list of works to be performed on monuments located in the territory of the country in agreement with the President's Scientific-Methodological Council. The Council is defined by the law On Cultural Heritage Protection and is to be established at the level of the President. It will consist of twelve highly qualified specialists for a 5-year term (afterwards to be renewed as necessary) and will function in accordance with the Charter approved by the President.

It is also noteworthy that the Constitution entitles autonomous units to undertake the responsibility to protect and maintain a monument (Government of Georgia, 1995). The laws *On the Local Self-Government and Local Government* and *On Tbilisi – Capital of Georgia* define these obligations very generally at the level of statements (which should be regarded as a significant drawback of the law). Local self-governmental and governmental bodies – city (region) municipalities, *Gamgeoba* (appointed bodies), *Sakrebulo* (elected bodies) and village (community) administration bodies (*Gamgeoba*) are held responsible for the protection of cultural monuments.

The issue is more concretely defined in the laws *On Culture* (1997) and On Cultural Heritage Protection. The law On Culture holds the local governmental bodies responsible for cultural heritage monument protection including the allocation of funds for this purpose in local budgets and the creation of bodies in this sphere. (These activities are carried out by the local bodies in agreement with the Ministry of Culture and under its supervision.) The law On Cultural Heritage Protection also provides concrete mechanisms for cultural heritage protection to be implemented by the local self-governmental and governmental bodies as well.

The Ministry of Culture, which co-ordinates and leads the sphere of cultural heritage, while the Department for the Monument Protection, created in the Ministry of Culture under the relevant law, cares for the protection and maintenance of monuments. It carries out the set goals and ensures settlement of all the numerous issues. The Ministry approves the functions of the Department in accordance with the principles prescribed by the law, as well as the frameworks of the activities. Unfortunately, it should be mentioned that until the law On Cultural Heritage Protection was approved in 1999, a specific service with a relevant budget for monu-ment protection and maintenance had not existed in Georgia (excepting the period when Georgia formed part of the Soviet Union). The law raises hope that special funds will be envisaged under the State (Department) budget for the year 2000.

The Department is directly responsible for the monument protection pro-cedure discussed above. It identifies and records the objects of heritage value, creates monument registration documents, defines and approves archaeological zones and other monument protection zones. The Depart-ment exercises these functions together with state organizations. It is authorized (together with other state bodies), to suspend all kinds of works that may endanger the cultural heritage. It further defines the respon-sibilities of natural and legal persons (disregarding the form of ownership of monument) for the execution of works, and supervises the implement-ation of works and their quality.

Furthermore, the concept of an object having heritage values is intro-duced in the law. In other words, items that are recognized as meriting protection may be afforded the same legal regime of protection in order to avoid any damage or potential danger against the cultural property that may later be granted 'monument' status.

The determination of a legal regime for each monument is a precon-dition for the application of procedures for the 'maintenance' activities, which, it turn, can be achieved through the inclusion in the List of Objects having recognized heritage value as a potential monument.

The owner of a monument is liable for, and is responsible for all expenses incurred in, protecting and maintaining a monument. An agreement on ownership must be defined. The Department will conclude an agreement with the owner referring to the ownership regime that identifies permissible uses and forms of activities and defines the protection regime. The owner is also required to assist the state bodies in examining the condition of the monument and must report any changes in the condition as part of the protection regime. In cases where an owner allows a third party rights to use a monument, the latter is under the same obligation as the owner.

The owner is authorized to use the monument only in accordance with the rule prescribed by the law. Written permission is required to alter, remove or dismantle the monument or any part of it (the Department only grants permission if it is necessary to save the monument from ruin or if there is a condition of utmost necessity). In cases of permitted alteration the data are entered into the monument registration documentation. The owner is also required to ensure that natural vegetation in the vicinity of a monument does not endanger its fabric (according to a defined protection zone around the monument). The right of alienation and transfer of ownership are also restricted – alienation of the monuments under state ownership is not allowed. Transfer is only permitted for the defined use and in accordance with the rule prescribed in the legislation.

In order to ensure monument preservation, the law also envisages the creation of protection zones around the monument, establishes the limits for the monument's use, i.e. the monument can be used only in its primary function within the limits of the regime established for the monument protection. With the aim of ensuring the protection of the cultural heritage, land cadastre and urban planning policies must be considered in relation to a monument and its protection zone. In other words, housing construction schemes, schemes and projects of regional planning, general schemes of populated areas and master plans, detailed planning, irrigation projects and so on, must respect the legal provisions for archaeological and architectural monument protection, urban development regulation and natural landscape protection zones. At present, planning mechanisms are being formulated through a draft law *On Territorial-Spatial Planning – Urban Constructions* which includes integrated conservation principles as advocated by the Granada and Malta Conventions. It is hoped that the draft will be completed in 2000. However, the implementation of a new planning system incorporating such principles will take some considerable time.

Procedures for the archaeological heritage
While the registration system for the archaeological heritage is still to be formulated the law On Cultural Heritage Protection nevertheless provides for the protection of the monuments of archaeological heritage. The Ministry of Culture ensures their protection, while the Centre for the Archaeological Research at the Academy of Sciences of Georgia is responsible for scientific research works in this field. The only law in the sphere of cultural heritage adopted in Georgia provides for the protection of archaeological heritage by identifying the types and conditions of works to be conducted. The works can be executed only on the basis of the pertinent licence issued by the Ministry of Culture and by the certified legal natural person. The Ministry issues a special licence in every case (it may cause some difficulties to the

executor, but it ensures a strong guarantee of monument protection). Responsibility lies with the person who undertakes the works in case of unsatisfactory execution of the works conducted on the monument.

Another important aspect of archaeological monument protection is that road and engineering infrastructure development, land and environmental works, mining activities, and other construction or reconstruction projects, can only be implemented on the basis of a conclusion reached jointly by the Ministry of Culture, the Department for Monument Protection and the Centre the Archaeological Research. Natural and legal persons intending to carry out these works should submit a suitable application to the Ministry of Culture and the relevant scientific-archaeological research institutions at least 3 months prior the execution of activities. These bodies will study the case and, if appropriate, will permit execution of the works on the monument on its area or in the protected area. The Centre for Archaeological Research will supervise the progress of the implementation of works. It is also important to note that the executor of works will be responsible for the expenses incurred for any necessary archaeological survey and other types of archaeological activities which may be determined as being necessary where the intended works may affect sites of the archaeological heritage. This may include the cost of archaeological excavations, supervision, prospecting, survey of historical and cultural heritage, scientific study, publications and protection measures.

Dissemination of information gained from these activities is achieved through the mass media; reports on excavations are published in the annual special collection: *The Results of Archaeological Researches in Georgia*. However, it should be noted that policy in this area is not fully developed and awaits the formulation of a law *On Archaeology*.

Conservation philosophy
According to the legislation of Georgia, conservation means a combination of activities aimed at preserving the condition of a monument. The law does not directly provide a list of the activities, but it defines the concepts of monument restoration, reconstruction, adaptation, application and maintenance, the unity of which, in fact, makes an accepted conservation philosophy. It is based on the recognized definition of conservation, according to which it encompasses all aspects of the protection of a site or of remains so as to retain their cultural significance. It includes maintenance and may, depending on the importance of the cultural artifact and related circumstances, involve preservation, restoration, reconstruction or adaptation, or any combination of these.

Conservation in Georgia is carried out in accordance with the methods and standards provided in the ICOMOS Venice Charter and other well-known guidelines applied in practice. Since 1978 the former State Body for Monument Protection (the Main Scientific Board for the Protection and Application of Historical Monuments) and the present heir-at-law bodies have applied the methods and principles prescribed by the Venice Charter. Translations of other charters have not yet been carried out and this, therefore, impedes their application. ICOMOS GEORGIA (created in 1993) is actively engaged in the popularization of the ICOMOS charters and other well-known documents. It serves also as UNESCO's consultant in Georgia.

ICOMOS GEORGIA co-operates with the non-governmental international organizations such as the Getty Grant Programme, the Foundation of World Monuments, Soros Foundation, World Bank, etc., and co-ordinates two programmes: 'Cultural heritage is in danger', and the 'Integration of cultural heritage protection in the process of risk prevention'. Tbilisi and Ikorta were entered on the list of 100 of the most damaged monuments as proposed by the ICOMOS GEORGIA. Together with the state bodies for monument protection, recommendations are being prepared for the insertion of Old Tbilisi in the UNESCO's list of World Heritage Sites and its sub-list 'World heritage is in danger'.

The 'Tbilisi Pilot Project' is being implemented within the framework of the 'Fund for the Preservation of Cultural Heritage of Georgia' in association with the Council of Europe (see above). Through this project research works in relation to Old Tbilisi are being conducted which should be reflected in the conservation-led revitalization of the area. This project will further facilitate the development of the conservation philosophy.

Sanctions and coercive measures

Legal obligations regarding the protection of cultural heritage in Georgia are primarily based on the Chapter II, article 34, of the Constitution (1995) which mentions the following:

1. The state fosters the development of culture, the unrestricted participation of nationals in cultural life, the expression and enrichment of cultural origins, the recognition of national and universal values and the deepening of international cultural relationships.
2. Each citizen is obliged to care for, protect and preserve the cultural heritage. The state protects cultural heritage by law.

Georgia's Laws On Culture, adopted in 1997, and On Cultural Heritage Protection, provide a broader definition and regulation of the above mentioned constitutional norms in legislative form.

The law On Culture actually represents a 'micro-constitution' in the field of culture, the implementation of which calls for the adoption of separate laws. The law set a goal of developing legislation in the field of culture and imposed liabilities on the state as well as society. The law holds state, local self-governmental bodies and individual citizens liable for the protection of the cultural heritage.

The law On Cultural Heritage Protection is a major legal act establishing legal relations in the field of cultural heritage. It defines what is meant by the terms 'monument protection' and 'monument'. It is noteworthy that the form of ownership is regarded as one of the decisive factors in defining the legal liabilities for the monument protection. The legal liabilities imposed on the state (as owner) and all other owners, emphasize that all the works intended for monument protection should actually be financed by the legal owner of the monument. Moreover, the right of ownership can be lost if the owner cannot ensure the funds needed for the required state of protection where there is a threat of damage, destruction or theft of items of heritage value. In a case of a threat of destruction due to the carelessness of an owner, the state is obliged to warn the owner and notify a deadline before which any necessary works must be completed. If the owner does not take into account the requirements of the state, then the court has the authority to expropriate the monument and transfer the ownership into state hands. The law also provides other methods to ensure the protection of a monument, namely, by requiring the owner to transfer the safekeeping of the monument to another body until it is possible to ensure its proper protection. If the owner does not take this requirement into account, the issue of expropriation may be raised again.

A different situation applies to the Orthodox Church of Georgia (Patriarchate). The church administers a major part of the cultural heritage of Georgia including many immovable (and movable) monuments used for religious purposes, many of them having 'international' protection status (Fig. 6.3). There is no regulating act concluded between the church and the state in the field of cultural heritage, especially, in terms of obligations to protect cultural heritage. The law On Cultural Heritage Protection, is vague in this context although it must be re-emphasized that it forms the basis of protection for all the monuments. However, the relationship of the church in

Fig. 6.3 Mtskheta: Svetitskhoveli Cathedral (1010–29), view from south-west, Shida Kartli, East Georgia.

this area is still being worked out on an informal basis between the church authorities and the state rather than by the strict rule of the law. It is also intended to conclude a Concordat between the State of Georgia and the Independent Apostolic Orthodox Church of Georgia. These actions will definitely make the legal situation regarding the liabilities for protection of monuments under the use of the Church more precise and comprehensive (Figs 6.4, 6.5 and 6.6).

Fig. 6.4 Ateni: Sioni Church. Annunciation – detail of Archangel (wall painting, eleventh century), Kartli, East Georgia.

Fig. 6.5 Tsalendjikha: Church of the Virgin. Detail of Archangel Michael (wall painting, fourteenth century), Samegrelo, West Georgia.

Fig. 6.6 Vardzia: rock-cut Church of the Dormition. Head of the Apostle (wall painting, 1184–6), Djavakheti, South Georgia.

Apart from direct powers of expropriation, the law has other coercive measures that provide extra guarantees to ensure the application of a whole set of protection measures monuments (disregarding the form of ownership). These provisions are as follows.

1 Supervisory control exercised by the state: the state is authorized to carry out all the legal activities within the limits of its competence, which are directed towards the monument protection. It can be reflected in written application, licensing or certification procedure, etc. Interestingly, in addition to the Ministry of Culture the Police and Prosecutor's Office and other state bodies for the protection of cultural heritage may participate in procedures for cultural heritage protection. In this regard, the state bodies apply the *Code of Legal Infringements* (civil and criminal code) as well as other numerous laws of Georgia indirectly related to the issues of cultural heritage protection.
2 The authority of the state to delegate powers to the local self-governmental and governmental bodies on the basis of the legal acts.
3 Constitutional rights and responsibilities of natural and legal persons to (a) protect a monument of culture; and (b) to notify the relevant authorities of damaging actions or the destruction of monuments.

The legislation of Georgia prescribes a liability for the illegal encroachment of cultural monuments. The law On Cultural Heritage Protection imposes moral as well as a material responsibility for the quality of works conducted on the monument. The permission for approved works may be withdrawn where the works to a monument are carried out in an unsatisfactory manner and other actions may be taken to stop damage or where a crime has been committed. The Criminal and Administrative Infringement Code also defines measures, e.g. 'infringement of the rules of protection and use of the monuments of history and culture', which can be applied where the damaging action is regarded as an administrative, rather than a criminal, infringement. In this case a formal warning may be given or a fine may be imposed.

Criminal prosecution for the crimes directed against monuments of culture is regulated by the Criminal Code (the Chapter on 'Crime Against Public Security and Order', article on 'Destruction, Ruin and Damage of the monuments of History and Culture'). The Code specifies the list of the activities (criminal activities and crime of omission), which may result in damage to a monument (these are: desecration of the monument, unauthorized use, ruin, destruction and damage caused by the use of explosives or vibrations, exhaust fumes and the like). In this case, to 'destroy' means to bring the monument to a condition where it is impossible to restore it. To 'ruin' means to cause such a danger to the monument that the original value of the monument is lost, but it is still possible to restore it. 'Damage' means to impair the historical, artistic and cultural properties of a monument. 'Unauthorized use' means the use of a monument against the regime envisaged by the protection contract.

The law defines that there can be different types of encroachment, which may alter (or have already altered) the original fabric (mechanical, chemical, biological) of the monument. It is interesting that the motive of the monument encroachment (financial gain, vandalism, revenge or other private interest), if directed against the state, and was intended to humiliate national self-respect and pride, can be regarded as a serious crime against the state, with grave outcomes. In case of negligence and unintended action, the damaging activity can be qualified as 'carelessness', and carries lesser consequences.

Movable objects of cultural heritage are protected with one more article of the Criminal Code, that has the sanction of imprisonment (for the illegal export and import of cultural property). The law 'On Cultural Heritage Protection' envisages the adoption of a law *On the Export and Import of Cultural Property* (which is an additional legislative provision that is proposed for adoption in 2000).

According to the draft version of this law, transportation of the property across the borders of Georgia without the relevant permission is to be regarded as 'contraband' whether it is granted with the status of a monument or not. The existence of the status of 'monument' aggravates the case since it might appear impossible to fix the value of a monument with respect to its rare historical, artistic and scientific significance. Unfortunately, numerous cases of illegal export of cultural properties have been reported. At the same time, many cases remain unreported because the economic situation of the country has not allowed the necessary measures to be adopted. The proposed law, when implemented, will help to resolve this situation.

However, while there are many general sanction measures in place to safeguard the cultural heritage, in many instances the regulations have not been applied in practice. At the present time the number of precedents are rare. The adoption of the laws On Culture and On Cultural Heritage Protection and other proposed laws give us a hope that mechanisms will be established to protect monuments more effectively in the future. At the moment it appears impossible to fully implement these procedures within a short period of time but the authorities are gradually moving towards being able to bring about effective solutions.

Integrated conservation

Georgia has old traditions of cultural heritage protection and enough experience in this respect to be able to integrate buildings, monuments and areas of cultural importance within the system of urban/town and rural/country planning.

At the same time, new realities of public life, particularly the movement towards the establishment of a market-based economy and the widening of private property interests in agricultural as well as in urban lands, etc., have raised new problems.

First of all this concerns the legislative position. All categories of monuments of the cultural heritage, except urban planning monuments, are ensured protection by the law On Cultural Heritage Protection. However, heritage protection has not yet been fully integrated into planning mechanisms for controlling land-use and development. The reason for this is that the 'Code on Urban Planning' (to regulate urban planning methodology, forms and content of documentation as well as other issues) has not been adopted. A draft law is under consideration (On Territorial – Spatial Planning – Urban Constructions) but even after it is adopted it will take some time before the administrative implementation of the proposed law will become fully operational. It is also planned to develop a law *On Urban Heritage* which will adjust specific problems concerning urban monuments.

In spite of this, the law On Cultural Heritage Protection provides an opportunity to exercise the protection of the largest part of material cultural monuments with the help of urban/town and rural/country planning. Several articles of the law cover this problem including: 'The system of protection zones and their regimes', 'Consideration of immovable monuments in land cadastre and urban planning documentation', 'Necessary terms for designing and executing large-scale construction and other types of works'. All the specific issues are covered in different chapters of the law.

It should be mentioned that in the early 1980s a system of subordinate normative acts to ensure the protection of the urban environment, as well as separate monuments, was developed by the state bodies for monument protection. A list of historical cities of Georgia was compiled and approved, for the majority of which a system of protection zones was elaborated. For example, in Tbilisi, the capital of Georgia, three protection zones were identified:

1   state protection zone for the historical part;
2   urban development regulation zone;
3   natural landscape protection zone.

For each zone an urban planning regime was established.

It should be emphasized that before the proposed Master Plan for Tbilisi is finalized (to be in force by the year 2000), the 'The detailed urban planning project of the historical part of Tbilisi' remains in force.

Unfortunately, at the present stage of public reorganization, relevant attention has not been devoted to the development of urban planning documentation. A vacuum will be apparent in this regard for most of Georgian cities/towns. Considering the fact that, at present, there is inadequate observance of legal procedures by new developers, the situation becomes more complicated.

Owing to the lack of legislation on urban planning and the imperfection of the legislation on land use it is practically impossible to work out and implement an integrated conservation policy to incorporate the architectural and archaeological heritage. Consideration of monuments in the procedures for granting permits for conducting certain works as provided in several articles of the law On Cultural Heritage Protection is not sufficient for the proper protection of monuments. Moreover, there are many issues that go beyond the framework of this law.

The legislation of Georgia fails to provide incentives for the development of programmes on heritage restoration and maintenance. The problems of conservation and development of the heritage are not adequately reflected in relation to environmental protection, land use and urban planning processes. It can be said that there are no regular relations and co-operation among the institutions for cultural and environmental protection, urban planning and land use. The allocation of lands for different purposes and the auction sale of lands in the regions have originated a serious threat to archaeological monuments since it is impossible to ensure scrutiny by archaeological experts.

Despite the fact that the law On Cultural Heritage Protection considers issues relating to the design and execution of large scale construction or other kinds of works, the documentation on land cadastre and urban planning deals with these issues in more specific terms. In cases where monuments will be affected by such works, a joint permission procedure is to be applied by the Ministry of Culture and the Ministry of Urban Development and Construction. However, the law only provides a basis for an integrated mechanisms – what is needed is a fully implemented planning system with its own legal basis which will cover other important aspects such environmental protection, land arrangement, etc. The issue of sharing responsibilities needs to be further explained by subordinate normative acts (currently in the process of development) to ensure the perfect implementation of legal provisions.

Access by visitors to the protected zones of architectural and archaeological heritage is to be encouraged in the development of such policies. However, tourist routes are not well arranged in many cases due to lack of resources, though the state cultural tourism policy and programme has already been created – covering thousands of monuments of cultural heritage (Fig. 6.7). The policy envisages infrastructure development and the arrangement of access roads.

Financial resources, funding mechanisms and the regeneration of historic environments

The grave economic condition of Georgia has had a negative impact on the cultural heritage. The scarcity of state budget resources means that there is inadequate financing of the activities to protect the cultural heritage. At the same time the state has incurred a legal obligation to protect cultural heritage. In this context the law identifies provisions to ensure there will be funding from the state budget and the establishment of a favourable taxation system. The state has also undertaken to provide grants, subsidies and other incentives (but this remains on the level of a declaration rather than having the legal force of law). The reason for this is well-known – the country's economic deficit and not the state policy.

In accordance with the law On Cultural Heritage Protection finance can be derived from all eligible income. This includes state as well as local budgets, and also funds obtained from the monument owner (user), specially

Fig. 6.7 Opiza: King Ashot the Great. Relief from the south façade of the church (826). Georgian State Museum of Fine Arts, Tbilisi.

created funds, rental taxes, contributions, grants provided by international organizations for the implementation of certain programmes and projects, credit proceedings and the means of natural persons (including foreigners). The problem is that nothing is certain – it is impossible to plan concrete actions on the basis of the above. It is hoped that the law On Cultural Heritage Protection will become the basis for the development of joint state, regional or municipal conservation-led regeneration strategies in time and when the economic situation in the country has improved. But there are other outstanding problems.

Tax exemptions established by the legislation of Georgia are not sufficient to be able to attract private sector investment or to develop sponsorship and patronage in this field. This makes it less realistic to obtain contributions from the private and voluntary sectors. Tax exemptions can be provided for works implemented under reconstruction, restoration and conservation projects under state programmes for monuments entered on the UNESCO's World Heritage List as well as for archaeological excavations. Expenditure incurred by the owner for the maintenance of monuments and the funds for archaeological works (and associated costs) envisaged in the cost estimates by the executor of the construction, land and other types of works can be considered. This represents the only real source of tax exemption provided by the law.

While interest by international bodies in the cultural heritage of Georgia is extremely valuable, it does not provide a stable source of funds. It is the state that should take care of the cultural heritage in the future.

Intellectual assistance for the reform of laws and other issues in the field of cultural heritage should be highlighted. In this respect, the Cultural Heritage Department of the Council of Europe has provided advice on the drafting of new laws and expert assistance for the Tbilisi Pilot Project (covering inventory of Zemo Kala and Kvemo Kala and the creation of thematic maps). As the programme of assistance develops in 2000 it is hoped that the process of implementation of legal reforms can be commenced in association with the pilot project which will assist in the preservation of the fabric of Old Tbilisi and aid the process of implementation elsewhere.

In 1996 a 'Cultural Heritage Initiative' was set up under the umbrella of the State Programme for the Preservation of Cultural Heritage through a grant provided by the World Bank. It was transformed into the 'Cultural Heritage Project' jointly undertaken by Georgia and the World Bank. On 18 February 1998 a 'Development Credit Agreement' was signed in Washington DC to set up this project. A legal body – the 'Fund for the Preservation of Cultural Heritage of Georgia (Project Implementation Unit)' (the *FUND*) – was set up. The World Bank provided finance of US $4.5 million and the Government of Georgia allocated an amount of US $480,000 under the agreement (as a co-financing share). On this basis the *FUND* was created as a legal body, under the Decree of the Parliament and the Presidential Decree. Together with the state bodies the *FUND* plays an important role in the preservation and protection of the cultural heritage of Georgia.

Other international organizations have provided grants for individual projects. For example, the Dutch Fund 'Horizon' is financing restoration works in Cauacasian House – which represents a house of the oldest traditions in Tbilisi. The Government of the Netherlands has also allotted a grant to finance restoration works on a rare monument of culture – the twelfth-century rock-cut monastery at Vardzia. But these are examples of only a small number of projects that have benefited from external assistance.

The role of agencies and specialist organizations
The role of the state and non-state structures (juridical persons of private sector, volunteers) in the field of cultural heritage protection has been established by different legislative acts (e.g. the laws On Culture and On Cultural Heritage Protection). These determine the responsibility and leading role of the Ministry of Culture and its structural subordinate – the Department of Monument Protection, Academy of Sciences of Georgia and other state bodies have been identified. All kinds of activities (scientific, practical, etc.) in the sphere of conservation are exercised through the observance of the principles established in these laws whether they are performed by the state bodies or by legal and natural persons involved in the private sector.

The issue of public awareness and the creation of a framework for consultations and collaboration among the state bodies, local authorities, associations and separate representatives of the society in the sphere of cultural heritage protection are not significantly developed at the present time. They are provided for in different chapters of the above-mentioned laws but they are not generally implemented. They await the formulation of separate independent norms under the joint decision of the President of Georgia, co-ordinating ministry or the creation of several Joint Ministerial Commissions. Some of them, however, are well expounded. For example: the norms for creating incentives for charitable activities, the creation of public organizations and promotion of private structures, the involvement of the community in the protection of cultural heritage, etc. But they still remain at the level of 'declarations' and the state is unable to ensure effective intervention.

In terms of the assistance to the state structures in their effort to ensure heritage protection, practical activities carried out by the *FUND* and supported by the World Bank and the Council of Europe are very important. The latter has a continuing programme of assistance in relation to draft laws concerning planning mechanisms, the import and export of cultural goods, museums, archaeology and the urban heritage.

Education and training
Georgia's cultural heritage is the spiritual and material chronicles of the country. Cultural heritage represents a precondition for the formation of the nation's self-cognizance representing a self-contained uninterrupted national culture. At the same time, it is an inseparable part of the Mankind's treasure. This is the starting point for the law 'On Cultural Heritage Protection'.

At present, when the grave economic condition of the country does not allow for new items to be added to the protected cultural heritage, the problem of safeguarding items currently protected and of passing them over to future generations, acquires particular significance. This highlights the need for a better comprehension of the role of cultural heritage protection by the public, the traditions of which already exist in the country.

It is well-known that traditions become out of date, and, as a part of national heritage, they also need care and popularization. The state strategy should be developed in this very direction. Though the protection of cultural heritage is envisaged in different state programs and conceptions, it is not realized because of lack of a budgetary resources.

Unfortunately, the curriculum of the Georgian educational system (except specialized schools) does not include a special course on cultural heritage. There is an opinion that archaeological studies should be included in the school syllabus of history and in the higher educational institutions. Moreover, practical field studies have been considered to facilitate the better comprehension of the remnants of the past by youngsters. The situation is more favourable in terms of acquiring specialist training as there are numerous state and non-state institutions of secondary and higher education.

Therefore, it is not surprising that there are many famous scholars, but this is not enough to raise the public consciousness. Moreover, it is also noteworthy that, owing to Georgia's financial problems, popular scientific publications are very limited at present and there is no opportunity to provide specialist cultural programmes through the television service.

Technical assistance rendered by foreign countries through different organizations is important in terms of staff training, material assistance and the conservation of archaeological finds, but too infrequently. One example is the conservation of the bronze objects revealed in Borjomy Gorge carried out in Germany (Bochum Museum of Mining Metallurgy). Some training assistance has also been provided by organizations from France and the United States of America.

Conclusions

Georgia has an ancient cultural heritage, which is an important part of the world cultural heritage (Fig. 6.8). At present a major part of it is in a grave condition. There is an urgent need for the adoption and implementation of

Fig. 6.8 Samtavisi: Church of St George (1030), east façade, Shida Kartli, East Georgia.

a serious legislative base and the provision of proper funds for safeguarding the cultural heritage of Georgia. This heritage is the spiritual wealth of the nation.

The law On Cultural Heritage Protection has been approved as part of the process of fulfilling the legislative and policy criteria of the Granada and Malta Conventions. Other laws (On the Export and Import of Cultural Property, On Museums, On Territorial–Spatial Planning – Urban Constructions) are also being prepared with this aim. The unity of the abovementioned laws creates a so-called 'Code of Culture', which will fill the legislative vacuum apparent in this field. The will enable the state to implement real mechanisms to protect the rich cultural heritage of Georgia.

Fortunately, Georgia has an intellectual sponsor in the Council of Europe. In terms of financial assistance, the contribution of the World Bank is very important. It is hoped that this will continue in the future and bring the results that are desired by the President: 'Let us save the culture and the culture will save the nation' (see the 'Introduction', above).

Note

The author would like to acknowledge assistance from the following in writing this chapter:

- Vladimer Vardosanidze – Architect-Urbanist, Professor of Architecture, Georgian Technical University Chairman, Corresponding Member, German Academy for City and Regional Planning (DASL).
- Vakhtang Licheli – Archeologist, PhD Historical Sciences, Deputy Director of the Center for Archaeological Research at the Academy of Sciences of Georgia.
- Leila Tumanishvili – Architect.

References

Council of Europe (1995): *Core data index to historic buildings and monuments of the architectural heritage*, and, *Recommendation R (95) 3 of the Committee of Ministries of the Council of Europe to member states on co-ordinating documentation methods and systems related to historic buildings and monuments of the architectural heritage.*

Fund for the Preservation of Cultural Heritage of Georgia (1999): *Tbilisi Pilot Project Framework Document.*

Government of Georgia (1995): *Georgian Constitution.*

Intskirveli, G. (1996): *State and Law Theory*, Tbilisi, Georgia

Pickard, R.D. (ed.) (2001): *Management of Historic Centres*, Conservation of the European Built Heritage Series, Spon Press, London (see Chapter 6 by Khimshiashvili, K. – Old Tbilisi, Georgia).

Shevardnadze, G.E. (1999): *Speech made by President George Edward Shevardnadze at the UN General Assembly Session of 20th September 1999* (published in *Saqartvelos Respublika* – daily newspaper, 21 September 1999).

Silvia Brüggemann and Christoph Schwarzkopf

Germany

Introduction

Although there had been a desire to place the care and preservation of historical monuments on a legal footing in the states making up Germany as early as the eighteenth century, the first law on the protection of historical monuments on a par with present-day legislation was passed in the Grand Duchy of Hesse-Darmstadt – one of the precursors of today's Federal *Land* (state) Hesse in 1902. It remained in force there until the Law on the Protection of Historical Monuments of the state of Hesse was passed in 1974. It afforded protection not only to the archaeological, natural and historical monuments themselves, but to their environs as well. This law also protected movable monuments. Provision was made for historical buildings to be listed, so giving them protection. A permit was required for alterations. It laid down maintenance requirements and the state's supervisory obligations and right of access to the monuments, as well as providing for the persons affected to be compensated.

It was in the 1970s that most of the other Federal German laws on the protection of historical monuments were passed. Even if this was not a direct consequence of the 1975 'European Architectural Heritage Year', the atmosphere of the time which was socially conducive to enactment of these laws was enhanced by this event. In addition to explicit laws on the protection of historical monuments, there are legal provisions relating to conservation matters in other Federal German and *Ländern* (states) statutes as well.

A survey of the situation pertaining to the preservation of historical monuments in Germany as a whole is not easy if it is to be based on the statutory provisions. As the *Ländern* have cultural autonomy, there are sixteen different laws on the protection of historical monuments. The laws are similar – but in some cases the law does indeed differ. This chapter will focus primarily on the situation prevailing in the state of Thüringia. Formerly part of the GDR, Thüringia has only been a *Land* of the Federal Republic of Germany since 1990. It goes without saying that the differences between the 'new', eastern Federal *Ländern* and the 'old' western ones in terms of the preservation of historical monuments are greater than between the two respective groups of *Ländern*. However, as the situation in the various *Ländern* has largely equalized in many sectors, it would seem possible to describe the overall position on the basis of the situation in Thüringia. Having said that, the position will not, as a rule, be illustrated by examples in this chapter. That has been assessed in a corresponding book (Pickard, 2001).

Definition of the heritage
General provisions
Only the laws on the protection of historical monuments define 'heritage' more closely. At the same time they leave considerable scope for interpretation. Section 2 of the Thüringian Law on the Protection of Historical Monuments of 1992 (the TLPHM 1992) determines what cultural monuments are. It states that these are 'objects, complexes of objects or parts of objects which it is in the public interest to preserve for historical, technical, folk-lore or urban design reasons and to preserve the historical aspect of villages'. As in most Federal *Ländern*, there are no precise instructions on how to execute this provision. Ultimately, therefore, it is the respective *Land* authority technically responsible that decides. Monuments above ground are the province of the Thüringia *Land* Office for the Preservation of Historical Monuments (*Landesamt für Denkmalpflege, Bau- und Kunstdenkmalpflege*) in Erfurt, whilst those on the ground fall to the Thüringia *Land* Office for the Preservation of Archaeological Monuments (*Landesamt für archäologische Denkmalpflege*) in Weimar. The latter also pronounces in individual cases on whether an object ranks as a cultural monument.

A working group composed of representatives of all the *Land* Offices for the Preservation of Historical Monuments seeks to have the 'inventory-taking', as the recording of monuments is called, conducted with a degree of homogeneity throughout the Federal Republic.

There is a relative amount of agreement on how to treat monuments dating up to about 1945. Views differ regarding the inclusion of more recent structures in the lists of monuments. The *Land* Government of Bavaria, for example, requires its *Land* Office for the Preservation of Historical Monuments to apply particularly strict criteria when selecting buildings built after 1945. In eastern Germany, moreover, many consider buildings of this period politically delicate. Whereas some feel that, as relics of a social system that is now passed, they should be demolished, others see them as symbols of a social order remembered as 'better' and consider them worthy of protection and preservation on those same political grounds. These very personal views are not always without effect on the deliberations of the authorities responsible for selecting the objects to be preserved.

Even without the structures dating from this period, the number of buildings registered as monuments today is steadily increasing. Conservationists officially reject accusations that today's term 'monument' is 'grossly exaggerated' (e.g. Petzet, 1993: 25). On the other hand, more and more conservation officials are calling for the number of protected objects to be limited. The reason for this is their concern that architectural history also suffers when structures can neither be maintained by qualified staff, nor funding be found for the extra cost that is regularly incurred when restoration or adaptation to present-day uses is carried out in a conservation-friendly manner. (The question whether that necessarily has to be the case is not for discussion here.)

All the laws on the protection of historical monuments give statutory protection not only to a monument's exterior but also to the respective structure including all its parts. In Thüringia, when an object is declared a monument, the parts worthy of protection are defined in the remarks attached to the declaration. Furthermore, Section 4(2) of the TLPHM 1992 provides that a cultural monument's movable accessories shall also be entered in the 'Monument Register' – the record of cultural monuments – 'if they are accessories of a historical building forming a unity with the main structure on artistic, historical or other grounds, or if they are items of fine art belonging historically in a specific place and it is in the public interest for them to remain there.'

Protection extends, however, not only to the monument and its parts, but to its surroundings as well. The TLPHM 1992 provides for this in Section 13 which lays down which measures in connection with monuments require a permit. Section 13 (2), like similar passages in other German laws on the protection of historical monuments, states that a permit is also required 'by anyone wanting to build, alter or demolish structures in the vicinity of an immovable cultural monument, if this could have an effect on the substance or appearance of the cultural monument . . .'. Such work can be prohibited if the 'project would result in the nature, the traditional appearance or the artistic effect of the cultural monument being impaired and there are important conservationist grounds for the present state being left unchanged.'

When implemented in individual cases, the way these very general provisions are applied differs depending on the situation. Neither should one overlook the differences necessarily resulting from the different standpoints of the conservationist responsible, given that the criteria defy objective definition. Moreover, more precise data are usually only provided for a particular monument when projects that might have an impact on it in some way are being planned in its vicinity.

Even though legislation in Thüringia does not provide for different categories of monuments, they are nevertheless treated differently in the day-to-day work of the responsible authorities. One reason for this is that it is practically impossible to devote equal attention to the host of objects recognized nowadays as cultural monuments. Another reason is that there is less pressure for change regarding monuments accepted as such in the public mind – the Wartburg in Eisenach for example (Fig. 7.1) – than with a freight shed at the station of the small community of Lauscha in the Thüringer Wald whose maintenance was no longer assured and demolition therefore approved (Fig. 7.2).

Fig. 7.1 Wartburg in Eisenach is an example of monument accepted as suc~ in the public mind. (Photograph: Thüringisch~ Landesamt für Denkmalpflege, Trefz.)

The GDR Law on the Preservation of Historical Monuments which remained in force until the Thüringian Law on the Protection of Historical Monuments was passed in 1992 had provided for such a gradation of monuments.

Monument ensembles in Thüringia's monument legislation
In principle, the same conservation provisions apply both to individual monuments and to ensembles of monuments. However, the TLPHM 1992 goes into much more detail on monument ensembles and defines criteria for them (Section 2(2ff.): monument ensembles comprise 'composite building complexes', 'typical configurations of streets, squares and localities', 'typical layouts of localities', 'historical parks and gardens' and 'historical manufacturing plant and equipment'. Except for the manufacturing plant, the law gives precise definitions for each of these categories of monument ensembles: 'Composite building complexes are groups of buildings in particular, blocks of buildings and housing estates of uniform design, and historical town centres along with the vegetation, open spaces and expanses of water associated with them'. What can also be described as a 'composite building complex' is an open question.

Fig. 7.2 Railway station in Lauscha in the Thüringer Wald: the demolition of its freight shed was approved in 1993.

Of 'typical configurations of streets, squares and localities', the Law states that 'the aspect of the area must be characteristic of a specific epoch or genre or of a typical building style, even featuring different architectural elements'.

Of 'typical layouts of localities' the Law states that 'the aspect of the area must be characteristic of a specific epoch or development, especially with regard to the form of the site and its settlements, its road systems, the structure of its plots of land and its fortifications'.

Of 'historical parks and gardens', which also feature under the term 'monument ensembles', the Law states that they are 'works of horticultural art whose location, architecture and vegetation bear witness to the site's function as a space in which earlier forms of society lived and moved, and the culture they represented.'

Whilst the topography of the conservation areas is also described, the land registered and numbered plots of land are always published when they are formally declared a monument.

In other Federal *Ländern* there are arrangements for more extensive sites of historical interest with provisions differing from those for cultural monuments. The GDR Law in force in Thüringia until 1992 also provided for 'monument protection areas'. Such provisions were not incorporated into legislation in the state of Thüringia, however.

Ground monuments as cultural monuments

Section 2(7) of the TLPHM 1992 defines 'ground monuments' as 'movable or immovable . . . testimony . . . to human culture . . . or animal or plant life . . . which is or was hidden in the ground'. Chance finds must be reported. This is provided for in Section 16 of the TLPHM 1992. Extension of the reporting requirement to all involved is intended to increase the likelihood of finds actually being reported. For Thüringia, Section 17 of the TLPHM 1992 relating to 'treasure trove' further provides that finds in the ground whose lawful owner is no longer ascertainable belong to Thüringia. Not all Federal *Ländern* have provisions on 'treasure trove'. On occasion, therefore, rogue diggers simply declare that their finds originate from elsewhere.

Where 'archaeological monuments' are concerned, there is no statutory timeframe. It is only since enactment of the Thüringian Law on the Protection of Historical Monuments in 1992, however, that the *Land* Office for the Preservation of Archaeological Monuments became responsible for ground monuments of modern times as well. This is not the case in all the Federal *Ländern*. In some of them, the responsibility of the competent authorities is limited to monuments dating from prehistoric and primitive times.

In order to protect areas which, in all probability, contain ground monuments, the supreme authority for the protection of monuments, the Thüringian Ministry of Science and Art (*Thüringer Ministerium für Wissenschaft und Kunst*) can, under Section 19 of the Thüringian Law on the Protection of Historical Monuments, define areas as 'archaeological protected areas'. So far, no such protected areas exist. Strictly speaking, the only legal difference between the provisions concerning the need for permits for excavation work within archaeological protected areas and outside them is the issuing authority responsible. Under Section 13(2), anyone 'wishing to carry out excavation work on a site known to or suspected of containing cultural monuments' requires a permit from the Lower Authority for the Protection of Monuments. Under Section 19(2), such work in a registered protected area requires a permit from the Higher Authority for the Protection of Monuments.

Identification of the heritage

Monuments in Thüringia are being recorded afresh following enactment of the Law on the Protection of Historical Monuments. Lists of monuments are being drawn up for all the administrative counties (*Landkreise*). The Law terms the recording of monuments a 'Monument Register' (*Denkmalbuch*), the system being a so-called 'notification' one, i.e. the monument's owner is merely notified that his property has 'monument status'. As this has no legal consequences initially, he cannot have the matter subjected to administrative scrutiny. Scrutiny by a Court of whether an object is a cultural monument might conceivably occur in an administrative court hearing following proceedings instituted against an administrative act in respect of it, for example, the refusal of a building permit because of its status as a monument.

By contrast some of the *Ländern* practise the so-called 'constituent' system. Here the object only becomes a cultural monument after being declared one by an administrative act. Such an administrative act can be appealed against and subjected to judicial scrutiny in Court.

The cultural monuments recorded in Thüringia's Monument Register are solely those that have been recognized for their monument status today. In addition, however, the Law on the Protection of Historical Monuments provides – in keeping with the theory of conservation – that cultural monuments are such, even when they have not yet been so recognized. In principle, the legal status of cultural monuments that have been identified as such and those that have not is the same. In practice, of course, it is not unproblematic to have to tell a person submitting completed planning documents that his or her building project cannot be approved because it has just been established that the property to be altered is a cultural monument. This has occurred on several occasions in recent years, in particular when many monuments were registered anew. This has made conservation of historical monuments unpopular. Therefore, it is and has been important to record monuments as fully as possible and to complete the process with all possible speed. In 1989, a monument registration, under GDR legislation, was completed. In what is now the State of Thüringia some 8,000 monuments were on record (Zießler, 1990: 20). The 7,300 monuments referred to there relate to a territory some 10 per cent smaller than today's Federal *Land*. According to the Home Page of the *Land* Office for the Preservation of Historical Monuments (http://www.thlv.de/denkmalpflege), there are ten times as many today.

New monuments began to be added at about the time that the Thüringian Law on the Protection of Historical Monuments was passed in 1992. The *Land* Office for the Preservation of Historical Monuments has a special department for this purpose. Under Section 2 of the TLPHM 1992, the prerequisite for inclusion of a cultural monument is that its 'conservation must be in the public interest for historical, technical, folk-lore or urban design reasons or to preserve the historical aspect of a village'. The procedure for identifying a monument is not laid down definitively anywhere, but is largely transmitted orally on an object by object basis. In order to ensure uniformity of registration, all monuments to be included in the Monuments Register are examined by the departmental and *Land* Office heads before being entered in.

The officials record monuments within the boundaries of a town or administrative district. Every site is inspected as a matter of principle. Initially, the existing GDR lists, as well as suggestions from local and regional associations or authorities, served as the basis for monument registration. In addition, the cut-back in tax concessions for building projects – except for the restoration of historical buildings – has resulted in developers and others who are commissioning building work increasingly requesting that something be declared a monument, thus drawing attention to further properties on occasion. If objects appear to be cultural monuments following notification or external viewing, they are inspected by way of verification. Prior to being recorded in the Monument Register, the building's particulars enabling it to be identified are noted. These include the place, street, house number, exact plot number and the name of the owner. These data are supplemented by a summary of what is known about the property. The exactitude of these data differs from object to object depending on the research conducted and the official's expertise. Before an entry is made in the Monument Register, the owner must be heard, and he or she is informed of the entry (Section 5(1) of the TLPHM 1992). Section

5(2) of the TLPHM 1992 provides for the entry of monument ensembles to be notified by publication in the *Land* gazette (*Staatsanzeiger*). As a preliminary to an object being declared a monument, the TLPHM 1992 provides for 'an object's provisional declaration as a monument' in a list. Entry in this list ceases to have effect after 6 months if the object has not been entered in the Monument Register by that time (Section 6 of the TLPHM 1992).

The area of Thüringia is covered by a virtually all-embracing inventory of monuments, largely drawn up between 1887 and 1932. Such 'old inventories' exist in all the Federal *Ländern*. The Thüringia inventory contains extensive information including detailed descriptions of the cultural monuments and precise data on sources, etc. This type of inventory, is increasingly being pushed into the background as legislation on monument conservation increases, because there is no time for in-depth research, the basis of such work, due to the host of everyday tasks (Brönner, 1990: 35).

At the end of the 1970s, the concept of 'monument topography' emerged, somewhat in competition with the 'grand inventories', and the first volume was published in 1981. Each of the volumes, which largely follow uniform Federal guidelines, is devoted to a region – usually an administrative district (*Kreis*) – and is divided up into a general section describing its settlement and architectural history together with a portrayal of phenomena characteristic of the area. A map section is provided in which the monuments are depicted, in some cases with the plot shown, depending on the scale. An index or catalogue section lists the individual monuments that may be supplemented by present-day and historical illustrations and plans. The object of topography is to portray the monuments in relation to each other and the surrounding landscape (Wulf, 1990: 28) The monument topography for Thüringia is under preparation.

In addition, the *Handbuch der Deutschen Kunstdenkmäler* (*Handbook of German Art Monuments*), known in brief as 'Dehio' after its founder, gives a brief description of the more important cultural monuments in Germany. Only the chief building and art monuments feature in it. The amount of text devoted to them depends on their importance. The volume entitled *Thüringen* was published for the first time in 1998. It was prepared with the assistance of the *Land* Office for the Preservation of Historical Monuments. 'MIDAS', a data bank for recording monuments, set up in 1991 is no longer used because of its inflexibility.

Ground monuments have to be recorded in the Monument Register only if they are visible above ground or are 'of particular importance' (Section 4 of the TLPHM 1992). Excavation is only conducted by the *Land* Office for the Preservation of Archaeological Monuments, but it draws on contract staff for assistance. Consequently, no commercial interests are involved in the excavation work. In other Federal *Ländern* commercial excavation firms are used as well, and here experience has been mixed. At present, excavation work is not usually done for the purpose of discovery in the sense of increasing the store of knowledge. It is generally an emergency measure to safeguard archaeological finds against destruction due to numerous building projects. In recent years aerial photography exploration has increasingly been used to record ground monuments in Thüringia too.

The protection of historical monuments

A comparison of the TLPHM 1992 with the provisions of the Granada Convention reveals that all the judicial tools provided for in the latter have been implemented in Thüringia. In general, this applies to the Federal Republic as a whole. The obligation to preserve cultural monuments is couched in Section 7 of the TLPHM 1992. Every owner is required to take all reasonable action to preserve his or her monument. Under case law, reasonable action is that which does not impose a burden on the owner's assets. Should any conditions or maintenance requirements be imposed that go beyond this, the extra outlay must be offset by subsidies. To this end, some Federal *Ländern* such as Bavaria or Saxony maintain so-called 'compensation funds'. In Thüringia such work is financed by promotion funding as required.

Damage and defects to cultural monuments must be notified to the competent authority for the protection of monuments by the owner (Section 8 of the TLPHM 1992). Changes in ownership of registered movable and immovable cultural monuments must also be notified (Section 8(2) of the TLPHM 1992). In order to ensure that monuments are maintained, the authority for the protection of monuments is permitted to view and enter monuments after notifying the owner. The constitutional inviolability of a person's home is limited to the extent that the authority may enter it even against the owner's wishes for the purpose of averting impending danger (Section 9(2) of the TLPHM 1992). If owners do not meet their maintenance obligation, they can be required to do so by the authority for the protection of monuments. Should they refuse, the authority is empowered by Section 11 of the TLPHM 1992 to carry out maintenance work at the owner's expense. The owner can be required to pay a reasonable portion of the cost.

Permit requirement for work on cultural monuments

All alterations to cultural monuments and their surroundings require a permit. This requirement far exceeds the need for a building permit under the Building Code. Under Section 13 of the TLPHM 1992, a permit is not only required *to* 'demolish, remove or transfer a cultural monument or parts of it elsewhere', it is also required by anyone merely wanting to 'remodel, repair or alter its outward appearance'. Strictly speaking, this makes a permit necessary for virtually any work on a cultural monument. Given the host of cultural monuments registered in Thüringia and the other Federal *Ländern* today, implementation of these provisions has its limits. Various solutions are under consideration. The most obvious – to increase the number of conservation staff – is out of the question in the foreseeable future, if at all, for financial reasons. On the other hand, it might help to limit the term 'monument'. There ought either to be greater selectivity in choosing from amongst the host of cultural monuments, or the term should be defined more narrowly. There is then the implicit risk, however, of not being able to preserve the profusion of historical buildings in existence. A third possibility is to pursue a course in monument preservation which is not fully consistent with today's 'purist theory' of conservation, but which can nevertheless be in the spirit of conservation if it safeguards a cultural monument's essence. It would, of course, be necessary to decide what the essence is. If it proves totally uneconomic to restore the windows of a large housing estate, perhaps the less expensive installation of a new window range could be regarded as a real solution in conservation terms. The same goes for the recurrent question of whether the materials used are appropriate. One should ask oneself why modern alternatives that 'blend harmoniously' within the meaning of Article 12 of the ICOMOS Venice Charter should not normally be used if they patently do not damage the building's substance.

Present-day standards also present problems when preserving cultural monuments. They do not generally have to be observed where existing structures are concerned, but 'existing building structures may be required to be modified if this is necessary to avert major hazards to life and limb' (Section 84(1) of the Thüringian Building Code). Consequently, this also applies to the parts not being restored themselves. The Thüringian Building Code contains no waivers for historical buildings such as those in the Building Code in force until the end of the GDR. Today there is merely a general exemption clause. Section 68 of the Thüringian Building Code states that the building supervisory authority may permit deviations from the provisions 'if these are in keeping with the public interest, bearing in mind the purpose of the respective requirement and taking the neighbours' interests into account'.

As conservation questions are usually discretionary decisions, implementation of conservation concerns primarily depends on the scientific and social competence of the conservation official responsible. His diplomatic skills are no less important, but without a clear strategy these cannot be successful either.

Putting monuments to alternative uses

There is no general 'Guideline' in Thüringia giving guidance on possible alternative uses. The conservation authorities in Thüringia are very flexible when it comes to altering monuments and putting them to alternative uses with a view to preserving them. In recent years it is mainly disused commercial buildings that have been put to new uses in many places. An example of this is the former slaughterhouse in Gotha which now houses numerous retail businesses (Fig. 7.3). In Rositz near Altenburg the former sugar factory is now home to a well-known manufacturer of windows. On occasion, major concessions have been made as part of such re-usage. However, without the host of compromises made in the last 10 years, Thuringia's monument landscape would be all the poorer.

Fig. 7.3 In Gotha the old slaughterhouse is an example of putting a disused commercial building to a new use. (Photograph: Thüringisches Landesamt für Denkmalpflege, Trefz.)

The independence of specialized conservation authorities

The tiered structure of Thüringia's conservation authorities with their autonomous specialist departments ensures as a matter of principle that decisions are not dependent on the politics of the day. Under Section 13 (3) of the TLPHM 1992, the Lower Conservation Authorities (*Landratsamt*), County Hall or the local authorities of county boroughs (*kreisfreie Städte*) decide on an application for a permit after hearing the conservation authority responsible, i.e. the *Land* Office for the Preservation of Historical Monuments or the *Land* Office for the Preservation of Archaeological Monuments. If agreement cannot be reached with the conservation authority, the Lower Conservation Authority must request the Higher Conservation Authority, the Thüringian *Landesverwaltungsamt*, in Weimar to mediate. If agreement cannot be reached at this level either, a decision must be sought from the Supreme Conservation Authority, the Thüringian Ministry for Science, Research and Culture (*Ministerium für Wissenschaft, Forschung und Kultur*). The latter decides after hearing the conservation authority responsible.

This system ensures – in principle – both that the conservation authorities exert a strong influence and can act independently. Given the decision-making procedures, the Lower Conservation Authorities who are more closely bound up in local politics cannot simply implement local government interests. On occasion, as for example when the regional Custodian of Monuments (*Landeskonservator*) consented a few years ago to the demolition of the railway station buildings at Erfurt, the *Land* Office for the Preservation of Historical Monuments is not above entertaining political considerations itself, although the Law on the Protection of Historical Monuments provides for a clear division of competences. Similar cases have occurred in other Federal *Ländern* too. Much as it makes sense for the conservation authorities to be directly involved in implementing the Law on the Protection of Historical Monuments, the public effect of doing so is risky. If – for whatever compelling reasons – consent is given in formal proceedings to a measure that is regrettable in conservation terms, the public perceive this as being conservationally correct.

Conservation philosophy

Conservation and the dispute about its proper implementation have a long tradition in Germany. Karl Friedrich Schinkel, the leading architect of the State of Prussia, was one of the first to call for a monument protection authority of one's own in 1815. He made himself the advocate of monuments. Even if he did not always implement his theoretical insights himself, many of his ideas run like a continuous thread through the history of German conservation to this very day: He called for an inventory of monuments, setting the upper limit at about 1,650. Less old buildings would scarcely be at risk, or he could see no artistic merit in them. On the other hand, he deemed the old architectural structure considered faulty in his day as worthy of preservation (Huse, 1984: 64). His approach to restoration was reflected in a decree of 1843 issued by the Prussian ministry responsible (Reimers, 1911: 440). It stated that restoration work must not erase the marks of time on a building. Despite that, another influence assumed greater importance in Germany: that of Viollet-le-Duc who took the view that one should immerse onself in what a monument sought to express, and that restoration work should recreate this, even if the end result achieved by this method had never existed in that form. This can produce very different outcomes. There are some well-known examples of such an approach: Cologne Cathedral or the Wartburg in Thüringia, as well as castles Hohkšnigsburg in Alsace and Marienburg in East Prussia, both of which were formerly part of Germany.

These models were drawn on in Thüringia over the years. It was not until 1900 that criticism of the standard restoration practice, such as Ruskin had voiced in England in the mid-nineteenth century (Ruskin, 1849), was reiterated in Germany. The well-known 'monument dispute' about the proposal to reconstruct the Palace of Heidelberg was conducted at the *Tage der Denkmalpflege* (Conservation Congress), a congress held almost annually since 1899. This brought together architects specializing in conservation, who espoused the ideals of Viollet-le-Duc, and a few art historians such as Georg Dehio or Cornelius Gurlitt who had previously also been an architect. Gurlitt began to resist the prevailing trend in restoration and won increasing support in this from younger architects such as Muthesius or Theodor Fischer. The latter complained in 1902 that

> in fifty cases out of a hundred, a major alteration is totally unneces-
> sary. Some bare patches of stucco, a weathered stone, a leaking roof –
> repair these and they would last for many decades still. Often ambition
> is the motivating force. The people in Adorf and Bestadt have restored
> their churches, so those in Cefeld must follow suit, that's clear. Often,

however, it's a matter of excessive tidiness and cleanliness: there is always so much that won't do. Here the paintwork is flaking, . . . here it is one thing, there another. It calls for a great deal of self-denial on the part of today's order-loving individual to see beyond the details bleached and broken down by time, and perceive the harmony of the whole'. (quoted from Huse, 1984: 117ff.)

Schinkel mentioned a further conservation problem in an expertise of 1832. He said that the monuments could not be restored under financial and time pressure. That is still true today. This is not to say that conservation work can be performed free of financial constraints and binding deadlines. Nevertheless, in many places these – as it were – age-old considerations are foreign even to the conservation authorities. They often accept that doubtful solutions must be tolerated so as to adhere to financial limits and deadlines. Instead, it is for conservationists to highlight these problems and indicate possible solutions well in advance of the work, which is usually conducted with the aid of government subsidies, and help to develop them.

The host of tasks to be performed by today's conservation authorities similarly prevents them from countering the trend toward 'full-blown' restorations. The object tends to be to have the work performed in such a way that the cultural monument is returned to a more or less well documented former state and that this be as permanent as possible. In the majority of cases, 'state of the art technology', which must be deployed if those involved in the restoration work are to accept liability, is accepted where it might make more sense to take out credit guarantees and pursue a course more commensurate with the monument.

Naturally, work is always based as a matter of principle on the appropriate guidelines, such as the ICOMOS Venice and Washington Charters. Usually, in Thüringia too, they form the substantive basis for conservation legislation. In practice, however, it scarcely seems possible for them to be applied consistently throughout. The reason for this is the generally contrary attitude of the monument owners. It is also worth noting, however, that the originators of the Charter could scarcely have anticipated the host of artifacts that would be deemed worthy of monument status. Documentation of the work on the monuments, as required by Article 16 of the Venice Charter, would itself be beyond the means of the archives of the *Land* Office for the Preservation of Historical Monuments if it were prepared with equal intensity for the 80,000 monuments now registered in Thüringia. There is no doubt that such documentation is requested and prepared when important cultural monuments are restored – even though officially no classification of monuments exists.

In order for official conservation circles, which are not organized on a national basis, to exchange views and – if possible – arrive at a consensus, the 'Association of *Land* Conservationists' was formed. It holds annual conventions and draws up common positions in nation-wide specialist working groups.

Sanctions and coercive measures

The Thüringian Law – like those of the other Federal *Ländern* – has various means of enforcing obligations under the Law on the Protection of Historical Monuments.

First, it is possible for the authorities to have the work performed themselves at the owner's expense in the event of neglect of his or her maintenance obligations (Section 11(2) of the TLPHM 1992). The authorities seldom resort to this course because of the risk of them having to bear the cost themselves should the owner be unable to pay. Under Section 15, the conservation authority can demand that a building be restored to its previous state should alterations have been made to a cultural monument or its environs illegally. In practice, of course, this is scarcely feasible in the case of alterations to the fabric of a monument, where the fabric has been destroyed in the course of the work.

For conservation purposes, expropriation is possible if this is necessary to preserve a cultural monument, or to secure and evaluate a ground monument scientifically or make it generally accessible. In Thüringia this is the responsibility of the respective conservation authorities. So far, however, no property has been expropriated in Thüringia on these grounds. It is not customary in other Federal *Ländern* either. In addition, when cultural monuments are put on sale, the local authorities have the right of first refusal which they can also exercise on behalf of another legal entity under public law. They can also exercise this right in favour of an individual under private law if his or her statutory purpose is to preserve cultural monuments and if their lasting preservation seems assured as a result. Such expropriations have not yet been carried out in Thüringia.

Fines of up to 250,000 DM can be imposed for unlawful work; the fine for demolition of a cultural monument can be as high as 1,000,000 DM. However, even relatively steep fines do not, as a rule, detract from the material gain that the owner enjoys as a result of disregarding conservation legislation.

Integration of monuments in the wider context

The overall planning instrument for conservation legislation in Thüringia is the 'Monument Conservation Plan' (*Denkmalpflegeplan*). Section 3(1) of the TLPHM 1992 reads as follows:

In concert with the conservation authorities, local authorities shall draw up monument conservation plans for monument ensembles . . . in statute form. The Monument Conservation Plan reflects the objectives and requirements of monument protection and conservation, and depicts and lays them down for town and country planning purposes. It contains: (a) an inventory and analysis of the planning area from a monument protection and conservation viewpoint; (b) topographical data on the location and extent of the monument ensembles and ground monuments in written form and on the plan; (c) conservation objectives to be observed in the care and maintenance of monument ensembles and ground monuments.

Preservation of the architectural heritage is a requirement not only of historical monument legislation but in regional policy and urban planning legislation too. The Regional Policy Law (*Raumordnungsgesetz*), as revised in 1997, lays down the following as a principle of regional policy (Section 2(2), sentence 13): 'The characteristic features of man-made landscapes, together with their cultural and natural monuments, shall be preserved'. The regional policy plans drawn up by the *Ländern* are to observe this. In the case of planning likely to have an environmental impact, as when building a new road or railway line, regional policy proceedings are to be instituted accordingly. Section 15 of the law calls for examination of the extent to which these plans meet the principles of Section 2. The responsible public authorities, i.e. the *Ländern* Offices for the Preservation of Historic Monuments, are also to participate in this.

Provisions concerning other planning affecting land are laid down in the Building Code (*Baugesetzbuch*) (BauGB). The realization that aspects of town and country planning, even if not in the immediate vicinity of a monument, can still affect the monument has led to the conservation authorities being involved in the drawing up of such plans as a matter of principle in their capacity as 'bodies representing the public interest' (Section 4, BauGB). Section 1 (5), BauGB, lays down, amongst other things, that when drawing up a development plan, i.e. a County/Town Map (*Flächennutzungsplan*) and Local Plan (*Bebauungsplan*), 'the interests of monument protection and conservation, as well as districts, roads and squares of historical, artistic or urban design importance that are worthy of preservation' shall be taken into consideration. These requirements actually go beyond what the conservation authorities might require as reasonable. Section 1(6) goes on to say: 'When drawing up development plans, a just balance shall be achieved between public and private interests.' Section 4 provides that bodies representing the public interest shall be given an opportunity to comment when the plan is being drawn up. Finally, after the public and private interests have been weighed against each other, the higher administrative authority responsible – in Thüringia it is the *Landesverwaltungsamt* – examines whether the Plan has been drawn up in accordance with the law, i.e. whether the hearings and the weighing up were conducted in due form.

In the course of these proceedings, the *Land* Offices for the Preservation of Historic Monuments not only have an opportunity to point to the direct effects of planning on monuments; they may also highlight the indirect effects. When commenting on the Town Map for the town of Hildburghausen in 1991, for example, the *Land* Office for the Preservation of Historical Monuments pointed out that to set aside land for retailers on the four main roads leading out of the town of just 10,000 inhabitants would mean the end of the old quarter which is a monument ensemble. Serious conservation problems would be the inevitable result. These warnings were to no avail; they were not heeded. Unfortunately, they proved true. By way of qualification it should be said that, after German unification, the new laws were not implemented to the full extent. Meanwhile, the higher supervisory authority would no longer accept such disregard of public concerns doubtless to be recognized when weighing up the pros and cons.

In addition to the conservation authorities' opportunities for participating in town and country planning, the Building Code also defines how local authorities can draw up statutes of their own to preserve the characteristic design features of an area.

The drawing up of a conservation statute is governed today by Section 172 BauGB. This states that a local authority can issue statutes for specific areas 'to maintain the structural character of the area resulting from its structural design'. First, the reasons why the conservation statute is being issued must be stated. In this case it is the proposed preservation of its structural character and maintenance of the population structure. To this end, all changes in the use to which buildings are put and structural alterations to them require a permit from the local authority. The permit can be refused if the building in question is of itself or in conjunction with others characteristic of the area or 'otherwise of urban, in particular historic or artistic importance'. It is also possible to draw upon a conservation statute (Section 174, 3 BauGB) to refuse a permit for buildings that would impair an area's development character.

Another tool for preserving the townscape is the 'design statute'. Based on detailed analysis, it is possible to define the character of specific parts of a city and arrive at rules for the design of roofs, building structures, façades, plot sizes, floor coverings, even going as far as regulations on materials and colours to be used. This is not without risk. It can result in uniformity of design, prevent good, new architecture and, on the other hand, not be a guarantee of producing design that really blends in. In addition, it is difficult to determine what is characteristic of particular sectors, given that design features have changed so often throughout the centuries. Good examples of the use of design statutes are always to be found where local government politicians show commitment in having them executed.

These wide-ranging opportunities for preserving the character of an area are understandably not always drawn upon by local authorities to an adequate extent on economic grounds.

The Building Code also provides for urban renewal procedures (Sections 136 ff.). Admittedly, this does not relate primarily to conservation work. However, Section 136(4) lays down that care be taken 'to take account of the demands of conservation'. In urban renewal, which is carried out in defined areas, the refurbishment objectives are drawn up in such a way as to integrate the monuments in the area on a permanent basis.

Lastly, there are the general tools of building legislation by means of which the building inspectorate (*Bauaufsichtsbehörden*) could outlaw building monstrosities anywhere and at any time in Germany without recourse to any of the other legal instruments. Section 34 lays down which structures may be erected in built-up areas in principle. These have to blend into the surrounding buildings in terms of size, design and also usage.

Similar provisions are found in the Building Ordinances (*Bauordnungen*) which vary only slightly between the Federal *Ländern*. Section 12(2) of the Thüringian Building Ordinance states the following: 'Building structures must harmonise with their surroundings in such a way as not to mar the aspect of the street, locality or landscape. . . . Account must be taken of features worthy of conservation.'

In order to be able to bring conservation interests to bear in area planning, it is essential to put them on a firm footing. In Thüringia, it is not possible to conduct systematic studies of our own on architectural history and the building structures of entire planning areas as the basis for advising on planning, such as the conservation authorities in Bavaria (Mosel, 1998; Ongyerth, 1998) or Baden-Württemberg do in this connection, because fewer staff are available.

Promotion of conservation work: financial resources and funding mechanisms

A Federal law provides for restoration work on historical monuments to attract tax relief. Over a 10-year period, all labour costs entailed in restoring a cultural monument and putting it to a meaningful use can be deducted from one's taxable income. In Thüringia, confirmation that the work has been carried out in a proper conservation manner is issued by the *Land* Office for the Preservation of Historical Monuments. This provides an effective means of influencing work on the cultural monument. Unfortunately, once again this opportunity can seldom be taken advantage of in full, due to the host of tasks to be performed by the conservation authorities. On average tax relief was applied for by some 250 persons commissioning building work per annum up to the mid-1998.

Thüringia also provides grants to promote conservation work. These currently total some 30 million DM per annum. Restoration work on historical buildings is further promoted as part of urban renewal. However, this does not relate explicitly to conservation measures. Nevertheless, historical buildings are still funded in large measure here as they tend to be concentrated in old quarters undergoing refurbishment. The purpose of this aid is to reimburse the owner for unprofitable expenditure, i.e. to make refurbishment economic in inner city problem areas. The various programmes are usually funded by the Federation (*Bund*) and the *Land* jointly. In Thüringia 1.78 billion DM were spent on refurbishing town centres and inner cities between 1991 and 1998.

Further funding is available within the framework of 'Village Renewal'. This programme provides for a proportion of the overall cost of refurbishment to be paid in villages that have been accepted into the promotion programme.

The Federal Interior Ministry contributes some 14 million DM per annum to preserving 'cultural monuments of national importance' in the new *Ländern* and Berlin. In addition to these government programmes, two semi-governmental foundations promote conservation work. Since its foundation in 1985, the *Deutsche Stiftung Denkmalschutz* (German Foundation for the Protection of Historical Monuments) has raised more than 320 million DM for conservation projects. The *Deutsche Bundesstiftung Umwelt* (German Federal Environment Foundation), founded in 1989, promotes projects linking environmental protection and conservation, or that specifically repair environmental damage to historical buildings and seek to avoid it permanently.

Several private law foundations also contribute appreciable sums of money for individual conservation projects. The work is classified as non-profit and the foundations' commitment is promoted by being made tax-deductible. In addition, the *Stiftung Thüringer Schlösser und Gärten* (Foundation for Thüringian Palaces and Gardens) was set up to look after and maintain important cultural monuments in Thüringia. So far it has been entrusted with some 40 properties, mainly palaces owned by the *Land*. This foundation is funded by the State of Thüringia.

In general, of course, it is the owner's responsibility to maintain the cultural monument, and this includes its financing. Furthermore, based on the causation principle (Section 14 (1) of the TLPHM 1992), the financing of conservation studies necessitated by building projects which could have an adverse effect on the cultural monument is a matter for the owner or the person commissioning the work.

The role of private agencies and specialist organizations

During the twentieth century, conservation changed from what was initially a virtually private endeavour to a function of the state. Admittedly, there are many local associations in Germany that have espoused the conservation cause, and even if they have next to no influence on government conservation policy as a whole, they form local initiatives in many places and make themselves heard.

When the Thüringian Law on the Protection of Historical Monuments was being drawn up in 1990/91, consideration was given to granting non-governmental conservation associations a statutory right to participate, similar to that in nature protection legislation. The Law passed in 1992 makes no provision for such participation, however.

The only conservation organization of note found throughout Thüringia is the *Deutscher Heimatbund* (German Homeland Federation). This organization, which operates nationwide, does not confine itself to conservation questions, but is active on interrelated issues. Other associations in Thüringia devote their attention to particular groups of monuments. For example, there is a Mill Association (Mühlenverein) and a *Land* group of the *Deutsche Burgenvereinigung* (German Castle Association).

In Thüringia, publicity for the protection of historical monuments is almost exclusively the province of the authorities, however. This is also true of the 'Monument Open Day' which is organized throughout Thüringia by the *Land* Office for the Protection of Historical Monuments. This 'Open Day' has meanwhile become a fixture in Thüringia and in many places it has a festive quality. In 1999 1,000 monuments throughout Thüringia were open to the public on this occasion.

The *Deutsche Stiftung Denkmalschutz* (German Foundation for the Protection of Historical Monuments) is active nationwide in seeking public support for the promotion of conservation – above all with its periodical *Monumente* (*Monuments*) – as is the *Deutsches Nationalkomitee für Denkmalschutz* (German National Committee for the Protection of Historical Monuments) which was set up to prepare for the European Architectural Heritage Year 1975. The latter organizes conventions and publishes their results, together with other leaflets giving instructive data on the protection and preservation of historical monuments. Both institutions receive financial support from the Federal Government.

The Thüringian Law on the Protection of Historical Monuments provides for honorary conservationists, but their participation in formal hearings is not laid down definitively, as is the case in Bavaria, for example. Neither have any honorary conservationists been appointed in most districts (*Kreise*) of Thüringia. On the other hand, there are administrative districts (*Landkreise*) where honorary conservationists exercise great authority.

In the archaeological monument sector, there is a whole network of honorary staff who work closely with the *Land* Office for the Preservation of Archaeological Monuments and regularly receive further training from it. On the authority of the *Land* Office, they also conduct emergency digs or inspect finds in the ground.

In addition, numerous associations have come into being to run job creation schemes in the field of conservation. However, their emergence and demise are usually closely linked with the availability of such programmes financed by the Labour Exchange (*Arbeitsamt*).

Last but not least Protestant – and Roman Catholic – Church authorities have their own building offices. They are responsible for their monuments also. In some *Länder* the church administration fulfils their work instead of the state Lower Conservation Authorities. In Thüringia the Lower Conservation Authorities are responsible for church buildings as well.

Education and training

Unlike archaeology, there is no separate university course for study of the care and preservation of historical monuments. Various universities and technical colleges that train architects have chairs in conservation. The material taught in the various educational establishments differs in some cases considerably. An association, the *Arbeitskreis Theorie und Lehre der Denkmalpflege* (Working Group on the Theory and Teaching of Conservation) organizes a nationwide exchange amongst the teaching staff.

In addition, some universities and technical colleges offer courses in restoration. This tuition is hampered by the fact that there are neither *Land* nor Federal provisions that protect the designation 'restorer'; neither are there guidelines that lay down minimum qualification standards.

In Thüringia there is a Chair of Conservation at the *Bauhaus-Universität* (Bauhaus University) in Weimar. The technical college in Erfurt has a department which trains restorers in different fields. The Architecture Department there has no conservation professorship of its own.

In addition to the courses of study mentioned, there are a great many further education courses in Germany addressed to craftsmen as well as architects and conservation authorities. The best known institution is the *Deutsches Zentrum für Handwerk in der Denkmalpflege* (German Centre for Craftmanship in Conservation) in Fulda which offers a comprehensive range of different courses geared to all the professions working in conservation. This centre also has a branch in Thüringia. In addition to the Centre in Fulda, there are other establishments in Germany of similar standing. The supplementary postgraduate course in 'Conservation' offered jointly by the University of Bamberg and the Fachhochschule (technical college) Coburg has a good reputation. There are similar postgraduate courses of study at other universities as well.

The same also applies, of course, to minimum standards of those working, or being allowed to work on a historical building. Section 14 (2) of the TLPHM 1992 addresses qualifications as a prerequisite for working on monuments as follows: 'Where required by the cultural monument's special character, its importance or the complexity of the work, permission will only be granted on condition that the preparatory study or work requiring special experience or knowledge is performed by suitably qualified conservation staff.' As long as standards or implementing regulations are lacking, the wording of this passage creates judicial uncertainty rather than being an expedient instrument. Furthermore, when applied as a requirement of conservation authorities that particular firms or individuals be commissioned with certain special tasks, the impression of illegal preferential treatment is given on occasion. This is another reason for requiring unequivocal provisions.

Conclusions

In the last 25 years of the twentieth century, interest in the care and preservation of the architectural heritage has become widespread. During this period the judicial position of conservation has improved appreciably. A variety of promotion schemes are helping to pass on the cultural monuments to future generations too, even though conservationists will always call for still more aid.

A problem lies in the fact that, at present, there is no consensus in society and professional circles about the right course to be taken in conservation. To address this issue will doubtless be the prime task facing German conservationists at the beginning of the new millennium.

References

Brönner (1990): Schicksal und Zukunft des Großinventars in der Bundesrepublik Deutschland, in Möller, Hans-Herbert (ed.), *Inventarisation in Deutschland* (Reports on Conservation Research and Practice in Germany 1), Hanover.

Huse, N. (ed.) (1984): *Huse-Denkmalpflege: Deutsche Texte aus drei Jahrhunderten*, Munich.

Mosel, M. (1998): Städtebauliche Denkmalpflege in Bayern, in: *Monumental*, publication in honour of Michael Petzet, Munich.

Ongyerth, G. (1998): Vorbereitende Denkmalpfelege, in *Monumental*, publication in honour of Michael Petzet, Munich.

Petzet, M. (1993): *Petzet/Mader, Praktische Denkmalpflege*, Stuttgart, Berlin, Cologne, p. 25.

Pickard, R.D. (ed.) (2001): *Management of Historic Centres*, Conservation of the European Built Heritage Series, Spon Press, London (see Chapter 7 by Brüggemann, S. and Schwarzkopf, C. on Erfurt, Germany).

Reimers, J. (1911): *Handbuch für die Denkmalpflege*, Hanover.

Ruskin, J. (1849): *The seven lamps of Architecture*, 'The Lamp of Memory', XVIII.

Thüringer Bauordnung (1999): *Re-publication of the Thüringian Building Code*, Thüringer Architektenhandbuch 1999, Leipzig 1998, pp. 143ff.

Thüringer Denkmalschutzgesetz (1999): *Gesetz zur Pflege und zum Schutz der Kulturdenkmale im Land Thüringen*, Thüringer Architektenhandbuch 1999, Leipzig 1998, pp. 252ff.

Wulf, W. (1990): Denkmaltopographie Bundesrepublik Deutschland, in Möller, Hans-Herbert (ed.), *Inventarisation in Deutschland* (Reports on Conservation Research and Practice in Germany 1), Hanover .

Zießler, R. (1990): Erfassung und Denkmalliste, in Möller, Hans-Herbert (ed.), *Inventarisation in Deutschland* (Reports on Conservation Research and Practice in Germany 1), Hanover.

Rachel MacRory and Seán Kirwan

Ireland

Introduction

This chapter outlines the policy and legislative framework for the protection of the built heritage in Ireland. It highlights key aspects of current legislation and policy and notes stages in its development. The account given here is not, of course, a legal interpretation and the focus is on developments in statute law rather than on case law relating to the protection of the built heritage.

Pre-1930 legislative background

Prior to the establishment of an independent Irish State in 1922 there was already a body of legislation in place which related to the protection of monuments, with some of this legislation applying to the United Kingdom as a whole and some applying exclusively to Ireland. Ireland was, in fact, the first part of the then United Kingdom of Great Britain and Ireland to have legislation relating to the protection of monuments. This came about in the context of the disestablishment of the Church of Ireland (i.e. the Anglican Church in Ireland) under the *Irish Church Act 1869*. The Act provided for medieval churches and other ecclesiastical features, which had previously belonged to the Church of Ireland, to be vested in the Commissioners of Public Works in Ireland if they were 'deserving of being maintained as a national monument by reason of its architectural character or antiquity'.

The *Ancient Monuments Protection Act 1882* was the first legislation in the United Kingdom aimed specifically at the protection of monuments of archaeological importance. The Act extended to the whole of the United Kingdom and applied in the first instance to 'ancient monuments' set out in a Schedule containing three separate lists for England and Wales, Scotland, and Ireland. The *Local Government (Ireland) Act 1898* established the basis for the modern system of local authorities in Ireland and gave local authorities a role in the protection of ancient monuments. The *Irish Land Act 1903* (the main aim of which was the division of landed estates) and the *Land Act 1923* also included provision for the protection of ancient monuments.

Current national framework

There is no single piece of legislation in Ireland, dealing exclusively with the protection of the built heritage, nor any single body vested with its responsibility. The two main areas of legislation are first, the *National Monuments Acts (1930–94)* and secondly, the *Local Government (Planning and Development) Acts (1963–99)*. (A further 'Planning and Development' Bill 1999 is expected to be enacted during 2000). The Minster for Arts, Heritage, Gaeltacht and the Islands (MAGHI) has responsibility for formulating national policy in relation to the physical heritage and for the implementation of the National Monuments Acts (Dúchas is the heritage service of the Department). The Heritage Council, as well as the cultural institutions that have responsibilities in the area of archaeological and architectural heritage, also come under the aegis of this Ministry. Physical planning legislation is implemented at local government level, under the policy direction of the Minister for the Environment and Local Government (MELG).

All legal provisions operate against the backdrop of the *Constitution* which takes precedence over any legislative enactment of the *Oireachtas* (Parliament) in the event of there being a conflict. Although provisions for the protection of the built heritage must be considered in the context of a citizen's constitutional property rights, individual rights and freedoms may be curtailed where such a restriction is deemed to be in the interests of the common good.

International framework

Ireland is party to the principal international conventions for the protection of the built heritage. The UNESCO *Convention concerning the Protection of the World Cultural and Natural Heritage* (World Heritage Convention) was ratified by the Republic of Ireland in 1992. To date Ireland has two sites included in the World Heritage List: 'Brú na Bóinne (1993), the archaeological complex of the Boyne Valley comprising the prehistoric sites of Newgrange, Knowth and Dowth, etc., and Skellig Michael (1996), an early christian monastery and hermitage on a remote island off the coast of Co. Kerry (Fig. 8.1). The Republic of Ireland is also party to the *United Nations Convention on the Law of the Sea* (1982), Article 303 (1) of which provides that 'States have the duty to protect objects of an archaeological and historical nature found at sea and shall co-operate for this purpose'. Ireland has signed the *Hague Convention for the Protection of Cultural Property in the event of Armed Conflict* (1954) and preparations for ratification are in train.

In 1997 Ireland ratified the Council of Europe *European Convention on the Protection of the Archaeological Heritage (revised)* (1992) (the Malta Convention) and the Council of Europe *Convention on the Protection of the Architectural Heritage of Europe* (1985) (the Granada Convention).

Fig. 8.1 Skellig Michael, an early Christian monastery and hermitage on a remote island off the coast of Co. Kerry, designated as a World Heritage Site in 1996. (Copyright: Dúchas, The Heritage Service.)

Definition of heritage

As there is no single piece of legislation in Ireland dealing with the archaeological and architectural heritage there is no single legislative definition in place, but rather a number of different definitions each specific to their legislative context. In general, legislative definitions, which form the basis of protection measures, tend to be broad and inclusive.

Definitions under the National Monuments Acts

The National Monuments Acts, 1930–94, are construed as one Act creating a broad piece of legislation for the protection of archaeological and architectural heritage. The basic definition relating to the built heritage contained in the act is that of 'monument'. This definition is extremely broad and is further qualified by definitions of 'national monument' and 'historic monument' to which a series of protective measures are applied (see below). Whilst the provisions under the National Monuments Acts contain no prejudice as to date, i.e. monuments of any period can be protected, the bias in their application has traditionally been towards structures of medieval or earlier date, or buildings of a later date not in active use. Churches in use for ecclesiastical purposes are excluded from the scope of the National Monuments Acts.

Definitions under the Acts

The 1930 Act (as amended by the 1987 Act) provides that a *monument* includes the following (whether above or below the surface of the ground or the water and whether affixed or not affixed to the ground):

(a) any artificial or partly artificial building, structure or erection or group of such buildings, structures or erections,

(b) any cave, stone or other natural product, whether or not forming part of the ground, that has been artificially carved, sculptured or worked upon or which (where it does not form part of the place where it is) appears to have been purposely put or arranged in position,

(c) any, or any part of any, prehistoric or ancient-
  (i) tomb, grave or burial deposit, or
  (ii) ritual, industrial or habitation site,

and

(d) any place comprising the remains or traces of any such building, structure or erection, any such cave, stone or natural product or any such tomb, grave, burial deposit or ritual, industrial or habitation site, situated on land or in the territorial waters of the State,

but excludes 'any building or part of any building, that is habitually used for ecclesiastical purposes'.

It can be seen that the term 'monument' as used in the Acts is a very broad one which, in effect, includes all artificial structures of whatever date regardless of whether or not they are of archaeological, architectural, or any other heritage interest.

The 1930 Act also provides for *national monument* to mean

. . . a monument or the remains of a monument the preservation of which is a matter of national importance by reason of the historical, architectural, traditional, artistic, or archaeological interest attaching thereto and also includes (but not so as to limit, extend or otherwise influence the construction of the foregoing general definition) every monument in Saorstát Eireann to which the Ancient Monuments Protection Act, 1882 applied immediately before the passing of this Act, and the said expression shall be construed as including, in addition to the monument itself, the site of the monument and the means of access thereto and also such portion of land adjoining such site as may be required to fence, cover in, or otherwise preserve from injury the monument or to preserve the amenities thereof.

It should be noted that this definition does not require a monument to be in state ownership or care, or to be formally designated or subject to any legal protection for it to be a 'national monument'. It should also be noted that scope of the term 'national monument' extends to monuments of historical, traditional and artistic interest as well as ones of archaeological and architectural interest and that there is no restriction regarding the date of monuments which may be considered to be national monuments.

The 1987 Act introduced the term *historic monument* which (under the Act) includes a prehistoric monument and any monument associated with the commercial, cultural, economic, industrial, military, religious or social history of the place where it is situated or of the country and also includes all monuments in existence before 1700 AD or such later date as the Minister may appoint by regulations.

Again, it should be noted that a monument does not have to be formally designated or subject to any legal protection for it to be a 'historic monument'. The reference to '*1700 AD*' means only that any monument dating to before AD 1700 is automatically a historic monument, but monuments dating to after AD 1700 may also come within the scope of the term 'historic monument'.

The 1987 Act also introduced the term *archaeological area* which means an area which the Minister for Arts, Heritage, Gaeltacht and the Islands

considers to be of archaeological importance but does not include the area of a historic monument standing entered in the Register.

The 'Register' being the Register of Historic Monuments established under Section 5 of the 1987 Act (see below).

It must be emphasized that 'monuments', 'national monuments', 'historic monuments' or 'archaeological areas' are *not* accorded any legal protection simply by being such; the circumstances or protective measures outlined below must apply before legal protection comes into effect. It should also be clear from the definitions set out above that there is no cut-off date for application of the Acts in respect of protection of monuments and that monuments of architectural or historic interest come within the scope of the Acts as much as ones of archaeological interest (Fig. 8.2).

Definition under the Local Government (Planning and Development) Acts

The *Local Government (Planning and Development) Acts 1963–99* form a broad framework for local authority planning, of which the protection of the built heritage forms just one part. Planning legislation in Ireland has provided for consideration of the protection of the built heritage as part of the planning process since the enactment of the first planning act in 1963, although the powers assigned to local authorities in this regard are discretionary. The planning legislation has in recent years been increasingly used to secure the protection of the archaeological and architectural heritage and, along with Environmental Impact Assessment (EIA), has provided a means of promoting the consideration of issues at an early stage in the development process. To date, EIA has been used more effectively in the context of archaeological rather than architectural heritage.

Archaeological heritage

In relation to the archaeological heritage the planning legislation does not specifically define 'archaeology' or 'archaeological interest', but includes provision for the setting of objectives for the protection of archaeological heritage. This will be discussed further below.

Architectural heritage

To date provisions, including definitions, governing the protection of the architectural heritage as part of the planning process have been quite general and non-specific. The key provision being the ability of a planning authority to include in its development plan objectives the 'Preservation of buildings of artistic, architectural or historic interest' and the 'Preservation of plasterwork, staircases, woodwork or other fixtures of artistic, historic, or architectural interest forming part of the interior of structures'. However the *Local Government (Planning and Development) Act, 1999* (the '1999 Act') which came into operation on 1 January 2000, replaces all earlier provisions and creates much greater clarity as to the nature and extent of protection extended to the architectural heritage.

Definition of 'structure'

The Principal Act (1963) provided a definition of *Structure* for the purposes of development control.

> 'Structure' means any building, erection, structure, excavation or other thing constructed, erected or made on in or under any land, or any part of a structure so defined, and where the context so admits, includes the land on, in, or under which the structure is so situate.

Under the provisions for the protection of the architectural heritage contained in the 1999 Act, this basic definition is extended:

'Structure' includes
(a) the interior of the structure
(b) the land lying within the curtilage of the structure
(c) any other structures lying within that curtilage and their interiors, and
(d) all fixtures and features which form part of the interior or exterior of any structure or structures referred to in paragraph a) or c)

Before the introduction of this legislation, the inclusion of an objective in a development plan for the protection of an individual structure was ambiguous as to the nature and extent of that protection, i.e. whether it extended to the whole building or just the external envelope or even a façade.

Since January 2000, planning authorities must include objectives in their development plans for the protection of structures, as defined above, 'or parts of such structures, which are of special architectural, historical, archaeological, artistic, cultural scientific, social or technical interest', through the inclusion of a Record of Protected Structures. (The qualitative criteria used in this definition have been based on those in the Granada Convention.) In this context the extended definition of structure is further clarified as follows: *Protected structure* means 'a structure, or a specified part of a structure, which is included in a record of protected structures, and where that record so indicates, includes any specified features which is within the attendant grounds of the structure and which would not otherwise be included in this definition'.

Architectural conservation areas
In addition to definitions and associated provisions relating to the protection of individual structures there is also a provision in the 1999 Act regarding complexes, groups of buildings or ensembles. It is now a mandatory statutory requirement for planning authorities to formulate objectives, as part of the development plan for their administrative area, for the preservation of the character of architectural conservation areas. For this purpose, *architectural conservation areas* are defined as

a place, area, group of structures or townscape, taking account of building lines and heights, which
(a) is of special architectural, historical, archaeological, artistic, cultural, scientific, social or technical interest, or
(b) which contributes to the appreciation of protected structures.

The Heritage Act
The *National Monuments Acts* and the *Planning Acts* provide the principal legislative framework for the protection of the built heritage. However there are other definitions which should be noted. Under the *Heritage Act, 1995*, which established the Heritage Council, an additional executive power was assigned to the Council in relation to heritage buildings in public authority

ownership, i.e. government departments, offices and agencies. In this context *heritage building* includes

> any building or part thereof, which is of significance because of its intrinsic architectural or artistic quality or its setting or because of its association with the commercial, cultural, economic, industrial, military, political, social or religious history of the place where it is situated or of the country or generally, and includes the amenities of any such buildings.

If a building meets this definition, and is in public authority ownership, the Heritage Council may advise the Minister (MAGHI) to designate the building as a 'heritage building'. This then requires the public authority in question to consult with the Heritage Council regarding action in respect of that building.

Identification of heritage

In relation to the identification of the built heritage in Ireland there are two principal programmes of recording at national level, both carried out by Dúchas (the Heritage Service of the Department of Arts, Heritage, Gaeltacht and the Islands). These are the Archaeological Survey of Ireland and the National Inventory of Architectural Heritage.

Archaeological Survey of Ireland

The purpose of the *Archaeological Survey of Ireland* is, in the first instance, to compile a base-line inventory of the known archaeological sites and monuments in the state. The large archive and the computer database resulting from the work of the Archaeological Survey of Ireland are in the care of Dúchas.

To date lists of all certain or possible archaeological sites and monuments dating to before AD 1700 (with some later ones also being included) have been completed for all counties in the state. These are referred to as *Sites and Monuments Records* (SMRs) and are prepared on a county basis. Approximately 150,000 archaeological sites and monuments have been included in the SMRs. SMRs consist of numbered lists of archaeological sites and monuments and accompanying maps on which the sites and monuments (other than certain ones for which a precise location is not known) are marked and numbered. These lists were in many cases based initially on examination of cartographic, documentary and aerial photographic sources with the results of fieldwork only being available for some counties.

The next stage of the Archaeological Survey is referred to as the *Inventory Stage* and involves field inspection of all the sites and monuments included in the SMR (if such has not previously been carried out) and the preparation of descriptions of those sites and monuments. The Inventory Stage is now well advanced and *Archaeological Inventories* are being published for each county. In addition to the Archaeological Inventories, one full survey volume has been prepared within the framework of the Archaeological Survey of Ireland. Several others have been prepared by locally based organizations with advice from the Archaeological Survey of Ireland. Such full volumes contain detailed descriptions and plans of known archaeological sites and monuments.

Dúchas also undertook an *Urban Archaeology Survey* which prepared reports on all historic towns dating to before AD 1700 with a view to delineating zones of archaeological potential within which archaeological deposits may exist as well as surveying upstanding pre-AD 1700 archaeological remains in such towns. The results of the Urban Archaeology Survey were included in the SMRs (under the classification 'historic town') and both the Urban Archaeology Survey reports and the SMRs were issued to all planning authorities.

The SMRs (as revised in the light of fieldwork) formed the basis for the establishment of the statutory *Record of Monuments and Places* pursuant to the National Monuments (Amendment) Act 1994. The Record of Monuments and Places, consisting of lists of monuments and places for each county in the state with accompanying maps, is comprised of the results to date of the Archaeological Survey of Ireland. (Certain sites and monuments listed in the SMRs for which a precise location is not known are not, however, included in the Record.)

It must be emphasized that the SMRs, the Archaeological Inventories, the full surveys and the statutory Record of Monuments and Places are not final lists of archaeological sites and monuments in each county. Other pre-AD 1700 archaeological sites and monuments with visible above ground features will be identified in the future if prospection fieldwork and further aerial photographic work take place. Without doubt many as yet unidentified archaeological sites exist which have no visible above ground features. The existence of a wide range of as yet uninventoried post-AD 1700 archaeological sites and monuments must also be taken into account.

Other archaeological survey work undertaken by Dúchas includes *peatland surveys* and the compilation of a *Maritime Archaeological Record* of historic wrecks and other archaeological sites in coastal waters.

National Inventory of Architectural Heritage
The *National Inventory of Architectural Heritage* (NIAH) was established in 1990 in response to the Granada Convention and was placed on a statutory basis in 1999.

The objective is to use computerized records for recording all structures to be included the NIAH. Survey work began with a pilot study of Carlow Town in 1991 and for the purpose of establishing the computer model, this survey was a combination of both paper survey work and a computerized database. Full computerization of the record for each structure has been used for each subsequent survey. The basic methodology for recording each structure is that of:

- a survey form, the content of which is entered in a text computer data-base;
- map identification on standard Ordnance Survey maps, each location is set out in GIS mapping database;
- a visual record, in the form of 35mm colour slide photographs is taken, which will be scanned at archival resolution and ultimately stored on CD-ROM.

The three computerized elements of each individual record, stored in different computer systems, are linked by a unique computer registration number.

In addition, research material, relating to each site and the overall survey area, is attached to each record. This research material encompasses material gathered from written sources, archival documents, interviews with people in the locality, architect's drawings, artist's sketches, engravings and prints, photographic collections, etc.

The records relating to structures gathered by the NIAH are primarily to be used in making recommendations to local planning authorities as to which structures should be included in a Record of Protected Structures. Under the 1999 Act, the Minister (MAGHI) may recommend to planning authorities specific structures which should be included in this record, and the Minister will make such recommendations on the basis of the information contained in the NIAH. The survey material is also available to members of the public at large, as well as professionals and educational institutions.

In order to assist the local planning authorities in giving protection to the architectural heritage of Ireland, two separate inventory processes have been undertaken. A system of making detailed town inventory surveys based on 1/1,000 scale Ordnance Survey maps is being carried out. In parallel, a system of initial surveys of geographical county areas based on 1/10,560 scale Ordnance Survey maps is also being undertaken over a 3-year period. These initial surveys will be extended in time by detailed surveys of geographical county areas carried out on 1/2,500 scale Ordnance Survey maps. It is intended that the primary detailed survey of the built environment will be completed within a 12-year timescale from current date.

The point of departure of the work of the NIAH in 1990 was the terms of the Granada Convention. The passage of the 1999 *Architectural Heritage (National Inventory) and Historic Monuments (Miscellaneous Provisions) Act* has placed the work of the NIAH on a statutory footing. The term *architectural heritage* is redefined in this piece of legislation, and now exceeds the definition given in the Granada Convention.

From its inception, the work of the NIAH has always been computer-based. The systems and procedures of the NIAH were reviewed at the introduction of the Core Data Index (CDI) (Council of Europe, 1995). It was found that the criteria of the CDI were either matched or exceeded in both the four primary levels and the five secondary levels. The NIAH is now setting out national standards for inventory survey work within Ireland. The basic content of the CDI will be included within those national standards.

The preservation and protection of the heritage

The principal legislative provisions for the protection of the built heritage as defined above, and other associated provisions, are set out below.

Protection under the National Monuments Acts

The National Monuments Acts 1930–94, are construed as one Act creating a broad piece of legislation for the protection of archaeological and architectural heritage. The *National Monuments Act 1930* repealed the Ancient Monuments Protection Acts and most of the related legislation referred to the section outlining pre-1930 legislative background, the main exception being the provisions of the *Irish Church Act 1869* relating to national monuments (Fig. 8.3). The 1930 Act was amended and extended by amending Acts of 1954, 1987 and 1994 which provided for further mechanisms for the protection of monuments, and dealt with issues relating to underwater archaeology, the use of detection devices to search for archaeological objects and the ownership of archaeological objects. The *National Cultural Institutions Act 1997* has also amended certain aspects of the National Monuments Acts.

The key provisions of the National Monuments Acts, 1930–94 as they currently stand are outlined below. Over the years there have been several changes in relation to responsibility for the various provisions under the Acts, and principal legislative responsibility now lies with the Minister (MAGHI). It should be noted that the National Monuments Acts provide a comprehensive system of protection for archaeological objects as well as for

Fig. 8.3 Rock of Cashel, Co. Tipperary, a complex of medieval buildings (twelfth–fifteenth centuries) constructed on a limestone outcrop. This complex of buildings was one of the first sites to come into state care under the first legislative provisions for the protection of the built heritage, the Irish Church Act, 1869. (Copyright: Dúchas, The Heritage Service.)

built heritage. These provisions are not dealt with in detail here, but in summary it may be noted that archaeological objects found in the state which have no known owner are state property, finds of such objects must be reported, and the alteration of archaeological objects is only permitted under licence. Export of archaeological objects requires a licence under the *National Cultural Institutions Act 1999,* which replaced previous legislative provision in that regard. The National Museum deals with the licensing of alterations and export of archaeological objects on behalf of the Minister.

A review of this legislation is currently being undertaken by the Department of Arts, Heritage, Gaeltacht and the Islands for the purposes of consolidation and amendment.

Preservation orders and temporary preservation orders
The 1930 Act (as amended) allows the Minister to serve a *preservation order* (to ensure the preservation of a national monument) where it appears that such a monument is in danger of being destroyed, injured or removed, or is falling into decay through neglect. It is unlawful for any person to do the following to a national monument in respect of which a preservation order is in force, i.e.:

(a)   to demolish or remove wholly or in part or to disfigure, deface, alter, or in any manner injure or interfere with any such national monument without or otherwise than in accordance with the consent hereinafter mentioned, or

(b)   to excavate, dig, plough or otherwise disturb the ground within, around, or in proximity to any such national monument without or otherwise than in accordance with the consent hereinafter mentioned, or

(bb) to renovate or restore a national monument without or otherwise than in accordance with the consent hereinafter mentioned, or

(c)   to sell for exportation or to export any such national monument or any part thereof.

The consent referred to is the consent in writing of the Minister (MAGHI). The Minister may give such consent whenever he or she thinks it 'expedient in the interests of archaeology or for any other reason so to do' and the Minister may 'attach to such consent all such conditions and restrictions' as he or she thinks fit. A preservation order may be revoked by the Minister following consultation with the Heritage Council.

The 1954 Act provided for the making of temporary preservation orders. These are similar to preservation orders in their effect, but lapse after 6 months.

Ownership and guardianship of national monuments by the Minister
for Arts, Heritage, Gaeltacht and the Islands or a local authority
The Acts provide for the Minister (MAGHI), with the consent of the Minister for Finance, to have the power to acquire, by agreement or compulsorily, any national monument.

The 1930 Act provides for the appointment of the Minister (MAGHI) as guardian of a national monument, either on the basis of agreement by the owner or on a compulsory basis where the national monument in question has been previously made subject to a preservation order. Local authorities also have powers to become guardians of national monuments, but only with the consent of owners. The 1930 Act requires the Minister and local authorities to maintain national monuments in their ownership or guardianship.

The provisions of the 1930 Act regarding unlawful actions to national monuments apply similarly to national monuments in the ownership or guardianship of the Minister or a local authority. However, in the case of local authorities consent to interfere with such a monument must be given jointly by the local authority and the Minister.

The Register of Historic Monuments
The 1987 Act provides that the Minister (MAGHI) shall establish and maintain the *Register of Historic Monuments*. The Register may contain any historic monuments or archaeological areas that the Minister considers appropriate to include in it. Notification of inclusion in the Register must be sent to landowners. Except in the case of urgent necessity, works may not be carried out by any person at a registered historic monument or archaeological area without the giving of 2 months' written notification to the Minister. Such works may not be commenced within that 2-month period without the consent of the Minister.

The requirements in the legislation regarding notification of individual owners have impeded the expansion of the Register of Historic Monuments. Currently there are approximately 5,000 entries in the Register. Only a very small number of these are archaeological areas as opposed to historic monuments.

The record of monuments and places
The 1994 Act provides that the Minister (MAGHI) shall establish and maintain a record of monuments and places where it is believed that there are monuments. The record is maintained on a county basis and is comprised of a list of monuments and relevant places and maps showing the location of each monument or relevant place. Regulations made under the Act provide for the relevant list and maps to be exhibited in the offices of planning authorities and in local libraries.

The level of protection afforded to a monument or place entered in the Record is similar to that afforded through entry in the Register of Historic Monuments. The Act does not specify what category of interest the monuments and places entered in the Record should be. However, in practice the lists and maps for each county issued so far are updated versions of the previous non-statutory Sites and Monuments Records. The Record of Monuments and Places therefore comprises the results of the Archaeological Survey of Ireland undertaken by Dúchas. The fact that there is no requirement of individual notification to owners or occupiers of monuments or places entered in the Record has allowed the process of providing a basic level of legal protection for all known monuments of archaeological interest to be speeded-up.

Control of archaeological excavation

The 1930 Act prohibits digging or excavating for archaeological purposes by *any person* except in accordance with a licence issued by the Minister (MAGHI), with a very limited exception in emergency circumstances. This requirement applies underwater as well as on land. Under the 1994 Act the Minister is required to consult the Director of the National Museum before issuing an archaeological excavation licence. Such a licence may include such conditions and restrictions as the Minister thinks proper.

Protection of historic wrecks and underwater archaeological objects

The 1987 Act prohibits diving on, or interfering with, any wreck that is more than 100 years old or an archaeological object situated underwater except in accordance with a licence issued by the Minister (MAGHI). The 1987 Act also provides for the Minister to have the power to designate a restricted area, by means of an *underwater heritage order*, any place underwater provided it is the site of a wreck or archaeological object and should be protected on grounds of historical, archaeological or historical importance. The provisions for the making of underwater heritage orders therefore allow for the protection of wrecks less than 100 years old as well as for the designation of areas wider than just a wreck or object itself. A restricted area is subject to the similar prohibitions on diving and interference as apply in general to wrecks over 100 years old and underwater archaeological objects.

The 1987 Act also includes provision for the mandatory reporting of finds of wrecks over 100 years old and underwater archaeological objects (to the Minister or the Garda Síochaná, and the Director of the National Museum respectively).

Control of use of detection devices

The 1987 Act provides for a general prohibition on the use of detection devices to search for archaeological objects anywhere in the state except in accordance with a licence issued by the Minister (MAGHI). There is also a prohibition on the use or possession of a detection device concerning any of the categories of protected monuments and in an archaeological area entered in the Register of Historic Monuments or a restricted area (i.e. an area subject to an underwater heritage order).

Protection under the Local Government (Planning and Development) Acts

The *Local Government (Planning and Development) Acts 1963–99*, are construed as one act (the 'Planning Acts'), forming a broad framework for local authority planning of which the protection of the built heritage forms one part. Each planning authority has a duty to prepare a development plan indicating development objectives for its area and to revise the plan at

5-year intervals and also from time to time as occasion may require. A planning authority has a general duty to secure the objectives set out in its development plan, and to take such steps as may be necessary to do so. In deciding on applications for permission to undertake development ('planning applications') a planning authority must consider the proper planning and development of its area, having regard to the provisions of the development plan. These plans, which consist of a written statement of the policy objectives together with a set of illustrative maps, are therefore the main vehicle for ensuring that conservation policies are co-ordinated and integrated with other planning policies affecting the built environment. The objectives that a planning authority should/may include in its development plan are set out in the 1963 Planning Act.

Regulations made under the Planning Acts provide for consultation by planning authorities with the Minister (MAGHI) and the Heritage Council *et al.*, in respect of draft development plans, so allowing an opportunity for recommendations to be made on protection of the built heritage.

The planning legislation has recently been reviewed for the purposes of consolidation and amendment. When enacted, the *Planning and Development Bill, 1999* (the 1999 Bill) will introduce a number of new planning provisions and also incorporate all the individual acts since 1963 (proposed in 2000).

Development plans and archaeological heritage
A planning authority may include in its development plan objectives for the: 'Preservation of caves, sites, features and other objects of archaeo-logical, geological or historical interest'.

No requirement is specified in the Act or Regulations for a planning authority to notify owners of such items of interest intended to be covered by an objective.

The inclusion of a relevant objective in a development plan removes the status of classes of development 'exempted' under regulations made by the Minister (MELG) where such development would interfere with any item covered by the objective.

The 1999 Bill, when enacted, will make the inclusion of archaeological objectives in development plans mandatory rather than discretionary.

Development plans and architectural heritage
From the introduction of planning legislation in 1963 until the commencement of the new legislation in January 2000, the protection of the architectural heritage was just one of a number of objectives which a planning authority could include in its development plan. In other words, a planning authority could set objectives for the preservation of amenities which included 'buildings of artistic, architectural or historical interest' (1963 Act) and also 'fixtures or features of artistic, historic or architectural interest and forming part of the interior of structures' (1976 Act). Over the years, most planning authorities have set such objectives through the inclusion of lists of buildings or parts of buildings in the Development

Plan, which operated to place those buildings or interior features outside the scope of the 'exempted development' provisions. These provisions were generalized, non-specific and non-directive with the result that there have been inconsistencies in the extent and nature of protection throughout the country.

The introduction of the 1999 Act, which came into operation on 1 January 2000, has provided a comprehensive system for the protection of the architectural heritage through the planning code. A development plan must now include the objective of protecting structures or parts of such structures which are of special architectural, historical, archaeological, artistic, cultural, scientific, social or technical interest and must for that purpose contain a Record of Protected Structures (as described above). The Record of Protected Structures can, however, be amended independently of the development plan review process and once a structure is proposed for inclusion in the Record, full protection is extended pending final determination. Development Plans must also include the objective of preserving the character of architectural conservation areas (as defined above).

The Minister (MAGHI), having consulted with the other relevant Minister (MELG), is obliged to issue guidelines to planning authorities concerning development objectives for protecting structures, and for preserving the character of architectural conservation areas. The guidelines must include the criteria to be applied when selecting proposed protected structures for inclusion in the Record. These guidelines, to which planning authorities must have regard, will be published in 2000.

Development control

The 1963 Act defines the meaning of *development* for the purposes of the Planning Acts as 'the carrying out of any works on, in, or under land or the making of any material change in the use of any structures or other land'. In this context '*works*' are defined as including 'any act or operation of construction, excavation, demolition, extension, alteration, repair or renewal'. In relation to the architectural heritage, the provisions for protected structures introduced in the 1999 Act extend the definition of works to include 'any act or operation involving the application of plaster, paint, wallpaper, tiles, or other material to or from the surfaces of the interior or exterior of a structure'.

There is a general obligation to obtain planning permission in respect of development of any land, unless the development is exempted development. The issue of exempted development is one which should be noted in the present context because it is a limiting factor regarding the role the Planning Acts can have in the protection of (in particular) the archaeological heritage. Categories of 'exempted development' are set out in the 1963 Act. These refer to the use of land for agriculture (including peat extraction) or forestry, development by local authorities within their areas, all local authority road works development and certain types of maintenance works by bodies with a statutory responsibility in that regard. In addition, the

Minister (MELG) may provide regulations to define other exempted classes of development. Such classes of development are set out in the *Local Government (Planning and Development) Regulations, 1994* (the 'Planning Regulations') (Fig. 8.4).

It should be noted that the 1999 Bill will, when enacted, end the general exemption of peat extraction and forestry (with some exemptions regarding the latter). It will then be a matter for the Minister (MELG) to decide to what extent these forms of development should be exempted under regulations.

With the commencement of the *1999 Act* for the protection of the architectural heritage, all works which 'materially affect the character' of a 'protected structure' (as defined above) now require planning permission. There is a provision in the Act for planning authorities to issue a *declaration* for a protected structure, on the request of the owner. Such a declaration must specify the types of works which would be considered by the planning authority to have the potential to materially affect the character of that particular protected structure and which will therefore require planning permission. Similarly, the planning authority may declare that certain works, for example – to an already much altered interior or to a recent extension, would not require planning permission as they would not be deemed to 'materially affect the character' of the particular structure in question. Such exemption through declaration can only apply in respect of works that would ordinarily be exempt if the structure were not protected. In the absence of a 'declaration' in respect of a particular protected structure, *all* works (as defined in the Act) to that structure require planning permission.

Notification of certain planning applications to the Minister for Arts, Heritage, Gaeltacht and the Islands
Under the Planning Regulations planning authorities have an obligation to send notice of a planning application to a number of prescribed bodies which include the Minister (MAGHI) and An Taisce (The National Trust), where it appears to the authority that

Fig. 8.4 Isolde's Tower, Dublin, a thirteenth-centu mural tower during excavation. (Copyright: A. Halpin.)

the development would be unduly close to any cave, site, feature or other object of archaeological, geological, scientific or historical interest, or would detract from the appearance of any building of artistic, architectural or historical interest, or, in either case, would obstruct any scheme for improvement of the surroundings of or any means of access to any such place, object or structure.

Development by a local authority within its own area is exempted from planning permission requirements. However, the regulations require a local authority proposing to undertake development, where it appears to the authority that such development would affect a site, site feature or object of interest in accordance with the list above, to notify the prescribed bodies.

The *Local Government (Planning and Development Regulations)*, introduced in 2000, provide for clear notification of planning applications in relation to protected structures, architectural conservation areas and archaeological sites and features.

Compensation

There is no general entitlement to compensation in cases where planning permission is refused or granted subject to conditions, but it may be payable in certain circumstances. These circumstances are, however, restricted under the Acts. These restrictions include:

- the refusal of planning permission on grounds that the development would interfere with a registered historic monument;
- the refusal of planning permission on grounds that it would involve demolition of a building, the preservation of which is an objective of a development;
- or the grant of planning permission subject to the imposition of conditions relating to the preservation of archaeological sites, features and objects.

Environmental Impact Assessment (EIA)

The *European Communities (Environmental Impact Assessment) Regulations 1989* (the EIA Regulations) and the *Roads Act 1993* provide for the implementation in the Republic of Ireland of the Environmental Impact Assessment Directive (*Council Directive 85/337/EEC*). As a result of the EIA Regulations an environmental impact statement (EIS) must be prepared in respect of a development which is of a class specified under the EIA Regulations. This requirement operates both within the framework of the Planning Acts and within the framework of other development control legislation such as the Foreshore Acts and the Roads Act.

The EIA Regulations amended the 1963 Planning Act so that the Minister (MELG) can define classes of development which may be subject to EIA and which also may require for planning permission even though they are specified in the 1963 Act as being 'exempted development'.

Under the regulations an EIS must include a description of the proposed development and a description of likely significant effects, direct and indirect, on the environment of the development by reference to its possible impact on (among other matters) the cultural heritage. As a result, impact on the architectural and archaeological heritage must be considered.

Other legislation relating to the functions of statutory bodies

The *Gas Act 1976* placed a statutory responsibility on Bord Gáis regarding protection of the archaeological heritage in the course of gas pipeline construction. The *Harbours Act 1996* provides that the harbour companies established under the Act shall have regard to heritage matters and the *Fisheries (Amendment) Act 1997* provides that natural and man-made heritage will be taken into account in aquaculture licensing. The *Turf Development Act 1998* provides for Bord na Móna (a state-owned company which carries out large-scale peat extraction) to have a responsibility to ensure that it affords appropriate protection to the archaeological heritage.

The Heritage Council was established under the Heritage Act, 1995. Apart from the definition of general objectives for the Council, there is also a protective provision under Section 10 of the Act whereby the Minister (MAGHI) can, on the advice of the Council, designate a building in the ownership of a public authority as a *heritage building*. In turn, this requires that advice must be taken from the Heritage Council in relation to the maintenance, preservation, restoration, upkeep and improvement of such a designated building. To date there have only been two structures designated under the Heritage Act, although the Heritage Council is actively involved in advising public authorities on the conservation of architectural heritage.

Conservation philosophy

The Malta Convention provides the basis for policy on the protection of the archaeological heritage. An official policy has been set out in a framework document (DAHGI, 1999) which sets out broad principles for the protection of the archaeological heritage in Ireland (with a particular focus on development related issues). Under the *Local Government Act, 1991*, local authorities are obliged in the exercise of their functions (including planning and development functions) to have regard to policies and objectives of Government Ministers.

The Granada Convention provides the basis for policy and legislation for the protection of the architectural heritage. While a conservation charter has not been specifically prepared for conservation in the Irish context, conservation work is carried out by Dúchas in cognizance of the international ICOMOS charters. Similarly, cognizance is taken of such international policy documents and guidelines in the preparation of policy and guidance documentation. Under the 1999 Act, the Minister (MAGHI) is obliged to issue guidelines for planning authorities regarding development objectives for the protection of the architectural heritage. These guidelines (to be published in 2000), will set out national policy and principles for the protection of the architectural heritage through the planning code and again are being prepared with consideration of international philosophy and principles as well as similar guidance documents prepared in other jurisdictions.

Sanctions and coercive measures

The National Monuments Acts and the Planning Acts, being the principal legislative framework for the protection of the built heritage in Ireland, provide a number of sanctions and coercive measures.

The National Monuments Acts provide for contraventions of their provisions to be deemed offences and for a range of penalties in that regard. The original penalties under the 1930 Act have been substantially increased. The 1994 Act sets penalties in respect of offences under that Act, the maximum being a £50,000 (€63,486) fine and 5 years imprisonment following conviction on indictment. The Minister may prosecute summary offences under the Acts.

The Planning Acts indicate that it is an offence to carrying out 'development' without planning permission (where such is required), or without adhering to planning conditions. Maximum penalties on conviction on indictment are a fine of £1,000,000 (€1,269,738) and/or 2 years imprisonment. Under the 1999 Act there arc a number of new provisions to safeguard protected structures. These include a new duty of care imposed in owners and occupiers of protected structures to ensure:

> to the extent consistent with the rights and obligations arising out of their respective interests in a protected structure, that the structure or any element of it which contributes to its special architectural, historical, archaeological, artistic, cultural or scientific, social or technical interest, is not endangered.

Following from this provision, a planning authority may require an owner or occupier to undertake specified work to prevent a protected structure from becoming or continuing to be endangered, or may undertake such work itself. In addition, a planning authority may also require an owner to undertake works to restore the character or an element of a protected structure, or a structure within an architectural conservation area. This may be in relation to 'the removal, alteration, or replacement of any specified part of the structure or element and the removal or alteration of any advertisement structure'. It is an offence for anyone, without lawful authority, to cause damage to a protected structure or to fail to comply with requirements under these provisions. There are penalties for such offences ranging from small fines or short imprisonment for summary conviction, to fines of up to £1,000,000 (€1,269,738) or up to 5 years' imprisonment for conviction on indictment. As these sanctions are new it is not yet possible to evaluate the effectiveness of procedures.

Where a protected structure is not an occupied dwelling, and where it appears to the planning authority to be necessary for the protection of the structure, the planning authority has the power to purchase the protected structure compulsorily. These sanctions are supported by provisions for planning authorities to provide assistance, including financial support, and for appeals against such sanctions through the District Court.

Integrated conservation

The legislative and administrative framework for the protection of the built heritage in Ireland involves shared responsibility between national and local level, as has been outlined previously. The Minster (MAGHI) has responsibility for formulating national policy in relation to the physical heritage and for the implementation of the National Monuments Acts. Physical planning legislation, of which the protection of the built heritage forms part, is implemented at local government level, under the policy direction of the Minister (MELG). The National Monuments Acts provide the specific legislative basis for the protection of the archaeological heritage, although there are provisions for its protection as part of the planning system which are generally the primary means of securing the protection of the archaeological heritage in development situations. The new legislative measures operating since January 2000 provide for greatly enhanced protection of the architectural heritage as part of the planning code and provide a legislative basis for the protection of architectural conservation areas. This legislation also creates, for the first time, a clear relationship between the Minister (MAGHI) and the local planning authorities in relation to the protection of the architectural heritage. Through the publication of guidelines the Minister sets national policy and also provides a conservation advisory service to the local planning authorities which have responsibility for the implementation of the legislation at local level.

Financial resources, funding mechanisms and the regeneration of historic environments

Incentives for the architectural heritage

Financial incentives for the conservation of the architectural heritage are still limited in Ireland, but there are two principal programmes of aid available. First, there is a programme of tax relief for expenditure on approved heritage buildings, gardens and objects in respect of repair, maintenance or restoration. Approved buildings and gardens are those 'intrinsically of significant architectural, historic, scientific, horticultural or aesthetic significance interest' as determined by the Minister (MAGHI). Owners of such approved buildings or gardens are required to open the buildings or gardens to the public for 60 days per annum in order to avail of tax relief, and certain conditions apply to the opening days and times. In this context, tax relief is also available against the cost of an alarm system and against the cost of public liability insurance. To date more than 270 properties have met this criteria, although not all the owners of these buildings may receive tax relief as all conditions must be complied with before such relief is given qualification for specific relief must be determined by the Revenue Commissioners.

Second, there is a new programme of grant-aid for the conservation of the architectural heritage, which is administered through local planning authorities in accordance with agreed national criteria set out by the Department of Environment and Local Government. This scheme was initiated in 1999 with budget of £3.9 million (€4,951,978) and from 2000 will be linked to the new system of 'protected structures'. Grants available under this scheme are small, within a range of £1,500–£10,000 (€1,269–12,697), although grants of up to £20,000 (€25,394) may be provided in exceptional circumstances.

The Heritage Council's functions include to 'promote interest, education, knowledge and pride in, and facilitate the appreciation and enjoyment of the national heritage'. In the context of meeting these objectives, the current Council has a number of grant aid programmes that include measures to support the architectural heritage. These include a programme of grant-aid for 'Buildings at Risk' identified primarily through submissions from owners as well as a number of research projects (Fig. 8.5).

Funding for the archaeological heritage

The 'developer pays' principle is extensively applied to fund archaeological work necessitated by development. This is generally achieved through the imposition of archaeological conditions on development authorizations issued under the relevant legislative code (e.g. the Planning Acts). The archaeological work itself is then normally carried out by archaeologists working in private sector consultancies and companies.

The work of the Archaeological Survey of Ireland is funded as part of the budget of Dúchas. Dúchas also provides grant assistance for a small number of research archaeological excavations on the advice of the Royal Irish Academy (total of c. £100,000 p.a. €126,973).

The Heritage Council provides a varying amount of grant assistance for archaeological research other than excavation. The Council also funds the Discovery Programme Ltd, an archaeological research company, to a total of c. £600,000 p.a. (€761,842). The Discovery Programme carries out wide ranging integrated archaeological research projects.

Other measures

In 1999 a new Urban Renewal Scheme was introduced by the Department of the Environment and Local Government under which fory-three Irish

Fig. 8.5 Mayglass, Co. Wexford, a traditional vernacular house which was seriously at risk and almost derelict. Repairs to the house are currently being funded by the Heritage Council and funding has been made available through the EU Raphael programme to promote traditional buildings skills. (Copyright: P. Ruane.)

towns and cities have been designated. Designations have been made on the basis of approved Integrated Area Plans prepared by the relevant local planning authority and one of the issues to be targeted is the conservation of urban fabric. Tax relief is available for certain types of development approved under the scheme. In addition to this programme, the Department of the Environment and Local Government is also responsible for a 'Townscape Restoration Scheme' which is a tax incentive based scheme aimed at the restoration and conservation of townscapes in smaller towns. Both of these schemes operate in accordance with monitoring and certification guidelines and the quality of development in respect of which relief is claimed is controlled through normal planning control procedures. As both schemes are new, it is not yet possible to evaluate their effectiveness with regard to the conservation of the historic environment.

The Rural Environment Protection Scheme (REPS) is the mechanism for the implementation in Ireland of *Council Regulation (EEC) No. 2078/92.* Farmers entering the scheme receive payments conditional on the preparation and implementation of a REPS plan for their farm. Protection of archaeological monuments, traditional farm buildings and other landscape features such as field walls is a condition of participation in REPS.

The role of agencies and specialist organizations
Dúchas
Dúchas, the Heritage Service, is part of the Department of Arts, Heritage, Gaeltacht and the Islands. The word '*dúchas*' has a number of meanings in the Irish language, including the terms 'native place' and 'heritage'. Heritage areas for which Dúchas is responsible include architectural and archaeological heritage, national parks and wildlife as well as inland waterways. In the context of the built heritage, Dúchas carries out, *inter alia*, those functions under the National Monuments Acts concerning the identification and protection of heritage under the responsibility of the Minister (MAGHI) as well as those functions assigned under the Local Government (Planning and Development) Acts and Regulations. Dúchas has a key role in providing advice to local planning authorities in relation to the protection of the built heritage through the planning control system (Fig. 8.6).

The Heritage Council
The Heritage Council, established under the Heritage Act 1995, is an independent statutory body appointed by the Minister for Arts, Heritage, Gaeltacht and the Islands and funded by that Ministry. The functions of the Heritage Council are to propose policies and priorities for the identification, protection, preservation and enhancement of the national heritage and, in particular, to:

- promote interest, education, knowledge and pride in, and facilitate the appreciation and enjoyment of the national heritage;
- co-operate with public authorities, educational bodies and other organizations and persons in the promotion of the functions of the Council;

Fig. 8.6 Heywood Gardens, designed by Sir Edward Lutyens and completed in 1912. The gardens have been in the care of Dúchas since 1993. (Copyright: Dúchas, The Heritage Service.)

- promote the co-ordination of all activities relating to the functions of the Council.

Non-governmental organizations (NGOs)

There are a number of very active NGOs in the built heritage field in Ireland. An Taisce (The National Trust for Ireland), which was founded in 1948, is actively involved in the promotion of the built, as well as natural heritage through lobbying, providing advice and commenting on policy proposals at national as well as local level, and commenting on planning applications. The Irish Georgian Society is similarly active in relation to the architectural heritage. There are also a number of active Civic Trusts, e.g. in Dublin, Cork and Limerick. The Irish National Committee of ICOMOS provides a forum for exchange of information and experience for professionals working in the conservation of the built heritage.

The Irish Association of Professional Archaeologists (IAPA) is the professional body for Irish archaeologists. The Irish Professional Conservators' and Restorers' Association (IPCRA) was established to promote the practice of conservation and restoration of cultural material to internationally accepted standards. Arising from this the Institute for Conservation of Historic and Artistic Works in Ireland was established as a more structured professional body with a system of accreditation. The Royal Institute of the Architects of Ireland (RIAI) is the professional body for architects, with a long established system of qualified membership on the basis of qualifications and experience. The RIAI also has a Historic Buildings Committee.

Cultural institutions
The two key cultural institutions with a role in relation to the built heritage are the National Museum of Ireland and the Irish Architectural Archive.

The National Museum
The National Museum is the repository of the national collection of archaeological objects, which now consists of in excess of two million such objects. It is also responsible for the collection relating to Art and Industry (which includes the decorative arts) and the National Folklife Collection. As previously noted, the National Museum is involved in licensing the alteration and export of archaeological objects and in the licensing of archaeological excavations.

The Irish Architectural Archive
The Irish Architectural Archive is a charitable company established in 1976 to collect and preserve records of Ireland's architectural heritage and to make those records available to those who wish to consult them. The IAA, which is primarily supported by the Department of Arts, Heritage, Gaeltacht and the Islands, provides an important information resource for the conservation of Irish architectural heritage.

Education and training
As yet there is no co-ordinated response at a national level in Ireland to the issue of education and training in the field of built heritage conservation. There have been several initiatives over the last number of years through which these issues have begun to be addressed. As yet there are no specific specialist qualifications, at either professional or craft level, required by policy or legislation in relation to the carrying out of works on protected elements of the architectural heritage. However, in relation to archaeological heritage, a licence is required in law to carry out an excavation and a policy on the issuing of excavation licences which sets out the basic standards required, has been published (DAHGI, 1999).

Archaeology is taught in three higher education institutions in Ireland. There are two university level courses for architecture and one specifically aimed at post-graduate study of urban and building conservation. While there is no system of Registration of Title of 'architect' at present in Ireland, proposals for the introduction of such a system are currently being developed. However, the Royal Institute of the Architects of Ireland is the professional body, which has clear criteria for membership, based on both qualifications and experience. Training with regard to building construction is also provided by a number of nominated agencies but has not been focused towards building conservation to date.

A government decision in 1998 has assigned to the Department of Arts, Heritage, Gaeltacht and the Islands the tasks of:

• undertaking research and developing skills related to the built heritage;

- raising the standard of conservation practice among owners, trades and professions;
- acting as a facilitator to the industry and training agencies.

At the same time the Construction Industry Federation in Ireland has been examining the issue of establishing specialist conservation contractors and is initiating a pilot project in this area. Also over the past number of years, Ireland has participated in a number of European-wide pilot projects on various issues relating to building conservation skills.

Conclusions

In recent decades attitudes in Ireland to the conservation of our built heritage have significantly changed and there is a shift at all levels towards a more active approach to ensuring the future of our historic environment. As can be seen in this chapter, there have been significant legislative changes in relation to the protection and management of the built heritage. There are also many additional initiatives, not discussed here, which are actively contributing to this climate change. As many of the legislative and associated administrative changes are new, especially in relation to the protection of the architectural heritage, it will take some time for all the mechanisms to be fully developed and before effectiveness of procedures can be evaluated. While there remain many further actions to be taken, the steps to date have been positive.

Note

*The Planning and Development Bill 1999 is expected to be enacted as the *Planning and Development Act 2000* and will incorporate all previous Local Government (Planning and Development) legislation (1963–99).

References

Council of Europe (1995): Core Data Index to Historic Buildings and Monuments of the Architectural Heritage: Recommendation No. R(95)3 of the Committee of Ministers of the Council of Europe to member states on Co-ordinating Documentation Methods and Systems related to Historic Buildings and Monuments of the Architectural Heritage.

DAHGI (1999): *Framework and Principles for the Protection of the Archaeological Heritage*, Department of Arts, Heritage, Gaeltacht and the Islands, 1999.

DAHGI (1999): *Policy and Guidelines on Archaeological Excavation*, Department of Arts, Heritage, Gaeltacht and the Islands.

Other sources of information

National Monuments Act, 1930–94

Local Government (Planning and Development) Acts, 1963–99

Planning and Development Bill, 1999*

Architectural Heritage (National Inventory) and Historic Monuments (Miscellaneous Provisions) Act, 1999

National Cultural Institutions Act, 1999

Heritage Act, 1995

Taxes Consolidation Act, 1997

Giorgio Gianighian

Italy

Introduction

Monument restoration in Italy is a rather recent subject, coming into existence as recently as the nineteenth century. The legislation governing this discipline was originally only meant to put a stop to the plunder of the archaeological and artistic heritage in churches and palaces. Subsequently, the government slowly started to take responsibility for the maintenance of monuments and then, much later, fort the protection of historical urban centres, of the 'minor' urban fabric, and of the natural environment including landscapes.

The most difficult step was to change the public perception so that the protection of these assets came to be recognized as a matter of public interest, even if they were privately owned. It took time to overcome the strong opposition of owners and antique dealers, whose interests were for the continuation of a very profitable trade, based around the plundering of an immense resource.

It was a bitter clash between public and private interests, during which the professional and academic worlds made a valuable contribution in favour of protecting the heritage of the country. The legislation was slowly improved, working on principles developed through the theoretic input of various intellectuals and architects and in this way the main requirements of the monuments' care and protection was identified.

The two main laws concerning the protection of the built heritage and landscape were passed by the Fascist government in 1939. They had their limitations and were rather dictatorial in their inspiration, but they strongly supported the principle of public interest in matters of conservation. These laws remained in force until 27 December 1999. We shall see that they sanctioned two different methods of restoration: preserving only the outer appearance of the monument or preserving it in its entirety, including the materials which make the monument what it is.

The enforcement of these laws was very much linked to the culture of the architect and of the *Soprintendente*, in charge of supervising the work of the architect. A good *Soprintendente* guaranteed a good conservation would be carried out, while a poor one meant enforcement of the law could be less effective, with the potential for serious damage or losses. This is the reason why substantial space is given to the historical background of conservation philosophy. The development of preservation laws in Italy is strictly dependent on the development of theories, so that legal actions, rules and Acts are inextricably mixed with Charters, debates and philosophies.

Historical profile of theories on conservation and restoration

When, in 1861, Italy first became a kingdom, Arrigo Boito wrote bitter rhymes commenting on the state of monument conservation: according to him the new country was mostly engaged in 'demolishing, destroying and ruining' in favour of new buildings (Emiliani, 1974: 49). Prior to Italian unification, the protection of what, today, we call cultural heritage was left to the initiative of the separate governments (Haskell, 1981).

The liberal nineteenth-century way of thinking, which guided the Italian ruling class at the time, was strongly against any government interference in free trade and any limitation on individual property rights. For these reasons, within the process of building a common legislation for the new country, there was little incentive to tackle the problem of protecting cultural heritage (Alibrandi and Ferri, 1995: 5). During this period, theoretical thinking on restoration was torn between the opposing views of Ruskin and Viollet-le-Duc. On one side practically no restoration, on the other stylistic restoration, which in Italy became analogic restoration: in the case of reconstruction, it was common practice to copy the characteristics of works of the same period and of the same cultural area (Bellini, 1978: passim). In July 1882, the Ministry of Education passed a decree and issued an accompanying circular on the restoration of monuments and monumental buildings. This was the first attempt to control the built heritage and was drafted according to the theories of Viollet-le-Duc.

The Fourth Congress of Architects and Engineers, held in Rome in 1883, was of great importance. Those participating upheld a motion (later known as the 'vote') proposed by Camillo Boito, criticizing the Act passed by the government in the previous year. Boito's theory is known as 'philological restoration', because he used a strictly scientific method in the preparation and in the execution of restoration work. He had learnt the lesson taught by the archaeologists of the period.

The 'vote' in many ways had its origins in Ruskin's theories. From him came the need to prove that the work was really necessary. The preference given to reinforcement rather than repair, to repair rather than restoration; the attention to 'the colour of old age', later to be called the patina, are also Ruskinian principles.

Boito's idea that the passing of time and the changes that it brings adds value to a monument was very modern. This concept should be kept in mind, because it disappeared quickly from restoration theories, reappearing only very recently.

In the wake of these debates, many bills were discussed in the Italian Parliament, but until 1902 none was passed. From this year dates the first law for the protection and conservation of monuments to be applied to 'monuments, immovable properties and movable objects endowed with artistic and historic value'. The Act implementing the legislation was passed 2 years later. It is no coincidence that the law was passed when Giolitti was Prime Minister: his was a more democratic government, and the economic conditions were more favourable to reform. Giolitti wanted to strengthen the powers of the central government, by asserting its right to protect public interests against private ones.

In the following years other Acts were passed, widening the range of heritage subject to protection of archaeological and palaeontological material, then parks, gardens and villas. In the meanwhile, the theory of philological restoration was increasingly able to back its principles with scientific evidence. The best expression of this is to be found in the work of Gustavo Giovannoni (1873–1947), an architectural historian and a professor of monument restoration at the university of Rome and one of the most important theoreticians of conservation in Italy. He was the main inspiration for the *Italian Restoration Charter* promulgated in 1932, ensuring through his influence that the principles of the *Athens Charter for Protection and Conservation of Monuments* (1931) were incorporated into the Italian document, together with some ideas of Boito's motion of 1883. In this way, the 1882 Circular was rendered largely obsolete.

A few years later the Education Ministry extended the 1932 Charter with *Instructions for the Restoration of Monuments*, underlining the philological basis of the discipline. Not a sign of stylistic restoration was to be found in the document, which underlined the great importance of maintenance and extended the concept of protection to fields other than the monumental heritage. Subsequently, in 1939, two very important laws were passed which remained force until the end of 1999 (see the subsection 'Revised definition of the heritage' and the 'Conclusions' below).

The destruction of the built heritage during World War II helped to inflame the debate on reconstruction. Different philosophies were debated in the two decades following the end of the war, but two of them became particularly important. The first was inspired by Benedetto Croce, the great Italian idealist philosopher, and was known as 'critic restoration'. The second was championed by Cesare Brandi, who favoured a philological concept of restoration, mingled with the recent phenomenological philosophy.

The debate by this time included the urban heritage. Architects as well as urban planners took part, while some General Master Plans turned their attention to the problem of protecting the historical parts of a city. This provided the impetus for the Gubbio Conference, discussed below.

By the beginning of the 1960s, the discussion was being held on an international level. In 1964, the ICOMOS Conference produced the Venice Charter, which is too well-known to require illustration. However, there is one important point in Article 9 of the Charter, which emphasizes that – in the course of restoration work – the ancient materials from which the building is made must be respected. This concept is derived from Ruskin (1849), and was to become the basis of the new school of conservation in Milan.

In the same year a Parliamentary Committee was established, chaired by Francesco Franceschini, charged with the task of carrying out a general survey of the state of the Italian cultural and artistic heritage. (The work of the Committee, formed by the law 310 of April 1964, is documented in AA.VV. of 1967.)

The Committee began with an analysis – very rich and deep – of the state of Italy's artistic heritage. The introduction to volume 2 of its report, 'Cultural heritage and parliamentary action post-War', began by expressing the Committee's concern at the lack of attention given to the problem of protecting cultural and natural assets. No new law had been passed, to reinforce and complete the old 1939 Act and very little money had been invested in the task.

The goal of the Committee was to draw up a new law for the cultural heritage. It was divided into several study groups, each composed of well known experts and scholars. They concluded their works by expressing dissatisfaction at the prevailing situation, especially with respect to the protection of the urban and natural environments (AA.VV., 1967: 6 –7).

Although the Committee's work had no positive outcomes, as no new law was drawn up, its efforts were not completely wasted. It helped to clarify which elements of the heritage had to be protected by the authorities, including both the historical urban centres and the landscape. Later government Acts, unfortunately passed in a piecemeal fashion, were to tackle those sections of the heritage identified by the Franceschini Committee as requiring attention.

The Committee's Proceedings also bear witness to the damages done to the built heritage by the growth in the economy during the post-War years and they thus contributed to a greater consciousness of the problems, and subsequently a few years later this did result in new legislation.

In 1972, the Ministry of Education produced another *Charter for Restoration* (inspired and in good part written by Cesare Brandi). The Charter was important because it included archaeological protection and restoration, guidelines for architectural restoration as well as for the restoration of paintings and sculptures, and also dealt with the protection of historical urban centres. This Charter and its accompanying detailed guidelines continues up to the present day to provide the framework within which the work of control and conservation of the heritage managed by the *Soprintendenze* is carried out.

The Charter defined those areas that are to be subject to restoration and protection. It made clear what was forbidden: mostly stylistic restoration and the elimination of successive layers accumulated on the monument through the passing of the time. Permitted practice included small additions for structural reasons, light cleaning, hidden structural reinforcements. The Charter prescribed that all restoration work should be reversible and new materials and techniques should be used only with the utmost care. Moreover, the document denounces the damage inflicted to the built heritage by pollution. (See Figs 9.1–9.6 for examples of recent major public works dealing with restoration in Italy.)

Identification of the heritage

Ever since the special Ministry was established to oversee the heritage, the cataloguing of cultural and environmental assets has been carried out by drawing up different files according to the asset to be recorded. The files are identified by means of acronyms: territory (T); urban sectors (SU); natural and built landscapes (TP); monumental architecture (A); parks and gardens (PG); archaeological monuments and ensembles (CA and MA).

The instructions for drawing up these catalogues complete the picture and offer sufficient information on the nature and state of each asset. Now the catalogues are being computerized, which will improve its efficiency as an instrument of both knowledge and control. What is still lacking is the political will to carry out an inventory of the whole of Italian cultural heritage. Some Ministries have started programmes for partial collections of information, of varying quality and importance. For instance, in the 1980s the cataloguing of the historical centre of Venice was begun, but this

Fig. 9.1 The church of San Giorgio al Velabro, Rome, restored after a mafia attack.

Fig. 9.2 Restoration of palazzo Barberini, main elevation.

valuable enterprise was stopped when only half complete. The problem is always a financial one, as budget restrictions frequently do not allow a general survey to be conducted.

The preservation and protection of the heritage
Protection of objects of artistic and historical importance
One of the high points for the protection and conservation of Italy's cultural heritage came in 1939, when two important laws were passed and the *Istituto Centrale per il Restauro* (Central Institute for Restoration) came into existence. Both the law and the Institute are still in operation and bear witness to thinking on, and practice in restoration in those years, including the obvious limitations due to the period.

Massimo Pallottino, in charge of the section for the archaeological heritage, when submitting evidence to the Franceschini Committee (AA.VV., 1967) makes clear, for instance, that the 1089/39 law is based on obsolete concepts concerning the objectives of archaeology. According to our present-day culture, archaeological research should aim to discover and analyse the physical records of the past, in order to obtain a better historical understanding of ancient civilizations. The philosophy guiding the 1939 law, on the contrary, implies that archaeology is mainly about the collecting of antiquities.

The law passed on 1 June 1939 is known as the law for the 'Protection of objects of artistic and historical interest'. It consists of eight chapters and seventy-three articles and is still in force except for several articles of Chapter VIII. This chapter contains the penalties provided for by the law, which have been adjourned in a law of March 1975 (see the section, 'Sanctions and coercive measures', below).

Fig. 9.3 Restoration of a section of Rome's city wall, known as Passetto di Borgo (after restoration).

The eight chapters of the 1939 law cover a very wide range of subjects, including the application of the law and statutory requirements governing every aspect of cultural heritage: how to preserve, protect, sell, and export cultural objects. It also contains provisions dealing with finds and discoveries, reproduction rights and public access, and sets out penalties for transgressions of the law.

Definition of objects to be protected

The first two articles of the 1939 law define the objects placed under protection: they are called 'things', both movable and immovable, having artistic, historical, archaeological, ethnographical, palaeontological or numismatic interest. Several categories of objects are specified, including manuscripts, incunabula, more valuable books and prints, villas, parks and gardens. Works produced by contemporary artists, or made less than 50 years ago, are not included.

The law protects immovable objects having significant cultural value: these must be 'notified' to the Ministry and the notification is registered in the Public Record Office and remains in force even if ownership of the asset changes. Notification or listing is therefore the instrument that the Ministry uses to give force to the national significance of a given object. The Ministry of Education is in charge of the protection of these assets and ensures that public rights of use and enjoyment are respected. The Ministry operates through the *Soprintendenze* located throughout the country (see section below on 'The role of public boards and specialist agencies').

Public bodies, including the Church, are obliged to submit to the Ministry lists of relevant objects in their possession. Once a property has been notified, it can be modified, destroyed or repaired only with the previous agreement of and permission from the Ministry. In the case of a

Fig. 9.4 Reggia di Venaria Reale, Turin: Galleria di Diana (after restoration).

property neglected by the owner, whether public or private, the Ministry has the power to enforce the carrying out of any necessary work and to require the owner to reimburse the costs.

Any work carried out on listed properties needs to be authorized first by the local *Soprintendenza*, and this body has the power to stop any work if it is not in agreement with the authorized project.

All the necessary powers intended to preserve the integrity of listed immovable assets, in terms of perspective, light, environment, are enjoyed by the Ministry, which can override any master plan or building regulations.

It is forbidden to dispose of listed properties belonging to the state or to public bodies, with very few exceptions. In the case of buildings in private ownership, the owner who means to sell must notify the Ministry of his intention to do so and the government has the right of pre-emption, paying at the same price, provided this right is asserted within 2 months.

The Ministry may carry out excavation works anywhere and on anyone's land, but has to reimburse the owner for any damage. All finds belong to the state, even when excavations are carried out by private agencies. There must be some form of public access to protected assets, when they are properties of the state or of public bodies. The same rule can be applied to privately owned assets, if they are endowed with exceptional value.

Protection of natural monuments

In the same year 1939, another important law was passed on 29 June, no. 1497, known as the law for the 'Protection of Natural Monuments'. Before the establishment of the united Italian Kingdom, the different governments had made some moves in this direction. For instance, the Bourbons in Naples had made rules banning buildings above a certain height, so as to protect the view in the most important streets of the city. Venice, on the other hand, had rules for the protection of certain types of trees, not only because they were needed for the construction of naval ships, but also so as to protect the mountain environment.

In 1905 the Italian government took measures to protect certain special marine areas, used for conservation and the reproduction of sponges, and banned fishing in them. Similar provisions were made to encourage the reafforestation of the Ravenna pinewood.

The first general legislation to promote the conservation of exceptional natural environments was contained in law no. 778 of 1922, known as the law 'For the protection of natural monuments and buildings of special historical interest' (Mansi, 1988: 18 and passim). Benedetto Croce was the principal force behind the drawing up of the bill and his guiding principle was to adopt parallel approaches towards the protection of cultural assets and natural environments. In the following decade, special provisions were passed for the protection of Portofino Mountain and the island of Ischia. The cited 1939 Act involved a general revision of the 1922 law.

Definition of items to be protected
This new legislation placed under protection:

- sites of special importance either for their natural beauty or because of geological significance;
- villas, gardens and parks of special beauty, which do not fall within the scope of the laws for the protection of cultural objects;
- environments composed of immovable objects with special characteristics, and of traditional or aesthetic value;
- panoramic views, regarded here as natural pictures, together with those sites, open to the general public, which offer a vista on to the same views.

Each Province elects a committee with responsibility for selecting the assets to be listed. The committee members include both local representatives and members nominated by the government. It produces two separate lists, one for objects, one for sites. These lists must be submitted to the Ministry, which, in turn, will notify the owner of the asset of its inclusion in the list. Decisions to include natural environments in protected lists are to be published in the Official Gazette and notified to the local council.

Once the lists have been drawn up, details of any proposed work must be submitted to the responsible *Soprintendenza*, in order to obtain permission for the works to go ahead. The *Soprintendente* can stop any work if not authorized and if any work has already been carried out, he or she has the power to order its demolition and any necessary reinstatement. The *Soprintendente* can intervene in the construction of roads and industrial

Fig. 9.5 The city walls of Recanati (during restoration).

installations, deciding distances and dimensions; he or she can also modify existing projects. If a city or town is included in the lists, its master plan must be submitted to the Ministry for approval. Advertising posters can only be displayed in protected areas if approved by the *Soprintendente*, who has the power to order the removal of illegal advertising.

The Ministry for Education has the power to require the *Soprintendenze* to draw up *Environment Plans* for the wider areas included in their list, in order to define:

- the zones to be subject to special protection;
- relationship between developed and undeveloped areas in each of the zones;
- rules for the various types of buildings;
- distribution and alignment of buildings;
- instructions for the choice and distribution of plants and vegetation.

Owners of listed buildings have no right to indemnification; however, in the case of a total prohibition on any new building compensation may be awarded and, if the listing diminishes the value of the property, a tax credit can be obtained.

Giovanni Astengo (AA.VV., 1967: 1: 455) is critical of this law, pointing out that in the course of almost 30 years only a very few 'immovable objects' of exceptional natural beauty have been included in the lists. The 1939 law has not proved effective so far as the listing and protection of geological and natural sites goes: this problem is therefore still with us and must be solved. Astengo also maintains that the law has proved useless for the protection of 'complexes of immovable things', which he correctly defines as 'historical urban centres'. Analysing several instances in which the law has not been enforced, he cites the Gubbio Conference of 1960. This meeting led to the drawing up of the Gubbio Charter in 1961. When, unfortunately much later, laws for the protection of historical urban centres were passed, they were based on the concepts and principles of this document.

Revised definition of the heritage

The old definition of 'things of artistic and historic interest', contained in the previous laws up to 1939 and in force until December 1999, was desperately inadequate. The Franceschini Committee (see above) numbered several merits, one of which is the proposal of a legal definition of cultural assets. The new definition is thus formulated: 'All the Assets connected with the history of civilisation belong to the cultural heritage of the country. Assets of archaeological, historical, artistic, environmental, archival and librarian interest are placed under the protection of the law, as well as every other asset which constitutes material evidence having a value of civilis-ation' (AA.VV., 1967: 1: 22). The proposals of the Committee were not passed as law. Therefore this definition can only be considered to show the progress made in updating the concept of heritage.

However, a new definition of a 'cultural asset' has recently been form-ulated in legislation approved on 29 October 1999, no. 490 (see below, 'Conclusions') which broadens the range of objects falling under the protection of the law (including photographs with their negatives – if rare and of historical/artistic value; films and other audio-visual documents – if older than 25 years; means of transport – if older than 75 years; and all the assets and tools related to the history of science and scientific techniques – if older than 50 years). Moreover, it is interesting to underline the introduc-tion of an important new concept in the chapter 'Definition of Restoration' (Article 43): a direct intervention is provided for, in order to maintain the material integrity of a given asset and to ensure the conservation and protection of its cultural values. The reference to the conservation of the physical elements composing the asset is rather clear and sufficient to protect it from any unwanted substitution of its parts. The concept that it is necessary to respect the subsequent layers, which form the asset as it is today and represent its changes in the course of time, is both new and clear, and is derived from the most advanced and most correct theories on architectural conservation.

Sanctions and coercive measures

The last chapter of the law for the 'protection of objects of artistic and cultural interest' contains the sanctions, which range from fines to custodial

Fig. 9.6 The restoration of the city walls in Gubbio (during restoration).

prison sentences. Heavy monetary penalties were provided for in cases of the law being broken, which have, however, been replaced by the *New Discipline of Sanctions*, contained in the law of March 1975, and which are still in force as we enter the twenty-first century. Local authorities failing to present a prescribed list of assets to be protected are fined. These fines are however less punitive than those set out in the former law, having been increased from L. 50,000 to L. 300,000 and from L. 1,000,000 to L. 3,000,000: 36 years have passed since these levels were initially set, with very high rates of inflation, meaning that this rise is not really significant. Moreover, no deadline is set for the presentation of the lists, which naturally tends to diminish the impact of the law.

In other cases, however, fines are heavier and may be accompanied by criminal prosecution. In the case of unauthorized work on any protected property, the law provides for the demolition of the work carried out and the penalty can be as much as a year in prison and a fine ranging between L. 750,000 and L. 37,000,000. The same penalty, with a higher fine, applies to local authorities found to have sold off protected assets. A heavy custodial sentence of up to 4 years faces anyone found guilty of exporting (or trying to export) any asset subject the protection of the law.

In relation to the law for the Protection of Natural Monuments, offences against this law fall under the criminal code and any illegal work is liable to demolition at the expense of the owner.

Urban laws and the restoration of historical town centres: integrated conservation

On 17 August 1942 a law was passed which dealt for the first time with the issue of the protection of the urban historical fabric. Its goal was to control the urban development of all built-up areas and to ensure that the traditional character of a given centre was respected, whilst at the same time promoting its renewal and further development.

The drawing up of *General Master Plans* was requested only for larger cities and was to be carried out through the *Detailed Plans*, in which 'buildings destined for demolition or reconstruction, or due to undergo restoration' are pointed out. This demonstrates that the law did not include the concept of protecting of a historical centre as a whole, even if the theory on this subject was already well grounded and developed, especially by Giovannoni (1931). Individual monuments were protected by the provisions of law no. 1089, while no. 1497 dealt with the surrounding environment of monuments and of complexes of immovable objects of special interest.

In the period after World War II protection of the heritage was limited, given the difficult conditions in the country, following heavy war damage. Only a few towns had drawn up a General Master Plan and the associated Detailed Plans, the only instruments capable of offering some protection to the historical urban fabric. Most towns and cities adopted the more flexible so-called '*Reconstruction Plans*'. But even in those cases where a General Master Plan had been prepared, the historic centre was left as an undefined gap, and urban planning was deferred to future Detailed Plans. Difficulties arose in turn both in the creation of these plans and in the obtaining of approval for them. During that period, the twin needs to heal the wounds inflicted by the war and to give homes to the many people left homeless, combined to fuel increasing land speculation. These factors wrought heavy destruction on the built urban heritage, whose only scant protection was in fact the poverty of the country at this time. In the meantime, the increasingly heady cultural and political discussions on the subject of urban conservation found an outlet in a new law (6 August 1967, no. 765), meant to put a stop to the damage which had been caused to the environment. It became compulsory for every municipality to draw up an *Urban Plan*: without such an instrument, building of any type was made very difficult. In historic centres, in the absence of a Plan, only the reinforcement and restoration of existing buildings was allowed and no 'filling of gaps' was permitted.

On 2 April 1968 a new governmental decree (no. 1444) of great significance was passed. It established limits for building intensity, the maximum height of and the distances between buildings, the relationship between residential areas and zones reserved for public infrastructures; moreover, the territory of the municipality was divided into different zones, each subject to special rules. Urban agglomerations of historic, artistic and environmental value were defined as 'A zones' in which, in the case of restoration and urban renewal, building densities, distances and height were not to be varied. As for new construction, the rules were even stricter.

This Act has a wide range of application, as it includes every kind of planning, from General Master Plans to building codes, to the allocation of land for public housing. Together with law no. 765, this decree created a series of checks and balances, which significantly reined in building speculation in historical urban centres. The protection of historical centres now had a foundation, that on which the theorists of urban planning had been working for a decade.

During the same period another measure came into being: in 1971 an Act, known as the 'law for homes' (no. 865), was passed. It provided financial assistance for public housing, including works of renewal and restoration of entire areas within historic centres. It was from this point on that the official action to save historical centres for which Italy has become famous, began to operate. This action, however, has been partly responsible for some heavy erosion of the physical fabric of the built heritage. The reason for this is the widespread practice of so called 'typological restoration': according to this theory, the plan and volume of a given building had to be retained, but very little attention, if any, was given to materials such as plaster, bricks, beams, tiles, etc.

According to law no. 10, of January 1977, the person or company intending to undertake a building project had to pay a fee in order to obtain planning consent. In this way people contributed to the costs incurred by municipalities in providing services and facilities. If the planning proposal concerns restoration or renovation work, the fee payable is either reduced or waived, thus making interventions on historic buildings more attractive.

The most recent law in this series is law no. 457 of August 1978, which defined categories of work for the rehabilitation of the heritage. These are as follows: ordinary and extraordinary maintenance, restoration and conservative rehabilitation, building conversion, urban restructuring. The law made it possible to identify run-down areas in the historical centres and to operate in these through a new urban instrument, the *Rehabilitation Plan*. This kind of plan is similar to the Detailed Plan, but can relate to either public or private action and can deal with very small areas, even a single building. The law also made available low-interest loans for restoration and rehabilitation work.

In 1972 (15 January) the power to legislate on urban planning matters was transferred to the regional administrative authority (*Regioni*) which made the whole system for the approval of new plans much faster, as it was no longer necessary to go through the Ministry of Public Work in Rome. Little by little, as each Region made its own rules, differences started to become apparent. These differences sharpened still further when protection of the environment was passed to the Regions and they were made responsible for the drawing up of *Regional Structure Plans*.

The whole system of planning, from General Master Plan to Detailed Plan to Implementation Plan to Local Plan, is very heavy and cumbersome. For this reason, most local authorities tend to define at the first and most superficial level (the General Plan) the rules to be applied to individual buildings. Only the most difficult and delicate areas, needing deeper analysis and more careful planning, are subjected to an Implementation Plans.

Special Laws have been passed to deal with exceptional natural catastrophes, such as earthquakes or floods in order to obtain faster results and to make the financing of projects easier.

The role of public boards and specialist agencies

The most important among the public boards involved in conservation is that of the *Soprintendenze ai Monumenti* (Board of Monuments), which has more recently become the Board of Architectural and Environmental Assets. The first to be established, as early as 1894, were the Board of Monuments for Ravenna and that for the Antiquities and Museums of Padua (Emiliani, 1973: 1633 and Dezzi Bardeschi, 1997: 46–51, date the Board for Ravenna three years later). Their role was, and remains, to be a practical link between the central power of control of the state and the need to delegate many tasks to local authorities. This role was made necessary less by political or administrative reasons than by the very nature of the heritage, scattered as it is throughout the country (Emiliani, 1973).

From 1904 onwards, local *Soprintendenze* were created, in three separate branches: for monuments, for archaeological assets and for galleries. Three years later there were eighteen Boards for Monuments, fourteen Boards for Antiques and fifteen for Galleries.

But World War I damaged the new organizational structure and the subsequent Fascist government ruined it even further. The *Soprintendenze* were more than halved, in 1923, and the *Soprintendente* became a mere civil servant, under the direct control of the state.

The work of today's *Soprintendenze* has already been discussed in connection with the two current protection laws (discussed above). Nevertheless, it is important to underline how extensive are the tasks entrusted to these Boards. They check restoration projects and the subsequent execution of the works, whether carried out by private individuals or by public bodies and they themselves undertake projects and works on any asset owned by the state (buildings, paintings, etc.). Moreover, the works undertaken by the *Soprintendenze* serve as a model for others to learn from in the still rather undeveloped but fast-growing fields of conservation and restoration. This is a heavy and often unrewarding task, the *Soprintendente* finding him- or herself in almost daily contrast with local authorities and public opinion, which is not yet mature enough to realize how essential the work of these bodies are, if our heritage is to be saved.

The *Soprintendenze* are heavily understaffed considering the gigantic task they have to deal with. The sector of the cultural heritage directly managed by the *Soprintendenze* is the largest within the country, in terms both of quantity and of quality, and on top of this they have to supervise all conservation programmes in the country.

The establishment of a new Ministry for Cultural Assets has given more strength and power to the *Soprintendenze*, but funding and staffing are still inadequate.

The year 1975 saw the establishment of the Ministry for Cultural Assets and the reorganization of its four Central Institutes, among which the Central Institute for Cataloguing and Documentation (ICCD), the Central Institute for Restoration (ICR) and the *Opificio delle Pietre Dure* are involved in the conservation of cultural heritage.

The ICCD, established in 1975, works in the field of cataloguing and documenting cultural properties of archaeological, artistic and environmental value. Its most important tasks are:

- to draw up programmes for the general cataloguing of the objects which form the cultural heritage and to define the methods for achieving this task;
- to create and maintain the catalogues of the aforesaid assets or objects;
- to issue publications on these activities;
- to manage relationships with similar foreign institutions, both private and public, and with international agencies engaged in this field.

The ICR was created by the 1939 law, mostly through the efforts of Cesare Brandi, who directed it for more than 20 years. Its role is to undertake and supervise the conservation of works of art and antiquities; it is also responsible for scientific research into methods of restoration and for assessing technologies for the conservation of cultural and historical heritage. It has the power to decide whether to proceed with any restoration and conservation intervention carried out on works of art. It is also responsible for the training in restoration and conservation of the administrative staff in charge of heritage.

The *Opificio delle Pietre Dure* is a special institute founded in 1588 by Ferdinando I de' Medici in Florence. This agency today plays a very advanced role in research and experimentation into new techniques for the conservation and restoration of works of art. It runs special courses for the restoration of decorative objects, mosaics and jewellery.

In addition to these government agencies, there are a few private organizations involved in the preservation of the cultural patrimony. In 1955, through the efforts of some leading figures in the cultural world, '*Italia Nostra*' was born. The aims of the association were 'to stop the process of destruction of our national heritage' and 'to arouse a more lively interest in the problems connected with the conservation of the landscape, of monuments and of the urban environment'. The society is still active and engaged both in commissioning and publishing studies and conferences on heritage and in fighting to protect cultural assets at risk.

The Gubbio Conference gave rise, in 1961, to the ANCSA (National Association for Historical and Artistic Centres), an association of certain towns promoting, together with politicians, scholars and civil servants, research into the protection of historical urban centres in Italy. The National Institute of Planning (INU), to which the most important Italian planners belong, is involved, among other things, in the protection and development of historical towns.

Financial resources, funding mechanisms and the regeneration of historical environments

The annual operational budget for the Ministry of the Environment and Artistic Assets enables the working of the structure, including the various

Soprintendenze, which manage the funding of restoration projects on the heritage belonging to the state, in line with an annual programme approved by the Minister.

As for the help granted to private owners, it consists mostly of fiscal exemptions. The 1982 law, no. 512, on 'Taxation on properties of high cultural interest' grants important fiscal benefits on income derived from the use of such cultural properties. The objective of the law is to involve the private owner actively in the preservation and maintenance of the cultural asset. The tax benefits aim to encourage the private owner to co-operate with the state in the work of conservation of the heritage (Alibrandi and Ferri, 1995: 711).

In the same spirit, properties turned to cultural uses are exempted from tax, as are the revenues from parks and gardens open to the public or listed by the Ministry as of public interest. The law lists many different tax concessions for private owners of cultural and artistic properties. Summarizing a very detailed and complex situation, it could be said that practically the whole cost of maintenance and restoration of listed properties are tax deductible. Moreover, inheritance taxes are significantly reduced or waived.

This law has proved very popular and requests to have one's property listed have significantly increased. This is a new attitude as the listing of a property was hitherto regarded as a burden, resulting simply in heavier controls over the management of the property. With this change, listing and its consequent restrictions have become a positive element, which people appreciate. To enjoy the fiscal concessions provided for in the law, requires various bureaucratic formalities the administration of which are an extra burden on the *Soprintendenze*. But normally they are able to meet the necessary deadlines and people are thus able to experience the advantage of owning a listed property.

In the last two decades of the twentieth century a number of other provisions have been passed, among which is the reduction of the Value Added Tax rate for building works on the built heritage. The rate is today of 10 per cent, in comparison with the standard rate of 20 per cent. In the 1980s it was lower, between 2 per cent and 4 per cent.

The several Special Laws passed on various occasions and discussed above always refer to financial contributions and the possibility of obtaining loans at especially low interest rates.

The Ministry for Cultural Assets and Activities has at its disposal a budget which is about 0.19 per cent of the entire national budget of Italy. It is obviously a very tiny percentage, but the amount has fortunately more than doubled in the last few years thanks to some important provisions. These so-called 'extraordinary' provisions are transforming the Ministry from a Cinderella of the national budget into a slightly more efficient structure.

In the last 5 years or so, the government has passed a number of provisions for the financing of the restoration of important monuments. First, there are the proceedings of the national lottery. Second, each tax-payer can choose to give 0.8 per cent of his tax to the Ministry of Cultural Assets, rather than to a church. Last but not least, for the Jubilee of 2000 a huge budget has been allocated to the Cultural Assets, with L. 445 billion distributed among 263 works, placed mostly in Rome and Lazio, with L. 340 billion for 211 works.

Education and training

One of the sub-committees of the Franceschini Committee, chaired by the illustrious architectural historian C. L. Ragghianti (AA.VV., 1967: 1: 737), was given the task of studying the crucial problem of training the staff of the organizations responsible for the protection and conservation of the heritage. The picture it drew of the current situation was far from optimistic. The sub-committee denounced the low standards of teaching of art history in secondary schools, which had an impact on subsequent university education. The result was that the numbers of skilled specialists, including teachers, were insufficient by a long way when compared with the needs of the artistic heritage, which had to be studied, protected and enhanced.

The sub-committee also judged that the state of the faculties of architecture was not satisfactory, in terms of helping the growth of scientific studies into the conservation, restoration and analysis of monuments. They signalled a 'general serious inadequacy in the teaching of restoration and allied subjects in architecture faculties and sometimes even a total lack of them' (AA.VV., 1967: 1: 737).

Schools of architecture had been founded from the beginning of the 1920s and generally included a course on Monument Restoration (in Rome this was taught by Giovannoni), a course on Stylistic and Building Elements and one on Architectural History. Because of the teaching of these subjects, the architect's is the only profession qualified in the restoration of listed buildings. The architecture faculties, nevertheless, have often proved to be insensitive to the problems of Italy's built heritage and have failed to train professionals equal to the difficult tasks facing them.

Only very recently have some faculties modified their curricula, turning their efforts towards the needs of a country that wishes to preserve what already exists and not only to build from new. At the same time, the architecture schools are undergoing a process of radical and rapid change, through which restoration is assuming a greater scope and importance.

In Italy there is a common opinion that intervention on the built heritage, both old and modern, makes up over the 50 per cent of the total building activity (Carbonara, 1996: 11). One would expect, given this situation, that the field of restoration would occupy a relevant place in Italian Architecture Universities and also in terms of the subjects taught in the faculty. It is not so: if one analyses the amount of teaching hours, one realizes that our discipline is underrated (Gianighian, 1994: 115–16). Architecture faculties are organized around 5-year courses, with a total of 4,500 hours of teaching. Of these, only 180 hours are dedicated to the two courses of our subject, which are Theory and History of Restoration (third year, one term's teaching, 60 hours) and Architectural Restoration (fourth year, two term's tutorial teaching, 120 hours). On the whole, there has been very little increase in the time given to restoration, in comparison with the old system. In the 1993 order, restoration took up 4 per cent of the courses. It is true, though, that there are more disciplines connected with restoration which can be taken by the students, but which are not compulsory. Other subjects connected with restoration and necessary for the training of a professional building restorer are those based around history. This is the share of each area of teaching, including the optional subjects, which cover the total of 600 hours:

*   architectural design – 23 per cent
*   history – 10 per cent
*   building science – 11 per cent
*   technology – 11 per cent
*   physics and technical services (sanitation, plumbing, heating, etc.) – 5 per cent
*   estimate – 3 per cent
*   planning – 9 per cent
*   economic, social and juridical subjects – 3 per cent
*   mathematics – 7 per cent
*   drawing – 11 per cent

The position of restoration and conservation is not the most favoured, but it is improved a little by the fact that restoration has a final workshop leading to the final exam (*laurea*).

The fact that subjects connected with conservation are taught in discipline areas which differ from that of restoration means that the problems of restoration are becoming more widely recognized as being an essential part of the training of an architect.

It is probably not necessary to have architects registered especially for restoration work. We need to offer a good general training on this subject to all architecture students. Once students have completed their courses, those who are interested in restoration will be able to undertake further study on a number of available post-graduate courses. Three universities offer PhD courses in Restoration and Conservation, in Milan, Rome and Naples.

There are four specialist courses (MA): in Milan, Rome, Naples and Genoa. They are full-time 2-year courses, with 250 hours of teaching and 250 hours of tutorials. In Milan, fifty graduates per year are admitted. There are also a number of post-graduate courses that offer opportunities for architects and engineers in practice to update their knowledge.

In the Architecture University Institute of Venice, about 18 per cent of the students gain a degree in subjects connected with Restoration and Conservation and are examined by two commissions out of eighteen.

Special attention should be given to the Course on the History and Conservation of Architectural and Environmental Assets opened recently at the University of Venice. It is a very good course with 4 years of study, but it does not allow the possibility of becoming a registered architect according to the present laws on professions, and this can be very difficult for graduates of the course.

Altogether, even if the new order of Architecture Faculties does not place the required level of stress on restoration and conservation, the time seems to be favourable for these subjects. The students have already realized this, and they devote more space to restoration subjects in their curricula; one final exam in five is being replaced by a thesis on the built heritage.

Now a new reform is under discussion, aligning the Italian School of Architecture to European standards. This means breaking the curriculum in two sectors, one 2-year course leading to a diploma, and a 3-year specialist course, which can be followed by a PhD. This new project greatly emphasizes the architectural design sector, at the expenses of other disciplines; it is probable, nevertheless, that a special diploma in restoration is going to be established.

Conclusions

The conservation of listed buildings is governed by means of a law that is 60 years old, while its implementation rules go back almost 90 years. In the meantime the concept of heritage has widened substantially in relation to the traditional idea of 'monument' and now includes so-called vernacular architecture as well as industrial archaeology, historical centres, gardens and parks.

Despite the age of the legal instruments, the quality of restoration work has not declined, in fact just the opposite has happened! Today, although still working on the premises of the old 1939 law, conservation of the heritage has reached new heights. We are aware of examples of works carried out 30 years ago on listed town or country houses, with the full permission of the *Soprintendenza* in charge. In many cases, these works have completely altered the inner volume, by rebuilding partitions, floors, etc., with modern materials. Today the same body, enforcing the same law, might well require the restorer to retain each floor joist or roof beam and even the old windows.

This change is thanks to the revisions that have occurred in restoration theory in recent years. It is increasingly widely accepted that the historical heritage is a not renewable resource and that this resource has not only a cultural but also an economic value. Moreover, the concept of restoration has shifted from an emphasis on preserving the 'quality' of objects, of the materials that are supposed most valuable, to an idea of 'quantity'. We want to preserve as much as possible of what has survived from the past, in this way adhering to the concept of 'material civilization'.

The definitions of what is meant by conservation, both of architecture and of the environment, has been debated and refined in successive Conferences held in many locations throughout the world over the past few years. The Granada Convention is not sufficiently clear in what it says about the conservation of historical materials. The Fourth European Conference of Ministers Responsible for the Cultural Heritage (Helsinki 1996) in its Declaration (point II/D.) states: 'the use of non-renewable assets

. . . this resource is transmitted to future generations, in a manner that preserves the authenticity of the heritage'. There is no mention of the fact that protection and conservation apply to the physical aspects of the existing heritage. This is more explicit, however, in the ICOMOS Washington Charter (1987), which numbers among its 'Principles and Objectives': 'Qualities to be preserved include . . . all those material and spiritual elements that express this character, especially: . . . c) the formal appearance, interior and exterior, of buildings as defined by scale, size, style, construction, materials, colour and decoration'.

We need to preserve a historical building respecting the materials with which it was been built and how it has changed over the course of time. This is very different from a restoration that effaces the physical elements of a building, considering them of little or no value, only preserving an architectural volume and the exterior appearance of the old construction. This is the concept known as *façadism*, which was declared to be unacceptable at the ICOMOS International Conference in 1999. 'To preserve can only mean to look for rules to manage a transformation which makes the best of permanence, adds its own sign and interprets without destroying' (Bellini, 1997).

The best restorations, such as those carried out by the *Soprintendenze*, are based on the principle of keen attention to the physical aspects of the object to be preserved. The work of the *Soprintendenze* influences both private and public professionals in their careers as conservators and restorers, but is not yet sufficiently known and understood. This is the lesson that one and a half century of thinking about conservation has taught us.

There is some important news from the world of the Ministry for Cultural Assets. In the first place, the Ministry has adopted a zero tolerance policy with respect to illegal building in protected areas. As an example, the demolition carried out under the protection of the *Carabinieri*, of the so-called 'monster of Fuenti' on the coast of Sorrento, may be cited. It was a huge hotel, the presence of which ruined one of the most precious and closely protected landscapes of Italy. The building was a symbol of the often-stormy relationship between central and local (Regional) government, the former having reversed the permission granted by the latter. This decision was a kind of miracle, certainly one that no government body had previously been able to achieve.

In another area of high archaeological value subject to a high degree of protection, the Valley of the Temples at Agrigento, the arrival of the bulldozers is also expected. It should happen at the beginning of 2000, almost as a celebration of the new attitude towards the protection of Italian landscape. Six concrete skeletons, multi-storeyed buildings never completed, and later 654 illegal constructions spread among the almond-trees are going to be demolished. Among them, there is even a church, built with no permissions of any kind!

These episodes induce reflection on the role of the local (regional) government for the protection of cultural assets. It is true that the Italian Constitution enshrines the legislative autonomy of these authorities – a reasonable democratic principle, and it is also true that the level of protection offered by any particular Region to its own heritage is linked to the cultural and economic conditions of the Region. Those Regions that are less developed can offer a lower level of protection and allow a larger number of illegal works, including in protected and listed areas. Unfortunately two laws, passed in 1985 and 1994, have given the green light to a great number of illegal buildings, some of them in protected areas.

In spring 1999 the Ministry set up a Technical Office for Programming, in charge both of the great projects of national importance and of programming the activity of the *Soprintendenze*, with a view to unifying and co-ordinating the various activities of the Ministry in the field of heritage protection.

Last but not least, the government has been working on a new Bill on the subject of cultural and environmental assets, revising the previous legislation. An Act was passed on 29 October 1999 (no. 490) and was published on 27 December 1999. It is to be hoped that this law will improve the general situation of the heritage.

References

Alibrandi, T. and Ferri, P. (1995): *I beni culturali e ambientali*, Dott. A. Giuffré Editore, Milano.

Autori Vari (AA.VV.) (1967): *Per la salvezza dei beni culturali in Italia. Atti e documenti della Commissione d'indagine per la tutela e la valorizzazione del patrimonio storico, archeologico, artistico e del paesaggio*, Casa Editrice Colombo, 2 voll., Roma.

Bellini, A. (1978): *Il restauro architettonico, in AA.VV., La difesa del patrimonio artistico*. Testi per ITALIA NOSTRA, Arnaldo Mondadori Editore, Milano, pp. 99–201.

Bellini, A. (1997): *Dal restauro alla conservazione: dall'estetica all'etica*, in *Ananke*, n. 19, sett. 1997, pp. 17–21.

Brandi, C. (1963): *Teoria del restauro*, Einaudi, Torino.

Carbonara, G. (ed.) (1996): *Trattato di restauro architettonico*, vol. 1°, UTET, Torino.

Dezzi Bardeschi, M. (1997): *Dietro le quinte: Corrado Ricci e la nascita della Soprintendenza di Ravenna*, in *Ananke*, n. 19, sett. 1997, pp. 46–51.

Emiliani, A. (1973): *Musei e museologia, in Storia d'Italia Einaudi*, V: I documenti, Einaudi, Torino.

Emiliani, A. (1974): *Una politica dei beni culturali*, Einaudi, Torino.

Gianighian, G. (1974): *L'enseignement de la restauration architecturale dans l'université italienne*, Les Cahiers de la Section Française de l'ICOMOS, Bâtiment, Patrimoine, Emploi. Les retombées économiques et sociales du patrimoine bâti, Poitiers, 24–25 Novembre 1994.

Giovannoni, G. (1931): *Vecchie città ed edilizia nuova*, Torino.

Haskell, F. (1981): *La dispersione e la conservazione del patrimonio artistico*, in AA.VV., Storia dell'arte italiana vol. 10, Einaudi, Torino, pp. 3–35.

Mansi, A. (1988): *Storia e legislazione dei beni culturali ambientali*, Del Bianco Editore, Udine.

Marconi, P. (1997): *Il restauro architettonico in Italia. Mentalità, ideologie, pratiche*, in F. DAL CO (a c. di), Storia dell'architettura italiana. Il secondo Novecento, Electa, Milano, pp. 370 sgg.

Price, N. S., Talley Jr., M. K. and Vaccaro, A. M. (eds) (1996): *Historical and Philosophical Issues in the Conservation of Cultural Heritage*, The Getty Conservation Institute, Los Angeles.

Rocchi, G. (1987) : *Teoria e prassi del restauro, bilancio: necessità di un cambiamento*, in Spagnesi, pp. 151– 8.

Ruskin, J. (1849): *The Seven Lamps of Architecture*, 'The Lamp of Memory' XVIII.

Spagnesi, G. (ed.) (1987): *Esperienze di storia dell'architettura e di restauro*, Istituto della Enciclopedia Italiana fondata da G. Treccani, Roma.

Juris Dambis

Latvia

Introduction

The territory of Latvia, which presently covers some 64,589 km^2, has been inhabited since 9000 BC. The population of the country was recorded as being 2,458,403 in 1998, and although the state language is Latvian, the composition of the population reflects different nationalities: Latvians 57.1 per cent, Russians 29.9 per cent, Belarussians 4.2 per cent, Ukrainians 2.7 per cent and Poles 2.5 per cent. The religious community may be similarly broken down: Catholic 38 per cent, Lutherans 30 per cent, Orthodox 14 per cent. The mix of cultures derived from such a multinational society is reflected in the heritage of Latvia.

The diverse nature of the Latvian cultural heritage can be revealed as follows:

- rural architecture consisting of individual farmsteads;
- an aesthetically attractive cultural–historical rural and coastal landscape. (Fig. 10.1);
- a framework for the cultural landscape in a countryside which is based on a network of manors associated with churches;
- Latvia's church architecture encompasses a wide range of religious denominations;
- a large dominance of wooden structures in urban and rural areas;
- a wide and diverse spectrum of evidence marking the presence of an ancient culture;
- a large proportion of art nouveau and functional architecture;
- a larger proportion of original materials in architectural objects in comparison to economically developed European states;
- church and secular buildings of the medieval Hanseatic cities;
- an archaeological heritage encompassing an underwater heritage;
- a significant proportion of historic military structures, including those of the twentieth century.

Fig. 10.1 A specially protected cultural and historical territory: the Abava Valley.

The first endeavours to preserve the cultural heritage in Latvia are connected with the reign of Swedish King Gustav II Adolph (1611–32) when the Swedish antiquarian Mārtiņš Ašaneus collected epitaphs and descriptions of church inventories and equipment in Vidzeme. A more earnest interest in registering the cultural heritage arose in Latvia with the establishment of several antiquity and art societies during the first half of the nineteenth century. A new period is connected with the first Republic of Latvia (1918–40) when in 1923 a special state institution – the Board of Monuments – was formed. There were 1,454 monuments under the protection of the state until the Soviet occupation in 1940. After World War II, different structures and subordinate institutions of the Council of Ministers and the Ministry of Culture, as well as institutions under their control, worked in the field of protection of the cultural heritage.

Today state administration and control over the protection and use of cultural monuments is provided by Cabinet of Ministers and is operated through the State Inspection for Heritage Protection, which was established in 1989 (Fig. 10.2).

Definition of the heritage
A cultural heritage is an evidence of a person's intellectual activity in a material or non-material form. The cultural heritage of Latvia contains works of artists, architects, musicians, writers and scientists, as well as works of anonymous artists, expressions of the spirit of humanity and system of values that imparts meaning of life.

The largest element of this cultural heritage, that being most directly perceptible as having the greatest potential, is of *toponyms* (cultural monuments). Under article 1 of the Latvian law 'On Cultural Heritage Protection', cultural monuments include:

Fig. 10.2 The edifices of the State Inspection for Heritage Protection in Riga. (Photograph: Robert Pickard.)

cultural landscape and separate territories (ancient burial grounds, cemeteries, parks, sites of historic events and workplaces of famous individuals), as well as separate graves, groups of buildings and separate buildings, works of art, furnishings and articles of historical, scientific, artistic or other cultural value.

The preservation of cultural monuments, for the benefit of future generations, corresponds to the interests of the state and to the nation of the Republic of Latvia, as well as conforming to international interests.

Categorization, significance and protection zones
Types of cultural monuments
The different forms of cultural monument are defined in article 2 of the law as follows:

1   Immovable cultural monuments include:
    * *separate objects*: buildings, works of art, furnishing and articles, and individual graves;
    * *composite objects*: archaeological sites, architectural ensembles and complexes, historical centres of towns or other populated areas, streets, squares, blocks, occupation layers, cemeteries, cultural landscapes, memorial places, historical sites and territories.

2   Movable cultural monuments include:
- *separate objects*: archaeological finds, antiquities, elements of immovable monuments, historical relics, pieces of art, manuscripts, rare publications, cinematic documents, photographic documents and video documents, audio records;
- *composite objects*: historically formed complexes, funds and collections of separate objects of inseparable cultural value;
- *objects preserved* in their original appearance as well as their separate parts and fragments that should be recognized as cultural monuments.

Significance
Cultural monuments are divided into those of state significance and those of local significance. The difference is in their historical, scientific, artistic or other value. A possible addition to the state cultural monument list is objects of the accounting group – according to investigation.

1   Archaeological monuments of state significance include:
- ancient grounds (settlements, castle mounds, ancient burial places, etc.) up to the thirteenth century (Fig. 10.3);
- all medieval castles, fortifications and historical centres of towns up to and including the seventeenth century;
- places of pagan cults with indications of artificial re-constructions or information about findings or a cultural layer;
- investigated archaeological monuments that have an outstanding scientific, historical, cultural or educational significance;
- sunk ships along with their cargo up to and including the seventeenth century.

Fig. 10.3 The Castle Mound of Daugmale on one of the Cultural Heritage Days.

2   Town planning and archaeological monuments of state significance include:
- all medieval castles, fortifications and historical centres up to the eighteenth century;
- all town halls and meeting houses;
- manors, dwelling and social constructions, defensive, industrial and technological constructions that have been erected up to the nineteenth century (Figs 10.4 and 10.5);
- building of cults that have been erected up to the twentieth century;
- folk construction objects that have been erected up to the twentieth century in the folk construction traditions and that are remarkable for their high craft quality;
- cemeteries, gardens and parks that have been formed up to the twentieth century.

A town planning and archaeological monument of state significance can also be an object that has been erected later than the periods mentioned if it is of extra significance for the whole of Latvia.

3   Art monuments of state significance include:
- artworks or their parts that represent a historical style of art and that have a high artistic value in terms of art traditions of their time in Europe and Latvia;
- professional artworks of Latvian national, as well as documented works attributed or signed by the authors of other nationalities considering their level of rarity, the author's personality and the quality of the work concerned.

4   Historical monuments of state value are buildings, territories and articles connected with:

Fig. 10.4 Ungurmuiža Estate.

Fig. 10.5 Ungurmuiža Estate with a fragment of a mural.

- the history of the Latvian nation;
- the formation of the Latvian state;
- outstanding people in the history of Latvia before 1945;
- the history of the world.

Reserves of cultural monuments
Ensembles and complexes of cultural monuments of particular historical, scientific or artistic value according to the resolution of Cabinet of Ministers may be declared to be *reserves of cultural monuments*, which should be protected according to regulations developed for each of these reserves. Regulations on the reserves of cultural monuments are made by the Cabinet of Ministers (Fig. 10.6).

Protection zones
In order to ensure protection of cultural monuments *protection zones* are defined around them. It is not necessary to obtain the consent of the user or owner of the land when creating a protection zone. The size and boundary of the zones (where fixed), and the regime of their maintenance, are determined by the State Inspection for Heritage Protection. Around cultural monuments that do not have an individually determined boundary, and newly discovered cultural monuments in rural, populated areas, the protection zone is 500m or 100m in towns. Economic activity within the

Fig. 10.6 A specially protected cultural and historical territory: the Abava Valley – the centre of Sabile.

protection zone of a cultural monument can only be performed with the authorization of the State Inspection for Heritage Protection.

According to the regulations of Cabinet of Ministers, the Head of the State Inspection for Heritage Protection may identify any object located within the protection zone of a cultural monument that may cause environmental damage. Such objects may be required to be dismantled, and, if so, their further development is not admissible.

Identification of the heritage

Cultural objects of state interest, as defined by the article 12 of the law, are required to be included on the state inventory, irrespective of their ownership, tenure or utilization. This requires their investigation and the preparation of inventory documentation. The state inventory of monuments includes an exploration and survey of each monument and a determination as to its historical, scientific, artistic, architectonic, ethnographic or other cultural value, as well as its fixtures.

Identification and protection by registration

The registration of cultural monuments for protection is provided for by the State Inspection for Heritage Protection. In the state 'list' of cultural monuments all monuments are listed, noting the:

* location (and whether open or closed to public);
* size (town planning ensemble or a separate article);
* possessor (whether the property of a private or corporate person);
* technical condition;
* period and circumstances of its origination.

213

Proposals for enlisting an object in the cultural monument list are put forward by:

- State Inspection of Heritage Protection;
- self-governments (local authorities);
- private and corporate persons.

Accounting material for each listed cultural monument includes:

- the title and addresses and the name of the proprietor;
- a description and a scheme of the location;
- photographic-fixation;
- accounting details of their foundation.

Typological groups of cultural monuments include:

- archaeological monuments;
- town planning (streets, plazas and their housing lines) and archaeological monuments
- constructions:
  - constructions of cults,
  - dwelling houses,
  - social constructions,
  - defensive and technical constructions,
  - folk construction objects,
  - cemeteries, gardens and parks;
- artistic monuments;
- historical monuments.

The state list of cultural monuments
The list of state protected cultural monuments is approved by the Cabinet of Ministers. Cultural monuments, according to their historical, scientific, artistic or other cultural value, are divided into monuments of state and local significance. The list of state protected cultural monuments is published in the newspaper *Latvijas Vēstnesis*.

In preparing the draft list of state protected cultural monuments, the State Inspection for Heritage Protection includes all objects deemed worthy of protection. The relevant State Inspector for Heritage Protection notifies the owner (possessor) in writing about the inclusion of the object, being in his or her possession (tenure), in the draft list. The owner (possessor) of the object has, within 30 days after receiving the notification in writing, to make representations to the State Inspection for Heritage Protection concerning the proposal to include the object in the draft list. However, the consent of the owner (possessor) is not required for inclusion. If an object is subsequently included in the state list, the owner (possessor) may be entitled to tax relief or compensation for damage if any such damage has occurred due to the limitations imposed on the use of the object or the associated land.

The State Land Service ensures that cultural monuments and their territories are marked in plans of administrative-territorial units and in documents of the state cadastral survey.

Although the Cabinet of Ministers is required to approve the draft list, the exclusion of an object from the list of state protected cultural monuments is generally admissible only if the object has fully lost its value as a cultural monument. Objects from the list of state protected cultural monuments are excluded by Cabinet of Ministers (until 1998, the Minister of Culture) upon the suggestion of the State Inspection for Heritage Protection.

Newly discovered cultural monuments
Newly discovered objects of historical, scientific, artistic or other cultural value, irrespective of their possession, are temporarily under state protection until a decision on the inclusion of these objects in the state list has been confirmed. This temporary protection applies for a period not longer than 6 months from the day when the owner has been notified of this situation.

Any person finding objects in the ground, on the ground, in water, in old buildings or their parts and remnants and with possible historical, scientific, artistic or other cultural value, must notify the State Inspection for Heritage Protection within 10 days of the discovery being made.

Number of state protected cultural monuments in Latvia
The historic centre of Riga is a place of international heritage importance and has been listed by UNESCO as a World Heritage Site.

Cultural monuments with state or local significance can be identified as shown in Table 10.1. Within this total there are 7,057 immovable cultural monuments, including those listed in Table 10.2.

Identification of the condition of cultural monuments
A large part of Latvia's cultural heritage is in a critical state because both the urban townscape and rural landscape was allowed to degrade in the period from 1940 to 1991. Furthermore, in the last 10 years significant changes have occurred in the ownership of cultural monuments. In 1990

Table 10.1 Latvian cultural monuments

Type of cultural monument	Total	State	Local
Archaeological monuments	2495	1482	1013
Architectural monuments	3364	1317	2047
Monuments of art	2414	2413	1
Territorial and urban monuments	44	39	5
Historical monuments	111	111	0
Total	8428	5362	3066

Source: National Programme for 'Culture': The Sub Programme 'Cultural Heritage', adopted by the Cabinet of Ministers on 8 February 2000.

Table 10.2 Latvian immovable cultural monuments.

Hillforts	474
Ancient burial sites	1233
Medieval castle sites and ruins	76
Manors	136
Lutheran churches	134
Catholic churches	48
Russian Orthodox churches	33
Residences of prominent persons	29

85 per cent of the cultural monuments within Latvia were in the ownership of state or municipal authorities, (with only 15 per cent in private
hands). Today this situation has reversed.

Unfortunately a large proportion of private owners are presently unable,
for reasons of financial hardship, to maintain their cultural monuments
according to the requirements of the legislation. Moreover, the state and
municipal budgets are not currently in a sufficiently healthy position to
support conservation activities (see below). The result is that the technical
condition of many cultural monuments remains critical.

In order to improve this situation the 'National Programme' of 'Culture'
(Sub Programme of Cultural Heritage) has identified the need to deal with
this problem. In 1998 a technical condition survey of cultural monuments
in Latvia was carried out. The results of this survey were as follows:

- good – 17 per cent
- satisfactory – 38 per cent
- poor – 37 per cent
- castastrophic – 7 per cent
- partially or entirely destroyed – 1 per cent

The survey has shown that at least 520 objects are in a catastrophic condition. However, in a more positive light, it should also be mentioned that
repair, restoration, reconstruction, adaption or conservation works have
been conducted on 27 per cent of the total number of cultural monuments
in the last 5 years.

The preservation and protection of the heritage
The current system of legislation and normative acts on cultural heritage
was established by the law 'On the Protection of Cultural Monuments'
(adopted by the *Saeima* (Parliament) in December 1992 and subsequently
amended in June 1993, December 1993, and February 1995). The State
Inspection for Heritage Protection also carries out its functions according
to the Regulations 'On Enumeration, Protection, Use and Restoration of
Cultural Monuments' (adopted by the Council of Ministers), the Statute of
State Inspection for Heritage Protection Regulation (adopted by the
Cabinet of Ministers in 1996), and thirty-seven other legal instruments
concerning the preservation of cultural heritage.

It is prohibited to destroy any cultural monument. Immovable monuments may be moved or altered only in exceptional cases with the authorization of the State Inspection for Heritage Protection. The alteration of a cultural monument or the substitution of its original details with new work may be admissible only in cases where it is the only possible way to preserve the monument, or when the alteration does not diminish the cultural value of the monument.

According to the law, private and corporate persons are responsible for ensuring the preservation of cultural monuments in their possession (tenure). This applies equally to state owned cultural monuments. The liability of the owner (possessor) of the cultural monument is as follows:

- to observe legislative and other normative bills as well as the directions of the State Inspection for Heritage Protection on the utilization and preservation of cultural monuments;
- to inform the State Inspection for Heritage Protection about any damage that occurs to the cultural monument being in their possession (tenure).

Scientific, educational and cultural use of cultural monuments is a priority. The use of cultural monuments for economic activities may be allowed only in where it does not damage the monument or reduce its historical, scientific and artistic value.

Cultural monuments may be conserved, restored and repaired only upon the reception of written authorization from, and according to the supervision of, the State Inspection for Heritage Protection. Similarly, any investigation of a cultural monument that may lead its alteration, including archaeological investigation, requires the written authorization and supervision of the State Inspection for Heritage Protection.

Before construction, melioration, building of roads, extracting of minerals or other economic activities can take place, the performer of these works must ensure that the potential cultural values that may be located in the zone of planned works are explored. Private and corporate persons who have discovered archaeological or other objects of cultural value as a result of their economic activities must immediately inform the State Inspection for Heritage Protection. The works must be halted to allow investigation by the State Inspection for Heritage Protection.

Conservation philosophy

The approach to conservation concerning the cultural heritage of the Republic of Latvia is based on the following principles:

- The destruction of any part of the heritage makes Latvia's culture become poorer. Cultural heritage is not a luxury – it is an economic value.
- The work of preservation should be open and information has to be widely accessible. Co-operation with the society is necessary – its precondition is an 'understanding'. Discussions on the most important matters should be accessible to the public.

- The idea of cultural heritage means not only separate objects or places, but also their place – the environment related to the history of the civilization. A cultural monument cannot be separated from its history – a witness of which it is and where it is located.
- The cultural heritage should be handed over to the future generations in an authentic form. Transformation or transportation of a cultural monument is admissible only if it is the only way to save the monument or if the result of transportation does not decrease the cultural value of the monument. Every period has its specific features and layers that are also historical witnesses and have cultural significance. In cases where new transformations of the monument become necessary, without which the existence of the monument will be under threat, or if the monument is in need of new details, these have to correspond to the principles of historical composition but with features relevant to the current time. The creation of a false image during the restoration is not admissible. Imitation or copying is not a means of preservation – restoration should not serve as an experiment to elicit historical and scientific presumptions. The main principle of cultural and historical protection is to preserve, maximally, the original building elements and details using traditional materials (Fig. 10.7).
- A significant constituent of preservation action for the cultural heritage is the investigation and documentation of cultural objects.
- The work of preservation is based on a co-operation and dialogue between official institutions and the proprietor/user of the monument. Juridical measures (fines) are the last step if this communication breaks down.
- The strategy devised by official institutions for preserving the cultural heritage must be realistic, i.e. feasible in the given time and economic

*Fig. 10.7: The Āraiši Castl
on the lake. A reconstructi
for scientific research and
craft training purposes.*

situations. Whilst dealing with the most important matters, details cannot be lost. Different economic situations may have different demands, however, they should be well-grounded.

- Specialist training has a significant role in the preservation of the cultural heritage.
- Timber, limestone and grout of their products are the main traditional building materials that are durable, environmental friendly and easy to look after. Non-critical usage of new building materials and ready-made products in historical buildings lead to their degradation.

Sanctions and coercive measures

Article 30 of the law 'On Cultural Heritage Protection' deals with liability for violations. Works performed on cultural monuments contrary to the 'schedule' of directions, contained in article 20 the law, are considered to be void.

Persons found guilty of failing to observe of the Regulations 'On Enumeration, Protection, Use and Restoration of Cultural Monuments', including violations of the regime of their protection zones, and other transgressions, can be called to criminal, administrative or other liability according to the legislation of the Republic of Latvia.

Cultural monuments, owners of which do not ensure their protection, on suggestion of the State Inspection for Heritage Protection may be alienated via litigation. In the case of alienation involving 'real estate', the rights of tenants are preserved according to the legislation of the Republic of Latvia.

Monetary fines can be imposed for the following actions:

- Persons found guilty of damaging cultural monuments or violating their protection rules can be fined up to 250 Lats.
- Persons found guilty of restoration, conservation and repair, as well as investigation and archaeological findings without the written permission of the State Inspection of Heritage Protection can be fined up to 250 Lats.
- Persons found guilty of damaging territories, protection zones or visual zones of a cultural monument, or responsible for their transformation, or allowing prohibited economic activities to be performed on them, can be fined up to 259 Lats.
- Persons found guilty of not carrying out an intended repair for preserving the monument, as a result of which the cultural monument is damaged, can be fined up to 150 Lats.
- Persons found guilty of damaging a burial place can be fined up to 250 Lats.
- Persons found guilty of befouling a burial place are imprisoned for a period up to 6 years or are fined up to 100 times the minimum monthly wage.
- Persons found guilty of destroying or damaging cultural monuments that are under state protection are imprisoned up to 4 years or are fined up to 80 times minimum monthly wage.

Integrated conservation

In Latvia, state institutions and enterprises co-operate with self-governments (local authorities) in the field of territorial planning. They provide information about relevant issues as indicated in the laws and, if necessary, direct a responsible official in territorial planning matters in this respect. State institutions work out the conditions for territorial planning within four weeks after a request from a regional, city or district council has been made. Within eight weeks, judgements are made on the first draft of the territorial plan (if there are further drafts and a detailed plan – within four weeks).

To work out the territorial planning requirements for regional, city or district areas, special protection and use regulations are necessary including nature protection plans and specific cultural territory protection mechanisms. In this respect national, regional and detailed planning are relevant as discussed here.

National planning is a territorial planning mechanism in which all the state's interest in land-use is defined for each territory within Latvia. It is binding on state government institutions and self-governments (local authorities) in terms of the decisions made over protection and use of territories, nature resources, and concerning the formulation of the territorial planning policies of a particular territory.

Regional planning is a planning mechanism for all the administrative territories of the region. It depicts existing objects and land-uses and defines the planned structure of the regional territory with a perspective ofr no less than 12 years. Regional plans determine:

- the disposition of immovable cultural monuments and specially protected cultural territories within a region
- significant territories for leisure activities and tourism – the objects of which concern the regions and are mentioned in the law 'About educational, cultural and scientific objects and national sports camps of state significance'
- other objects, territories and claims corresponding to necessary works and ecological assignments.

Each city and district must also have a valid territorial planning scheme at their disposal. Plans that have been worked out for the territory of all of a district or a city (general planning) depict the existing objects and land-uses, and permitted uses, within a local authority's territory for 12 years, as well as defining objects, territories and claims defined in the territorial planning.

The *detailed planning* involves the planning of a part of a district or city that concretizes and specifies proposals and claims of the general planning. Detailed plans define:

- red lines (borders of a street or road), construction distances (the minimal distance from the red line to the existing or planned construction), all kinds of shelter belts, burdens and requirements for the use of immovable property (for each plot);

- housing regulations – at a the level that ensures the introduction of concrete claims for each plot or parcel (designed plot).

It should be stated, however, that the territorial planning system is still in the process of development. Therefore, it will take time before the integration of conservation objectives within territorial planning mechanisms can be fully implemented.

Financial resources

The conservation, maintenance, repair, and restoration of a cultural monument is performed by its owner (possessor) at his or her own financial cost (Fig. 10.8). In general there is very little finance within the state budget to offer financial support to private owners directly, at the present time. In fact the level of state funding has been estimated at one tenth of the minimum that is required to support the required action. However, a few measures have been made available and will be considered here.

Following proposals made by the State Inspection for Heritage Protection, the state budget provides some finance (50 per cent of the cost) for the investigation of cultural monuments and for the conservation and restoration of cultural monuments of state significance that have no economic use. Finance is also provided by municipal budgets – for the conservation and restoration of cultural monuments of local significance with no economic use.

The State Inspection for Heritage Protection signs a contract with each owner (possessor) of a cultural monument with respect to the granting of resources from the state budget for cultural monuments of state significance, and controls the use of these resources. The cost of investigations necessary

Fig. 10.8 Repair and restoration of cultural onuments on a large scale are performed by the proprietors: the reconstruction of Rāmava Estate.

for construction works, melioration, building of roads and for other economic activities is financed by the performer of the work at the customer's
expense.

Financial resources are made available to municipalities by renting out
cultural monuments and by profit deduction obtained as a result of commercial activities connected with cultural monuments. Money is also received
from fines imposed as a result of prosecutions for damage or the unauthorized demolition of cultural monuments – the adjustment of connected
damages are remitted to incomes of the special budget of *pagasts* or the town
municipality. These different forms of income may be used only for investigation, conservation, repairs and the restoration of cultural monuments.

In addition, a *Cultural Capital Fund* was established in Latvia in 1998.
The objective of the Cultural Capital Fund is to accumulate, raise and distribute capital and is generally aimed at the development and preservation
of creative work (including the cultural heritage). The fund will also be used
to encourage the development of international contacts, as well as to
popularize the culture and art of Latvia in the world.

Defined tax easements are also available for cultural monuments. The tax
normally levied on immovable property is not applied to:

• the ground where economical action is prohibited by the law;
• immovable property that has been recognized as a cultural monument of
  the Republic of Latvia and the land for its maintenance – except for
  dwelling houses and associated land for its maintenance, and immovable
  property in commercial use.

The role of agencies and specialist organizations
The Cabinet of Ministers insures the state administration of the protection
and use of the cultural heritage which, in practice, is implemented by the
State Inspection for Heritage Protection (a subordinate of the Ministry of
Culture). Administrative acts and directions on the use and preservation of
every single cultural monument are issued by the Inspection and are binding
to every owner and landlord of the cultural monument. State Inspection for
Heritage Protection appoints an inspector for heritage protection, directly
subjected to the devolved inspection service in every region and city of the
Republic (in total thirty-three administrative units). Municipalities have
been requested to set up local services for cultural heritage – so far, these
have been established within Riga, the Riga region, Jūrmala, Ventspils and
Daugavpils (Fig. 10.9).

The main tasks and rights of the inspection service are to:

• implement state control on the protection of cultural monuments;
• carry out state enumeration of cultural monuments, register and research
  cultural monuments;
• examine documentation on works connected with cultural monuments;
• issue directions for owners of cultural monuments on the use and
  preservation of the corresponding cultural monument;

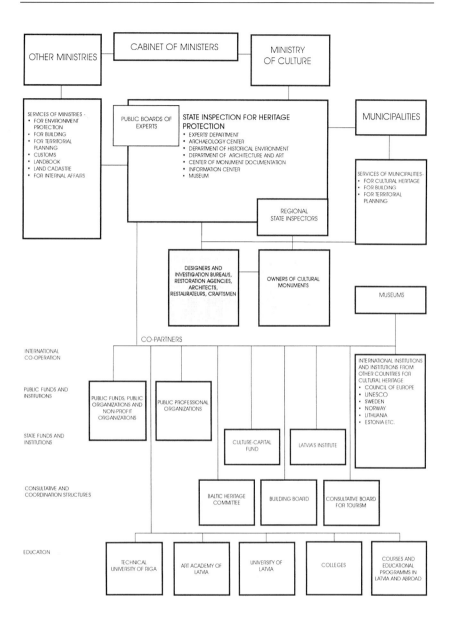

Fig. 10.9 Cultural heritage department structure scheme

- issue licences for the approval of definite patterns for conservation, restoration, repair and reconstruction works relating to cultural monuments;
- carry out examination of objects of art and antiquity, and issue licences to export them abroad;
- finance works on research, preservation and restoration of cultural monuments from specially allocated resources;
- suspend economic activity if regulations on the protection of cultural monuments have been violated and the cultural monument is endangered; fine with an administrative punishment; to file a petition on remedies.

The activities are carried out with the assistance of seven constituent bodies subordinated to the state inspection:

- Administrative Department;
- Experts' Department;
- Archaeology Centre;
- Department of Architecture and Art;
- Department of Historical Environment;
- Museum of Architecture;
- Centre of Monument Documentation.

There are also seven voluntary boards of experts working within the inspection service. These are:

- Board of Architecture Experts;
- Board of Restoration Certification;
- Board of Organ Experts;
- Board of Archaeology Experts;
- Board of Art and Antiquity Experts;
- Board of Architecture and Art Listing Experts;
- Board of Art Restoration Experts.

In order to fulfil its tasks, the State Inspection for Heritage Protection collaborates directly with municipal authorities and their services, as well as other ministries (Environment and Regional development, Interior, Justice, and finance Ministries) and their services.

Education and training

Institutions and organizations connected with education in the field of cultural heritage include the following:

- *Latvijas Restauratoru biedrība* (Latvian Society of Restorers);
- *Latvijas Amatniecības kamera* (Latvian Crafts Chamber);
- *Latvijas Mākslas akadēmija* (Latvain Acadamey of Arts);
- *Amatniecības vidusskolas un celtniecības koledžas* (Craft Secondary Schools and Building Colleges);
- *Rīgas Tehniskā universitāte* (Technical University of Riga);
- *Latvijas Universitāte* (University of Latvia);
- *Latvijas Kultūras akadēmija* (Latvian Cultural Academy).

In Latvia, there are 111 certified restoration architects, three certified building engineers, and 108 other certified restoration experts. There is a distinct shortage of specialists and everything must be done to increase their numbers.

Education in this field is also provided though general programmes provided by Latvian schools and separate specialised subjects. Different courses are organized in this context (Fig. 10.10). Objects of the cultural heritage

Fig. 10.10 Training of the blacksmith craft: Vārnu House: the blacksmith's yard.

are 'signposts' for the development of a sense of place for young people. An ability to understand and evaluate the cultural heritage, taught and acquired in childhood, provides the nation with citizens who have a well-developed national consciousness and assists in fostering a sense of civic responsibility.

The culture–historical environment is the most easily perceived link with the past. It has been rooted in the character of the national identity. The educational process cannot be envisaged without visible witness to the presence of culture.

Conclusions

There is a persistent state administration and control system established in Latvia in the field of cultural heritage that is based on specialized laws, regulations and thirty-seven other legislation acts. The law 'On Cultural Monument Protection' passed in Latvia was the first specialized law of this kind in the former states of the Soviet socialistic regime. Owing to the support of the Council of Europe and other states, a cultural heritage policy has been created in Latvia that corresponds with the principles and philosophies of the states of Western Europe; merely the financial resources are different. Within the National Programme for Culture a sub-programme 'Cultural Heritage' has been formulated for the period up the year 2005, and it provides visions for the year 2020. The basic tasks for the arrangement of the cultural heritage protection activities have been assigned. These include some necessary juridical modifications, as well as undertakings for the development of cultural tourism, arrangement of the educational system, involvement of children and youth, popularization of the cultural heritage, and availability of information.

References

Code of Administrative Trespasses, adopted in 1994.

Criminal Code, adopted in 1998.

Law of Cultural Capital Foundation, adopted in 1997.

Law 'On Cultural Monuments Protection', adopted in 1992 (amended in 1993 (twice), and in 1995).

Law 'On Immovable Property Tax', adopted in 1997.

Legislation booklet, issued by State Inspectorate for Heritage Protection in 1999.

National Programme for 'Culture': The Sub-Programme 'Cultural Heritage', adopted by the Cabinet of Ministers on 8 February 2000.

Regulations No. 509 'On cultural monument registration, protection, use and restoration', issued by the Cabinet of Ministers in 1992.

Regulation No 62 'On Territorial Planning', issued by the Cabinet of Ministers in 1998.

Anthony Pace

Malta

Introduction

The protection and conservation of Malta's cultural heritage is governed by
a number of institutions and a set of legal instruments some of which date
back to 1925. In effect, the history of heritage protection legislation of the
Maltese islands does not span more than 90 years. During this time, the
enactment and amendment of legal instruments took place in stages that
were very much isolated in time. Due to this, legislation often became
isolated from contemporary developments in other socio-economic sectors.
It is for this reason that the government of Malta is currently reviewing all
heritage protection legislation with a view to enacting new legal instruments
and establishing new operational frameworks. It is envisaged that a new
heritage act for the Maltese islands will be submitted to cabinet during the
year 2000.

The regulation of the Maltese cultural heritage was established on a proper
footing during the first three decades of the twentieth century. This was a
pioneering period for innovation and discovery. In the space of a few years a
number of major archaeological sites were identified and excavated. Among
these were the prehistoric Hal Saflieni Hypogeum and the Tarxien Temples,
two of Malta's World Heritage Sites. Such discoveries led to the growth of
public awareness of the richness of the archipelago's antiquities. In time,
awareness led to mounting pressure in favour of the introduction of a
suitable protective mechanism. In 1903, Governor Lord Grenfell established
the *Museum Department*. At first this department was entrusted with accumul-
ating the various collections that were deemed to be public property under
one roof. But at the same time, the Museum Department also served as the
central government agency that had responsibility over the protection
of antiquities and historic buildings. To this day, the present *Museums
Department* (the plural denoting a number of off-shoot museums that have

developed since 1903) still has a two-fold responsibility over the collection, management and display of the country's antiquities (Pace, 1998) (Fig. 11.1).

For about seven years, the Museum Department operated without any form of heritage protection legislation. In 1910, a Preservation of Antiquities Ordinance was enacted (Malta Government, 1910). The Ordinance provided a simple framework for the protection of antiquities. It was inspired in the main part by the Italian legislation, which had just been freshly enacted in 1909. Following amendments and improvements in 1922 and 1923, a final *Antiquities Protection Act* was enacted in 1925 (Malta Government, 1925; Buhagiar, 1985). The 1925 Act provided for the establishment of an Antiquities Committee which, before being disbanded in 1992, assessed and advised government on the protection of heritage assets. It is the Antiquities Protection Act that, to this day, regulates some of the more important functions and procedures that concern the protection of cultural heritage.

It was only after 66 years had passed that two new legal instruments, having some bearing on heritage issues, were enacted. The first of these acts was the *Environment Protection Act* of 1991 (Malta Government, 1991). This law served to focus on environmental protection, with provisions for the safeguarding of cultural heritage. In respect to cultural heritage, however, the Environment Protection Act did not suffice to provide a comprehensive framework that would have enabled broader heritage management structures

Fig. 11.1 Sixteenth-centur interior of the Inquisitor's Palace, Birgu, the site of a 1930s restoration exercise an urban environment by th Museums Department.

to develop. Moreover, the Act was not considered to provide adequate cover for a series of important provisions that were enshrined in the Antiquities Protection Act of 1925. It is for this reason that the older Act is still in force.

A year later, the *Development Planning Act* (1992) was enacted to regulate and establish modern planning procedures. The Act established a central Planning Authority as an autonomous agency to regulate development. This important Act established the critical principles of scheduling and grading of historic buildings. The Act also introduced the concepts of urban conservation areas and protective zoning. Moreover, the Act marked a historical development in that, unlike the Antiquities Protection Act and its Italian background, most of the planning principles and procedures have been imported from British legislation and practice. Although greatly influenced by British practice, Malta's planning framework has para-doxically not adopted the critical presence and contribution of strong heritage institutions, such as English Heritage, or even policy guidance documents that have been adopted throughout the United Kingdom (Pickard, 1998).

Current national legal framework

Malta has a composite framework of institutions and legal instruments that, in varying proportions, govern the protection and conservation of the cultural heritage. There is no single legal instrument that has sole jurisdiction over heritage issues. Legal action in heritage protection matters is therefore not limited and can be initiated under any active law. Currently the three main legal instruments that have a direct bearing on cultural heritage are the *Antiquities Protection Act* (1925), the *Environment Protection Act* (1991) and the *Development Planning Act* (1992). These three instruments lay down definitions of heritage as well as the different levels of control and intervention available to government where necessary protective action is required. While the Antiquities Act and the Environment Act have a pro-heritage perspective, the Development Planning Act is primarily devoted to promote and regulate development.

The Antiquities Protection Act (1925) is primarily devoted to safeguarding cultural heritage. The Act defines the regulatory role and responsibilities of the state in matters related to the sale or exportation of art or archaeological objects, demolition or alteration of historic buildings in case of development, the regulation of excavation and the publication of a list of protected monuments. The Act established operational responsibilities that are vested in the Minister in charge of heritage, the Director of Museums and an Antiquities Committee – which is chaired by the Director of Museums. The Antiquities Committee was entrusted with the formulation of advice on heritage matters; this advice was to be given to the Minister responsible for heritage assets. As the Antiquities Committee has not been instituted since 1992, responsibility currently resides with the Minister who exercises authority through the Director of Museums. Although dating to 1925, the Antiquities Protection Act does not contradict the Granada or

Malta Conventions. However, while the Act does in fact fulfil a number of articles of the conventions, the law does not cover the innovative cultural heritage management principles that have developed internationally since 1925 and which were enshrined in the Council of Europe's documents. In spite of a number of amendments, the Antiquities Protection Act remains very much tied to the structures that were formulated 70 years ago in 1925.

The Environment Act (1991) was designed to place heritage in its broader environmental context. In a sense, this principle is reflected in the envisaged composite framework of Council of Europe Conventions, including the Granada and Malta documents, should the draft European Landscape Convention on the management and protection of the landscape become effective in the future. Technically, the Environment Act combines a limited selection of a number of provisions of the Antiquities Protection Act in a new framework that also protects the natural environment. The Act incorporated the regulation of excavations, exportation and conservation. The Act provides for the publication of listed buildings and monuments. For the first time, the Environment Act introduced the protection and conservation of historic centres. The Act was not extensive enough to enable the repealing of the Antiquities Protection Act which, therefore, has not been repealed. In many ways, the articles of the Environment Protection Act concerning the heritage can be considered to be complimentary to the principles of the Antiquities Protection Act.

The Development Planning Act (1992) established a proper planning process and operational structures to deal with development control. The Act is significant because it established a central Planning Authority and development control mechanisms and bodies. The Act provides for drawing up of policies, a Structure Plan as well as a series of subject, local and action plans. The Act also lays down application procedures for development, the decision-making process, as well as appeals. The Development Planning Act therefore treats heritage conservation within the broader context of development control. The Act lays down important articles that establish the listing and graded scheduling of monuments and conservation areas.

National operational framework
The three national legal instruments cover areas that can fall under the responsibility of different Ministries, depending on the formation of Ministerial or Cabinet portfolios. Currently, the areas broadly covered by the three legal instruments fall under the Ministries of Education, Environment and that for the Interior respectively. These Ministries are in turn responsible for a number of departments and agencies. The Ministries for Education and that for the Interior are each responsible for a single institution (the Museums Department, in the case of the former, and the Planning Authority, in the case of the latter). While the Museums Department is a government agency, the Planning Authority is an autonomous body. In contrast, the Ministry for the Environment is responsible for the *Restoration Unit* (a government department) and three semi-autonomous

Rehabilitation Committees that operate within the walled cities of Valletta, Mdina and the Cottonera (the 'three Cities'). The Rehabilitation Committees combine a number of executive and policy design functions.

Other government departments and high level offices can have direct or indirect impact on cultural heritage. The most important of these are the Lands Department (the state agency responsible for state properties of all ages), and the Housing Authority (the state agency with executive and policy functions on housing, often in historic town centres). There are also numerous state agencies and departments that are housed in historic buildings or that have some bearing on heritage resources.

The role of the Museums Department in the field of heritage is two-fold: that of undertaking superintendence functions and that of operating heritage resources such as museums and sites. The department is legally bound to step in and take any necessary remedial action in case of infringement of legal provisions in the case of development that affects monuments and historic buildings. To do so, the department follows two autonomous but related activities. The first is the formulation of responses to consultation requests from the Planning Authority. The second is autonomous action, often consisting of legal proceedings that are deemed necessary for the preservation and conservation of heritage resources. The department carries out such activities without the Antiquities Committee, which has not been constituted since 1992.

In the case of the Planning Authority, the Development Planning Act lays down provisions for the establishment and functioning of a number of bodies. These include the Planning Authority itself, which is convened on a regular basis. The Act also regulates the establishment of a Development Control Commission. The Planning Authority and the Development Control Commission are serviced by a Planning Directorate. The Act supports independent bodies, namely, the Planning Consultative Commission and the Appeals Board. The planning framework has been designed to guarantee independence of component bodies. In heritage matters, applications involving or having an impact on heritage assets are treated through the established development control procedures. However, the Planning Directorate has made sure that heritage matters are dealt with internally by an Environment Management Unit and a Heritage Advisory Committee. These bodies remain internal components of the Planning Directorate and submissions regarding protection and development are subject to planning control procedures through the scrutiny of development applications.

The Restoration Unit of the Environment Ministry operates entirely in the field of architectural conservation. The unit tackles specific projects related to the conservation and restoration of historic buildings and monuments. Being operational in nature, the remit of the Restoration Unit is therefore clearly specified and has no legal bearing on the superintendence or regulation of heritage resources. The Ministry also includes within its structures three Rehabilitation Committees that operate entirely in the designated walled city areas: Valletta (Figs 11.2 and 11.3), the Cottonera area and Mdina (Fig. 11.4). The committees have broad functions that are

Fig. 11.2 Aerial view of Valletta, Malta's modern capital. Built ex novo in the sixteenth century, Valletta an excellent example of Renaissance and Baroque urban form. The illustration clearly displays the tightly packed urban landscape characterizing the Maltese islands.

Fig 11.3 St John's Street i Valletta – an early twentie century photograph of one the approaches to the Valletta harbour, showing lively community life that still characterized Malta's historic towns prior to the 1950s.

limited to specific actions, management plans and other initiatives related to urban embellishment and conservation. Like the Restoration Unit, the Rehabilitation Committees have purely advisory and operational functions with no bearing superintendence.

In spite of this composite operational framework, there is currently no legally defined mechanism that binds or co-ordinates these various bodies

Fig. 11.4 A characteristic medieval urban streetscape in Mdina.

in a common working framework. Interaction depends on *ad hoc* measures or legal obligations defined in existing legislation in matters that mostly concern development. Development applications, even those affecting historic monuments, are made to the Planning Authority which has the power to exert selective consultation with state agencies or non-governmental organizations (NGOs). In effect, therefore, the only channel open for consultative functions is that of development control, which is the over-riding remit of the Planning Authority.

International conventions

Malta is also party to a number of international conventions related to the protection of the cultural heritage. In particular, Malta has ratified the Council of Europe *Convention on the Protection of the Architectural Heritage* (1985 – the Granada Convention) and the European *Convention on the Protection of the Archaeological Heritage* (revised) (1992 – the Malta Convention signed in Valetta).

The archipelago is also party to the UNESCO *Convention Concerning the Protection of the World Cultural Heritage* (1972 – the World Heritage Convention). Malta has been an active participant in the proceedings of the World Heritage Committee. The country has three sites on the World Heritage List: a composite listing of five separate megalithic sites representing a single cultural phenomenon (Tarxien – Fig. 11.5, Hagar Qim, Mnajdra, Ta' Hagrat and Ggantija), the Hal Saflieni Hypogeum and the fortified city of Valletta (Fig. 11.6).

Fig.11.5 The megalithic site of Tarxien, part of a composite listing of five separate sites designated a World Heritage Sites by UNESCO. (Photograph: Council of Europe.)

Fig. 11.6 Verdelin Palace one of the more spectacular examples of baroque art applied to the Maltese urban architectural fabric and located within the UNESCO designated World Heritage Site of the fortified city of Valletta.

Definition of the heritage

The Maltese legal system provides direct and indirect definitions of heritage. Because Malta has three legal instruments that regulate activities surrounding cultural assets, it follows that the definition of heritage is a composite matter. The three Acts do, however, complement one another and provide a broad definition framework.

The Antiquities Protection Act (1925) defines 'monuments and other objects whether movable or immovable having geological, palaeontological, archaeological, antiquarian or artistic importance' as being those objects older than 50 years. By virtue of the Act, this broad all-encompassing definition can technically be narrowed by actual identification of assets through published listing of assets (article 6) which however, does not exclude non-listed heritage resources (article 6 (5)).

Definitions in the Environment Protection Act (1991) follow closely those of the Antiquities Act with the difference that the all-encompassing principle is extended to establish heritage as part of the human environment. In the Act environment is defined as 'the whole of the elements and conditions, natural and man-made, existing on earth, and in particular . . . (e) the landscape, taken to mean both open country, village and town aspect, (f) the cultural and historical element'. Historically, the Environment Protection Act was the first to parallel closely the principles of the Granada Convention. Like the Antiquities Protection Act, the Environment Protection Act has provisions for the identification of heritage assets through published listing.

The Development Planning Act (1992) adopted the all-encompassing philosophy used in previous Acts. The Development Planning Act, however, refers to a process of scheduling. Similar to the Environment Protection Act, but distinctly different from the Antiquities Protection Act, the Development Planning Act extends definitions geographically and spatially to include areas. The definition contained in this Act (article 46 (1)) is therefore not focused entirely on the individual monument. It states that the Planning Authority shall prepare 'a list of areas, buildings, structures and remains of geological, palaeontological, archaeological, architectural, historical, antiquarian or artistic importance, as well as areas of natural beauty, ecological or scientific value . . . which are to be scheduled for conservation.' As in the case of the Environment Protection Act, the Development Planning Act provides a legal framework that conforms to the Granada Convention and the later Malta Convention.

Depending on the choice of legal instruments, heritage assets can be safeguarded as individual buildings, sites or monuments as well as assemblages or composite sites as defined in Article 1 of the Granada Convention and Article 1 (3) of the Malta Convention. In particular, the Development Planning Act enables groups of historic or archaeological monuments or buildings to be collectively listed as conservation areas with boundaries that are map based and legally binding. Conservation areas are mostly applied to historic urban centres, but the principle is extendable to rural areas where composite sites, combining the works of man and nature, are more evident. The conservation area principle enables stricter control on such elements as streetscapes and urban aesthetics apart from the problems related to structural deterioration and architectural conservation. In the case of non-urban monuments and ensembles, the principle of conservation areas is applied to tracts of landscape that may include archaeological monuments or historical assemblages such as rural settings. Such areas may also be designated parks, an example being the World Heritage Sites of Hagar Qim, Mnajdra and Ggantija. The walled Cittadella, on Gozo, has been scheduled along with the entire hill on top of which this town is located. In many instances, monument or architectural groups can be given protective buffer zones. These zones help fortify protection levels.

Planning legislation enables buildings to be protected at various levels. Although in principle graded buildings are protected *in toto*, there have been instances where façadism has been allowed as a form of compromise. Scheduling or listing has followed Core Data principles, yet unlike practice in the United Kingdom, very little attention has been given to building interiors. The Planning Authority's Heritage Advisory Committee holds regular weekly inspections in order to tender advice on the interior of historic or scheduled buildings for which development applications have been submitted. Such inspections often include open spaces, such as grounds or gardens, belonging to 'inspected' properties. Where large private gardens are concerned, protection can be augmented through the designation of an urban conservation areas. Within historic town centres, designated urban conservation areas restrict, but do not exclude, development. This means that such areas offer a higher level of protection through more detailed attention of development applications.

Graded listing of buildings and archaeological sites

Individual buildings and monuments can be scheduled under the provisions of the Development Planning Act. The grading of buildings is at three levels (1, 2 and 3) depending on a number of factors. In the main part, considerations for grading levels are based on the significant value of a building (for example a historic parish church, a palace or cathedral), history, architectural features, aesthetic qualities and so on. While the historical elements of a building influences grading, age is not an over-riding parameter. Several early twentieth-century buildings have in fact been listed in certain areas, such as Sliema, that have also been designated urban conservation areas. The Structure Plan for the Maltese Islands (1992) identifies the grading levels and their description provides a clear indication of the levels of protection (Structure Plan, 1992: 88).

• *Grade 1*: Buildings of outstanding architectural or historical interest that shall be preserved in their entirety. Demolition or alterations, which impair the setting or change the external or internal appearance, including anything contained within the curtilage of the building, will not be allowed. Any interventions allowed must be directed to their scientific restoration and rehabilitation. Internal alterations will only be allowed in exceptional circumstances where this is paramount for reasons of keeping the building in active use.
• *Grade 2*: Buildings of some architectural or historical interest which contribute to the visual image of an Urban Conservation Area. Permission to demolish such a building will not normally be given. Alterations to the interior will be allowed if proposed to be carried out sensitively

and causing the least detriment to the character and architectural homogeneity of the building.

• *Grade 3*: Buildings which have no historical importance and are of relatively minor architectural interest. Demolition may be permitted provided the replacement building is in harmony with its surroundings.

The concept of the Grade 2 level is currently being revised, an undertaking parallel to developments in the United Kingdom.

In the case of archaeological heritage, another grading system is provided for in the Structure Plan (1992: 102). Scheduling of archaeological sites and monuments follows the same system as that used for historic buildings and conservation areas. In certain cases, the local context of certain arch-aeological monuments makes scheduling and related conservation decision-making more difficult and less clear cut. Examples of such situations are the numerous underground monuments, such as the World Heritage Site of the Hypogeum and various early Christian catacombs, all of which lie underneath urban centres that in most cases qualify for lesser grading levels. There are, therefore, several areas of conflict in which the decisions regarding surface re-development of early twentieth-century Grade 3 buildings may not be compatible with the Class A grading for underground archaeological sites. The Hypogeum underlying streets and turn of the century housing blocks at Paola, and numerous catacombs in the Rabat area present such a dilemma.

In the non-urban areas, archaeology presents less of a technical problem in that protective buffer zones, that can also be augmented by the designation of rural conservation areas and coastal areas, provide added protection to scheduled monuments.

The grading levels for archaeological heritage are indicated in the Structure Plan for the Maltese Islands (1992: 102) and are as follows:

• *Class A*: Top priority conservation. No development to be allowed which would adversely affect the natural setting of these monuments or sites. A minimum buffer zone of at least 100m around the periphery of the site to be established in which no development is allowed.
• *Class B*: Very important and to be preserved at all costs. Adequate measures to be taken to preclude any damage from immediate develop-ment.
• *Class C*: Every effort must be made for preservation, but may be covered up after proper investigation, documentation and cataloguing. Provision for subsequent access shall be provided.
• *Class D*: Belonging to a type known from numerous other examples. To be properly recorded and catalogued before covering or destroying.

Although there are similarities between the grading system for the archi-tectural heritage and that for archaeological sites, the respective systems also reflect marked differences. For instance the grading of archaeological monuments and sites automatically assumes, in the highest grade, geographical dimensions to protection. This principle is absent in the case of graded buildings. Class B grading is designed to focus on the immediate archaeological monument, thereby implying that development can take place in the vicinity. In cases such as that of the Hypogeum, this principle presents contradictory perspectives to grading a World Heritage Site which underlies the building area. Class C presents a compromise approach to protection, with a 'planning gain' being made by allowing surface development and protection of underlying archaeological remains. Class D enables destruction, the planning gain being represented solely by records. This particular grade can lead to controversial decisions in that it technically allows the destruction of archaeological sites on the principle that numerous other examples exist. Such a principle is not applied to architectural monuments and buildings where the quantity of examples is not the primary decision-making criteria.

Conservation areas

The Development Planning Act provides for the designation of various types of conservation areas. Scheduled buildings and monuments can also be located within designated conservation areas. The principle of a conservation area is therefore that of safeguarding the spatial dimension as well as the localized or individual monuments, buildings, sites or features. In the case of Urban Conservation Areas, the main aim is the preservation and enhancement of buildings, spaces (gardens, squares, etc.) townscapes and streetscapes (Structure Plan, 1992: 88–90). Although the accent is on a level of architectural protection, urban conservation areas provide a 'carpet cover' protective measure for component buildings. Policy UCO 4 of the Structure Plan (1992) states that all buildings in urban conservation areas and village cores are to be treated as listed buildings of architectural and historic interest. The policy also establishes a 'presumption against the demolition of any building of Architectural or Historical interest' within such designated areas.

Non-urban areas can be protected by designated Rural Conservation Areas (Structure Plan, 1992: 92–3). It is within such areas that numerous archaeological sites are located. Rural conservation areas have the same legal force of other designated conservation areas, the main difference being the context that rural conservation areas propose to protect. Marine Conservation Areas provide yet another protective dimension especially in areas where archaeological sites are located in coastal zones or on the seabed (Structure Plan 1992: 103–7).

Identification of the heritage

The Antiquities Protection Act (1925), the Environment Protection Act (1991) and the Development Planning Act (1992) all provide for the creation of inventories (article 6(2)). During the 1930s, the Museums Department had published a list of protected monuments. The list was very limited and was never revised or augmented. Given the limited extent of the list, heritage protection action has traditionally been taken on the basis of article 6(5) which provides cover for monuments that were technically not listed, but nevertheless possessed value in terms of the legally defined heritage assets. No listing has ever been undertaken under the provisions of the Environment Protection Act.

Since 1992, the Planning Authority has undertaken to compile and publish a list of scheduled monuments and sites as provided for in the Development Planning Act. This new listing has been undertaken in a more systematic manner with along lines that are very close to the Core Data Capture System as prescribed in Recommendation No. R (95) 3. The system adopted by the Planning Authority has the added advantage that recording is also carried out on a Geographical Information System (GIS). Furthermore, in the case of archaeological monuments and conservation areas, map-based indication of the designated protected areas or scheduled monuments are published in the official *Government Gazette* as required under article 46 of the Development Planning Act (1992). Present day scheduling of monuments is therefore legally binding.

Currently, scheduling or listing forms part of the responsibilities of the Planning Authority. Scheduling criteria are closely linked to the previously indicated grading levels and definitions of heritage as expressed in the three legal instruments. The scheduling process is clearly stipulated in the Development Planning Act. Following identification, including basic on-site assessment in cases of lesser-known monuments, site nominations are examined by the Planning Directorate and the Heritage Advisory Committee prior to publishing in the *Government Gazette*. Article 46(1) of the Development Planning Act (1992) directs the Planning Authority to inform property owners of scheduling. By virtue of article 46(8) of the same Act, owners can demand a reconsideration of property scheduling, conservation orders or other requests imposed by the Planning Authority.

Unlisted properties can be protected through the issue of Emergency Conservation Orders that have a legal life span of 6 months. While bestowing the same status of listed properties on endangered buildings, Emergency Conservation Orders allow sufficient time for properties to be nominated for scheduling. Conservation Orders as well as Emergency Conservation Orders come into effect after publishing in the *Government Gazette*.

To date, the Planning Authority scheduling exercise has listed about 10,000 buildings following systematic field assessments in selected towns and villages. Historic centres have received primary attention. Around 300 archaeological sites have been listed. The Structure Plan (1992) further indicates a number of conservation areas in various parts of the Maltese islands and its towns.

The preservation and protection of the heritage

The three main legal instruments concerning heritage protection and management provide a composite framework of policies and legislative procedures for the preservation and protection of cultural assets. The legal instruments can technically be used independently or together.

Article 6(1) of the Antiquities Protection Act (1925) stipulates that development involving historic buildings or antiquities requires permission

from the Minister in charge of heritage assets. The Act stipulates that
ministerial approval is required in cases where demolition or alteration is
requested. For the purposes of regulating procedures, the Act provides for
the creation of a published list of protected sites and monuments. The list
does not diminish the importance of non-listed monuments, which are
technically subject to ministerial approval (article 6(5)). Prior to its dis-
banding in 1992, the Antiquities Committee examined and tendered advice
on development applications. By virtue of article 7 of the Antiquities Act,
the Church is exonerated from the provisions of the Act. Development in
ecclesiastical property is, however, subject to a Church-appointed board
following approval of the Minister. Article 10 of the Act empowers government to carry out necessary work in order to safeguard buildings, sites or
monuments owned by private owners.

The Environment Protection Act (1991) is slightly looser in matters
concerning development applications involving buildings and monuments.
The Act does however make provisions for Environment Impact Assessments to be carried out where projects are concerned (articles 39–43). The
terms of reference for such impact assessments include considerations of
historical heritage.

The Development Planning Act (1992) takes a different approach by
submitting all development applications to a standard regime. On considering applications however, the Planning Authority places special attention on
scheduled buildings and monuments as well as conservation areas. In
particular article 46(3) and 46(4) prohibit or restrict development,
demolition, alteration or similar activity in scheduled buildings. Remedial
action included in article 46 consists of the issue of a Conservation Order
or even a Stop Notice as stipulated in article 52. Conservation Orders may
include the imposition of any remedial action and conservation measures
that the Planning Authority may consider necessary for the protection of a
listed building or monument. In the case of non-listed heritage assets the
Act provides, under article 47, for the issue of an Emergency Conservation
Order. With an expiry date of 6 months, an Emergency Conservation Order
allows sufficient time for formal listing as well as the imposition of
necessary conservation measures. The Development Planning Act does not
distinguish between historic buildings, archaeological sites, monuments and
other sites in the application of development control procedures as
stipulated in articles related to heritage protection.

Preservation and protection policy guidance
The Development Planning Act as well as Structure Plan policies are not
averse to the re-use of listed historic buildings or the re-use of buildings in
conservation areas. The graded schedule or listing system lays down
restriction parameters and conditions within which changes could possibly
be allowed after careful consideration. This regulatory structure also serves
as a policy framework. Since the introduction of Urban Conservation
Areas, there developed new pressures related to demolition and alterations
within historic building areas. Restrictions on urban sprawl have added

further pressure and demand for the reutilization of buildings within historic centres. The Planning Authority's Design Guidance on *Development Control Within Urban Conservation Areas* (1995) spells out a clear policy direction towards an evolutionary approach to the conservation of urban centres. This identifies that 'evolutionary changes such as the reuse and adaptation of historical buildings, the provision of community facilities . . . are not only desirable but necessary to sustain livability within the village and town context. So long as change is generated from within and is compatible with the historical continuum, then the evolutionary process is a healthy and progressive one.'

The pressures on managing such an evolution are inevitably strong. Requests for demolition of houses, in-filling of gap spaces, façade and interior alterations, the construction of additional floors, the use of non-traditional materials and others have had several negative results. Among these, the loss of traditional social spaces – such as town and village squares as well as gardens – to demolition, street widening and similar development are most evident. These problems have led to a severe deterioration of the quality of street and townscapes.

It is because of such factors that severe steps have had to be established at planning policy levels. Thus, any form of alteration to or demolition of Grade 1 buildings is prohibited under Structure Plan Policy UCO 7. The same policy states that while normally excluding demolition, alterations to the interiors of Grade 2 buildings could be considered if proposals still respect the character and architectural homogeneity of buildings. In this case, however, alterations to architectural features such as staircases, mouldings, barrel vaults, stone carvings, etc. are prohibited. It is only in the case of Grade 3 buildings that the prospect of demolition becomes easier, 'provided that replacement is in harmony with its surroundings'. All in all however, the Structure Plan declares a presumption against demolition (policy UCO 9), thus giving urban conservation areas more stability.

Where interior alterations or demolition are to be permitted within the context of the grading policy, the *Development Control Within Urban Conservation Areas* (1995) stresses a number of important criteria that have to be followed in assessing development applications related to historic buildings. Applications for demolition will entail a clear exposition of such factors as the state of a building's repair, fabric or structural deterioration, sanitation, levels of lighting, external and internal features and other significant elements. Should demolition be allowed to proceed, the Planning Authority retains overall powers to exert restrictions on building height, alignments, architectural features where the preservation of street and townscapes require priority consideration.

Finally, issues related to the re-use of conservation areas and historic buildings for commercial, residential, cultural and tourism purposes retain a foremost position in development considerations. A number of urban centres, Valletta being the most important one, are the focal point of state administration, commerce and tourism. Such factors have created a number of imbalances leading to some areas becoming lifeless. While Structure Plan

Policies (Policies COM 1–COM 3) discourage commercial and administrative re-use in favour of the residential and cultural use of historic buildings and conservation areas, such measures depend on the development of
adequate facilities and infrastructure outside protected areas.

Conservation philosophy

Recourse to an applicable conservation philosophy is a fairly recent
development in Malta. The archipelago does not posses a long tradition of
conservation philosophy based on established practice, schools of thought
or written policies. Prior to 1992 and the enactment of the Development
Planning Act, policy making and execution depended on the committee
framework that was supported by the existing legislation. The Planning
Areas Permit Board (PAPB), the Aesthetics Board and the Antiquities
Committee in addition to other boards brought together leading professionals and practitioners in a decision-making process involving development matters. In effect, conservation measures have traditionally been
isolated from broader development concerns, which themselves were devoid
of any clear strategy. The general policy of treating cases on their own
merits meant that development as well as protection measures were a piece
meal affair. The period after World War I in particular led to a steady decay
of the traditional morphology of historic town and city centres. The causes
were not limited to development pressure. The substitution of traditional
building materials and idioms by modern ones, the abandonment of characteristic features such as mouldings or wooden balconies and the introduction of new building specifications that distorted streetscapes or skylines led
to an overall degradation of traditional built-up areas. The negative effect
was by no means negligible and everywhere the quality of the environment
had 'deteriorated significantly in comparison with what it used to be, and
with the equivalent standards in Europe' (Structure Plan, 1992: 5).

The introduction of new planning legislation and the Structure Plan in
1992 meant that such problems could be addressed in a radical manner even
though results could realistically be felt on a long-term basis. The plan sets
forth a framework within which a broader philosophy of rehabilitation can
be put into practice (Structure Plan, 1992: 8). At the heart of this philosophy, such elements as the re-vitalization of historic centres, the conservation of valuable urban fabric, the introduction of grants, public sector
investment and other fiscal measures all bear the hallmarks of integrated
conservation policies.

The 1992 planning legislation also introduced the principle of urban
conservation areas, scheduling in addition to conservation orders a framework that governed individual development applications. Although still
considered on their own merits, development applications are therefore
considered within a policy framework as well as an urban-environmental
context.

Finally, the 1990s witnessed a radical shift in sensibilities and awareness
to the needs of Malta's built and natural environment. Historically, this
decade has seen a sharp rise in the number of new professions related to a

number of academic and scientific fields, following the complete restructuring of Malta's only university. The positive impact this had on a wide range of sectors occurred within a relatively short time-span with a number of specialist services being made available. This has made it possible for such activities as policy design and Environment Impact Assessments to be carried out on a sounder basis with the participation of planners, environmentalists, archaeologists and other professionals. The use of international conventions, charters and standards related to conservation therefore became more widespread. The government became more aware of the urgent need to draw up new legal instruments. Within the space of a few months between 1991 and 1992, the Maltese government enacted a new environment bill, ushered in a Development Planning Act and published a nationwide Structure Plan, and hosted the signing of the Malta Convention on the protection of the archaeological heritage. It was therefore inevitable that following such developments, legislation, planning procedures and several other operations related to safeguarding the heritage came into line with international thinking on such issues as integrated conservation, restoration and protection (Pace, 1999a).

Sanctions and coercive measures

Maltese legislation offers a number of alternative forms of sanctions and coercive measures. Under current Development Planning legislation, initial measures are in many ways implied in the general requirement for development to be preceded by a formal application.

The principle of state intervention in the safeguarding of heritage can be traced to the Antiquities Protection Act of 1925. The introduction of fines and the possibility of imprisonment established a deterrent against offences involving the heritage. However, the powers of the act were not limited to inflicting penalties. Under the provisions of the act, offenders are liable to reinstate the damaged, altered or demolished parts of historic buildings. Furthermore the act gives the state the right of preference in the acquisition of cultural property for reasons of protection. Expropriation legislation extends these powers through other legal instruments.

Such principles are similarly enshrined in the Development Planning Act of 1992. Apart from submitting all development to an application procedure, the act also provides for immediate and timely action in cases of contravention. The Act in fact establishes a broad time framework for protective action. Long-term precautions are embedded in the concept of scheduling, which, apart from providing a basic inventory of listed properties, provides a policy framework for development consideration. Short-term action is supported by Conservation Orders as well as Emergency Conservation Orders. Such orders can often include preventative and remedial action as may be deemed necessary for protective purposes. The act enables 'stop works' procedures to be followed where unauthorized development takes place. 'Enforcement Notice' procedures allow for remedial action to be taken, in default of which, offenders are liable to daily fines apart from penalties incurred for general offences related to development.

As the majority of applications dealing with cultural property concern urban conservation areas, a special treatment of procedures is followed. Development applications involving historic centres and scheduled properties have to be accompanied by a detailed 'Method Statement'. This requires details to be provided regarding the history of subject buildings or monuments, the presence of particular features, a condition survey form, and a preamble to outline proposals of intended works and a detailed implementation schedule. Thus, such applications have to outline, for example, technical aspects involving cleaning methods for building fabrics and materials, the extent of materials to be replaced, any proposed chemical treatment as well as the installation of services. Policy guidelines 'Access for All', dictate the user-friendly aspect of buildings that would allow access to persons with special requirements. These requirements must be considered along with the method statement accompanying development applications. The process of submitting a method statement with development applications presupposes a degree of technical dialogue, which is itself an important method of detailed control, standard setting and monitoring.

Integrated conservation

The enactment of the Development Planning Act of 1992 led to an integrated policy framework for planning processes. The framework includes several policies covering conservation that vary in the level of applicability and context. Nevertheless, while the act embodies principles of policy integration, its main focus remains the proper regulation of development and not integrated conservation. Conservation concerns form part of broader planning processes with conservation principles being applied mostly to listed buildings and designated conservation areas. In practice, planning control within such designated areas is not conducted on the principle of a holistic policy of integrated conservation, but rather on the status of individual monuments and properties within the framework of listed properties or areas requiring protection.

Although the concept of a unified policy of integrated conservation has not been overtly adopted at a national state level, several principal elements of Resolution (76) 28 (on the application of Integrated Conservation) have been enshrined in the Development Planning Act and the Structure Plan. In particular, the development of 'Local Plans' and the management of Urban Conservation Areas (Policy and Design Guidance 3, *The Planning Fact Book*), has enabled government to adopt a more holistic approach to conservation. This policy guidance establishes the need for an evolutionary process of change that enables a steady rehabilitation of historic urban centres. The 1990s have seen a growing tendency for historic properties to be rehabilitated as individual dwellings. This phenomenon, in the most part supported and promoted by real estate interests in the sale of character houses, has led to a change in the perception of the historic significance of town centres. These changing social trends have in turn acquired wider political attention, with local authorities turning their attention to embellishment programmes and other initiatives.

Policy Design Guidance 3 is the first coherent attempt to bring together a concerted approach to planning processes within Urban Conservation Areas. The policy document seeks to control demolition and actively promote protective measures for the safeguarding of monuments and historic properties. The policy outlines restrictions on the alteration of façades, balconies and other elements of the architectural heritage. The document emphasizes the need to halt the deterioration of the urban context by means of discordant aesthetic qualities, the deterioration of design standards, the use of inappropriate materials and fabrics. Mindful of the need for there to be a rehabilitation of historic properties, the policy document outlines principles of a 'Method Statement' which is a pre-requisite for development application within urban centres. The Method Statement is designed to be a document containing proposed alterations to interiors as well as a historic document recording such changes for eventual inclusion in the state National Archive. The policy also stresses guidelines with regards to such aspects as shop fronts, street furniture, signage, the enhancement or re-introduction of traditional street paving, the protection of urban fabric, restrictions on land use as well as traffic management. In effect, therefore, the policy design guidance document supports a decision-making process aimed at enhancing the exterior character of urban centres together with a policy of building rehabilitation and protection. In the absence of a fully developed approach to the revitalization of urban centres, Policy Design Guidance 3 goes a long way to support a healthy balance between preservation and social development in historic centres.

Financial resources, funding mechanisms and the regeneration of historic environments

By far the largest allocation of financial resources for conservation initiatives is that available to the national government. Grant schemes are still very limited and at an experimental stage. These deal mainly with the restoration and re-integration of traditional wooden balconies. Indirect funding opportunities are available for private property owners especially through special interest rate schemes that support property rehabilitation. Although not specifically designed for conservation schemes, a system of bank loans is available for the purchase or upgrading of dwellings and home ownership schemes.

Where state funding is concerned, this is normally concentrated on the conservation or maintenance of public buildings of an historical nature. Such initiatives are taken at the level of ministries or departments, being the main bodies using public buildings. Conservation initiatives mostly follow *ad hoc* decisions and are building specific.

Increasingly, local authorities are turning their attention to enhancing the historic fabric and spaces located within council boundaries. Street paving projects, traffic taming schemes and the enhancement of public areas are becoming more important in local government agendas and are proving to be of great benefit to urban conservation areas. Such initiatives are enabling community investment in embellishment and preservation projects. Such schemes are beginning to attract a degree of private support.

Finally, the Maltese government has established a limited number of rehabilitation projects which are focused on Valletta (a UNESCO World Heritage City), the Cottonera area (comprising three Baroque walled cities) and Mdina (the seat of Melita, Malta's ancient capital). The projects are run on a long-term committee basis in which specific actions and initiatives are normally taken. Being funded entirely by the state, these rehabilitation projects also tend to concentrate mostly on historic public buildings, common public spaces, gardens and monuments.

The role of agencies and specialist organizations

The role of agencies and specialist organizations is somewhat limited due mainly to the paucity of such bodies and also, to the objectives of the few active organizations. Agencies and organizations fall mainly into three categories: state departments, professional bodies and NGOs (non-governmental organizations).

The principal state bodies having a direct involvement in conservation are the Planning Authority, the Museums Department and the Restoration Unit in the Department of Works. While the Planning authority plays the role of development regulator, the Restoration Unit is mainly an operating agency focused on the conservation of historic public buildings. The Museums Department has the dual role of regulator and operator.

The main professional body having direct links to conservation issues is the Chamber of Architects. The role of the Chamber is mostly directed towards the regulation of Architectural and Civil Engineering standards and professional interests. The Chamber interfaces in the main with the Planning Authority, other professional bodies and educational institutions.

NGOs represent a mixture of roles. Two leading trusts often undertake and fund conservation projects, but these are normally directed towards buildings that fall outside urban conservation areas. Typically, such NGOs focus their efforts on military installations, historic towers and small monuments. NGOs also act as 'watch-dogs' raising public awareness and communicating policy positions to the Planning Authority and other government bodies.

Education and training

Training in conservation and planning skills has traditionally been extremely limited in Malta. Significant changes have occurred since 1987, as the revitalization of Malta's only university increased the number of professionals operating in the field of conservation and planning. The Malta University now runs academic courses in the conservation of fabrics, planning and restoration. Other important areas such as archaeology, anthropology and art history are also being catered for. The graduate output of the university is supplemented by a number of professionals who seek specializations in foreign institutions. Over a decade of sustained growth in the tertiary education sector is now having a significant positive impact on the conservation and protection of the cultural heritage. This impact has been registered at various levels, be they purely academic and technical or, more importantly, at the level of policy development. Other important developments emerged from this process of broader skill development. Certain institutions, such as the building restoration unit, have been re-vitalized (for example, as the Restoration Unit within the Works Division in the Environment Ministry). Within the Ministry of Education, a Centre for Restoration Studies has also been established with the primary aim of conferring higher diplomas, degrees and certificates in restoration studies. These two initiatives will no doubt contribute further to the development of professional skills at higher and technical levels.

A post script: towards legislative reform

Over a decade of sustained planning policy development and the enactment of the Development Planning Act in 1992 have led to significant changes in Malta. Equally drastic have been the numerous changes that have been witnessed in Malta's heritage sector throughout the twentieth century, especially since 1910 and 1925 when the first legal instruments regulating heritage protection were enacted. The institutionalization of heritage management and the status of heritage are rapidly gaining more and more attention at the political level.

The nature of Malta's heritage management has also changed throughout this century. The establishment of the Museums Department, the enactment of the Antiquities Protection Act (1925) and other developments preceded such phenomena as post-war industrial activity, urban spread and development, mass tourism and cultural tourism. While the establishment of the Museums Department in 1903 encompassed the regulation of the archipelago's antiquities, the institution developed very little beyond its original operational structure to cater for the profound social and economic changes that took place throughout the entire span of the twentieth century (Pace, 1999b; Mallia, 2000; Schembri, 2000).

At another level international charters and legal instruments have raised standards and obligations on several states across the globe. In many ways, these developments have placed new legal obligations on Malta. At the same time, the archipelago's Structure Plan has been submitted for public and institutional consultation as part of a revision process.

In the year 2000 Malta has to contend with different parameters and responsibilities. The nature and extent of Malta's cultural heritage assets and their place in society are now perceived differently (Boissevain, 2000). On the one hand, perceptions now depend on how values are bestowed on heritage by different social groups. Values themselves are not static, for their evolution through time is a cultural construct which changes from one generation to another (de la Torres and McLean, 1997). While meaning and significance of heritage change through time, it is the responsibility of the state to ensure that cultural values retain a social significance. For Malta, the manner in which seemingly competing values of cultural heritage contribute to the country's sense of cultural identity is gaining greater public and sectoral attention (Pace, 2000).

These changes have raised several concerns regarding the need for reform of Malta's heritage sector (Pace, 1999b). In spite of much progress in various areas, an institutional imbalance has been perceived in the current state of heritage management (Pickard, 1998). Improved practices and policy development in the field of conservation and heritage protection need to be augmented by other changes so that the concept of development planning can be further supported by independent heritage management institutions. In this regard, the year 2000 will see two important developments taking place within Malta's Planning Authority and the Museums Department. In the case of both institutions, legal as well as operational reform will be underway. These changes will, however, consolidate, rather than diminish, Malta's commitment to heritage protection. In particular, the Planning Authority has embarked a revision of the archipelago's structure plan. Coming eight years after the publication of the first Structure Plan (1992), the Planning Authority is certainly in a better position to evaluate its practices in the field of heritage. The process of revision includes consultation with institutions and NGOs working in the field of heritage. In particular, the revision of the structure plan will entail a new look at the incorporation of integrated conservation policies and how these could be put into action.

The Museums Department and the Antiquities Protection Act of 1925 are also being reviewed. A draft Heritage Act has been drawn up stipulating the establishment of a regulatory and policy making body (a Directorate of Superintendence), a separate operational agency and a Committee of Guarantee. While the operating agency will be entrusted with the day to day running of museums, sites and other heritage assets, the Superintendence Directorate will be laying down the ground rules for the entire sector. The new law provides a framework that will enable 'stakeholders' to participate in the widest possible sense (Pace and Cutajar, 1999).

At the heart of all heritage activity will be the creation and management of inventories and the active superintendence of such operations as conservation, restoration and the study of cultural property. The provision of access to cultural heritage is also enshrined in the new law. In essence the basic principles underlying many heritage site management policies have been transformed into fundamental legal instruments. The new legislation empowers the Superintendence Directorate to prosecute court cases against heritage related offenses. Another innovation is the recognition of international conventions and charters. The new law calls upon the Minister responsible for heritage to convene a national forum on cultural heritage on an annual basis, thus ensuring that consultation will be widely and more regularly applied. As opposed to the 1925 Antiquities Protection Act, the new legislation provides a better mechanism for stronger control but at the same time, it enshrines democratic principles allowing access to culture and active dialogue.

In the preambles of the new law, the protection of Cultural Heritage is given 'priority in establishing public policy in all fields of activity in Malta whether economic or social'. This important article is designed to transpose heritage protection from the level of policy to that of executive legislation. This significant step suddenly gives a humanistic dimension to heritage protection and conservation. Traditionally, public policy has focused in the main part on other areas social concern. The principle that cultural heritage actively contributes to the quality of life and enrichment of society is steadily gaining importance.

This social element is embodied in the principle of Integrated Conservation, as defined by the Council of Europe, which attempts to 'maintain a balance between man and his traditional environment and prevent the debasement of those assets inherited from the past on which the quality of the environment largely depends' (Council of Europe, 1976).

References

Boissevain, J. (2000): 'Changing Maltese Landscape: From Utilitarian Space to Heritage', in Vella, C. (ed.), *The Maltese Islands on the Move*, Central Office of Statistics, Malta Government, Valletta.

Buhagiar, K. (1985): 'Evolution of Conservation Legislation in Malta', *The Sunday Times Building And Architecture Supplement*, Progress Press, Valletta.

Council of Europe (1976): *Resolution (76) 28 Concerning the adaptation of laws and regulations to the requirements of integrated conservation of the architectural heritage*, Strasbourg.

De la Torre and McLean, M. (1997): 'The Archaeological Heritage in the Mediterranean Region', in *The Conservation of Archaeological Sites in the Mediterranean Region*, 1995 Conference Proceedings, The Getty Conservation Institute, Los Angeles.

Mallia, E. (2000): 'The Environment: Prospects for the Millennium', in Vella, C. (ed.), *The Maltese Islands on the Move*, Central Office of Statistics, Malta Government, Valletta.

Malta Government (1910) *Ordinance VI*, Malta Government Gazette No 5270, Government Printing Press, Valletta.

Malta Government (1925): *Antiquities Protection Act*, Malta Government Gazette, Government Printing Press, Valletta.

Malta Government (1991): *Environment Protection Act*, Malta Government Gazette, Government Printing Press, Valletta.

Malta Government (1992): *The Development Planning Act*, Malta Government Gazette, Government Printing Press, Valletta.

Pace, A. (1998): 'The National Museum of Archaeology Permanent Exhibition Project', in *Vigilo* (October 1997–January 1998), Din l-Art Helwa, Valletta.

Pace, A. (1999a): 'A Common Space: The Council of Europe, Malta and the European Perspective on Cultural Heritage', in Saliba, G. (ed.), *A Council for All Seasons*. 50th Anniversary of the Council of Europe, Malta, Ministry of Foreign Affairs.

Pace, A. (1999b): *New Directions in Malta's Heritage Management*, (forthcoming publication of Calpe 1999 Conference proceedings, Gibraltar).

Pace, A. (2000): 'Cultural Heritage Values as Expressions of Identity: the Maltese Context in Vella', C. (ed.), *The Maltese Islands on the Move*, Central Office of Statistics, Malta Government, Valletta.

Pace, A. and Cutajar, N. (1999): *Report on the Situation of Urban Archaeology in Europe*, Council of Europe, Strasbourg.

Pickard, R.D. (1998): *Specific Action Plan For Malta*, Cultural Heritage Committee, Permanent Legal Task Force Legal Assistance (Technical Co-operation and Consultancy Programme), Council of Europe, Strasbourg.

Planning Authority (1995): *Development Control Within Urban Conservation Areas*, The Planning Authority, Malta.

Planning Authority (1997): *The Planning Fact Book*, Malta, The Planning Authority, Malta.

Schembri, J. (2000): 'The Changing Geography of Population and Settlement in the Maltese Islands', in Vella, C. (ed.), *The Maltese Islands on the Move*, Central Office of Statistics, Malta Government, Valletta.

Vella, C. (ed.) (2000): *The Maltese Islands on the Move*, Central Office of Statistics, Malta Government, Valletta.

Saskia Richel-Bottinga

The Netherlands

Introduction

In The Netherlands the systematic governmental care of its cultural heritage started in the second half of the nineteenth century. Victor de Stuers (1843–1916) is regarded as the founder of 'organized' conservation. Under his leadership a number of volunteers itemized and documented the most important buildings. This inventory led to the Provisional List of Dutch Monuments of Art and History (1903–33), on which the official list of historic buildings and monuments was later based.

There was a reason for this sudden interest in conservation. Many valuable old buildings had been demolished at the end of the century, because as the Industrial Revolution progressed the demand for new housing, factories and railways grew enormously. Victor de Stuers and his volunteers wanted to slow down these demolition activities and this marked the start of protection and conservation of the built heritage.

The preservation of historic buildings became a task of the national government, which set up a special Arts Department for the purpose. This department started on a systematic description of historic buildings. In 1903 the department was replaced by a National Committee headed by the well-known Dutch architect P. J. H. Cuypers. Ultimately, the Netherlands Department for Conservation was set up in 1947, with the protection and preservation of historic buildings as its foremost task. However, legislation for this task was still missing; not until 1961 was the first *Historic Buildings and Monuments Act* passed.

This Act arranged for the legal protection by the state of exceptional historic buildings and of historic sites. The Act regulated the powers of the public sector and the rules which the owner of a protected historic building must adhere to. The first Act of 1961 has been superseded by the *1988 Historic Buildings and Ancient Monuments Act*, which is still in force. There have been a few changes from the 1961 Act. Under this first act conservation was centrally controlled, whereas the 1988 Act imposes more tasks and powers on the municipalities which have been given more responsibilities and also have the task of informing and guiding owners, users and other interested parties. The task of registering protected buildings and historic sites has remained with the government.

The Ministry responsible for the protection and conservation of the Dutch cultural heritage is that of Education, Culture and Science. The work itself is done by the Department for Conservation, a governmental organization which resides under the Ministry. The Department is the central point for knowledge and research in the field of conservation. It is responsible for implementing the 1988 Historic Buildings and Ancient Monuments Act and the regulations governing subsidies. The Department does not concentrate solely on buildings but also on the protection of the historical environment, such as city and urban structures and the culturally and historically valuable landscape.

The protection of archaeological monuments is also controlled by the 1988 Act. The Netherlands Department for Archaeological Research is engaged in this respect. It nominates archaeological monuments and sites and once this is done, the monument is placed on the list of protected buildings kept by the Department for Conservation.

Definition of the heritage

Article 1 the 1988 Historic Buildings and Ancient Monuments Act defines monuments and sites as follows:

1 Objects constructed at least fifty years ago, which are of public interest because of their beauty, scientific significance or cultural and historic value (Fig. 12.1).

The article goes on to specify the difference between a monument and a protected monument. The last is recorded in the official Registers established by the Act. At the moment there are 48,474 protected monuments.

The monumental value of a protected monument can be found in the description of that object in the Register of Protected Monuments. The structure of the building is always part of that value and consists of weight-carrying parts like the foundation, walls and beams. This also applies to the floors and the outer walls and roof. The monumental value is further designated by those parts that define the architectural and historical characteristics of the building, such as gables, stoop or interior details like stucco, chimneypieces and wainscoting.

When an object is given protected status, it means that the owner has to follow the regulations laid down by the 1988 Act. The protection regime for monuments applies to the whole building, even if only a part of it is found worthwhile. It is possible to protect a building just because of the presence of a specific cornerstone. In practice this means that any alteration of the structure can take place only after a permit has been given.

Fig.12.1 Haarzuilens: Castle De Haar. Although it looks medieval, the castle was built at the end of the nineteenth century. Unfortunately the cracks in the wall are twentieth century. The castle is used as a museum and summer dwelling for the owner. (Photograph: Bert and Lilian Mellink, D-Vorm, Leidschendam, The Netherlands.)

It is also possible to protect the garden or the estate surrounding the building. In that case the historic estate will consist of the main building, the economy buildings, a stable, a hothouse and even garden vases or footbridges. Furthermore the terrain will be described, including streams, orchards and woods. This is all mentioned in the description as found in the official register.

2   Sites which are of public interest because of the presence of objects referred to under 1. Article 1 also gives a definition of a historic site: a group of immovable objects, which are of public interest because of their beauty, their spatial and structural relationship or their cultural and historical value and which includes at least one monument. This does not necessarily have to be a protected one. Public as well as private property can be part of the protected site.

If the Minister of Housing, Physical Planning and Environment and the Minister of Education, Culture and Science together designate such an area, it becomes a protected historic site after publication in the *Government Chronicle*. There are now about 340 protected sites. The total surface area is unknown. The size of such sites can range from a very small village to a large section of a city.

Archaeological monuments also come within the definition of sites and separate monuments. Most of the archaeological monuments consist of sites, but in some cases there are single objects, like dolmen or medieval basements.

Apart from protection by the government, provinces and towns can also designate monuments inside their territory. The 1988 Historic Buildings and

Ancient Monuments Act, however, does not apply to these monuments. Instead the protection is based on the municipal or provincial heritage ordinance. In practice this will follow the regulations of the 1988 Act.

Identification of the heritage

All protected monuments are recorded in the official Register of Monuments, which is kept by the Department for Conservation. This not only applies to all built objects, but also to archaeological monuments and historic sites.

Protected monuments

An object which is at least 50 years of age and meets with the other conditions of the 1988 Act can be designated as a *protected monument*. Until 1985 attention had been focused almost exclusively on the older historic buildings. The description of these buildings entailed so much work that hardly any time was left for more recent buildings. The 'younger' architecture was only incidentally designated. In 1985 a national inventory of the period 1850–1940 was started. This period is one in which enormous changes took place in The Netherlands. The pace of industrialization accelerated and with it urbanization (Fig. 12.2). Railways were laid, factories built and worker's houses erected. New materials, such as concrete, were used in the construction. New techniques were used, made possible by the use of cast iron, for example. Much of this more recent architecture still remains.

Fig.12.2 Geldrop: textile factory. The façade of the factory is to be restored and the interior will provide accommodation for a library and a cultural centre. (Photograph: Bert and Lilian Mellink, D-Vorm, Leidschendam, The Netherlands.)

Because concern was expressed about the historic buildings of this period an inventory was set up. Every town listed the buildings and other objects belonging to this period. In 1995 the inventory was completed and a start was made on the selection of national, regional and local monuments for protection. The town councils select those objects which they find of national importance. They do this in accordance with the province. Their proposal for protection is then sent to the Department for Conservation, where it is submitted to the Minister who will usually be in agreement. From the other objects a selection is made for the provincial or the municipal lists.

Before officially protecting the building all parties concerned are invited by the town council to a hearing. The Minister is at the same time advised by the council, the province and the Council for Culture. The Council for Culture is an advisory body which advises the Minister on request or otherwise about all aspects of conservation by the state. It will also submit recommendations on the designation.

After taking the decision to protect a certain object, any party which has an interest in the case can lodge an appeal. This will lead to a public hearing and the decision will be reconsidered. After that an appeal to the court is possible, sometimes followed by an appeal to the Council of State. Its decision is final.

When the building is finally protected its records are included in the official Register of protected monuments. The records consist of the address, the town, the province and the owners. Added to this are the cadastral numbers and also a description of the building. All this makes it possible to identify the monument. The Register has a legal basis and can be consulted by the public. Prints of the records can be ordered at cost price. At this moment an attempt is being made to actualize the Register.

The many data which ensued from the 1850–1940 inventory process have been published in a series of books which depict a number of exceptional and typical historic buildings in each of the twelve provinces and also in the four major cities (Amsterdam, Rotterdam, The Hague and Utrecht).

In the year 2000 the project 1850–1940 will be concluded and the next project started. This will consider the architecture of the Reconstruction period, the period when the damage caused during World War II was repaired. For this project a new policy on protection will be announced.

Sites

Sites can be designated by the Minister of Housing, Physical Planning and Environment and the Minister of Education, Culture and Science in cooperation. This is done after recommendation has been given by the town council, the province and the State Planological Committee and the Council for Culture. The public is not directly consulted, nor do they have rights of redress. The notification of the designation is published in the daily newspapers. After designation, the town council has to establish an urban zoning plan, in which the monumental values are guaranteed. The Minister has to approve zoning plans. Another way to protect sites is to have them designated as nature reserve by the Ministry of Agriculture.

Inventories of sites are made by order of the Ministers mentioned above. They contain general information on the site including buildings, landscapes and town planning. The inventories are financed by the Ministers and published as books which include a map of the designated area. A list of all protected historic sites can be obtained from the Department for Conservation.

Archaeological monuments

Archaeological monuments and sites are nominated by the Department for Archaeological Research. The same procedure is followed as for protected monuments. After designation the monument is placed on the list of protected buildings kept by the Department for Conservation.

In addition to national protection of historic or archaeological sites, an international level of protection is possible: the UNESCO World Heritage List, which can also be applied to single monuments.

The preservation and protection of the heritage

The owner of a protected monument requires a permit to restore, reconstruct or demolish of his or her property. An application must be submitted to the municipality for this. No restoration or rebuilding may be undertaken without a permit. Most Dutch towns have a heritage ordinance through which an advisory committee on heritage is appointed. These municipalities will issue the permit after recommendation by the Department for Conservation, within at least 6 months. This is a statutory limit, which can only be extended once. In cases of towns without an ordinance, the permit is issued by the Department.

After receiving the permit according to the 1988 Act, the owner then requires a permit in accordance with the Housing Act to be issued by the municipality. Both permits can be used only after six weeks, the time available for an appeal to be lodge against the permit(s). No permit is needed for regular maintenance of the building.

A permit is issued in accordance with the usage of the building. In practice this means that a building which has lost its original function, can be re-used in another way (Figs 12.3–12.5). For instance, if a church has been disposed of, it can be transformed into an apartment building without losing the monumental value it originally had. In this way it is possible for owners of factories, water towers or warehouses to restore and re-use their property.

The central government is responsible for the protection of historic sites. As legal instruments it uses the Monument and Historic Buldings Act 1988, the Urban and Village Renewal Act and the Town and Country Planning Act. The rules are laid down in the above mentioned Acts and zoning plans, authorized by the town council. The procedure is regulated in a local act on building, in accordance with the zoning plan. The rules that apply to the works are the same as those that apply for regular building permits. It is prohibited to demolish buildings in historic sites either entirely or partially without a demolition permit from the town council.

Fig.12.3 Diemen: Roman Catholic Convent, called 'The Hope', before restoration. After restoration in 1997 it is now used as a venue for exhibitions and concerts. (Photograph: Bert and Lilian Mellink, D-Vorm, Leidschendam, The Netherlands.)

Fig.12.4 Gulpen: Castle Neubourg. Used as a boarding school during World War II it is empty at the moment, but will be used for hotel accomodation in the future. (Photograph: Bert and Lilian Mellink, D-Vorm, Leidschendam, The Netherlands.)

Archaeological monuments are also the responsibility of the central government. This means that carrying out excavations without a written permit from the Minister is prohibited. The permit is issued to the Department for Archaeological Research, a university or a municipality. The excavation must be carried out by qualified personel. The Minister can also designate a building as a repository for archaeological finds.

Fig.12.5 Hellevoetsluis: the marine dock. It was designed in 1767 and used by the Dutch Navy until 1930. It will be used for yachts and pleasure boats. (Photograph: Bert and Lilian Mellink, D-Vorm, Leidschendam, The Netherlands.)

The Minister can determine that the owner of a site must tolerate, in the interest of science, the taking of measurements or the carrying out of excavations. Insofar as the owner suffers a loss through this, the state will pay compensation. On the other hand, if an owner disturbs the site in any way he or she will be held legally liable and have to pay any costs.

Moveable objects which are found during excavation and for which no one can prove title to ownership will become property of the state. If these objects are found during legal excavations by a municipality they will become the property of this municipality. The owner on whose land the objects are found shall receive an amount equal to half the value of those objects from their owner, i.e. the state or municipality. Any person who finds, other than during an excavation, an object which he or she may reasonably expect to be a monument is bound to report the find to the municipality within three days.

Conservation philosophy

In the past, restoration philosophy was aimed at erasing any restoration history from a building. It was seen to be necessary to return a building back to its original design. Any later addition was broken away and the remains were then supplemented to make it look old. However, the general restoration philosophy of today is that of *conservative repair*. This means consolidating and undertaking only those actions that are necessary for preservation, to halt degradation and to do everything essential to ensure future use. The history of the building, including earlier additions or restorations, are left intact as far as possible.

If an owner requires a subsidy for *restoration* he or she will only be eligible if the plan concentrates on the reparation of the monumental value of the building. Modern conveniences, like isolation or living comfort, cannot be subsidized. It is, of course, permitted to add these and the (future) use of the monument is always taken in consideration.

When, during restoration, a find of architectural and historical importance is made, the owner is obliged to allow scientific research of the find. In this way the restoration is documented for further study.

Sanctions and coercive measures

The Minister may, insofar as he or she is the authority issuing a permit, prevent actions which are in conflict with the regulations of the 1988 Act. The Minister may do this with the assistance of the police, but only after the offender has received a written warning. In urgent cases the written warning is, of course, not issued. Furthermore, the Minister can order the offender to restore the building as far as is possible and at his or her own cost. The Minister can also order the work to be executed by someone else, at the cost of the offender.

If the municipality is the authority issuing the permit, it can take coercive measures of its own, which are usually related to the building regulations of the town.

Any person, who wilfully alters, demolishes or removes a protected monument without a permit, can be penalized with a prison sentence of one year at the most or with a fine of approximately 50,000 euro. This also applies to a person who wilfully and without a permit carries out an excavation. The offence is a crime. If these actions are taken unintentionally the penalty is 6 months in prison or a fine of 50,000 euro. This offence is a misdemeanour.

Integrated conservation

At the start of July 1999 the Ministries of Housing, Physical Planning and Environment, Education, Culture and Science, Agriculture and Transport published the policy document *Belvedere*. Through this document the government has attached greater importance to the cultural-historical values of environmental development. Cultural history and environmental planning will therefore be associated with each other to a greater extent than in the past.

In environmental planning the values of archaeology, historic architecture and historic landscape will have more influence and this is done by establishing the following aims:

- the recognition and acknowledgement of the cultural-historic identity as the starting point for further development in urban as well as in rural areas;
- the designation of so-called *Belvedere* areas for further development, which are, in the cultural-historical view, the most important areas.

The aim is, of course, to safeguard the rich cultural history, which still exists. Therefore a map has been drawn intensively describing 76 areas. Next to a cultural-historic description, the important developments for each area are noted. Those subjects which can give a start to the strengthening of the cultural-historic value are described and finally, proposals for a possible approach to these areas are made.

Within the existing environmental procedures an obligation to consider the cultural history has been initiated. This applies to the entire country, but especially to the *Belvedere* areas. Several instruments can be used in the consideration of values. First of all there is the *Key Planning Decision*, in which the government can determine where there is room for agriculture, nature, industry, housing or infrastructure. This is then implemented in the zoning plans. This procedure can take up to 5 years.

Next there is the possibility of defining an area as a nature reserve. This procedure does not takes as long as a *Key Planning Decision* – it can be completed in 2 years. Nature reserves are designated by the government and, by way of regional planning, are established in the municipal zoning plan.

Still another way to protect scenically important areas is the *Ecological Headstructure*. The province has to determine the boundaries between which nature can be developed. In this way it is possible to discourage large-scale farming.

To realize the aims of the *Belvedere* policy, extra funds are made available for a period of 10 years.

Financial resources, funding mechanisms and the regeneration of historic environments

Grant assistance

Grants for restoration

In 1997 a new regulation for state *grants for the restoration* of protected monuments came into operation as a substitute for the regulation of 1991.

A grant can be given for restoration projects, which are listed in a municipal or provincial programme of restoration. Every 4 years the municipalities are requested to list the technical need of future restorations. These lists are then used by the department to calculate the budget for each town. These budgets have to be divided as follows: for dwellings and farms 50 per cent of the budget, for churches 30 per cent and for other objects (castles, windmills, watertowers, etc.) 20 per cent (Figs 12.6 and 12.7).

Towns that have 100 or more protected monuments and a heritage ordinance have responsibility for their own budget. The budget for towns with fewer monuments are put together in each province. These towns are allowed to make a list of priorities and the province has to take these into consideration. The reason for collecting money in this way is that the provinces are thus able to distribute more money to certain objects, which would otherwise never receive enough financial help.

Application for a grant should be made to the town council. There the costs of restoration will be calculated and the application form with the calculation will be sent to the Department. In the case of the smaller towns the application will be sent to the province, which – after verification – will

Fig.12.6 Zaltbommel: ruins of the castle of Nederhemert which burnt down in World War II. Due to a lack of financing it has never been restored. (Photograph: Bert and Lilian Mellink, D-Vorm, Leidschendam, The Netherlands.)

Fig.12.7: Utrecht: Roman Catholic Church of Saint Willibrordus. After considerable water damage the restoration is now underway. Apart from state and local grants, a European subsidy has also been made available. (Photograph: Bert and Lilian Mellink, D-Vorm, Leidschendam, The Netherlands.)

send it to the Department. Both authorities will define the year in which the grant should be made payable. The Department will then issue a decision on the application and at the same time notify the *National Restoratie Fond* (National Restoration Fund), which arranges the payment.

The grant amounts to a certain percentage of the restoration costs and varies from 20 per cent up to 70 per cent, depending on the type of building and on whether the owner is liable to taxation. For instance, a foundation which restores monumental buildings cannot deduct the costs of maintenance or restoration from income tax. Therefore it will receive a grant for 70 per cent of the restoration costs. This also applies to a parish which wants to restore its church. For private persons 20 per cent is the standard, but if they do not have tax exemption they will receive 50 per cent.

The National Restoration Fund is a private foundation, which arranges the payment of grants and, if applicable, a low interest loan. It administers the budgets allocated to a municipality or province and pays out the grants. Interest and instalments on these low interest loans are returned to the fund, thus creating a revolving fund, which can be used again and again for restoration activities.

In addition to the restoration grant there exist two other regulations for state grants. One is a grant for the maintenace of certain, specified objects. The other is a grant for protected historical country seats.

Maintenance grants
The *maintenance* grant is intended for those objects, which have a unfavourable economical market value and are difficult to maintain after restoration. The categories for which this grant is intended include, amongst others, churches, castles, fortifications, windmills and factory chimneys. Houses and farms are exempted from the grant, because the owner can deduct the costs of maintenance from his or her income tax.

The grant is given for keeping the object protected against wind and water and consists of 50 per cent of the total costs, within certain limits.

Grants for country seats
The grant for *protected historical country seats* gives the owners the opportunity to apply for payment of the maintenance of objects situated within their grounds. For example, the garden vases, bridges, hen houses and other objects intended for decoration of the grounds or buildings with a functional use, like a hothouse. The main building or the outhouses are excluded from this regulation. For the maintenance of 'green' elements of a country seat a grant can be sought from the Ministery of Agriculture.

Other grants
Incidentally there are grants for special purposes. At this moment there is a grant to finance the damage caused by *acid rain*. It is used for the restoration of stonework or metalwork on monuments. It follows the regulation of the restoration grant.

These regulations will also apply to a new grant which will be used for *large-scale restorations* which surpass the 500,000 euro figure. In these cases the objects are likely to be churches, castles or windmills.

Tax deductions

In The Netherlands the owner of a state-protected historical building has the opportunity to benefit from several *tax deductions* for his or her property.

- *Income tax*: deduction of the costs of maintenance if they surpass a certain sum. Owners of historic monuments protected by province or municipality are not able to use the income tax deduction.
- *Corporation tax*: tax exemption for certain institutions in the field of restoration or public housing.
- *Wealth tax*: tax exemption on rural estates recognized by the Nature Act 1928.
- *Conveyance tax*: tax exemption for foundations for the benefit of restoration.

There is no exemption for VAT or property tax for repair or restoration work.

As far as is known, there has been no evaluation of the effectiveness of the tax relief measures. The tax system is in the process of revision at this moment and may have consequences for owners.

Other assistance

In addition to these ways to keep a protected monument in good order, there are private funds or other grant regulations, for which an owner can apply. In these cases it is not a legal requirement that the property is a protected historic object. There is, for instance, the Urban Renewal Grant, used for the revitalization of the built environment.

The role of agencies and specialist organizations

The field of conservation and preservation of historic buildings and monuments is not only the concern of the government. The Netherlands has many private organizations, some large and many smaller ones, which are involved in the care of the cultural heritage.

Probably the most important is the National Contact Monuments (NCM) which was founded in 1972 and is the platform for the private organizations on conservation. More than 340 organizations are associated to the NCM (examples include Stadsherstel and Hendrick de Keyser). The NCM organizes many initiatives in the field of monuments. For instance the National Open Day for Monuments, on which certain private historic buildings are open to the public. Furthermore, it has started a course on conservation in practice, aimed particularly at local government officials.

A special note must be made concerning the Federation Monument Watch (*Monumentenwacht*). This organization offers owners of historic buildings, on subscription, a yearly check-up of their building. The owner receives a report on the technical state of his or her property and can thus decide whether restoration is required or whether straightforward repair or maintenance of the monument is called for. The reports are accepted by the Department for Conservation as technical proof when an application for a grant is received.

Education and training

Specialist training in conservation work is organized by private institutes in The Netherlands in co-operation with the government. One of these institutes gives professional training for building companies for the purpose of creating a group of specialists in restoration. There is also a course given to young construction workers who have become unemployed.

Apart from these technical courses much is done by government and private institutes to teach children and students more about their cultural heritage. There is, for instance, a project in which schools adopt an historic building and use this object as part of their educational programme.

Conclusions

At this moment the preservation and conservation of historic buildings and monuments in The Netherlands is subject to change. The *Belvedere* policy is an example, but also the forthcoming changes in the 1988 Act or the increased sophistication of the regulations for grants. This, in combination with the growing number of protected historic buildings and sites, will keep the preservation of the Dutch cultural heritage very much alive.

Marina San Martín Calvo

Spain

Introduction

The beginnings of historical and artistic regulation in Spain goes back to
the eighteenth century, with the creation in 1752 of the 'Academia de las
Nobles Artes', that later on would become 'Academia de San Fernando',
and take charge of the approval of building designs erected in public places.

The nineteenth century began with the 'Novissima Recopilación' that,
following an official order from Carlos IV (1803), set up the notion of
'monument' for the first time in Spain's regulation history. According to this
definition, the idea of 'antiquity' is the hinge on which this concept is
based. Very soon, this idea was transcended by different regulation arrangements, and the 'monument' was no longer recognized as an object belonging to a certain historical period, its artistic value becoming the determining
factor for protection to be given by law. Anyway, it should not be forgotten
that, during the nineteenth century, a monument was always an individual
and isolated good, still a long way from the time when the law of guardianship would be appied to the architectural whole.

On the other hand, only the state's properties and those belonging to the
Catholic Church were under the auspices of the Administration, whilst the
private possessions, whose owners did not face any artistic or aesthetic
limitation to their right, even when a Royal order from 1950 restricted the
owner´s faculties in public opened buildings (although these limitations
only referred to the outward appearance of the buildings), were excluded
from any control.

Thereby, it could be said that the nineteenth century produced certain
rules inspired by a conservative thesis about heritage. However, these rules
were not sufficient to avoid catastrophic acts like the ransacking and
destruction of the Spanish heritage by Napoleonic troops, the neglected
state of works of art, the degradation of hundreds of historical buildings

together with their libraries and furniture, or the destruction of the greater part of our cities' walls to facilitate the enlargement of villages.

The twentieth century is distinguished by a pronounced desire to protect the cultural heritage, although at the same time many serious mistakes, leading to an important degradation of our *historical heritage,* were committed. It is in this century that a specific, though scattered, legislation relating to heritage protection appeared.

In the legal context we can highlight the Act from 1911 which established the rules that control those excavations in which there were signs of archaeological sites; the *Monuments Act* from 1915, where for the first time a process of formal integration of goods in the historical-artistic heritage was controlled, and the most important Decree from 1926 passed on the *Protection and Preservation of the Artistic Richness*, in which the *National Artistic Treasure* is defined. This rule extended the guardianship of the state authority to private monuments. Under this decree, protection in favour of urban areas and buildings as a whole overcomes the protection of isolated effects, anticipating by some years the Athens Charter of 1931.

Five years later, the Republican Constitution from 1931 declared (section 35) that 'all the historical and artistic richness of the country, no matter who the owner may be, forms the cultural treasure of the nation and will be under the auspices of the State'.

The development of the Constitution was carried out by the 13 May Act 1933, in force for more than 50 years, and completed with a Regulation published a few months before the outbreak of the 1936 Civil War. In spite of its great legal value, this Act did not reach a solution for Spain's heritage problems, as no inventory had been elaborated and the application of this measures was ineffective, although it is true that the circumstances were not propitious.

The 1933 Act defined the 'historical-artistic heritage' as being made up of all the moveable chattels and real properties with artistic, archaeological and historical interest with an antiquity of no less than a century. In addition, it meant the generalization of the direct supervision principle of the authorities in private historical-artistic goods. The 22 July 1958 Decree, pronounced to develop and apply the 1933 Act, enlarged the domain of the Administration over the environment of the historical-artistic real properties.

By means of the 1964 'Instructions' the protective prospects of the 1933 Act would be transcended. In fact, these Instructions (which applied characteristic techniques from urban development) gave place to a new concept of a 'historic site' as something alive, perfectly integrated in its surroundings. In the international level, this idea, preceded by the Charter of Quito (1967) found its ultimate shape in the 1976 Nairobi Declaration, which asserted that historical sites must be considered 'as a coherent whole whose balance and specific character depends on the synthesis of its forming elements and which includes both human activities and buildings, spatial structures and surroundings norms'.

On the other hand, the ancient 'Ley del Suelo' of 9 April 1976 (a Spanish act that governs the use of the ground) introduced a new idea in the property law concerning urban development schemes, through which defence of the historical-artistic heritage became part of the global framework of town planning action.

This introduction would not be complete without mentioning the *Local Ordering*, a tradition in our positive law. This gave Town Councils an outstanding role in the conservation of the historical areas of our cities.

The legislative sector has always been sensitive to the protection needs of the historical city areas, but due to differing circumstances, its rules have been ineffective. The necessity to develop cities relegated monument conservation to a lower level, a situation which lasted until the 1980s, when a restoration regulation favouring historical city conservation at last emerged to the detriment of those wanting to create excessive development.

To conclude, we can affirm that the regulations developed by the 1933 Act offered sufficient instruments and structures for an effective policy for historical heritage preservation, but the non-fulfilment of the regulations and the lack of material means have made this law ineffective.

This Act was in force for 50 years, until it was replaced by the actual 16/1985 Act, of 25 June, about 'Patrimonio Histórico Español' (Spanish Historical Heritage) (LPHE). The publication of this Act shaped the new juridical regime for the Spanish historical heritage, thus concluding the preceeding legislation´s dispersion and fragmentation.

The institution of this new legal order was due to two reasons.

*   The reorganization of the principles, aims and instruments of guardianship that took place after World War II, mainly through the action of international institutions such as UNESCO, the Council of Europe or ICOMOS, that demanded the adaptation of the different regulations to the new principles.
*   The promulgation of the 1978 Spanish Constitution, that established the notion of a historical cultural artistic heritage and the transfer of heritage responsibilities to the autonomous regions (Castillo, 1997).

Spain's important ecclesiastical cultural heritage deserves a special mention. Traditionally, our historical legislation took control of the Catholic Church´s heritage regulation, which over a number of centuries has gathered together such an artistic richness that, even nowadays, and in spite of incidents like the 'Desamortización de Mendizabal' (the sale of church lands and properties in the nineteenth century), the Catholic Church is still the main historical real property owner in Spain. This legal tradition has its sequel in the present day LPHE, and in the Agreement between the Spanish State and the Holy See about education and cultural matters (3 January 1979), still in force and in accordance with which this Act must be interpretted.

Definition of the heritage
Obviously, the new Act increases the 1933 Act limits. Section 1 from the LPHE states:

1   The purpose of this Act is to protect, to increase and to transmit the Spanish Historical Heritage to future generations.
2   The Spanish Historical Heritage is composed by real properties, and movable chattels of artistic, paleontological, archaeological, ethnographical, scientific or technical interest. The documentary and bibliographic heritage, archaeological sites and areas, and also natural places, gardens and parks possessing any artistic, historical or anthropological value form part of this heritage as well.
3   An inventory must be made of the most outstanding goods from the Spanish Historical Heritage or, on the contrary, they must be declared Assets of Cultural Interest, according to the terms of this Act (Figs 13.1–13.6).

Similar definitions can be found in Autonomous Regions Acts that have been developed in the field of heritage preservation: Act 4/1992, 30 May, for the Historical Heritage from Castilla-La Mancha; Act 7/1990, 3 July, for Basque Cultural Heritage; Act 1/1991, 3 July for Andalusian Historical Heritage; Act 9/1993, 30 September for Catalonian Cultural Heritage; Act 8/1995, 30 October for Galician Cultural Heritage; Act 4/1998, 11 June, for Valencian Cultural Heritage; Act 10/1998 9 July for the Historical Heritage from the Autonomous Region of Madrid; Act 11/1998, 13 October, for Cantabrian Cultural Heritage; Act 12/1998, 21 December, for the Balearic Islands Cultural Heritage; Act 4/1999, 15 March, for the Canary Islands Historical Heritage; Act 3/1999, 10 March, for Aragonese Cultural Heritage; and finally, Act 2/1999, for Extremaduran Historical Cultural Heritage.

Fig.13.1 Santa Maria Cathedral in Burgos, in the Autonomous Region of Castilla-Leon, Spain. Designated a World Heritage Site by UNESCO in 1984. (Photograph: Fotoceteca del Patrimonio Histórico IPHE MEC.)

Fig.13.2 Royal Monastery of Santa Maria of Guadalupe, in Guadalupe, Cáceres, Autonomous Region of Extremadura, Spain. Designated a World Heritage Site by UNESCO in 1993. (Photograph: Fotoceteca del Patrimonio Histórico IPHE MEC.)

Fig.13.3 Church of Santa Maria del Naranco, pre-Roman Asturian site, in the Spanish region of Asturias. The church forms part of a World Heritage Site 'Monuments of Oviedo and the Kingdom of the Asturias) designated by UNESCO in 1985. (Photograph: Fotoceteca del Patrimonio Histórico IPHE MEC.)

All these Acts allude to the historical, architectural, archaelogical, ethnographical, scientific or technical interest of the protected cultural goods.

Section 1 from the LPHE consists of three separate paragraphs. The purpose of the Act is defined in the first paragraph, the delimitation of the application area (i.e. applied to the historical heritage) in the second, and specific systems of protection in the third (discussed below).

Concerning the first paragraph, suffice it to say that this Act introduces the term *historical heritage* omitting other similar terms such as 'cultural

Fig.13.4 Cathedral in Santiago de Compostela, part of the Historic and Artistic Santiago de Compostela site in the Spanish region of Galicia. Designated a World Heritage Site by UNESCO in 1985. (Photograph: Fotoceteca del Patrimonio Histórico IPHE MEC.)

heritage', 'artistical heritage', or 'historical artistic heritage', terms possessing a traditional character in our law. The reason for this is that, although the field controlled by law is more extensive than it was in preceding laws (as for the first time the documentary, bibliographic, ethnographical and submerged archaeological heritage are included plus there are concrete references to historical gardens, historical sites and picturesque landscapes) this Act does not take in the whole cultural heritage. In fact, other fine arts such as music or literature remain outside the remit of this Act.

In spite of the above mentioned notions, the use of the term 'Spanish Historical Heritage' has been criticized by many involved in the subject who would have preferred the term 'cultural heritage' because it is in accordance with the international standard. Anyway, as we have noticed, a large part of the published Autonomous Regions Acts use the term 'cultural heritage' instead of 'historical heritage'.

With regard to the second paragraph, the Spanish Historical Heritage includes the following assets:

- movable chattels and real properties of artistic historical, paleontological, archaeological, ethnological, scientific or technical interest;
- documentary heritage;
- bibliographic heritage;
- archaeological sites;
- Natural places, gardens and parks of artistic, historical or anthropological value.

Fig.13.5 Aqueduct in the town of Segovia, Autonomous Region of Castilla-Leon in Spain. The Old Town of Segovia and its aqueduct were designated a World Heritage Site by UNESCO in 1985. (Photograph: Fotoceteca del Patrimonio Histórico IPHE MEC.)

This study will focus on the different notions given by the LPHE concerning real property and the archaeological heritage (and not on the different autonomous rules which contain similar definitions). The LPHE states that 'the real properties forming the Spanish Historical Heritage can be stated as Historical Monuments, Gardens, Sites and Places as well as Archaeological Areas, all of them considered Assets of Cultural Interest' (section 14.2)

Monuments

Objects considered as monuments are 'those real properties which constitute architectural or engineering structures, or colossal sculpture works whenever they hold historical, scientific or social interest' (section 15.1).

The *architectural structures* relate, according to the notion of traditional architecture, to any kind of buildings, whereas *engineering structures* refer to constructions built by the application of special and scientific techniques (aqueducts, bridges, buildings dating from the beginning of the Industrial Age, etc.). Finally, the term *colossal sculpture works* seems to relate to those human works liable to be inserted in the classical sculpture concept and which are fixed to the ground, being part of the landscape. This would confer them the condition of 'real properties', that, at first, they lacked. That would be what the civilian Spanish doctrine calls 'real properties by sumptuary destiny'.

Fig.13.6 The Alhambra Palace in Granada, in the Autonomous Region of Andalucia, Spain. The Alhambra, Generalife gardens and Albayzin quarter were designated a World Heritage Site by UNESCO in 1984 (Photograph: Fotoceteca del Patrimonio Histórico IPHE MEC.)

Historic sites

A *historic site* comprises a group of real properties 'that form a township unity, either continuous or scattered, conditioned by a physical structure representative of the evolution of a concrete human community, thus being evidence of its culture or a valuable and useful thing for the collectivity. In the same way, any individual settlement of real properties forming part of a superior population unity, gathering together the same characteristics and being easily delimited can be considered as a Historical Site' (section 15.3).

This is one of the most important categories of the Spanish Historical Heritage. In fact, the 'Historical Site' means the inclusion in the heritage of urban settlements, being either continuous or scattered, as long as they can be considered as a unit.

An essential condition for the set to be considered as 'historical' is that it forms a physical structure representative of the evolution of a concrete human community, that is to say 'urban weft' architecturally speaking, because the aforesaid structures are an evidence of the people´s culture. For instance we can cite the differences between a medieval city such as Toledo and a moslem city such as Seville.

Historical gardens

A *historical garden* is 'the delimited space obtained as a result of the arrangement of natural elements by human beings, sometimes complemented with manufactured structures, and considered interesting because of its origin, its past or its aesthetic, sensorial or botanical values' (section 15.2).

In comparison, the ICOMOS-ILFA Florence Charter (1981) defines 'historic gardens' in quite similar terms. Actually, its first section defines the historic garden as 'an architectural and horticultural composition of interest to the public from the historical or artistic point of view'.

In short, the subject of protection are those properties that are the result of human action on nature, emphasizing the 'historical origin' of the garden and its 'aesthetic, sensorial and botanical values', mentioned in the fifth section of the Charter as well, considering the historical garden as 'an expresion of bonds existing between civilization and nature, a place for joy, propitious to meditation or dream . . .'

Moreover, the expression 'sensorial values' seems to justify the garden preservation for the sense of pleasantness, whereas the 'botanical value' covers the human actions on nature, what article 1.3 of the Granada Convention calls: 'the combined works of man and nature', a concept that must include Historical Places. These are defined in the LPHE as 'natural places and spots linked to past events or memories, popular traditions, cultural or natural creations and human works possessing historical, ethnological, paleontological or anthropological value' (section 15.4 LPHE).

The notion of historical place has recently appeared in our legal nomenclature and is explained as 'the setting of relevant events for the knowledge of the people´s public life or that having signs which express a certain way of land working that provides these places of an undoubted interest concerning the behaviour of men in former times' (Barrero, 1990).

The archaeological heritage and archaeological areas
The *archaelogical heritage* is controlled in the Title V from the Act as a Special Heritage. It is formed by

> movable chattels or real properties which may be studied by archaeological methods, being extracted or not and whether they are placed in the surface or in the subsoil, in the sea or in the continental platform. Likewise, geological or paleontological elements linked with human history, origins and background form part of this Heritage (section 40.1)

whereas an *archaeological area* is a place or natural spot where items of the archaeological heritage can be found, and thus it has been declared (Fig. 13.7).

Thereby, we can assert that, independently of its movable chattel or real property quality or its concrete location, an archaeological asset can be described by its own values or its historical meaning. The difference lies in the varied methodologies used to declare it as a *asset of cultural interest* (CIA). For instance, caves or places containing paintings are declared a CIA by the Act, whereas the archaeological areas are individually declared a CIA by the Administration through the appropriate procedure.

We must still clarify what our legal ordination means by 'assets which may be studied by archaeological methods'. The LPHE considers excavations, archaeological explorations that do not imply ground removal, and casual discoveries, as such assets.

Fig.13.7 Archaeological zone in the Sierra de Atapuerca in Atapuerca, Burgos, in the Autonomous Region of Castilla-Leon, Spain. Declared immovable property of cultural interest in 1991. (Photograph: Fotoceteca del Patrimonio Histórico IPHE MEC.)

Goods found in archaeological sites cannot be considered private property, as they are deemed to be public assets. The LPHE provides that the character of every object and material remaining possesses specific Spanish Historical Heritage values.

The environment

With regard to the *environment*, it is officially included in the historical heritage as an area forming part of CIA real properties, becoming its territorial delineation, and therefore one of the most important aspects of its regulation. However, the LPHE does not establish any form of standard to define the area. In general terms the *environment* can be defined as 'a surrounding space inseparably linked to the Cultural Interest of real properties, forming part of them, having either an urban or territorial nature and liable to be controlled in order to protect, physically and visually, the real properties which it has an effect on' (Castillo, 1987). Both the LPHE and its Attachment Regulations demand the environment delimitation of every property, meaning not only monuments in a strict sense but also archaeological sites, historical sites, historical gardens and historical places.

Generally speaking, this Act states that a 'a real property declared of cultural interest is inseparable from its setting' and, in the same way, the ICOMOS Venice Charter (1964) states that 'the monument is not separable from the history it has been witness of, neither from the environment in which it is situated'.

In relation to the single objects of real property, that is to say, monuments and historical gardens, the regulations insist on the need for a specific permission from the responsible government organs for every work executed on its environment.

Concerning the environmental regulation of monuments and historical gardens placed inside of historical sites, historical places and archaeological areas, the situation is very complex. The general arrangements for environmental protection can be applied, as well as the dispositions established for the monuments and historical gardens considered individually. On the other hand, they are governed by the rules provided by the Act and must assume the supervision proposals required by the Special Plans.

Identification of the heritage

The LPHE classifies the Spanish Historical Heritage on three levels:

1 An *upper* level, that grants the highest protection degree for movable chattels or real properties, and requires their statement as Assets of Cultural Interest (CIA). Assets thus stated must be inscribed in the General Register of Assets of Cultural Interest.
2 An *second* level of protection that only has effect on movable chattels of exceptional importance, which must be declared as well and must be inscribed in the General Inventory for Movable Assets of Cultural Interest.
3 There is a *third* basic level, applied to all assets belonging to the Spanish Historical Heritage, simply for what they are. They are not inscribed anywhere, although there are certain Autonomous Regions Acts that have created a special inventory in order to inscribe these goods.

The Autonomous Regions Acts also have their own systems for identifying the heritage. While every inscription made in the Autonomous Registers must be notified to the General Register of Assets of Cultural Interest, the regions use a variety of approaches for their own purposes.

The Castilla-La Mancha Act was the first of the autonomous Acts concerning this subject and is less innovative in relation to the LPHE. The Historical Heritage Act from the Canary Islands keeps the LPHE scheme concerning the separation between movable chattels and real properties as well, including in its Register of Assets of Cultural Interest every movable chattel or real property declared CIA, but keeping the Regional Inventory for the movable chattels that have 'special artistic, ethnographical or historical values'.

The Act 7/1990 of Basque Cultural Heritage has created the Qualified Cultural Assets Register, where those assets from the Basque Cultural Heritage whose protection is of public interest are inscribed, and the Cultural Heritage General Inventory, in which are inscribed the Cultural Assets that, being of less importance, form part of the Basque Cultural Heritage. This Act does not include the basic level of protection.

The Historical Heritage Act from Andalusia follows the LPHE scheme concerning the protection degrees, but not in relation to the nature of the inscribed goods, as incriptions can be either specific, equivalent assets to CIA, or generic, and both movable chattels and real properties.

The Act 9/1993 of Catalonian Cultural Heritage also includes the three protection levels. A Cultural Assets Register of National Interest has been created, where the mentioned Cultural Assets, equivalent to CIA, are inscribed. It also includes the Catalonian Cultural Heritage Catalogue, where those cultural assets that do not fulfil the conditions of the National Interest Cultural Assets will be registered. As a novelty, this Act contains an inventory called the Catalonian Cultural Heritage Inventory. This includes registered and catalogued goods, and all those which 'deserve' to be preserved.

The Cultural Heritage Act from Galicia, very similar to that of Catalonia, contains the three levels of protection and has created the Galician CIA Register, the Galician Cultural Heritage Catalogue and the Galician General Inventory of Cultural Heritage. All assets here inscribed can be both movable chattels and real properties.

The same scheme is adopted by the Aragonese Cultural Heritage Act, which keeps the three categories of assets: CIA, catalogued and inventoried assets. The first ones are registered in the Aragonese CIA Register, the second in the Aragonese Cultural Heritage Catalogue, and the third in the Aragonese Cultural Heritage Inventory.

The Act 11/1998 of the Cantabrian Cultural Heritage also keeps the three level scheme. To the General CIA Register can be added the Cantabrian Cultural Heritage Catalogue, which includes the local interest assets or catalogued assets. The registered and catologued assets and other assets that deserve to be preserved form the Cantabrian Cultural Heritage Inventory.

In the Historical Heritage Act from Madrid, the second level disappears, being movable chattels and real properties declared CIA inscribed in the Cultural Interest Assets Register of the Autonomous Region of Madrid and the remaining assets of the historical heritage from this region are inscribed in the Cultural Assets Inventory of the Autonomous Region of Madrid.

The Act 12/1998 of Historical Heritage from the Balearic Islands pretends to follow the legal techniques designed by LPHE, focusing its protection in the CIA and catalogued assets categories, although their inscription presents certain peculiarities. In fact, there are two different Cultural Interest Assets Registers, one created by every Insular Council concerning its territorial limits, and another one for the whole autonomous region. There are also two catalogues, an Insular one and a General one.

The Historical and Cultural Heritage Act from Estremadura establishes the following categories for historical and cultural assets: assets declared cia, inventoried assets and some others that 'without reaching the previous categories, still deserve protection for its latent value'. The first ones are inscribed in the Cultural Interest Assets Register, the second ones in the Cultural and Historical Heritage Inventory of Estremadura and the last ones (only real property that deserves to be preserved) will be inscribed in a new register that has not yet been created.

Some of the state autonomous regions have not developed their own Heritage Act yet. The Cultural Legislation from the Autonomous Regions of Asturias, la Rioja, Murcia, Navarra, and Castilla y León, as well as the autonomous cities of Ceuta and Melilla, are currently developing their own rules, although all these regions have sectorial norms on these subjects (to indicate responsibilities and procedures) and Acts to preserve the archaeological heritage, files, library collections and museums.

Assets belonging to the Spanish Historical Heritage that have been expressly or individually declared in the Historical Heritage Act by a Royal Decree or another similar norm from the autonomous regions are considered to be Assets of Cultural Interest (CIA).

Works by living authors cannot be declared as CIA except if it is expressly authorized by the owner or if they are acquired by the Administration.

Assets specifically declared
Certain assets are expressly declared as CIA by the LPHE. These are:

- assets inscribed in the Spanish and Archaeological Heritage Inventory according to the preceding regulation;
- all Spanish castles;
- emblems, heraldic stones, law scrolls and any monument of a similar kind older than 100 years;
- 'horreos' and 'cabazos' (typical rural structures found in northern Spain) older than 100 years;
- caves and shelters containing cave paintings;
- real property assigned to state use, libraries and museum installations or movable chattels forming part of the Spanish Historical Heritage maintained within them;
- assets declared CIA by law.

Administration of protection procedures for assets individually declared
Concerning the CIA that must be individually declared, the autonomous regions are generally responsible for the legal procedures which deal with their protection. However, the state will be responsible for assets assigned to public services managed by the State Administration, those being part of the National Heritage and those belonging to an autonomous region affected by pillaging when that autonomous region has been requested by the Administration to act in defence of endangered goods but has adopted a passive attitude.

The files to declare an asset as a CIA can be commenced by a court or at the request of any person, and must be notified to the Council in which the landed property is situated. When the files relate to monuments and historical gardens similar provisions exist. The details of an intention to protect must be published in the State Official Journal and communicated to the CIA General Register so that it can be preventively registered. The LPHE provides the basis for this provisional procedure to protect an asset.

In order for an application to protect to be administered the file must contain a favourable report from any of the consultative institutions established in the LPHE or in respective rules from the autonomous regions. A CIA declaration must be fulfilled by a Royal Decree or an equivalent rule from the respective autonomous region, which must contain the asset's environmental delimitation, the definition and enumeration of its essential parts, its possessions and accessories and the movable chattels placed into the landed property.

Once this procedure has been completed an asset will be inscribed in the suitable Register from every autonomous region, and, subsequently, in the State CIA General Register, specifying whether it is a monument, a historical garden, a historical site or an archaeological area. When dealing with monuments or historical gardens, the Administration will urge its free inscription in the Land Registry.

The preservation and protection of the heritage

At the present time the law provides two kinds of intervention instrument. First, there is a legal instrument that provides compulsory purchase powers. Second, there are tools that possess technical characteristics, such as for preservation, consolidation and restoration interventions, that tend to assist a re-evaluation of assets of the historical heritage, especially those declared CIA.

The compulsory purchase instrument

The LPHE provides for the use of this mechanism in two cases.

1 When there is a threat of destruction or deterioration for an affected asset or a usage incompatible with its values. The instrument can cover the whole of the protection area for real estate that forms part of the cultural scene of monuments and historical gardens.
2 When dealing with real properties that could disturb or obstruct the contemplation of CIA or when an asset may be endangered.

Technical interventions

In this context, every action in relation to a CIA must be designed in favour of its conservation, consolidation or restoration. Reconstruction must be avoided, except for when the original elements of the assets are used. Otherwise, any addition should be recognizable and must not mimic the exisiting fabric.

The restoration of landed property must respect the contributions from every period. The exception to this rule is where the contributions of a certain period have degraded the quality of the asset. In such circumstances the removal of damaging elements may be authorized as long as there is documentary evidence to prove that this is the case.

Landed property preservation techniques

Specific techniques are authorized, and prohibitions may be applied, to individual landed property assets that are considered to be historical monuments or historical places.

With respect to authorization techniques, the authorization of the Administration is compulsory in the following activities related to monuments and historical gardens:

- the realization of any inner or outer work which has an effect directly on the landed property or on any of its integral parts and accessoires;
- the placing of any label or symbol in façades and roofs;
- the realization of works in the cultural scene affected by a CIA declaration.

As far as prohibitions are concerned, it is not permitted to place either commercial advertisements or any kind of wire, aerial or pipe in historical gardens or in the façades and roof belonging to a cultural interest monument. Furthermore, the construction of new structures in such a way as to cause alteration to the character of such real property assets, or otherwise disturb them, is forbidden.

The simple inception of a CIA declaration file implies the withdrawal of any licence permitting partition, construction, or demolition and creates a provisional control which is the same as the regime that is applied to CIA already declared.

Techniques applied to real properties forming a historical site
The guardianship provided by the LPHE to historical sites, historical places and archaeological areas pretends to ensure the necessary conservation of their cultural values, warranting the intervention of the Heritage Administration. This need has to be harmonized with the essential work of the Town Councils, the real promoters of urban development, especially through the use of Preservation Special Plans in the context of municipal planning.

Thus, the historical site, historical place or archaeological area declaration as CIA states that the affected Council has the duty to create a Preservation Special Plan. This should contain the criteria relative to façades and roof preservation and modification, as well as the possible integrated conservation approaches that may permit the residential rehabilitation.

The plan approval will require a favourable report from the competent Administration for the CIA preservation. Once this has been undertaken, the Council will be the only institution authorized to allow the works through appropriate planning approval tools. This is that these works do not have a detrimental effect upon monuments, historical gardens or real estate included in the environment of a site. In such a case, the responsibility to authorize any work does not rest with the Town Council, but with the State Heritage Administration.

Where CIA landed property is in a ruinous state, the general rule giving Councils the exclusive responsibility to authorize works is replaced by a specific rule that requires the necessary supervision of the Heritage Administration. The question of demolition is conditioned by the aforesaid Administration authorization.

This reserved area in favour of the Heritage Administration can be found as well in historical places and archaeological areas, in which 'any planned work or ground removal will require the previous authorization' from the Heritage Administration. The Administration may order this before agreeing to authorize the works, or may decide on the need for some prospection activity or, when necessary, archaeological excavations, in any public or private land that may contain historical remains or archaeological sites.

Some autonomous regions have improved this 'presumption' by the creation of specific concepts such as 'Archaeological Obligation Areas' (in Andalusia), or the 'Archaeological Protection Spaces' (of Catalonia), following the outline of Article 4 of the Malta Convention, despite the fact that this convention is still not ratified by Spain.

In relation to preservation rules for fortuitous archaeological discoveries, the LPHE admits that the discoverer has a 'prize right' amounting to 50 per cent of its estimated value of the 'find'. The prize must be shared with the owner of the land in which the discovery was made. If the discoverer fails to observe the obligation to notify its discovery to the competent Administration, this right is lost.

Landed property assets not declared as being of cultural interest
Another supposition that must be taken into account is that real property of cultural value, but not a declared CIA, may still be subject to control over demolition, i.e. those assets belonging to the historical heritage that, not being included in any catalogue or register, deserve to be preserved and belong to the so-called 'third protection level'. In this case, the competent Heritage Administration may order the total or partial interruption of demolition works for a period no longer than 6 months. During this period the affected Town Council must take a decision about the suitability of the initial approval of a Special Plan or other protective measures provided in the urban legislation. If no action is taken in this respect, the 'interruption' is lifted and demolition works may proceed.

Conservation philosophy
'Spanish Historical Heritage is the main witness of the Spaniards historical contribution to the universal civilization and its contemporary creative capacity . . .' Thus begins the LPHE Preamble, and it follows that 'the preservation and enrichment of its goods are the basic obligations of every public authority, according to the order addressed to them in the 46th section of the Spanish Constitution'.

Section 46 of the 1978 Constitution confirms the need to defend and preserve the heritage and its priority as a main element of the social and economical policy. By this the guardianship of the historical heritage has become an essential value of legal regulation, to whose attainment all public authorities are bound.

This basic rule places the cultural value (historical and artistic) under the guardianship of the legal regulation in force. As a consequence of this 'cultural spirit' that pervades in the 1978 Constitution, the cultural heritage is considered as an autonomous legal asset, worthy of guardianship by itself, irrespective of whether its owner is private or public. In fact, it can be said that the heritage is formed by a set of assets 'whose togetherness derives from its own qualities, being the bearer of cultural values' (Barrero,

1990). All these things turn them into general interest assets, originating a collective right over them, and this implies the necessity of a regulation rule to preserve its integrity, whoever the owner may be.

The preservation duty is made concrete in the culture 'access right' mentioned in section 44.1 of the constitutional text, which states that 'the public authorities will promote and protect access to culture as a common right'. The right of access has two different aspects: the capacity to estimate its products (which implies a right of educational benefit), and the capacity to approach those goods and products (which implies the right to see, to study and to participate in them) (Alvarez, 1989).

Laws in force about this subject essentially search the easiest access to the goods that compose our historical heritage. All established rules make sense if, finally, the number of citizens who can enjoy and contemplate the works of the people's collective capacity has increased.

Sanctions and coercive measures
Administrative infringements and sanction regulations
Every law in force concerning heritage, except the one from Castilla-La Mancha, establishes a series of infringements against the historical heritage, and their respective sanctions.

The LPHE includes two large sections corresponding to two types of infringement: section 75, concerning the illegal exportation of historical heritage assets, and Section 76, that determines the non-fulfilment of legal obligations that lead to administrative infractions. We can classify these infringements as light faults, serious faults and very serious faults.

Light faults includes a list of activities concerning the infringement of the obligations imposed on the owners and heritage goods possessors by law, for instance the non-fulfilment of the preservation, maintenance and safe keeping duties or the non-communication of an archaeological discovery in the required period by the methods determined by law. *Serious* faults are concerned with procedures for the granting of licences and the realization of works, excavations and archaeological explorations in monuments, historical places, archaeological areas or historical gardens without the compulsory authorization. Finally, *very serious* faults relate to the destruction or illegal exportation of CIA.

Concerning sanctions, the LPHE states that, when injury to the Spanish Historical Heritage may be economically calculable, a fine amounting to quadruple this sum would be imposed; and in cases where the damages may not be economically calculable, fines would amount to up to ten million pesetas for light faults, up to twenty-five million pesetas for serious faults, and up to one hundred million pesetas for very serious faults. In the Autonomous Regions Acts published to date, the same sanction scheme is basically reproduced with some additional specifications.

Penal infractions
The new Penal Code of 1995 includes for the first time a chapter (II, Title XVI, Book II) entitled 'About Offences to Historical Heritage', although

heritage is preserved by other precepts which are not included in this chapter.

We will not study now specific criminal patterns such as theft, robbery with violence, swindling or illegal appropiation, as they mainly affect movable chattels, although the limit between movable chattels and landed property categories difers between criminal law and civil law. Thus, the criminal law states a broader movable chattel category, for it includes all those movable chattels that could be moved.

Thereby, the criminal law provides that the appropriation of a heraldic stone placed against a CIA can be considered as theft or robbery as much as the appropriation of a sculpture, and it may give place to the application of specific aggravating circumstances provided for this offence in the Penal Code. In this context, the normative sections that consider damaging actions to the historical heritage may be analysed.

In Chapter I (Title XVI), and relating to territorial arrangement misdeeds, the landed property's historical, artistic or cultural environment is protected for the very first time, punishing illegal or non-authorized constructions in 'soils assigned to roads, green areas, public property goods or places possessing a scenic, ecological, artistic, historical or cultural value legally or administratively recognized, or for the same reasons are considered worthy of special protection', with penalties of fines or imprisonment and special disqualification for promoters, builders or technical directors.

The Penal Code of 1995 examines the role of the authorities and the behaviour of civil servants in situations when they provide favourable 'reports about demolition or alteration projects or protected buildings' or when they decide or vote in favour of action in circumstances which they know are unjust.

The demolition or serious alteration of a specially protected building is punishable under section 321, whereas any other damaging behaviour against this kind of building, a wider notion, that includes damaging conduct concerning movable chattels and the archaeological heritage, is punishable under section 323. The same material subject is considered in section 324, although this section deals with damage caused by a serious imprudence. These three sections consider that any person can be subject to imprisonment, fines and disqualification when necessary.

Likewise, the Penal Code identifies the possibility of weekend arrest and fine penalties for actions against the well-being of the community (according to certain legal duties that must be observed), or for theft. On the other hand, the Title XXIV from the Penal Code, concerning 'Offences against the International Community' penalizes whoever attacks or takes reprisals against cultural assets.

Finally, and apart from the Penal Code, the Organic Law 12/1995, 12 December, concerning Smuggling Repression, penalizes whoever takes Spanish historical heritage goods older than 100 years, and inventoried real property items, out of Spanish territory without an appropriate exportation licence.

Integrated conservation

The 'Ley del Suelo' of 1992 identifies different urban schemes categories.

- The first category is formed by the *Order National Plan*, on a state scale, and includes the main urban guidelines.
- The second category, probably the most effective, is formed by the *Territorial Director Plans* adopted in the autonomous regions territories in which special measures for historical heritage 'preservation' are indicated.
- A third category is that of the *Municipal General or Urban Order General Plans*, concerning municipal areas, the aims of which are to determine land-use and urban order, to preserve land (i.e. to leave it free from development), and to take suitable measures to protect landscape, territory and historical sites. In this repect, their contents must be adapted to the policies of the *Territorial Director Plan*.

The Municipal General Plans are the basic tools used to control territorial order. The Complementary Planning Rules detail the General Plans, although they are not basically altered. For smaller townships the law provides Subsidiary Rules. These also contain qualifications about the ground and establish heritage protective norms.

From all these categories, the tool most frequently used to protect the historical heritage is the *Special Plan*, which cannot qualify ground by itself, but it can provide order to areas and historical sites (see the section above, 'The preservation and protection of the heritage'). Suffice it to add that historical site preservation implies 'the maintenance of its urban and architectural structure, as well as the general character of its setting' (section 21.3 LPHE). It follows that new development may exceptionally be allowed within an historical site as long as it would contribute to the general preservation of the site's character.

The LPHE makes the conservation of the goods which form part of the historical heritage fall on its owners, or on possessors. This duty implies the realization of every work needed in order to protect the aforementioned assets in the public interest. This means, through simple ordinary works, the recovery of its former healthiness, security and decoration conditions. However, repeated jurisprudence doctrines have established that a legally declared ruinous state excludes the conservation duty.

When an owner´s behaviour does not observe what the LPHE demands, the Administration has the power to impose the duty. In this context, the LPHE provides a series of measures which tend to perform the required proceedings. The Administration may make a 'refundable' advanced grant of financial assistance or the works may be directly undertaken by the Administration. The measures also provide an expropriation procedure as a sanction for not observing the required actions (see the section above, 'The preservation and protection of the heritage').

Other duties of the owners of Spanish Historical Heritage goods consist of permitting archaeological excavations and CIA Administration inspection, and allowing the free public visits for people of Spanish nationality.

On the other hand, in a case of the owner wishing to sell a movable chattel declared CIA (we should not forget that archaeological goods may be either movable chattels or landed properties), he or she must communicate this decision to the competent Administration, together with the price and sale conditions. In such cases the Administration may purchase the asset within a period of 2 months.

Financial resources, funding mechanisms and the regeneration of historic environments

Non-fiscal promotion measures

The LPHE states that 'the Government will arrange the necessary measures to provide financing for the rehabilitation, maintenance and preservation works, and that prospections and excavations carried out in assets declared of cultural interest may have preferential access to the official credit' (section 67, LPHE).

In addition, the LPHE identifies that the State Administration must assign at least 1 per cent from its budget to finance public works, to subsidize, totally or partially, 'Spanish Historical Heritage preservation or enrichment works or artistic activities promotion' (section 68, LPHE). The regulation of this measure is included in the LPHE and coexists with the regulation from the autonomous regions where they have developed their own historical heritage regulations. In such cases, the regions have acquired a similar obligation to totally or partially fund works through their own budgets.

Fiscal measures

There are a number of fiscal measures included in the Income Tax Act 40/1998 (IRPF). The following state deductions may be provided:

- 10 per cent on CIA inscribed in the CIA General Register inversions;
- 15 per cent on CIA inscribed in the General Register acquisition inversions;
- 15 per cent on the amount of conservation, repairing, restoration, diffusion and exposition expenses of CIA inscribed in the General Register;
- 20 per cent on donations towards assets being part of the Spanish Historical Heritage when inscribed in the Cultural Interest Goods General Register or included in the Spanish Historical Heritage Goods General Inventory, provided they are made in favour of the beneficiary institutions;
- 20 per cent on the amount of donations assigned to the above mentioned Spanish Historical Heritage Goods conservation, reparation and restoration, provided they are made in favour of beneficiary entities;
- 20 per cent on the amount of works of art donations made in favour of beneficiary entities and institutions that carry out museum and promotion activities, provided they promise to assign them to public exhibitions;

Beneficiary Entities and Institutions are, among others, the following:

- the state, autonomous regions, local corporations and public universities;
- the Catholic Church, and churches, confessions and religious communities which have suscribed to collaboration agreements with the Spanish state;
- national heritage foundations;
- the Prado Museum and the Centro de Arte Reina Sofia;
- the National Library.

Fiscal reductions made by the autonomous regions
Some autonomous regions have acts to establish their own deductions for heritage protection. Thus, Act 11/1998, 28 December, of Financial, Administrative and Regional Public Function Measures from the Autonomous Region of Murcia provides economic donations deductions whose aim is to develop the Murcian Region Historical Heritage preservative actions. The Act 10/1998, 28 December, of Fiscal, Management Administration, Financial and Organization Measures from the Generalitat Valenciana provides donations related to the Valencian Cultural Heritage. Likewise, the Act 13/1998, 23 December, of Economical, Fiscal and Administrative Measures from the Autonomous Region of Castilla y León introduces deductions for Community Heritage Investments.

Other fiscal reliefs
Enterprises liable to the 'Impuesto de Sociedades' (Corporation Tax) may deduct 15 per cent on the amount of money assigned to the acquisition, preservation, restoration, divulging and exhibition of CIA. Fiscal exemptions in the IRPF and 'Impuesto de Sucesiones' (Inheritance Tax) are provided as well.

Concerning indirect taxes, exemptions are provided in the 'Impuesto sobre el Valor Añadido' (Value Added Tax) in relation to assets of the historical heritage.

Finally, in the context of local taxes, the CIA are exempted from the payment of urban or rural contribution taxes.

The role of agencies and specialist organizations
Apart from the competences corresponding to the Ministry of Culture and Education and to the Fine Arts General Office, the LPHE and its regulations mention certain consultative or advisory institutions, the most oustanding are:

- *Consejo del Patrimonio Artístico*, whose essential aim is to facilitate communications and information, and procedure programmes exchanged between the state and the autonomous regions.
- *Junta de Calificación, Valoracion y Exportación de Bienes del Patrimonio Histórico Español*, qualified to judge the exportation requests for goods inscribed in the General Inventory and for those forming part of the Spanish Historical Heritage older than 100 years.

- *Junta Superior de Monumentos y Conjuntos Históricos*, entrusted with the safeguarding of any report concerning provisions designed to obtain the CIA protection, restoration and defence.
- *Junta Superior de Arte Rupestre*, that gives information about any activity related to cave paintings including investigation, conservation, preservation, excavation, prospecting or fortuitous discoveries, and works and constructions performed in their environment.
- *Junta Superior de Excavaciones y Exploraciones Arqueológicas,* which, among other competences, is responsible for reporting every disposition designed for the Spanish Submerged Cultural Heritage and Archaeological Heritage preservations, defence and investigation.
- *Consejo Superior de Investigaciones Científicas,* whose main function is to assist in the elaboration of national scientific policy.
- *Reales Academias,* firmly rooted in the Spanish cultural tradition, among which the most notable are the Real Academia Española, the Real Academia de la Historia, the Real Academia de Bellas Artes de San Fernando and the Real Academia de Jurisprudencia y Legislación.
- *Universities.*

On the other hand, autonomous regions possess their own consultative and advisory institutions, among which we can mention the *Consejo Asesor del Patrimonio Cultural de Cataluña* (Catalonia), the *Comisión Superior de Valoración de Bienes Culturales de Interés para Galicia*, the *Junta de Valoración de Bienes del Patrimonio Cultural Valenciano*, the *Consejo Regional de Patrimonio Cultural de la Comunidad de Madrid*, the *Consejo Extremeño de Patrimonio Histórico y Cultural* (Extremadura) or the *Consejo de Patrimonio Histórico de Canarias* (Canary Islands). Other autonomous regions are in a position to create them, for example the Basque Country or Cantabria.

As well as these public institutions, the state admits the contibution of private individuals to preserve and divulge the Spanish Historical Heritage. The activities of such so-called '*maecenas*' or 'sponsors' are regulated in Spain by Act 30/1994, 24 November, about Foundations and Fiscal Incentives for Cultural Interest Activities Private Cooperation, or 'Ley del Mecenazgo', and hold special fiscal advantages.

Education and training

The idea that education is the best way to avoid the destruction of the historical heritage has been accepted, internationally, for a long time. The 1969 European Convention for the Archaeological Heritage Preservation compelled the signatory countries to fulfil an educational programme in order to arouse and develop knowledge about the past for public benefit. Recommendations, Charters and Conventions published subsequently have widened this aim. After the agreement of Spain to the 1969 convention, the least that could be expected was a change in the content of educational programmes, but this did not happen, except for certain autonomous Acts that have required the historical heritage to be considered in their educational programmes (Querol and Martinez, 1996).

Until the 1991 reforms, references to heritage preservation in the elementary education were hardly noticed. The secondary education curriculum contained two subjects: *Civilizations and Art History* and *Spanish Geography and History*, which emphasized the basic cultural and ethnic issues that have contributed to Spanish historical development. The University Preparation Course (COU) included visits to museums and monuments, but there were no allusions to the concept of the historical heritage concerning art history. In a general sense there remains a need to promote and develop the constitutional desire (contained in section 44.1 of the Spanish Consitution) to educate the public in this field.

However, there are some specialist courses designed for architects which are held in the cities of Valladolid, Madrid, Barcelona and Granada, although this training is not obligatory. There are official training courses given at the Higher Colleges for Conservation and Restoration of cultural asscts (LOGSE). Spain also provides some training in trades for the maintenance of the architectural heritage. Thc Ministry of Labour, with the various departments of the autonomous regions and local institutions has also implemented a professional training programme in the field of historical heritage for unemployed young people.

Conclusions

From all that has been discussed in this chapter, it must be concluded that, although the development of the Spanish cultural heritage regulations has not been completed, a great effort is being made. It must be taken into account that, in Spain, there are eighteen responsible administrations in charge of the protection, conservation and preservation of the historical heritage, as well as the bodies holding official responsibilities, especially in urban matters.

Today, a state field act, the LPHE, and twelve autonomous Acts coexist in Spain, and the legislation in the autonomous regions, whose historical heritage is partially controlled by sector rules, is being developed.

The LPHE has consolidated the provisions for the protection of the Spanish Historical Heritage. Thus, the designation of assets, the determination of the legal categories of protection and the control of foreign trade are exclusively under the state authority. Autonomous regions maintain legal authority over their own heritage, provided that this authority has not been through the state legislation and does not affect the basic conditions for equality amongst citizens.

This distribution of authority is ordered simultaneously, as the LPHE requires that the state and the autonomous regions work together on most of the actions carried out in relation to heritage guardianship through several levels of co-operation.

For example, if we consider the steps taken to ensure the protection of already identified heritage assets, first we find a group of dispositions applicable to every asset of the historical heritage. Then, we find two higher levels that gather together protective dispositions, the CIA declarations being the highest level of protection.

The legal development is being carried out in accordance with the guidelines established by the conventions supported by Spain, such as the Granada Convention and the Charters and Recommendations that have been published on this subject, whose postulates are followed almost exactly. Concerning archaeological heritage, although the 1992 Malta Convention has still not been ratified by Spain, the state rules, and, most of the autonomous legislation provisions that have been developed or are in the process of development, are working towards the aims of this convention.

References

Alvarez, J. L. (1989): *Estudios sobre el Patrimonio Histórico Español*, Civitas.

Barrero Gómez, C. (1990): *La Ordenación Jurídica del Patrimonio Histórico*, Civitas.

Castillo Ruiz, J. (1987): *El entorno de los bienes inmuebles de interés cultural*, Servicio de publicaciones de la universidad de Granada.

Querol, M. A. and Martinez Díaz, B. (1996*): La gestión del Patrimonio Arqueológico en España.*

Other sources of information

Alegre Avila, J. L. (1994): *Evolución y Régimen Jurídico del Patrimonio Histórico*, Ministerio de Cultura, Colección Análisis y Documentos, no. 5.

Alonso Ibañez, M. R. (1992): *El Patrimonio Histórico. Destino público y valor cultural*, Civitas.

Basque County Official Journal 6 August 1990.

Benitez de Lugo y Guillen, F. El Patrimonio Cultural Español. Aspectos jurídicos, administrativos y fiscales, Comares 1988.

Region of Murcia Official Journal 31 December 1998.

Salinero Alonso, C. (1997): La Protección del Patrimonio Histórico en el Código Penal de 1995, Cedecs.

State official journals 1985–1999.

Valencia Government Official Journal 4 November 1993.

John Pendlebury

United Kingdom

Introduction

In relation to many other European countries the legislative history of British conservation started late and modestly with the Ancient Monuments Act of 1882. However, subsequently legislation and policy have developed enormously, especially in terms of their inclusiveness and in terms of the restrictions placed on owners. From inadequate measures to protect a handful of prehistoric monuments, the system has developed to encompass a significant part of the British town and landscape within an often strict legal framework. Evolution has been incremental; monuments, buildings and areas each have their distinct category of protection. Similarly recent inventories of historic parks and gardens and battlefields, started in the 1980s, have created their own registers. Early legislation was quite separate from early town planning legislation, and though post-war conservation legislation was found in the planning Acts it was often treated as a separate activity. However, since the 1967 *Civic Amenities Act* there has been a steady convergence and integration of conservation activity into planning processes.

Today the British system of heritage protection is both extraordinarily extensive and relatively flexible; both of which can be argued as a strength or a weakness. Conservation has enjoyed remarkably stable political support over the last 20 years and seems to remain a popular cause. However, there are, of course, enduring issues and topics of debate. The philosophical underpinnings for conservation action have arguably not been sufficiently evolved to deal with a more extensive and complex definition of heritage and there are inevitable questions over the adequacy of resources to manage the system. This has perhaps been particularly the case with 'conservation areas'. Flexibility is a characteristic of the discretionary British planning system. The scope this gives for negotiation can allow for sensible and creative solutions to conservation problems, but the absence of fixed rules can create confusion and poor compromises.

This chapter's principal focus is on the situation in England. Though the essence of the conservation system is similar throughout the United Kingdom, there are some differences in Wales, Scotland and Northern Ireland and these are briefly reviewed at the end of the chapter.

Definition of the heritage

As previously remarked, distinct categories of monument, building and area have been defined, which have conceptual differences from those categories set out in the Malta and Granada Conventions.

Definition of the archaeological heritage

In the United Kingdom the term 'monument' is associated with the archaeological heritage, as broadly defined in the Malta Convention. It can include unexcavated archaeological sites where there is evidence of archaeological significance, such as may be visible through crop marks, for example. Also included are upstanding remains and industrial and pre-industrial artifacts. The emphasis is on sites, buildings and structures which do not have a current utility (other than as cultural heritage), though, for example, working bridges maybe classified as monuments (Fig. 14.1). *Scheduled ancient monuments* are those afforded statutory protection.

Fig. 14.1 The Swing Bridge, Newcastle upon Tyne, built 1868–76, is scheduled as an Ancient Monument because of the significance of the Armstrong Hydraulic engines which enable the bridge to swing open and allow navigation. The illustration also shows a rich urban townscape.

The primary legislation for the protection of the archaeological heritage is the *Ancient Monuments and Archaeological Areas Act* 1979. It is notable that this element of the heritage remains legislatively separate from town and country planning, though planning guidance is set out in Planning Policy Guidance Note (PPG) 16, 'Archaeology and Planning' (Department of the Environment, 1990). Key criteria for assessing archaeological monuments for scheduling are historic period, rarity, existence of documentation, group value, survival/condition, fragility/ vulnerability, diversity (scheduling may be suitable because of a combination of factors or a single attribute) and, importantly, archaeological potential. However, only a limited number of potential sites are given statutory protection, more commonly these are addressed through planning policies (see below).

Definition of the architectural heritage

The architectural heritage, as defined under the Granada Convention, is protected through the categories of *listed buildings* and *conservation areas*, which do not neatly map on to the categories of 'monuments', 'groups of buildings' and 'sites'. Individual buildings defined as being of architectural or historic interest are 'listed', though a factor in the decision to list might be the 'group value' of an ensemble of buildings. Such a grouping may also be defined and designated as a 'conservation area', as may larger or less coherent areas of architectural or historic interest. Thus, though the Granada Convention category of 'monument' broadly equates to buildings, and 'groups' to conservation areas it is not a perfect match. Furthermore, unlike the homogeneity suggested by the Granada Convention (and evident elsewhere; see Hamer, 1998), there is a long tradition in the United Kingdom of acknowledging the picturesque qualities caused by heterogeneous and accidental groupings, as evidenced in early listing criteria (reproduced in Delafons, 1997). Finally there is no direct equivalent of the 'site' category set out in the convention, though such ensembles clearly exist. Examples of the suggested synthesis of cultural and natural landscape may have a variety of designations. For example, Fountains Abbey/Studley Royal in North Yorkshire, comprising major monastic remains and a historic garden, contains *scheduled ancient monuments* and *listed buildings*, is registered as an historic park or garden and is inscribed as a *World Heritage Site*. Some areas of field barns and walls in the countryside in the Yorkshire Dales are designated as *conservation areas*. These areas also form part of a *National Park*, and indeed it is perhaps in the English National Parks that the principal recognition of cultural/natural landscapes occurs.

Listed buildings

The duty on the Secretary of State to compile lists of historic buildings is currently set out in the *Planning (Listed Buildings and Conservation Areas) Act* 1990. Listed buildings are defined as being of 'special architectural or historic interest'. Government guidance on listed buildings is set out in PPG 15 'Planning and the Historic Environment' (Department of the Environment and Department of National Heritage, 1994: 6.10) and defines architectural interest as 'all buildings which are of importance to the nation for the interest of their architectural design, decoration and craftsmanship; also important examples of particular building types and techniques (e.g. buildings displaying technological innovation or virtuosity) and significant plan forms'. Historic interest is defined as 'buildings which illustrate important aspects of the nation's social, economic, cultural or military history'. However, also included in these broad parameters are 'close historical associations: with nationally important people or events;' and 'group value, especially where buildings comprise an important architectural or historic unity or a fine example or planning (e.g. squares, terraces or model villages)'. Though buildings may be listed purely for their historic associations this is relatively rare in the UK; much more common is listing on the basis of architectural merit or rarity. Though age is not an explicit criteria, the overall emphasis is for increasing selectivity the closer the construction of a building was to the present day. Thus it is suggested that most buildings of before 1840 that survive in reasonable condition are listed whereas relatively few twentieth-century buildings are included. In general there is a 30-year cut-off rule, i.e. buildings younger than 30 years are not listed. However, this rule may be waived where buildings of exceptional quality are threatened. So, for example, the Wills Coroon building in Ipswich, designed in 1974–5 by Norman Foster (now Lord Foster), was listed grade I in 1991 (Fig. 14.2).

Buildings are categorized into one of three grades (I, II* and II), with grade I the most important. Most buildings are grade II (94 per cent); buildings in the higher grades are far less numerous with grade II* accounting for 4 per cent of listed buildings and grade I a mere 2 per cent. The system of control is the same for each of the three grades, the grading

Fig. 14.2 The Wills Coroon building in Ipswich, designed by Norman Foster in 1974–5 and listed grade I in 1991.

system merely illustrates the importance of the building. So, for example, listing extends protection to the whole building, the interior as well as external envelope, whatever the grade of the building. The protection afforded by listing can also include fixtures within the building and the building's curtilage. However, the definition of these has been a grey area, subject to a series of legal cases as indeed have other matters, including the definition of 'demolition' (see Mynors, 1999). The setting of a listed building is a 'material' (relevant) consideration in planning decisions, though there is no system of defined 'zones of protection'.

Conservation areas
The national system for the protection of historic areas, introduced in 1967, is quite distinct and different from that for monuments and buildings. Though conservation areas are defined by the same national legislation as listed buildings, and the subject of central government policy advice in PPG 15, the primary responsibility for defining and designating conservation areas lies with local planning authorities. No attempt has been made at a national level to prescribe criteria for which areas are suitable beyond the statutory definition of 'areas of special architectural or historic interest the character of which it is desirable to preserve or enhance' (s. 69 of the 1990 Act). Furthermore, there is no grading of the relative importance of conservation areas, so the legislative framework is the same for conservation areas covering major historic cities as for far more modest ensembles of cultural heritage. This lack of prescription reflects a philosophy that conservation areas are locally valued environments. English Heritage has produced a range of guidance in recent years, geared principally at assisting local authorities in the management of conservation areas (see, for example, English Heritage, 1988; English Heritage, 1995; English Heritage, 1997a).

Other defined sites
In the last 15 years three new inventories of cultural heritage have appeared in English conservation. These are the *Register of Parks and Gardens of Special Historic Interest*, the *Register of Historic Battlefields* and *UNESCO World Heritage Sites*. In the mid-1990s discussions were held on the desirability of a register of 'Historic Landscapes' but an alternative approach of a more broadly based assessment of the whole countryside through *Historic Landscape Assessments* has been pursued (Fairclough, 1999).

Identification of the heritage
The responsibility for scheduling monuments and listing buildings rests with central government, advised by *English Heritage*, an independent state agency. Historically scheduling and listing have been carried out by different parts of government which has led, for example, to some structures being both scheduled and listed. In recent years efforts have been made to more closely define and co-ordinate these two processes. The *Department of Culture, Media and Sport* (DCMS) is responsible for the identification of both categories (though not conservation planning, see below). In both

cases no statutory criteria exist for the inclusion of sites in their respective inventories, but non-statutory guidelines have been developed and published. It is important to note that with both categories there is no right of appeal against inclusion and no right to compensation.

Until relatively recently monuments were added to the schedule incrementally, and somewhat haphazardly. After the creation of English Heritage in 1984 it was decided that a more systematic approach was needed. This eventually led to the on-going *Monuments Protection Programme* (MPP), whereby particular categories of monuments were surveyed, for example, the coal industry. There are now over 18,000 scheduled monuments in England (covering some 30,000 archaeological sites) and it is estimated that on the completion of the MPP there will be 45,000–50,000 scheduled monuments. Local government county authorities also maintain their own more inclusive *Sites and Monuments Records* (SMRs) at the sub-regional level, and though non-scheduled monuments do not have statutory protection, they may be afforded some protection through planning policies. It is estimated that these SMRs will soon contain over 1,000,000 archaeological records (Bournemouth University and English Heritage, 1997).

Historically the principal means of 'listing' buildings has been through comprehensive area surveys, though the provision also exists for individual buildings to be instantly 'spot listed', particularly used when a building is under threat. However, following the completion of a national re-survey in 1989, emphasis has increasingly shifted to thematic surveys. This has included building types thought to be under represented on lists, e.g. textile mills, and post-war buildings, the latter often with controversial results such as the proposal (now confirmed) to list Park Hill, a large local authority deck-access housing estate in Sheffield from the 1950s. The process of thematic survey has allowed a more selective approach to listing to be pursued, but the traditional more inclusive area survey has resulted in quite staggering numbers of listed buildings when set next to other countries. The number of listed buildings in England stood at over 453,000 at the beginning of 1999 (Hanna, annual).[1]

Information on listed buildings is published in area based documents, compiled by parish, the smallest unit of administrative area. In addition to basic information on the building, such as its address and date of listing, these include a description. The descriptions are not, however, statutory or intended as an exhaustive schedule of the building's historic interest, but as a more general guide. The non-inclusion of an element of a building cannot be taken to imply that it is of no interest. This may be particularly important with complex buildings with concealed layerings of historical evolution. Furthermore, many historic buildings were only inspected externally at the time of listing.

Recording of monuments and buildings has been undertaken as a largely separate activity from their identification for statutory protection. For much of the twentieth century the key recording body has been the *Royal Commission for the Historical Monuments of England* (RCHME), established in 1908, though the RCHME was merged with English Heritage in 1999.

Constrained resources have meant that only a small fraction of the identified heritage has been systematically recorded. Mechanisms exist in the planning process to allow for the recording of buildings threatened by demolition. Local planning authorities may also require developers to make records of buildings (typically photographic) before undertaking works. Quite different from the scholarly recording of the RCHME is the English Heritage initiative *Buildings at Risk* (BAR), developed as a planning tool and discussed below.

Numbers of conservation area designations have steadily risen since their introduction in the *Civic Amenities Act* 1967 and in England now stand at nearly 9,000, a far greater numbers than was originally forecast (Smith, 1969). This is largely a reflection of both the incredible flexibility of conservation areas as a policy tool and the way notions of historic cultural value, and therefore environments which should be protected, have progressively broadened over the last 30 years. So from an initial focus on historic towns and villages (Fig. 14.3), conservation areas now encompass, for example, 1930s suburbs of speculatively built semi-detached houses and operational transport corridors such as the Settle-Carlisle Railway in the north of England. This conservation area, which is over 100 kilometres long and never more than a few hundred metres wide, stretches the whole notion of what might be considered an 'area' (Fig. 14.4).

Fig. 14.3 Louth, Lincolnshire, a typical English conservation area seen with buildings of varying ages leading to the medieval parish church.

Fig. 14.4 The Ribblehead Viaduct, the most famous structure on the Settle–Carlisle Railway, part of which runs along the watershed between the north-west and north-east of England.

This steady increase of conservation area numbers has led to criticisms that the system has become devalued as, it has been asserted, areas of less than special interest have been designated (Morton, 1991). The government has not sought to limit the freedom of local authorities in designating areas, but more recent policy advice in PPG 15 has put stress on authorities establishing consistent local standards and publishing 'conservation area appraisals' which describe an area's interest. Ultimately, however, recording of conservation areas is restricted to those surveys and records local authorities choose to compile, and are therefore inevitably highly variable.

The Registers of parks and gardens and battlefields are both compiled by English Heritage. The first of these currently contains around 1,300 sites. It is numerically dominated by country house parks but also contains a wide diversity of sites including municipal parks and cemeteries. These will often contain listed buildings and are now frequently designated as conservation areas by local authorities. The Battlefields Register has less than 50 sites. Finally, there are eleven UNESCO Cultural World Heritage Sites in England, one in Wales and one in Scotland. These reflect a wide-range of contributions to the cultural heritage from prehistoric ceremonial monuments (Stonehenge, Avebury and associated sites) to the industrial revolution and Britain's global influence as an imperial and trading power (Ironbridge and Maritime Greenwich) (Fig. 14.5). The government has recently put forward a list of eighteen further sites within the UK for nomination in the next 5–10 years.

The preservation and protection of the heritage
The protection of scheduled ancient monuments
Scheduled monuments have the strictest series of statutory controls of the various heritage categories, reflecting a policy emphasis on preserving as

*Fig. 14.5 Stonehenge,
part of a group of
prehistoric ceremonial
monuments in the west of
ngland which together form
a World Heritage Site.*

found. Though this cultural heritage category probably has the highest proportion of any in state ownership or care, the vast majority of monuments are in private hands. All works to a scheduled monument, including works of maintenance, require *scheduled monument consent* from the Secretary of State. No right of appeal exists against the refusal of permission, though an applicant does have a right to an informal hearing or public inquiry prior to the determination of an application. *Class consents* exist to allow certain bodies (for example, English Heritage) and certain operations to be carried out without the need for applications. This allows for management agreements between the government and owners, whereby owners can proceed with a defined series of works and/or management operations over a period of time without the necessity of continually applying for scheduled monument consent. Indeed, much of the effort of English Heritage on monuments over recent years has been devoted to securing their proper management.

The protection of listed buildings

Works affecting the *character* of a listed building as a building of special architectural or historic interest are subject to *listed building control*. Consent is not generally required for works of 'like for like' repair. Most decision making has been delegated by the Secretary of State to local authorities, though applicants have the right of appeal against the refusal of permission. Applications for works to grade I and II* listed buildings, and for the demolition of grade II buildings, are subject to greater scrutiny due to various requirements placed on local authorities to consult on and to refer such applications to English Heritage, the *Department of Environment, Transport and the Regions* (DETR) and national amenity bodies (see below). PPG 15 sets out criteria against which all applications should be appraised. These are the importance of the building (which may be suggested by its grading), the particular features of the building which justify its listing, the building's setting and contribution to the wider townscape and the extent to which the works proposed would bring substantial benefits for the community, including the regeneration of an area or the enhancement of its environment.

Government policy emphasizes a general presumption in favour of the retention of listed buildings and sets out further criteria for those applications involving total or substantial demolition. These are: the condition of the building; and the cost of repairing and maintaining it in relation to is importance and the value derived from its continued use; the adequacy of efforts made to retain the building in use; and the merits of alternative proposals for the site. This last criterion is considered only of relevance in exceptional cases where a substantial community benefit would result; claims for the architectural merits of proposed replacement buildings are not seen in themselves as justifying the demolition of listed buildings.

In practice the number of buildings given consent for demolition, set against the total number of listed buildings, has dropped dramatically over recent decades. In 1997 58 consents for the demolition of listed buildings were granted out of a total of 451,287 listed buildings, a proportion of 0.013 per cent. This contrasts with 1977 when 306 consents were given, out of the then 251,570 listed buildings, a proportion of 0.122 per cent (Hanna, annual).[2] Thus consents for demolition set against the stock of listed buildings are now one tenth of 20 years ago.

In addition to listed building consent, works to listed buildings may require *planning permission* for alterations or changes of use and *building regulation approval* (principally covering health and safety considerations). The process of planning consent is usually run in parallel with listed building control and is rarely problematic. Because of the importance of securing the future of historic buildings, land use planning policies may be relaxed and allow changes of use not normally permissible. More difficult may be the need to obtain building regulation approval. Standards are formulated with modern construction in mind and may be wholly inappropriate for historic buildings. Fire safety regulations have often proved particularly problematic. For example, historic joinery may be damaged to achieve fire resistance and achieving means of escape may lead to unsympathetic external staircases or clumsy fire lobbies in circulation spaces. Discretion exists in the *building regulations* to take account of the particularities of historic buildings and creative solutions can be found to achieving fire safety and means of escape. An exemplar is provided by the solution found for the Society for the Protection of Ancient Buildings (SPAB) in its London headquarters. The building has only one staircase, with timber panelled wall linings, providing escape from four floors of the building. Smoke detectors activate an air in-take fan which pressurizes the escape route by forcing air out of the building and thus preventing smoke entering the fire exit route (Pickard, 1993/4). However, what can be achieved may depend on the flexibility and imagination of individual fire officers.

Two further issues which can be significant in achieving the successful continued use of listed buildings are adaptive re-use and enabling development. Government policy on the former is cautious, stating that 'the best use will very often be the use for which the building was designed, and the continuation or reinstatement of that use should certainly be the first option when the future of the building is considered' (Department of the Environment and Department of National Heritage, 1994: 3.10). This attitude perhaps in part reflects concerns that unskilful adaptation can destroy much of the character of a building. However, the need for adaptive re-use of some buildings is generally accepted, and if undertaken skilfully can enhance the qualities of the building (Fig. 14.6).

Enabling development has become a controversial issue in recent years. This means the granting of planning permission for development proposals which would not normally be allowable, in order to cross-subsidize the repair or restoration of historic buildings which in themselves are not economically viable. The affects on historic gardens and on the setting of historic buildings have been particular concerns. The problems caused have recently led to the production of an English Heritage policy statement which has as a starting point a presumption against enabling development (English Heritage, 1999).

Fig. 14.6 St Ninian's Manse, Leith, Edinburgh, where a disused seventeenth- and eighteenth-century residential building, latterly used as a seed mill, has been repaired and restored as offices for rent by the architects Simpson and Brown for the Cockburn Trust. (Photograph: John Sanders.)

Policy on conservation areas

The controls that exist in conservation areas are more modest by comparison with listed buildings. When introduced in the 1960s conservation areas were primarily regarded as a means of achieving positive enhancements in an area. However, as numbers have grown without a parallel growth in resources, the balance has swung in most areas towards the control of development. The added weight conservation area status gives to normal planning decisions is a key factor (though again the precise weight of this has been the subject of case law) (Mynors, 1999). So, for example, a local authority will often find it easier to resist a planning application on design grounds in a conservation area than elsewhere. The key additional control a conservation area brings is control over demolition, though this has been subject to the same problems of definition noted for listed buildings. The power of control over demolition has been argued as one of the motivations for local authorities continuing to increase the number of designated conservation areas (Morton, 1991).

Other modifications to the planning system within conservation areas are controls over works to trees and more limited rights for householders to undertake minor works, known as *permitted development*, without requiring planning permission. However, extensive permitted development rights do still exist and this has been a matter of controversy and lobbying throughout the 1990s. Groups such as the have argued that through incremental change the cumulative impact of these works can severely damage the character of a conservation area. Such works might include, for example, the replacement of traditional joinery with PVCu or a change in roofing material. The means of bringing these works within planning control, known as Article 4 Directions, are generally thought to be cumbersome, bureaucratic and confusing; though in 1995 the government did make it easier for local authorities to implement these, removing the need for government approval in some situations.

Policy for other defined sites

The Registers of Historic Parks and Gardens, Battlefields and World Heritage Site status do not bring additional statutory controls, though following government guidance in PPG 15 they should be the subject of planning policies in development plans. Their status is also a material factor in the decision-making process for determining planning applications where proposed development activity may affect such sites.

Conservation philosophy

'Modern' approaches to conservation in the United Kingdom developed from the nineteenth-century writings of John Ruskin (see, for example, 'the Lamp of Memory' in Ruskin, 1855) and William Morris. Morris's Manifesto for SPAB has been especially influential (Morris, 1877). It is an approach that stresses the retention of historic fabric and can be best encapsulated by the phrase 'conservative repair'. Integrity or honesty are considered vital. 'Restoration', and especially the use of conjecture, are considered to be unacceptable. From its nineteenth-century origins it has evolved to encompass principles such as the reversibility of contemporary intervention. The SPAB tradition is still influential in its most conservative form today, through such bodies as the Ecclesiastical Architects' and Surveyors' Association and SPAB itself. The stress placed on the repair of historic fabric and the antipathy towards conjectural restoration or reconstruction has become embodied in international statements of conservation philosophy, such as the ICOMOS Venice Charter (ICOMOS, 1964). Working out of this tradition is the recent *British Standard* on architectural conservation: 'The principles of the conservation of historic buildings' (British Standards Institution, 1998). This document accepts the concept of 'restoration' in certain circumstances, such as completing a coherent design or where restoration is based on good evidence and would contribute towards the restoration of the cultural significance of the building.

There is also a very strong visual/aesthetic tradition in British conservation and architecture, albeit not articulated as coherently as the conservative repair tradition. This visual approach was evident in the formulation of the system of conservation areas where initially emphasis was placed on visual enhancement. This was evident in the Civic Trust's pioneering schemes in historic areas from the late 1950s. In the same period written works of enduring influence, such as Cullen's 'Townscape' (Cullen, 1961) were being published and stressing the importance of the visual qualities of place. SPAB and visual approaches to conservation may conflict. For example, '*façadism*', the building of a new structure behind a retained historic façade, is defended as a means of retaining familiar historic streetscapes or formal set pieces of urban design (Richards, 1994). However, using SPAB philosophy façadism is considered inherently dishonest, and though still practised, is frowned upon in official guidance (Department of the Environment and Department of National Heritage, 1994).

A third philosophical tradition, relating specifically to historic areas, is that of urban morphology derived from academic writing by, for example, M. R. G. Conzen (Whitehand, 1981). It is an approach based on the study of the historical development of a settlement. The development of the townscape is a physical manifestation of the development of society and is imbued with cultural meaning, and becomes the spirit of the place, the *genius loci*. Townscape form is derived from three principal components; the town plan, building form and land-use. The town plan is considered as generally the most enduring of these and land-use the most ephemeral. For conservation, an appreciation of urban morphology means valuing this historic form and 'grain', as well as the buildings which occupy it. Over the last decade or so these ideas have increasingly been incorporated into policy and practice, albeit often in a much diluted form.

The British Standard is arguably one of the first major United Kingdom statements on conservation philosophy since the publication of the SPAB Manifesto in 1877, though it is too early to say what influence this will have in practice. Recent years have also seen other publications such as English Heritage's 'Principles of Repair' (English Heritage, 1991). Though British conservationists have been active in the formulation of the various ICOMOS international charters, the direct influence these have had on wider conservation practice is, at best, opaque. Though as noted many of the principles incorporated in these charters are evident in current practice, others can be argued to be absent. For example, the social emphasis of the ICOMOS Washington Charter 'on the Conservation of Historic Towns and Urban Areas' (ICOMOS, 1987) has been largely absent in Britain, where conservation remains object focused. There are some signs of change. The ICOMOS charter which has probably received most debate in recent years is the ICOMOS Australia Burra Charter 'for the Conservation of Places of Cultural Significance' (1981) (revised in 1999), written specifically for an Australian context (Marquis-Kyle and Wlker, 1992). Perhaps its key concept of relevance is its emphasis on the conservation of the cultural significance of place, whereby historic fabric is only one potential element of place. Indeed some culturally significant places (such as Aboriginal sites) may have no historic fabric as such. Cultural significance may need to be determined partly through discussion with the people who use the place. Attitudes of conservation professionals towards the role of the general public in conservation are highly variable, ranging from an emphasis on a didactic wish to educate the public with a particular set of values to attempts to engage in a more open dialogue (Pendlebury and Townshend, 1999).

The United Kingdom is a full signatory of the Malta and Granada Conventions (with the exception of a partial non-ratification for Northern Ireland with the latter) and a member of the UNESCO World Heritage Convention. The spirit of these conventions is found within United Kingdom law and policy, though neither the Malta or Granada Convention or other acknowledged international standards (such as ICOMOS charters) are explicitly referred to. The one exception is the policy weight which is given to UNESCO World Heritage Site status (Department of the Environment and Department of National Heritage, 1994).

Sanctions and coercive measures

Contravention of planning control is not, in the first instance, a criminal offence in the United Kingdom. However, in recognition of the irreversible damage which can result, unauthorized works to a scheduled ancient monument or a listed building are a criminal offence. Importantly public officials have *rights of entry* which enable inspections to be carried out. The provisions for the two systems are different, with the ancient monument system being rather more loosely drafted. Despite clear weaknesses in this system, for example both ignorance of the status of a monument and the need to undertake urgent works can form a legitimate defence, there have been successful prosecutions. The system for listed buildings is tighter; so, for example, it is not necessary to prove intention. There are more plentiful examples of successful prosecutions and Mynors (1999) detects a trend of increasing fines, though fines above £10,000 are still rare. A recent exception was a fine of £200,000 for the partial demolition of a grade II listed building based on the likely profit from the redevelopment of the site; an action which was described by the judge as a 'cynical commercial act' (Mynors, 1999: 483). With both scheduled ancient monuments and listed buildings the facility also exists for the relevant public body to seek a *court injunction* to stop damaging works. This would be sought to prevent works when they are proceeding or known to be imminent, and the court can set unlimited fines in cases where injunctions are taken out.

The listed building system also contains a series of other provisions, not available on scheduled ancient monuments, to help public bodies (usually local planning authorities, though English Heritage/the Secretary of State usually have reserve powers) secure the future of buildings. *Listed Building Enforcement Notices* maybe used in conjunction with, or instead of, prosecutions for unauthorized works. These can require an owner to return a building to its former state or, if that is not practicable, to undertake works to alleviate the effect of works carried out without consent. Furthermore, local authorities have two potential courses of legal action in the case of buildings in poor repair. If works are needed urgently and the building is unoccupied an *Urgent Repairs Notice* may be served whereby the owner is obliged to undertake 'emergency repairs'. If these are not carried out the local authority can undertake the work itself and recover the cost from the owner. Typical works might encompass preventing the ingress of water or intruders, or structural collapse. A different procedure is the service of a full *Repairs Notice*. This specifies all the works necessary for the repair of a building to proper (rather then temporary) specifications and can apply to occupied buildings. If not complied with it can lead to the expropriation of a property through a *Compulsory Purchase Order*. Research has shown that the fear of acquiring potentially problematic buildings is a factor in deterring local authorities from using this power, identified in a survey of the use of repairs notices (Kindred, 1992). However, it was also demonstrated that generally repairs notices are an effective means of prompting repair, rarely resulting in compulsory purchase. Of the 287 notices authorized during the period covered by the survey only five led to compulsory purchase and in the majority of cases they led to owners undertaking repairs or disposing of the property. Indeed, it was found that the threat of such a notice is often a spur to action. In cases where compulsory purchase takes place a local authority may immediately sell the building to a *building preservation trust* (see below) or other organization or individual, in 'back to back' deals. Where deliberate neglect of a listed building can be demonstrated provision exists for minimum compensation in the event of compulsory purchase. Though this is rare, there have been significant cases such as the grade II* listed Pell Wall Hall, designed by Sir John Soane, where compensation for the house and 4.35 acres of land was set at £1 (Pickard, 1996).

Integrated conservation

The systems of town planning and heritage protection that evolved in the nineteenth and early part of the twentieth century were quite separate. Even though the listed building system created in 1944 was to be found in the planning Acts, in practice conservation was not regarded as a mainstream planning activity. The sea-change occurred in the 1960s. In large part this was a reaction to the town planning of the time, which through comprehensive redevelopment and road building was in itself the largest threat to the cultural heritage. In reaction against this loss of treasured and familiar environments conservation developed a broader base of interest and support than its traditionally rather narrow and patrician image. The momentum of redevelopment was only halted in the mid-1970s and subsequent years have seen conservation transformed from a protest movement to become, increasingly, a mainstream planning activity. This is perhaps not surprising given the extent of the cultural built heritage now protected in the United Kingdom.

The government has increasingly emphasized the importance of integrating conservation into the preparation of development plans (Department of the Environment and Department of National Heritage, 1994). Development plans, though not legally binding in the manner of some countries' planning systems, have, in the 1990s, acquired a key status in the policy framework for planning decisions. In addition to specific conservation policies local authorities are expected to demonstrate co-ordination with other planning policy as conservation has become more integrated with, for example, urban regeneration (see below). They are also exhorted to include policies on development control, to set out their approach to enhancement and to give broad criteria for the designation and review of conservation areas. This leaves local authorities considerable freedom to develop their policies and approach to conservation area designation, but they are exhorted to do this systematically and transparently.

The relationship between planning and conservation is mostly closely integrated with conservation areas. Except where English Heritage are involved in funding works in a conservation area, the conservation area system is almost wholly a local government responsibility. PPG 15 and recent guidance produced by English Heritage and local authority bodies (English Heritage, 1995; English Historic Towns Forum, 1998) has emphasised the importance of positive conservation area management. A key element of this is the *character appraisal* – an assessment of the characteristics of areas which make them 'special' and worthy of designation. Local planning authorities have in recent years often developed a more sophisticated understanding of historic areas. So, for example, historic towns and villages defined largely in terms of fabric and aesthetics in the 1970s have often subsequently been reappraised with a more holistic understanding of settlement form including, for example, the historic morphology. Perhaps less satisfactory has been the record of integrating new development in conservation areas. Given the heterogeneity of conservation areas it is difficult to generalise, but it has been argued that design in historic areas has often resorted to weak pastiche (Larkhan, 1996).

Conservation has increasingly been associated with economic development and urban regeneration. Since the 1970s conservationists have been arguing the economic case for conservation (SAVE Britain's Heritage, 1978). As the national mood has swung away from modernism towards a more heritage based culture this has increasingly been accepted. Areas of generally well-maintained historic buildings may be used as the basis of tourism promotion or more broadly as part of a process of 'city imaging', establishing a location as a good place to live, work and invest. Conversely, areas of run-down listed buildings may form the focus for regeneration efforts. A well-known small town example of this was the regeneration of Wirksworth in Derbyshire by the Civic Trust Regeneration Unit and others (Pickard, 1996). At a city-scale, the currently in progress Grainger Town Project in Newcastle upon Tyne is a £120 million regeneration programme intrinsically linked with the conservation and re-use of an extensive ensemble of historic buildings which form the major component of this part of the city centre (Pickard, 2001).

In contrast to those areas where conservation is being used as part of a strategy of revitalization, some historic places face development or tourist pressures which jeopardize their historic character. The city which has perhaps done most in trying to understand these forces is Chester. Chester has considered conservation in terms of sustainability through its Environmental Capacity Study (ARUP Economics and Planning, 1995). The objective was to scope development options which ranged from major development to managed reduction. The study concluded a selective growth option could be accommodated within the City's capacity, though this finding was contested by local conservation groups (Strange, 1997).

In historic cities archaeology often presents complex issues for the planning process. Scheduled monuments represent only a small part of the known archaeological record. Furthermore, much archaeological potential is, by its nature, not currently identified. The importance of addressing archaeology in planning and development issues was recognized in the Ancient Monuments and Archaeological Areas Act 1979, and, more significantly, with the publication in 1990 of Planning Policy Guidance Note 16, 'Archaeology and Planning' (Department of the Environment, 1990). The latter effectively superseded the system of 'areas of archaeological importance' enabled in the 1979 Act. Both are attempts at improving the situation that previously pertained, whereby archaeological matters were principally dealt with by the attachment of conditions to planning approvals. This could lead to uncertainty and delay for developers.

Emphasis has increasingly shifted to early discussions between developer and local authorities in order to identify potential archaeological constraints. This process should be helped, and underpinned, by appropriate development plan policies. Policies can identify areas of archaeological potential and reinforce the importance of archaeology as a material planning consideration. If the outcome of early consultations is that a site is considered to be archaeologically sensitive this may lead to a developer commissioning an independent archaeological assessment, based on desktop research and field visits. As archaeological advice stresses the desirability of preservation *in situ*, this initial assessment may include early advice on mitigating the impact of development proposals. An initial appraisal may lead to a field evaluation which might include, for example, a trial trench. The results of initial appraisals or evaluations may be a material factor for the local authority in taking planning decisions. They may lead to the redesign of a development scheme. If preservation *in situ* is not possible planning permission may still be granted subject to the recording of archaeological deposits prior to their destruction.

Though the government has not explicitly said so, the emphasis has increasingly been on developers paying the cost of archaeological requirements, effectively following a 'polluter pays' principle. Moreover, the British Archaeologists' and Developers' Liaison Group devised a national Code of Practice in 1984 (revised 1988) to assist in this process. The Code of Practice can sometimes be used as a basis for voluntary agreements instead of applying planning conditions so that appropriate archaeological investigations can be carried out prior to construction works being commenced by a developer (Pickard, 1996).

Financial resources, funding mechanisms and the regeneration of historic environments

Tax provisions

Financial assistance for private owners of the cultural heritage is mostly oriented around different grant regimes. There is no general scheme of tax assistance. Tax concessions exist on inheritance tax for buildings of 'outstanding' historic or architectural interest provided some measure of public access exists. There is also the peculiar structure of the Value Added Tax (VAT) system. VAT is not chargeable on alterations to historic buildings (generally defined as works requiring listed building consent) but is payable on routine repairs. This incentive to change the character of buildings, and disincentive to undertake proper maintenance, has been the subject of long and bitter protest by the conservation community, but thus far without success. *Unoccupied* listed buildings and scheduled ancient monuments are also exempted from the Uniform Business Rate (which is a property tax based on the rental value of non-domestic buildings).

Grant-aid and linked schemes

The pattern of grant provision for conservation projects has changed rapidly over the last few years. Grants provided by English Heritage have undergone a number of changes, particularly for conservation areas, now focused on *Heritage Economic Regeneration Schemes* (HERS). Grants exist for the conservation of each of the principal categories of heritage (archaeology, buildings and areas) but are extremely limited relative to the overall heritage resource. The strategic change English Heritage has made is to take a problem oriented approach, rather than focusing purely on architectural or historic merit. This is evident with HERS and the *Conservation Area Partnership* schemes which preceded them. Thus the emphasis shifted from providing grant-aid in the architecturally finest conservation areas, to areas where a demonstrable need for public sector intervention is evident and where a credible argument can be made that grant assistance will be instrumental in achieving the regeneration of the area. This has allowed for very high rates of grant-aid, tailored to achieving results, rather than the fixed percentages (typically 40 per cent or 25 per cent) English Heritage had previously used.

This problem solving approach is also seen with the *Buildings at Risk* (BAR) initiative (shorthand for 'historic buildings at risk through neglect or decay'). On the creation of English Heritage in 1984 it was realized that no information existed on the condition of the country's stock of listed buildings. BAR surveys were piloted from 1986 and were designed to quickly survey building condition and occupancy and identify those 'at risk', as a preliminary to targeting effort and resources on these buildings. Thus buildings would usually be subject to a brief visual inspection, rather than any more comprehensive survey, and buildings graded in 'degrees' of risk on this basis. Local authorities were strongly encouraged to undertake BAR surveys, often with financial assistance from English Heritage. English Heritage's BAR scheme was relaunched in 1998 . A greater emphasis is now placed on catching buildings before they deteriorate badly, i.e. 'prevention rather than cure'. In addition to providing grants, generally restricted to grade I and II* buildings, resources are targeted at helping local authorities take action. A *Monuments at Risk Survey* (MARS) has also been undertaken (Bournemouth University and English Heritage, 1997.

Limited English Heritage grants also exist for 'rescue archaeology', grade I and II* listed buildings and cathedrals and churches in use for worship. This latter scheme is jointly funded with the *Heritage Lottery Fund* (HLF), part of the *National Lottery*. The major change in public sector funding of the heritage in recent years has been the creation of the National Lottery. This has generated huge new resources for heritage projects (though the government's assertion that it would not lead to a drop in English Heritage funding is generally considered false). Allocation of funding has included some specific themes, including a programme of investment in historic urban parks. Also, there has been the *Townscape Heritage Initiative*, effectively a successor to the English Heritage Conservation Area Partnership scheme, though no longer confined to England. When created the HLF received 20 per cent of the money allocated to 'good causes', though this has subsequently been cut to 16.67 per cent. Perhaps inevitably expectation now exceeds availability of resources and the HLF has become significantly overbid. However, the sums are substantial. In 1998–99 the HLF disbursed £290 million throughout the United Kingdom, over £75 million of which was for the conservation of the built heritage. Some of the other grant would also have been spent on building conservation through, for example, the allocation of money to historic parks and museums. By contrast English Heritage's grant budget in 1998–99 was £35.5 million out of a total expenditure of £131 million.

The other principal source of public sector grant assistance is local authorities. Local authority provision is highly variable between areas, depending on local priorities. However, funding is generally assumed to have declined with increasing constraints placed on local authority funding throughout the 1980s and 1990s.

Also acting at a local level are *building preservation trusts* (BPTs). These are charitable bodies with the objective of rescuing and restoring historic buildings, often on a revolving fund basis. A revolving fund allows for the capital received from the sale of a completed scheme to be reinvested in the next project. BPTs have access to a range of funding sources including low interest loans and grant assistance to undertake feasibility studies through a national organization, the *Architectural Heritage Fund*.

Other associated regeneration activity

As conservation has become increasingly linked with regeneration, so conservation projects have been able to access funds earmarked for regeneration projects. Various central government funded regeneration initiatives have existed over the last 20 years, such as *Urban Development Corporations*, *City Challenge* and the *Single Regeneration Budget*. These have been utilized on some major prestige conservation schemes, such as the restoration of the Albert Dock in Liverpool (Fig.14.7). This major complex of grade I listed warehouses has been restored and put to new uses including the Tate Gallery and a maritime museum. The regeneration agency, *English Partnerships*, is currently involved in some major conservation related schemes, such as a commitment of up to £25 million to the Grainger Town Project, Newcastle upon Tyne (Pickard, 2000).

The role of agencies and specialist organizations

Within central government there is a basic split between the two relevant departments DCMS, responsible for the identification of the heritage and

Fig. 14.7 The restored grade I listed warehouses of Albert Dock, Liverpool, now incorporating retail, office, leisure and cultural uses. The flagship scheme of the Merseyside Development Corporation. (Photograph: Robert Pickard.)

the administration of scheduled monuments and the DETR responsible for conservation planning. Both are advised by English Heritage which was created in 1984, principally by placing functions previously undertaken directly by government in this new independent arms-length agency. The appropriate Secretary of State is at liberty to accept advice or not. With much of the casework undertaken, such as the listing of buildings, advice is routinely accepted. However, with more controversial work, such as the listing of modern buildings or some of the planning casework this might not be the case. As an independent state agency English Heritage has a freedom to state its case in a way which was not possible when its functions were undertaken directly by government. In creating English Heritage it seems to have been the intention of the then Secretary of State, Michael Heseltine, to create a strong and independent voice for conservation (Kennet, 1991, cited in Larkham and Barrett, 1998). English Heritage also manages historic properties in state care. The development of a more entrepreneurial approach to the heritage described above is also evident in the way that English Heritage manage and promote this historic estate. A further body linked to the state is the *Commission for Architecture and the Built Environment*, which in 1999 replaced the now disbanded Royal Fine Art Commission. One of the functions of the new Commission, like its predecessor, is to comment on planning applications of major design significance, many of which are in historically sensitive locations.

Most conservation planning work in the United Kingdom is, however, undertaken by local planning authorities. The 1970s, 1980s and 1990s has seen planning authorities increasingly employ specialist conservation staff, commonly termed 'conservation officers'. Though the administration of the scheduled monument system is still largely undertaken by a partnership of DCMS and English Heritage, most control over works to listed buildings is devolved to local authorities. English Heritage and DETR normally only become involved in listed building case-work where it involves works to a grade I or II* building or where total or substantial demolition of a grade II building is proposed. Thus proposals for alterations to the vast majority of listed buildings are left to local authorities, alterations which may fundamentally transform the character and interest of a building. For example, a particular concern over recent years has been the destruction of character that often occurs when farm buildings are converted to residential use (English Heritage, 1993).

An important and unusual part of the English system is the statutory role of amenity societies in conservation planning decisions. At least since the formation of SPAB in 1877 the amenity movement has played an important role in the development of conservation legislation and practice. A number of amenity bodies form part of the statutory framework. Local authorities are obliged to consult the *Ancient Monuments Society*, the *Council for British Archaeology*, *SPAB*, the *Georgian Group*, the *Victorian Society* and the *Twentieth Century Society* on proposals involving the total or partial demolition of a listed building, and in practice these bodies may be involved in commenting on a range of other applications. Other societies such as the *Garden History Society* and the *Theatres Trust* have to be consulted on applications in their particular spheres of expertise.

There are many other voluntary sector or charitable bodies in the conservation field. They are far too numerous to do more than briefly mention some of the most important here. The *Civic Trust* has been mentioned in this chapter a number of times, and this body, created in 1957, has been influential in particular in the sphere of conservation areas. *SAVE Britain's Heritage* has, since the 1970s, been an important campaigning body on particular sites or particular groups of endangered buildings. The *National Trust*, created in 1895, manages a huge portfolio of historic buildings and environments (Fig. 14.8). Building preservation trusts (BPT) (discussed above) have been a major contributor to the rescue of historic buildings across the country. There are currently approximately 150 BPTs, most of which are based around a particular town or locality. The *Landmark Trust* has become particularly known for its conversion of often derelict historic buildings to holiday accommodation.

Education and training

At a professional level, conservation skills historically resided in a small number of architects and surveyors specializing in conservation work. However, as the conservation system has become more extensive and more integrated with the system of town planning this picture has changed. The development of a specialist skill base in local authority planning departments led to the creation of the Association of Conservation Officers in 1981. This group has now become sufficiently established to form the core of a new professional body for the cultural built heritage, the Institute of Historic Building Conservation, created in 1997, and with a wider

Fig. 14.8 Little Moreton Hall, Cheshire – one of the many historic properties in the care of the National Trust.

membership of conservation professionals than its local government origins. This professionalization and skill development in local authorities has been of key importance but is far from uniformly developed across the country. Established professional institutes such as the Royal Town Planning Institute, the Royal Institute of British Architects and the Royal Institution of Chartered Surveyors (RICS) have recognized the growing importance of conservation with varying degrees of enthusiasm and belatedness.

The growth of conservation, and the development of career possibilities, has been paralleled by developments in further and higher education. A number of well-established courses, which have historically focused on the development of mid-career skills for those already working in conservation, have been joined by a number of new undergraduate and postgraduate courses for those interested in acquiring a conservation training and education from the outset of their careers. Similarly, attention is being given to the development of craft and vocational training through the efforts of bodies such as the Conference on Training in Architectural Conservation (COTAC).

Wales, Scotland and Northern Ireland

The differences between England and these other principal components of the United Kingdom are mostly procedural. However, there are some more significant differences worthy of brief mention. None of these countries has the direct equivalent of English Heritage. These functions are either carried out by executive agencies much more closely bound into the structure of government (*Cadw* in Wales and *Historic Scotland* in Scotland) or directly by the Secretary of State (in Northern Ireland). The principal significance of this is that these arrangements, unlike those for English Heritage, do not allow for an independent line to be taken separate from government policy or allow for these bodies to appear at public inquiries.

The primary legislation in Wales is the same as England. However, policy guidance takes a different form and there is no direct equivalent of PPG 15. In 1999 there were nearly 23,000 listed buildings in Wales and just over 500 conservation areas. In Scotland the primary legislation is different from, though very similar to, England and Wales. Buildings are graded differently (A, B and C) with the top grades forming a larger proportion of the listed building stock. In 1998 there were nearly 44,000 listed buildings and over 600 conservation areas in Scotland. In Northern Ireland all planning functions are undertaken by central government. In 1995 there were approximately 8,000 listed buildings and in 1998 54 conservation areas in Northern Ireland.

Conclusions

The United Kingdom system for the protection of the cultural heritage is extraordinarily extensive. Furthermore, it is supported by a highly developed (and rather complex) legal and policy framework. On the whole this must be considered a good thing. Inevitably some conservationists always want the system to be further developed, though this is now largely related to relatively narrow particular concerns or to perceived technical deficiencies.

Conversely some see the extent of heritage protection as a blanket smothering innovation. However, there is little systematic evidence for this and the system is in many ways extremely flexible. Change is embedded in the concept of conservation, generally taken as meaning protecting key qualities but with scope for evolution.

The extensiveness of protection does raise some issues, however. As the extent of the culturally valued heritage has grown, so have a range of ways about thinking about the management of this resource. Applying strict conservative repair principles to over 500,000 listed buildings and to a whole range of other historic environments is impractical. However, an accepted and coherent philosophical framework which embraces this wider historic environment has yet to be evolved, though efforts have recently been made in this direction. In practice the various philosophical strands described are combined in different ways by different agencies and individuals and the very flexibility of the system can lead to tensions and inconsistencies.

Compared with many other countries, the British system of protection has developed a high degree of integration with the system of town and country planning, and this is arguably one of its great strengths. However, it can also be argued that there remain issues which are yet to be satisfactorily resolved. So, for example, adequate conservation skills and political support for maintaining the cultural built heritage do not exist in all local authorities, there are difficulties in, and uncertainty over, the appropriate architectural form of new buildings in historic areas and the role of the general public in conservation planning.

Finally, there can be no doubt that conservation in the United Kingdom has enjoyed popular and political support over the last 25 years or so of the twentieth century, as evidenced, for example, by the large number of protected heritage assets. However, conservationists should not be complacent; the public's mood can swing and governments change. There are perhaps two particular areas to which attention is needed which have recently been given recognition in an English Heritage discussion paper (English Heritage, 1997b). First, the emergence of the sustainability agenda has had a fairly marginal impact on conservation practice to date. Second, the extent of the historic environment, and the pluralistic society in which it exists, means that a system which is largely expert-driven and object-focused is no longer adequate. As suggested by the Burra Charter (Marquis-Kyle and Walker, 1992), there is a need to ensure attention is given to place rather than merely fabric, and to do this involves engaging beyond expert communities with those who use these places.

Notes

1 Statistics on listed buildings are the subject of confusion. Figures used here are derived from statistics held by DCMS. The number of list entries is approximately 370,000 but in early lists a list entry may include, for example, a whole terrace. Other attempts to extrapolate entries into numbers of buildings have estimated the numbers of listed buildings to be in the region of 500,000.

2 Note the problems of listed building statistics described above.

References

ARUP Economics and Planning (1995): *Environmental Capacity: A Methodology for Historic Cities*, ARUP, London.

Bournemouth University and English Heritage (1997): *The Monuments at Risk Survey of England 1995: Summary Report*, Bournemouth University and English Heritage, Bournemouth and London.

British Standards Institution (1998): *Guide to the Principles of the Conservation of Historic Buildings, BS 7913*, BSI, London.

Cullen, G. (1961): *Townscape*, The Architectural Press, London.

Delafons, J. (1997): *Politics and Preservation*, E & FN Spon, London.

Department of the Environment (1990): *Planning Policy Guidance 16: Archaeology and Planning*, HMSO, London.

Department of the Environment and Department of National Heritage (1994): *Planning Policy Guidance 15: Planning and the Historic Environment*, HMSO, London.

English Heritage (1988): 'Shopping in Historic Towns: A Policy Statement', *Conservation Bulletin*, 1–2.

English Heritage (1991): *Principles of Repair*, English Heritage, London.

English Heritage (1993): *The Conversion of Historic Farm Buildings*, English Heritage, London.

English Heritage (1995): *Conservation Area Practice*, English Heritage, London.

English Heritage (1997a): *Conservation Area Appraisals*, English Heritage, London.

English Heritage (1997b): *Sustaining the Historic Environment: New Perspectives on the Future*, English Heritage, London.

English Heritage (1998): *Buildings at Risk: A New Strategy*, English Heritage, London.

English Heritage (1999): *Enabling Development and the Conservation of Heritage Assets*, English Heritage, London.

English Historic Towns Forum (1992): *Townscape in Trouble: Conservation Areas – The Case for Change*, EHTF.

English Historic Towns Forum (1998): *Conservation Area Management: a practical guide*, EHTF.

Fairclough, G. (1999): 'Protecting the Cultural Landscape: National Designation and Local Character', in J. Grenville (ed.), *Managing the Historic Rural Landscape* (pp. 179), Routledge, London.

Hamer, D. (1998): *History in Urban Places: The Historic Districts of the United States*, Ohio State University Press, Columbus.

Hanna, M. (annual): *English Heritage Monitor*, London: English Tourist Board.

ICOMOS (1964): *International Charter for the Conservation and Restoration of Monuments and Sites: 'The Venice Charter'*, ICOMOS, Paris.

ICOMOS (1987): *Charter on the Conservation of Historic Towns and Urban Areas: 'The Washington Charter'*, ICOMOS, Paris.

Kindred, B. (1992): *Listed Building Repairs Notices*: Association of Conservation Officers.

Larkham, P. (1996): *Conservation and the City*, Routledge, London.

Larkham, P., and Barrett, H. (1998): 'Conservation of the built environment under the Conservatives', in Allmendinger, P. and Thomas, H. (eds), *Urban Planning and the British New Right* (pp. 287), Routledge, London.

Marquis-Kyle, P. and Walker, M. (1992): *The Illustrated Burra Charter*, Australia ICOMOS, Sydney.

Morris, W. (1877): *Restoration*, reprinted by the Society for the Protection of Ancient Buildings as their Manifesto, SPAB, London.

Morton, D. (1991): 'Conservation areas: has saturation point been reached?' *The Planner*, 77(17), 5–8.

Mynors, C. (1999): *Listed Buildings, Conservation Areas and Monuments*, 3rd edition, Sweet and Maxwell, London.

Pendlebury, J. and Townshend, T. (1999): 'The Conservation of Historic Areas and Public Participation', *Journal of Architectural Conservation*, 5(2), 72–87.

Pickard, R. D. (1993/4): 'Fire Safety and Protection in Historic Buildings in England and Ireland – Part 1', *Structural Survey*, 12(2), 27–31.

Pickard, R. D. (1996): *Conservation in the Built Environment*, Longman, Harlow, Essex.

Pickard, R. D. (ed.) (2001): *Management of Historic Centres*, Conservation of the European Built Heritage Series: Spon Press, London (see Chapter 13 by Lovie, D. 'Grainger Town, Newcastle upon Tyne').

Richards, J. (1994): *Façadism*. Routledge, London.

Ruskin, J. (1855): *The Seven Lamps of Architecture* (2nd ed.), Smith Elder, London.

SAVE Britain's Heritage (1978): *Preservation Pays: Tourism and the Economic Benefits of Conserving Historic Buildings*, SAVE, London.

Smith, D. (1969): 'The Civic Amenities Act: Conservation and Planning'. *Town Planning Review*, 40(2), 149–62.

Strange, I. (1997): 'Planning for change, conserving the past: towards sustainable development policy in historic cities?' *Cities*, 14(4), 227–33.

Whitehand, J. W. R. (ed.). (1981): *The Urban Landscape: Historical Development and Management: Papers by M. R. G. Conzen*, Academic Press, London.

Robert Pickard

Review

Introduction

This study of legal and policy issues for the conservation and protection of the immovable heritage in thirteen different countries within Europe provides an opportunity to reflect on the different approaches. Without further detailed examination it will not be possible to determine ideals of best practice. ('Guidance on the development of legislation and administration systems in the field of Cultural Heritage', including the architectural, archaeological and movable heritage and drawing on examples from different countries, has been published by the Council of Europe in 2000). Nevertheless, the study sheds light on the complexity of provisions utilized in practice in comparison to the brief framework of articles identified in the Granada and Malta Conventions.

Definition of the heritage

The way in which items of the immovable cultural heritage are defined for protection generally do not follow the terms used in the Granada and Malta Conventions but nevertheless they can be said to be similar.

The interest factors used for the purpose of selecting objects for protection – conspicuous historical, archaeological, artistic, scientific, social or technical interest for the architectural heritage (and 'collective memory' in the case of the archaeological heritage) – are generally followed by a combination of the same or similar terms or other terms. For instance, 'landscape' (Wallonia, Belgium), 'revolutionary' (Czech Republic), 'architectural' (Denmark, Malta and United Kingdom), 'aesthetic' (Georgia and France), 'palaeontological' (Italy, Malta and Spain), 'ethnological' (France, Italy and Spain), 'spiritual' and 'religious' (in Georgia and Ireland respectively), 'urban design' and 'folk-lore' (Thüringia, Germany), illustrate the different 'interest', 'quality', 'value' or 'significance' factors. Social interest may also be represented by 'public interest', 'events' or 'persons of note in history' and 'military significance', while environmental and economic considerations may also be used.

The definition of 'monument' categories is wide. There are also different approaches as to whether there should be one single category or different levels of protection. The argument for different levels of protection would seem to be tied to the question of economics. A higher level may warrant priority support (largely due to the limited funds available to support conservation action), whereas countries that have chosen one level have decided not to discriminate on the basis that all monuments should be equally eligible or for other reasons. For instance, Denmark used to have both A and B levels of listed buildings but due to a reassessment of the selection criteria (which recognized the importance of industrial buildings for example), the distinction was removed. A brief summary of the terms of definition can be identified as follows:

- Belgium veers towards the simple definitions in the conventions (monuments, groups of buildings, sites and archaeological sites) in the case of the Walloon region. The main level of protection is by 'listing', although there are 133 items that are listed as 'exceptional immovable heritage', and there is also the 'safeguard' (for temporary protection) and the possibility of *ad hoc* designations from the inventory. The Brussels-Capital and Flemish regions use different approaches.
- In the Czech Republic assets are defined as immovable and movable objects and sets of objects (from the oldest time to the present) – items of the cultural heritage defined as national cultural monuments.
- Denmark adopts the concept of listed buildings (with an age criterion of being more than 50 years old) and a lower level of 'buildings worthy of preservation' which are dealt with more in relation to local planning mechanisms and the SAVE system. With respect to archaeological heritage these are categorized as ancient and recent monuments as well as underwater monuments.
- France uses an all-encompassing system of 'historic monuments' on two levels: 'classification' and 'inclusion on the supplementary list of historic monuments' (with no age distinction – the most recently classified item dates from 1998).
- Legislation approved by the Georgian government in 1999 has defined five types of monuments (archaeological, urban park and landscape art, architectural, monumental fine art, and monuments associated with the development of science, technology and industry). Three levels of significance have been identified (international – i.e. sites that are included on the UNESCO World Heritage List – national and local).
- The German state of Thüringia defines the concept of 'cultural monument' including objects, groups of objects and parts of objects, ground monuments and archaeological monuments and while there is only one level of protection, in practice the authorities prioritize action on certain monuments. A similar approach is used in other German states.

- Ireland has a system of national/historic monuments (in existence before 1700 although later monuments can be protected), heritage buildings (in public ownership), and a new system (operational from the beginning of 2000) to give greater protection to buildings of the architectural heritage through locally based development plan objectives.
- Italy has had a fragmented system of definition including objects of artistic and cultural importance and monuments in nature, but legislation from the end of 1999 has redefined the concept of monuments.
- Four types of monuments of 'state' significance (which incorporate different age criteria) are defined in Latvia: archaeological, town planning and archaeological, art, and historic monuments. Monuments of local significance can also be defined.
- Malta defines, through its structure plan policies, listed buildings at three levels (which may soon be revised), and classification of the archaeological heritage according to four types.
- The Netherlands, in its historic buildings and ancient monuments Act, defines objects (generally buildings more than 50 years old) and sites (including archaeological sites).
- In Spain the 'real property' heritage items include monuments, sites, gardens, archaeological sites and areas, and environments. Autonomous regions also have their own system of local designations.
- In the United Kingdom items of the architectural heritage (listed buildings) are categorized according to three levels (generally they must be at least 30 years old), whereas assets of the archaeological heritage are defined as scheduled ancient monuments ('areas of archaeological importance' have now been largely superseded by other methods of protection through the planning system).

In general terms, monument protection is with respect to the 'whole' monument. However there are different methods of identifying the scope and regime of protection. In the United Kingdom, case law has been used to define the fixtures, objects, structures and land associated with a listed building which often causes disputes, but the idea of defining items or boundaries remains a question of discussion. Moreover, the context or 'setting' of a listed building exists but does not extend to an actual definition. New legislation in Ireland has attempted to deal with this problem by making a 'record of protected structures'. In Germany the exterior and movable parts can be protected as well as the surroundings. In Belgium the opportunity exists to protect different items so that even the frontage/façade can be singled out. Protection zones can be defined on a 'case by case basis' (Belgium, Czech Republic, Georgia) or by a defined radius (France, Latvia and Denmark in relation to ancient monuments)

One marked difference between a number of countries seems to be in relation to the issues covered by laws and also the different types of laws used as the basis of protection. Most of the countries use all encompassing laws for the protection of the 'cultural heritage' in its widest sense – immovable, movable or other. However, Denmark, Ireland, Malta and the United

Kingdom use different legislation and policy mechanisms for the architectural and the archaeological heritage, although there is a degree of overlap in the management of these issues. Concerning the architectural heritage, individual objects that can be protected include 'listed buildings' (Denmark, Malta, United Kingdom) which are based on national criteria. In Malta the definitions are provided through the 'structure plan' and the United Kingdom uses planning legislation for the protection of buildings of 'special architectural and historic interest' (the same applies in the Walloon region of Belgium but not in the other two regions). In comparison, in Ireland recent legislation requires local planning authorities to devise protection objectives for 'structures' in relation to the preservation of buildings according to defined interest factors, but there is also the category of 'heritage building' which is defined at the national level. In these four countries the archaeological heritage is protected through separate legislation. In England 'scheduled ancient monuments' and in Ireland the protection procedures grew out of early legislation concerning ancient monuments dating from the late nineteenth century when Ireland formed part of the United Kingdom. In both countries there is a degree of overlap: in theory some protected buildings can also be protected monuments.

In Denmark ancient monuments are protected under nature protection legislation. Similar approaches have been used in Malta and in Italy where the idea of nature monuments has existed alongside the protection of cultural objects and has included items that may generally be regarded as items of the immovable heritage.

Historic parks and gardens and other combined works of man and nature, making reference to the concept of 'sites' in the Granada Convention and the 'context' of monuments in the Malta Convention are also considered in different ways. In Italy, villas, gardens and parks and other environments composed of immovable objects have been protected under legislation for the protection of nature and buildings. In England, the register of historic parks and gardens has not been given a statutory footing but they may be safeguarded through being a 'material consideration' in decisions concerning new development activity. In France, Belgium (Wallonia), The Netherlands and Spain, monument protection can cover sites such as parks and gardens, while in Georgia an 'urban park and landscape monument' can be specifically defined. In Germany (Thüringia) a 'monument ensemble' can be designated for this purpose, in Latvia a 'cultural landscape' can be classified as a 'composite' immovable cultural monument, and in the Czech Republic landscape conservation sites and zones may be defined.

The concept of 'sites' and 'groups of buildings' (the latter mentioned in both the Granada and Malta Conventions) are often not specifically used in the sample of countries examined. Apart from the designation possibilities for parks, gardens and landscapes mentioned above (in relation to cultural heritage protection), many countries have adopted environmental and nature protection laws and policies which can be used to protect the combined works of man and nature. However, with respect to cultural heritage legislation, the consideration of sites and groups is more generally approached through area-based mechanisms such as *secteur saugardé* and ZPPAUPs (France), conservation zones and sites (Czech Republic), monument ensembles (Thüringia, Germany), the SAVE system (Denmark), urban parks including ensembles and complexes (Georgia), architectural conservation areas (Ireland), town planning monuments and reserves of cultural monuments (Latvia), and conservation areas (Malta and the United Kingdom). Historic sites that form a townscape unity or groups of immovable objects can be specifically designated in Spain and The Netherlands respectively.

Buildings can be listed for 'group value' in the United Kingdom, 'sets' of objects and 'composite' objects can be declared in the Czech Republic and Latvia, whereas the *à la carte* approach in Belgium can consider different choices depending on the merits of the case. Similarly in France the law allows the possibility of applying historic monument status to entire areas of cities, towns and villages.

Archaeological sites, apart from individual archaeological monuments, are generally recognized within the sample of countries. The question of protection of 'perceived remains' is generally implicit – the contributions from Belgium, France, Germany and the United Kingdom indicate that protection methods can be defined for this purpose although it is in relation to integrated conservation systems that this issue should be further scrutinized (discussed below).

One outstanding difference between the countries is the number of 'monuments' defined for protection. In the United Kingdom, taking into consideration England, Scotland, Wales and Northern Ireland, approximately 575,000 items have protection as 'listed buildings' and approximately 10,000 conservation areas have been established. There are also approximately 18,000 scheduled ancient monuments in England and their number is expected to increase to over 40,000 once the current review of the ancient heritage has been completed. By contrast, in France, there are currently approximately 40,000 buildings that have been 'classified' or included in the supplementary inventory of historic monuments as well as 92 *secteur sauvegaurdés*. This does not mean to say that there are fewer items of cultural heritage value in France, it is more a reflection of policy designation, as an historic monument is tied in with a commitment to financial support, which cannot be guaranteed for all listed buildings in the United Kingdom. Moreover, for unprotected historic buildings and areas other methods are used to financially support rehabilitation through the ANAH/OPAH arrangement.

In contrast to other countries, it would seem that the approach taken in the United Kingdom is quite remarkable. For instance, in The Netherlands there is a total of 48,474 protected monuments. In Denmark there are 9,200 listed buildings and some 30,000 ancient monuments. In the Czech Republic there are 38,700 immovable monuments and 389 conservation areas in total, and in Latvia there are 8,428 cultural monuments of all types. The higher number of protected items in the United Kingdom has been the subject of critical comment in recent years. In turn, this has led increasingly towards area-based systems of funding in the last 10 years. A new major review of the 'historic environment' commenced in the United Kingdom in 2000 from which there may be some reappraisal of the general approach to protection. Notably a review conducted in the mid-1990s put forward the idea of listing 'façades' and questioned the number of conservation area designations – largely due to the cost implications of having so many protected items. However, although there has been concern at the shortage of supporting funds, the Heritage Lottery Fund has provided a level of financial support that could be envied by many other countries.

Identification of the heritage

Since the Granada and Malta Conventions came into being, identifying the need to maintain inventories and to document threatened items of the heritage, further work has been developed at the international level to identify core data information (Council of Europe, 1995 and 1999; Getty Information Institute/Council of Europe, 1998). Moreover, the development of geographical information systems (GIS) and other new information technology methods have provided the means to improve recording methods. It is clear that these are now beginning to be used in a number of countries, particularly in those countries where laws and policies have been reviewed in recent years.

In Denmark and Ireland new inventory systems have been developed in response to these countries signing the Granada Convention. Furthermore recording systems have been developed along the lines of the core data index/standard in Belgium, Georgia, Ireland and Malta and most countries are now recording inventory information on computer databases. The 'index' was developed by a working group, with members drawn from heritage organizations in France, Germany, The Netherlands, Sweden and the United Kingdom, established under the aegis of the Council of Europe (Getty Information Institute/Council of Europe, 1998). The 'standard' has drawn on the experience of organizations that have already implemented heritage databases, for example, DKC (Denmark), MONARCH (England), DRACAR (France) and ARCHIS (The Netherlands) (Council of Europe, 1999). The MIDAS (Monument Inventory Data Standard) is being developed to provide an on-line information system in England (http://www.rchme.gov.uk/survey.html) but in Thüringia (Germany) the MIDAS system has been found to be inflexible. GIS systems are now being used in Belgium, Czech Republic and France (where the concept of a 'heritage atlas' is being considered to combine all heritage data in a given region – similar to the 'preservation atlas' developed through the SAVE system in Denmark). Pilot projects have been developed to examine the potential of GIS in the United Kingdom. Other new technologies have been used to document the heritage and include the use of CD-ROM (for example, to create a 'virtual' record in Ireland and also in France).

Work to record the heritage began in the nineteenth century in the Czech Republic, but for most countries in this study serious attempts to develop inventories commenced much later. The last ten years has seen this action escalate due to improvements in information technology, political changes (particularly in the new independent republics of central and eastern Europe), and the need to reassess the methods by which the immovable heritage and the environment are managed.

• In Belgium, an inventory for the Walloon region was completed in 1998 and a new inventory is to be developed which will recognize a wider concept of the heritage, taking into consideration the interplay between built 'landscapes', economic and social history and the morphology of territories. The aim is to develop this work as a management tool for decision makers in relation to land-use planning of the 'living environment'. Furthermore, the inventory of the architectural heritage has been an important instrument for *ad hoc* protection of assets and a benchmark for framing integrated policies.

• In the Czech Republic, there has been a need to revise inventory records since the 'velvet revolution' in 1989, particularly due to the restitution of property to private owners and also due to a new wave of building and development pressure. In this respect the up-dating process is to be used to assist authorities in the granting of permits and for land-use planning. The Central list is not the basis of protection, but the information contained in it is used to determine items for protection.

• In Denmark, the inventory records developed in the 1960s–1980s are now being augmented by 'thematic surveys' (for example, to re-evaluate the industrial heritage) and by the topographical assessment of areas through the SAVE system to assist in the management of the cultural built environment. With respect to the latter, the aim is to produce a 'preservation atlas' for each of the 267 municipal areas, of which approximately 60 have been surveyed so far.

• In France, the general inventory was set up in 1964 which, so far, has covered 25 per cent of the French territory. This work does not form the basis of protection but the results are increasingly used in this context. Current action is also concentrating on developing a 'heritage atlas' for each region and further studies are being carried out to assist in management activities.

• As a new legislative framework for cultural heritage protection is being developed in Georgia and new systems for recording the heritage are in process. A new form of identification was adopted for the architectural heritage in 1997, however the recording of archaeological heritage awaits the approval of legislation in this field which is being developed over 2000. Planning legislation also still awaits approval and it will therefore take some time before the information can be integrated with land-use planning to assist in the management of the heritage.

• In Germany, at the national level, a handbook of the most important building and art monuments was completed in 1998. Following the monument topography survey, which commenced in Thüringia in the 1970s, monuments are now being re-examined in this state. Similar action has taken place in other former GDR states, the need for which has arisen due to the re-unification of Germany, the restitution of property to private owners and the enactment of new laws and policy on heritage protection.

- In Ireland, the national inventory of the architectural heritage was placed on a statutory footing in 1999 and survey action has occurred over the last decade, and is on-going, to develop inventories for towns and also for geographical county areas. This information is to be used as a management tool for the protection of structures under planning legislation following the commencement of a new legislative regime at the beginning of 2000. Work is also on-going to develop and publish a survey of the archaeological heritage and other inventories are being developed including for urban archaeology and a record of monuments and places.

- In Italy, work to catalogue the heritage assets has been in process for a long period of time. The process of recording has considered the relative values of each asset as well as their condition. However, the political will to complete a full inventory of the Italian heritage has been lacking (partly for financial reasons). A new legislative regime, which came into being at the end of 1999, may assist in developing this work.

- Surveying work in Latvia has concentrated on reviewing all cultural objects of state interest (and then to divide them into state and local significance) in the context of the new legislative regime developed in the last decade. Work has also commenced to assess the condition of the heritage in order to determine appropriate courses of action.

- Since 1992 the Planning Authority in Malta has been compiling lists of scheduled monuments and sites which presently include 10,000 buildings and 300 archaeological sites. This information is being utilized by the Planning Authority in relation to the structure plan and (proposed local plans) for the Maltese Islands.

- All protected monuments dating from before 1850 have been recorded on the official register in The Netherlands and from 1985 to 1995 the heritage from the period 1850–1994 was recorded and subsequent registrations have been made. In 2000 a new project has begun to record items from the period of reconstruction following World War II.

- Identification of the Spanish Historical Heritage has concentrated on recording items in a General Register (for protection) and the autonomous regions have also been involved in developing their own special inventories which can be used to as a management tool.

- In the United Kingdom, the Sites and Monument Record plays a similar role to the same named record used in Ireland. A re-survey of the architectural heritage was completed in 1989 and has played the most significant role in determining which assets should be put on the statutory 'list'. Since the mid-1990s recent survey work has been of a thematic basis, looking in particular at buildings of the twentieth century. The on-going Monument Protection Programme is expected to more than double the number of 'scheduled ancient monuments'. Other work to assist in the management of the immovable heritage includes the building-at-risk and monuments-at-risk surveys that have been developed in recent years to prioritize action. Non-statutory registers for historic parks and gardens and battlefields have also been formulated; registered sites are now regarded as being 'material' matters in the planning and development decision-making process.

In general inventories are not normally utilized as the basis for protecting assets, but as a means to determine which assets should be protected, although in some cases the inventory (or register) is used directly to define items for protection. It is clear that the information contained in inventories and the development of new recording techniques and technology will increasingly have an important role to play in protection decisions especially in developing management tools for integrating heritage protection and land-use management.

The preservation and protection of the heritage

Once heritage assets have been identified and designated for protection legal implications necessarily follow to ensure that preservation objectives are met through the authorization and supervision of activities.

In relation to the architectural heritage this concerns control over activities such as repair and maintenance, use and adaptive re-use, demolition and other activities. In some countries there is an implied, or even an explicit, duty of care imposed on owners and failure to observe this can lead to sanctions and coercive measures being applied (see below).

There are many different approaches to the administration of control procedures. A single-track permission procedure (linked with the planning system) exists in Wallonia (Belgium) and similarly in Ireland planning permission is required for changes to protected structures (which are controlled through planning legislation). In Malta there are two consent procedures, but unless historic buildings are protected under both Antiquities and Planning legislation, the control of activities in relation to 'listed buildings' (as defined in the structure plan) will only require planning consent. In Spain, town councils regulate matters according to Special Preservation Plans (which are approved after the heritage authority has commented on them) – but there are reserve powers of control by the heritage administration. Elsewhere the control of activities concerning heritage assets is more usually independent from associated development control procedures although integrated forms of planning help to ensure that there is a link between conservation and development control.

The general theme for control procedures is related to whether proposed actions will materially affect the character of a particular architectural asset. To some extent this depends on the philosophy of conservation (see below) adopted within a particular country but in general there is a movement towards encouraging maintenance and conservative repair rather than restoration – the idea of conjectural restoration or reconstruction finds little support now.

The idea of allowing new uses for historic buildings is generally accept-able if it helps to maintain the long-term preservation of the assets. Alterations to accommodate a new use may be permissible if they do not materially cause detriment to the character or values for which the item has been protected. It is difficult to apply precise rules in this context and the general principle is that each case should be looked at on its merits. In Georgia there is the concept of 'eligible uses'. In France there is a greater likelihood of permission being granted for a new use for items contained on the 'supplementary' list as compared to classified monuments (as is the case for lower grades of listed buildings in the United Kingdom and Malta).

Authorization of works is often delegated to a local level such as town councils in Spain, the local *Soprintendenza* in Italy, or local planning authorities in the United Kingdom (reserve powers of control are usually maintained by a higher authority). In other countries the authorization procedure is exercised by a higher authority (for example, the state auth-orities in the Czech Republic, France and Latvia).

For the archaeological heritage there is generally a much stricter control over activities in most countries with authorization often being required at the higher level (for example, by the relevant Secretary of State in the United Kingdom and the relevant Minister in Ireland). A common feature seems to be that there is a mandatory requirement to report the discovery of archaeological items to the appropriate authorities.

The Malta Convention highlights the need to preserve the archaeological heritage *in situ* – preservation *by record* is therefore a less desired option. New pressures on archaeological sites led to the revised European Conven-tion in which the integrated approach to management has been advocated – similar to the Granada Convention. Pre-development recording and investig-ation is therefore becoming increasingly important – the only danger with this is that it may encourage destruction of actual assets and safeguarding them may only become a process of recording. For some countries there are insufficient resources to monitor this problem and there remains problems concerning the cost of investigation and the type of agencies that conduct the investigation (i.e. public or private). This issue has been further scru-tinized by the Council of Europe through a study on practice concerning archaeology in the urban context (1999a).

Another aspect that the Malta Convention has addressed is the need to prevent the illicit traffic of movable items found in archaeological sites. For countries where legislation is still in the process of formulation, and where staff resources are scarce, this issue is of particular concern. Within a wider framework this problem was considered in the 4th European Conference of Ministers responsible for the Cultural Heritage (in Helsinki, 1996). Following on from this the Council of Europe has promoted a dialogue between states, international organizations and interested groups (such as law enforcement agencies, customs services, representatives of the art market, and religious authorities) to help resolve this issue. This will culminate in an International Forum on this problem area to be held in Strasbourg at the end of 2000.

Conservation philosophy

Approaches to the way work is carried out in relation to the architectural heritage reflect the debate that has occurred on conservation philosophy over the last 150 years or so. On one hand evidence of the principle of 'unity of style' following Voillet-le-Duc's theories on *restoration* (1866), as well as others who have advocated the restoration approach, has certainly had an influence within the sample of countries (i.e. the idea that restoring a building is to bring it back to completeness). On the other, the influence of Ruskin (1849) is evident, as well as those who have advocated the *conservation* approach (i.e. that the patina of time should be safeguarded and that maintenance should be pursued on the basis that the worn original material is immeasurably more important than a modern imitation, not matter how carefully it has been forged). The distinction between these two theories is clear, and the conservative/maintenance approach is certainly the most important now.

However, practice in different European countries is not so clear. There is an element of merging of the two approaches in some cases. Moreover, the Venice Charter (ICOMOS, 1964) remains an important document for several countries. In article 9 of the charter, the process of restoration is acknowledged so long as it is based on respect for original materials and authentic documentary evidence. It further states that any restoration work must not be conjectural and infers that such work should be honest, showing a 'contemporary stamp'. Thus a compromise may be achieved where evidence allows the restoration approach to be used, but at the same time respecting the contributions of all periods. Other documents have developed the debate on this issue further (notably the 1981 ICOMOS Australia Burra Charter – which has recently been revised) and some countries have chosen to issue their own guidelines on conservation and restoration.

Since the Venice Charter was formulated, the philosophical debate has extended to other issues. In particular, the notion of allowing alterations to accommodate new uses was encouraged by the *Amsterdam Declaration* (Council of Europe, 1975) and there has been a movement away from the singular importance of individual buildings to area-based and integrated methods of conservation. Moreover, the argument for rehabilitation has gained greater ground in recent years as society moves towards more sustainable ways of living.

A brief summary of the approaches adopted in the countries under examination identifies current thinking on conservation philosophy:

- In all the regions of Belgium there is an obligation to carry out 'necessary conservation and maintenance work'. Restoration is still considered but maintenance and preventative action are the preferred courses of action, avoiding the cost of expensive restoration, and this approach is encouraged partly by policy and also by the *Monumentenwacht* through its subsidised survey system (which can be linked to grant aid). Moreover, the need to safeguard 'living environments' has given support to the idea of rehabilitation.

- The debate between the restoration and conservation approaches has moved backwards and forwards over time within the Czech Republic. For a large part of the twentieth century the conservation approach has been advocated but the 'synthesized-reconstruction' has remained and conservation theory has retained an element of flexibility. The present generation of experts has rejected the concept of costly reconstruction which was encouraged by the socialist building contractors of the 1970s and 1980s and preference is now being given to 'timely repairs' although many owners of cultural monuments continue to prefer substantial renovation. To increase the quality of techniques the State Institute for the Preservation of the Cultural Heritage started publishing a series of methodological handbooks from 1996.
- The basic premise for preservation work in Denmark is to strive to maintain as much as possible of the original material for as long as possible. Where substantial work is necessary it is subject to stringent assessment in terms of necessity and authenticity. Re-use is encouraged where it can help to prolong the life of a listed building. Each case is looked at on its merits and requires a detailed plan to be produced for the proposed works – the over-riding consideration being that the more authentic the building is, the less one should plan for changes.
- In France the method of intervention advocated by Voillet-le-Duc, to-wards the restoration of a monument to its so-called 'ideal' original state was advocated until the 1960s. Since the Venice Charter, the concept of restoration has changed in favour of the conservation of an entire building, authenticity and respect for the strata of history. Another evolutionary influence has also occurred – that of linking the monument to its environment – which has addressed the needs of society in terms of rehabilitation and reuse.
- In Georgia, various approaches may be accepted as appropriate – the combined actions of 'restoration, reconstruction, adaption, application and maintenance' are said to form a conservation philosophy. In practice, there has been little debate on the principles of conservation particularly as international guidelines, such as the Venice Charter, have not been translated into the Georgian language. Moreover, as Georgia is currently in the process of reforming legislation in the field of cultural heritage it will take some time before new thinking on conservation methods can be formulated and implemented.
- German debate on conservation philosophy has seen a movement from those who advocated the approach of Voillet-le-Duc towards the approach of timely maintenance. Financial as well as philosophical arguments tend to counter the idea of 'full-blown' restorations today although more 'doubtful' solutions can still be tolerated. Alternative uses are encouraged on the basis that, without the inevitable compromises that are necessary for this (i.e. a purist theory of conservation is not always followed), the monument landscape would be much poorer.
- Until recently the protection of the architectural heritage in Ireland remained in a weak position. By signing the Granada Convention and

reforming and strengthening legislative provisions, this situation is now very different. However, while work is carried out with cognizance of the ICOMOS Charters, no principles of conservation have been developed yet. Nevertheless, there is an intention to issue guidelines to planning authorities in relation to development plan objectives for the protection of the architectural heritage.

- The historical profile of theories on conservation and restoration in Italy again reveals the early debate between the opposing views of Voillet-le-Duc and Ruskin. However, the 1932 Italian Restoration Charter, extended by the subsequent 'Instructions for the Restoration of Monuments', advocated the importance of maintenance and avoided any discussion of stylistic restoration. Moreover, since the Venice Charter, the 1972 Charter for Restoration made clear that stylistic restoration and the elimination of successive layers built over time was forbidden as well as advocating the concept of 'reversibility'.

- The Latvian approach to preservation work is based on 'understanding'. The transformation of cultural monuments is permissible only when it is necessary to save a monument and when a 'contemporary stamp' is used for new work while safeguarding the original values. In other respects, the need to pass monuments to future generations in an 'authentic' form is the defined rule, reflecting the different historical layers, and the advocated approach is against false restoration and imitation.

- The situation in Malta is less clear, partly due to the fact that policy for the architectural heritage has only recently been strengthened. For the most important grade 1 listed buildings interventions have to be carried out according to scientific analysis. In other respects, the structure plan encourages a broader philosophy of rehabilitation.

- In The Netherlands the general approach today is 'conservative repair' and this has been supported by the work of the *Monumentenwacht* organization (where the system first started) although restoration work is still allowed if approved through the agreement of a plan which safeguards monumental values. Grant aid has supported restoration action but the authorities are increasingly moving against costly restoration work and in favour of regular maintenance.

- In Spain technical interventions in assets of cultural interest are permitted according to a number of different approaches: conservation, consolidation and restoration and as long as the interventions respect the contributions of every period. Reconstruction and imitation is not permitted.

- Modern approaches to conservation in the United Kingdom are based on ideas developed in the nineteenth century by Ruskin and Morris (1877) – essentially 'conservative repair'. The importance of this approach has recently been reflected in *Principles of Repair*, published by English Heritage in 1991, a British Standard published in 1998, and guidelines to fundamental courses of action based on the theories developed in various international charters published by Historic Scotland (Bell, 1997). Re-use is actively encouraged where an original use has been lost, and also rehabilitation on a wider scale.

The evidence of this study suggests that conjectural major restoration work is generally not pursued today. The debate is more about whether restoration, in an authentic form, respecting the changes of time and originality of materials or methods should be pursued, or whether conservative repair and timely maintenance is more important. There is no clear answer to this: the most important cultural objects are likely to demand restoration where maintenance has not been continued on a regular basis. However, it is more likely that the question of economics and principles of good management will direct endeavours more towards maintenance and rehabilitation if the cultural built heritage is to be sustained in the future. Much depends on the level of resources that are available to support activities, and in this respect there always seems to be a shortage, whatever the economic resources of a particular country. This may lead policy towards the integrated approach to conservation as advocated by both the Granada and Malta Conventions, a movement away from the attention that has been concentrated on individual buildings and more towards the preservation of living environments that incorporate the cultural heritage.

Sanctions and coercive measures
In all of the countries under examination the legislative provisions for cultural heritage protection (and in some cases through other legislation) provide sanction and coercive procedures which usually combine both administrative and criminal measures.

Administrative procedures include reparation measures, i.e. in the case of the architectural heritage, to reinstate the situation that existed before unauthorized work was carried out (for example, in Belgium, Denmark, Ireland, Malta, The Netherlands and the United Kingdom). In some instances the relevant authorities are permitted to enter premises to undertake necessary repair works. In France, Germany and the United Kingdom the relevant authorities can enter premises through a formal notice system to carry out urgent repair work if this work has not been undertaken. In the case of France half the costs can be recovered, in Germany such action is rarely taken because of the difficulty recovering the costs, and in United Kingdom the full cost can be recovered but the procedure is subject to appeal on such grounds as 'financial hardship'. In Denmark the preferred approach is to use counselling and subsidies or loans to correct the situation.

In the United Kingdom, a Repairs Notice provision can require that a detailed schedule of works be carried out with the ultimate sanction of compulsory purchase if the works are not undertaken within a specified period. Such notices are rarely served, but the threat of this action is often enough to induce the required works. Should expropriation follow there exists the ultimate sanction of a 'minimum compensation order' if deliberate neglect can be proved (in practice this is very difficult). Expropriation provisions have also been highlighted in relation to the Czech Republic, Georgia, Germany (in the case of the state of Thüringia there have, in fact, been no such cases since the new legislation came into force in 1992), Malta and Spain.

Administrative measures can also be taken in relation to the archaeological heritage (for example penalties exist for failing to report 'finds' in France). However, as the legislation in many of the sample of countries is combined (with cultural heritage protection) it is less easy to identify specific measures in this context.

Action to stop damaging activity can be quite effectively pursued (for example, through the assistance of the police in France and The Netherlands, and other provisions in Malta and the United Kingdom).

One problem that exists generally is that the evidence shows the sanction and coercive measures to be ineffective because they are not often applied (for example, in Denmark – although juridical orders are increasingly being served; and France – where the provisions are currently under review). In Georgia there are not enough precedents of prosecutions, although this is not the case in the United Kingdom. Another problem is the low level of fines (Czech Republic) or the fact that the level of fines is not sufficient to act as a deterrent (Germany). In Italy, Ireland, Latvia and the United Kingdom the level of fines have been increased in recent years. The maximum level of fine of IR £1 million that can be applied in Ireland for carrying out 'development' without permission or for not carrying out specified work to 'protected structures' – appears to be a significant deterrent, but the effectiveness of these procedures has not really been tested yet.

Criminal proceedings can extend to imprisonment though it appears that this is a measure of last resort. The maximum period of imprisonment varies between 6 months and 5 years amongst the sample of countries.

Integrated conservation

Integrated conservation is one of the main themes of both the Granada and Malta Conventions. The concept has been important in widening the approach to cultural heritage protection from individual assets to whole areas and environments, which in turn is now being developed in the context of policies for 'sustainable development'.

Within all of the countries under examination there is a degree of integration between heritage protection and management, and land-use planning and associated issues. Today the issues of rehabilitation, and of protecting the concept of 'living environments', has become important since the term sustainable development was coined. Some countries are more advanced in this area. Where integrated approaches are well developed the idea of establishing sustainable approaches to heritage management is being actively pursued. However, for the purposes of this study this issue cannot be explored in depth (see Pickard, 2001). Nevertheless a reflection as to the extent and effectiveness of integrated approaches can be summarized.

- In all the three regions of Belgium there are strong links with planning mechanisms (in Wallonia monument protection is directly incorporated in the spatial, town planning and heritage code). Belgium has not signed the Malta Convention but, for example, in the Brussels-Capital Region there is increased protection of the archaeological heritage through regional and communal development plans. These plans, as well as regional and specific land-use plans, town planning regulations and other planning procedures provide a vehicle for the integrated protection of the architectural heritage. These can cover strategic (regional) and specific policies to preserve and enhance the architectural heritage (including specific provisions on individual and groups of buildings of exceptional quality), policies to guide developers, the safeguarding against damage to the heritage from disuse, as well as other characteristics and elements to be preserved.

- The Czech republic has a long tradition of integrated conservation and land-use planning. Today the state protection authority has a binding opinion when land-use plans are being prepared and approved. And development policy involves (at the local level) programmes for the regeneration of urban conservation sites and zones which are linked to the organization of grant policy. But development pressures are now pointing to the need for measures to be strengthened and action in this respect has included the formulation of plans to define the principles for the protection of cultural heritage items within territories.

- The protection of listed buildings and archaeological monuments is recognized in the general plans implemented by regional and local authorities in Denmark. Focus is also directed at urban landscapes (townscapes), features of towns and buildings 'worthy of preservation' in local plan policies at the municipal level. Further co-operation with local municipal authorities is provided through the SAVE system (developed as part of a commitment to the principles of the Granada Convention) which is increasingly being used as a basis for local preservation plans and linked to supporting financial provisions.

- The Town Planning Code in operation within France provides mechanism for safeguarding the archaeological heritage particularly through the *Plan d'Occupation des Sols* (POS). Government agencies provide information to municipal authorities for sectors to be designated or where permits are to be subject to conditions to safeguard preservation aims. Major infrastructure routes can be re-routed where they may affect archaeological assets. Procedures for environmental assessment and preventative archaeology are less satisfactory – at present cases are considered on the basis that the 'developer pays' which is not entirely effective – but new procedures have been proposed to improve this situation. In relation to the architectural heritage, protection zones or rules incorporated into the ZPPAUP (as an annex to the POS) and *secteurs sauvegardés* ensure an integrated process which is further assisted by spatial development schemes that include measures to safeguard the unprotected heritage. For the latter, economic development policies are geared towards the conservation and rehabilitation of traditional buildings and procedures for designating heritage-based economic growth areas.

- The Georgian authorities are currently in the process of drafting a law on territorial and spatial planning and development control. This aims to fully integrate heritage protection within a code on urban planning, but it will take some time before proposed mechanisms can become fully operational. The proposals include a system of protection zones and planning regimes. These provisions are urgently needed due to the fact that new development pressures have arisen within Georgia.

- In Thüringia (Germany) it is a requirement of law that local authorities, in association with relevant conservation authorities, prepare a 'monument conservation plan' to highlight policy on protection and conservation for town and country planning purposes. Regional policy law, building code plans (at county and local levels) and design statutes all form part of the process for defining conservation policies for monuments and areas. Urban renewal procedures also indicate the means by which the demands of conservation are to be taken into account, for example, through refurbishment objectives to safeguard and integrate monuments. Building inspectors also have powers to outlaw development that does not blend within existing surroundings. The over-riding consideration is for conservation officials to ensure that issues are fully covered in planning objectives. In Thüringia there is a shortage of such staff, though this is not the case in other states within Germany.

- Planning legislation in Ireland does not specifically define matters in relation to the archaeological heritage but the development plan objectives can be defined for this purpose. A Bill, proposed for approval as law in 2000, will make this a mandatory requirement. A similar requirement to define objectives for preserving protected structures of the architectural heritage and for architectural conservation areas was made at the beginning of 2000, and will be followed by guidelines to assist planning authorities in this respect. There has also been a widening of the definition of matters that will require planning permission, for example, work that is deemed to 'materially affect the character' of a protected structure will require consent. These changes have been part of a process of reform aimed at satisfying the requirements of the Granada and Malta Conventions (both of which were ratified in 1997) and have included new financial support regimes and specific provision to create positions for officials to deal with conservation matters.

- Control of development within Italy's historic urban fabric first came under the law in 1942 and through the years since then a series of different plan mechanisms (at different levels) have been created although the process of implementation was slow in the early years. In the late 1960s and 1970s further consideration was given to integrated systems of conservation especially through the definition of zones for urban agglomerations of historic, artistic and environmental value and also through rehabilitation plans. The latter have been used to identify areas under threat in historic centres and to link financial mechanisms to rehabilitation and restoration action. Plan implementation has been swifter since their preparation has been transferred to regional authorities but the process has remained cumbersome. Detailed levels of planning do not appear to have fully safeguarded the heritage, as is evidenced by the fact that the process has suffered from damaging illegal building activities. However, a new law, approved at the end of 1999, aims to improve the co-ordination of cultural and environmental issues, but it will take some time before proposed procedural improvements can be implemented.

- A framework for integrating conservation within the land-use planning system has been introduced in Latvia in recent years as the country has gone through a period of post-independence reform. But the concept of national, regional and detailed plans are still in the process of development. Two important examples of this process are the on-going work to develop a preservation/rehabilitation plan for the UNESCO World Heritage Site of the Historic Centre of Riga, and the development of an integrated process of management for the Abava Valley in the rural context. At present, co-operation between the environmental Ministry and the state preservation authority is assisting the process of integration at a national level. However, much work still needs to be undertaken to ensure effective integration can be implemented at the regional and local levels.

- The Development Planning Act 1992 provided the basis for an integrated policy framework for development control in Malta. This was not specifically directed at conservation goals and a united policy awaits formulation through the introduction of a local level of planning. In the meantime, design guidance policy documents have highlighted issues to be safeguarded including monuments, historic properties and other qualities in the urban context as well as rehabilitation issues. Policy on listed buildings, urban and rural conservation areas and assets of the archaeological heritage have also been highlighted in the structure plan for the Maltese islands. However, the position of underground monuments is less clear in cases where there are redevelopment proposals for certain listed buildings above them, revealing a potential conflict between priorities for different types of heritage assets.

- In The Netherlands, a policy document produced jointly by several Ministries (*Belvedere*) was published in 1999, aimed at improving the integration of conservation within environmental planning, although an integrated approach has been evident for sometime. An obligation to consider cultural history has been made but this new procedure will take some time to implement, particularly in relation to zoning plans (which can take up to 5 years to prepare).

- Different levels of plans are used to control development and preserve heritage assets within Spain. The Special Plan is of particular importance for the maintenance of the urban and architectural structure and the general character of the settings of historical sites, as well as other historical places and archaeological sites. For the latter, the heritage authorities are able to control development work and in some autonomous regions specific protection areas have been created despite the fact that Spain has not yet ratified the Malta Convention. Special Plans may also be used to co-ordinate rehabilitation activities.

- Since the 1960s, the United Kingdom government has emphasized the importance of integrating conservation into the preparation of development plans which may include policies on development control and preservation and enhancement. Planning and conservation is most closely integrated through conservation areas designated by local planning authorities. A joint policy statement made by the government departments responsible for environment and cultural matters (in England and Wales) has further stressed the integrated approach including the safeguarding of historic parks and gardens and other non-statutory heritage sites. Policy mechanisms to deal with the issue of development in areas of archaeological importance (known or perceived) were defined in 1990, prior to the changes recommended by the Malta Convention. Furthermore, an archaeologists' and developers' code of practice has influenced the drafting of a 'European Code of Good Practice' by the Council of Europe (2000a). Planning policy in the United Kingdom is now moving towards defining and implementing sustainable goals and in this respect the immovable heritage has become an important consideration. Identification of assets at risk has assisted the development of management strategies and the prioritising of financial assistance.

The concept of 'integrated conservation' is accepted (in different degrees) in all the sample countries. Significantly many of the countries have recently (in the last decade) implemented or are in the process of implementing or elaborating integrated management tools. Since 1999 new laws have been approved in Italy and Ireland and Georgia is in the process of drafting a series of laws – covering both heritage and planning matters – at the same time. New policies have been approved in the Czech Republic and The Netherlands and further changes are expected to occur in France and Malta, while in Latvia the process of implementation has commenced. The integrated approach is perhaps most developed in Belgium and the United Kingdom where aspects of heritage protection are linked through planning legislation rather than specific cultural heritage legislation.

Financial resources, funding mechanisms and the regeneration of historic environments

The cultural heritage is not a primary target for public funding but the need for support is widely recognized. In some countries the shortage of finance is a particularly acute problem as state budgets are not in a position to provide subsidies and other assistance. Nevertheless, the heritage is an asset that should be maintained for future generations as a sustainable activity as it can provide employment, skills training, and functional benefits and it also reinforces identity and community values. In this context it is not just individual assets that are important – an integrated approach to the management of heritage assets can bring wider benefits to society and the environment.

In relation to the architectural heritage there are three principal methods by which conservation action is supported: subsidies (grants), loans, and fiscal (tax) relief. In some countries one of these methods is the main source of funding, whilst in others different types of support are used either in combination or separately. In most cases financial support is subject to an agreed plan of works for maintenance, repair or restoration work (but not improvements such as the provision of new utilities) and may be subject to public accessibility requirements. Grants can be prioritized according to the quality of the protected item or due to its condition. Moreover, research into the condition and occupation of assets has proved to be a useful basis to assess where support action should be directed (for example, the BAR system in the United Kingdom, and surveys of condition have been used for this purpose in Denmark, Latvia and the Czech Republic). Financial support may also be linked to other activities such as urban renewal programmes and other activities to regenerate historic environments. Private and charitable foundations and trusts may also play an important role in providing financial support.

- In Belgium there are two principal forms of financial assistance: grant subsidies and income tax relief. Grant aid can be for both maintenance and restoration work and the rate of grant can be in the range of 40–90 per cent (and exceptionally 95 per cent in the Walloon Region). Provinces and communes may also contribute to the total grant figure. Income tax relief is given for maintenance and restoration for property that is not commercially let and some other forms of fiscal relief can be provided on sponsorships, cash donations and legacies bequeathed to the regions or foundations.
- Since 1989 the restitution of property to private owners in the Czech Republic has taken the onus of responsibility for many properties out of the public hand, but research has shown that the architectural heritage has inherited a debt from a past lack of maintenance. The main form of assistance is grant aid provided through various supporting programmes for repair, renovation and redevelopment action, for the countryside and for assets under threat, which have been provided since 1996. Some additional support is provided through an exemption from real estate tax for a period of 8 years after a permit for agreed works has been granted.
- In Denmark a combination of methods is used. Grant aid is the main form of support (usually 20–50 per cent) but low interest rate loans (at 2 per cent in 1999) can be provided for substantial work and there is a special system of income tax relief for owners of listed houses. Foundations can also support substantial conservation projects and work to accommodate new uses – this source can be used when there is insufficient finance available from public sources. Other programmes can be used to stimulate action such as urban renewal grants, special housing grants (which can be provided to create work in times of high unemployment) and through schemes operated with municipalities, for instance in association with the SAVE system.
- France provides grant aid for all classified property (30–50 per cent) and those on the 'supplementary' list (15–25 per cent) and income tax relief

on works (the rules vary according to whether the asset is open to the public). Municipal authorities may also provide some grant assistance for other historic properties. Tax incentives can be provided to owners of properties located in *secteur sauvegardés* and ZZAUPs and state funds are provided to subsidize rehabilitation work on old houses located within an OPAH programme. A system of foundations is well established and sponsorship can be provided through 'enterprise foundations' and other non-profit-making foundations.

- At present the Georgian state budget is unable to provide much support although the cultural heritage law has identified provisions to allow for subsidies and tax relief to be provided and a proposed new law on sponsorship and charitable activities is in preparation. The World Bank has provided some support for specific projects.

- In Germany the federal government provides tax relief for work on historic monuments spread over a period of years. Various other national stimulation programmes indirectly support the heritage. Each State has its own system of providing funding and in Thüringia a grant system is operated and there is a village renewal programme. Foundations also play an important role (quasi-public and private, for the latter conservation work is regarded as a non-profit making activity and is tax deductible).

- A new grant system has recently been set up in Ireland to support 'protected structures' (grants are limited to IR £1,500–10,000 and exceptionally up to IR £20,000). There are tax relief provisions for a limited number of properties (270 have benefited so far). Other forms of assistance can benefit heritage assets through urban renewal schemes (via tax incentives) and townscape restoration schemes.

- In Italy the main form of assistance is via income tax relief on conservation work and properties used for cultural purposes are exempt from tax. A lower rate of indirect tax (VAT) is applied to building works on heritage properties (at 10 per cent instead of 20 per cent). There are also limited possibilities for low interest loans. A new provision has allowed the National Lottery to support restoration work on important monuments.

- The state budget in Latvia is only able to provide limited assistance at the present time – estimated to be 10 per cent of that needed – which includes grant awards of up to 50 per cent. Tax easements can be created to provide some fiscal relief where immovable assets are not in commercial or residential use. A 'cultural capital fund' was established in 1998 to accumulate and redistribute funds for cultural activities including conservation and restoration work.

- In Malta grant aid is still at an experimental stage and awards are mostly determined on an *ad hoc* basis at present. There are also possibilities for low interest loans for 'rehabilitation' work and a number of other rehabilitation projects have been set up to concentrate on public buildings, gardens and common public spaces.

- A combination of different methods can be used in The Netherlands. Grants are provided for restoration work (20–70 per cent) and are increasingly being provided for maintenance work. The grant system is dependent upon whether an owner is liable to pay tax as, for example, a foundation cannot deduct costs from tax if it is not liable. Grant aid is most commonly at 20 per cent where tax relief is also claimed but can be 50 per cent where tax relief cannot apply. The National Restoration Fund (a private foundation) operates within this framework as well and can provide loans at a low rate (currently 1 per cent) and it administers budgets allocated to municipalities. Tax relief relates to income tax, corporation tax, wealth tax (applied to rural estates) and conveyance tax (for foundations). Other sources of finance are available from urban renewal grants for the revitalization of the built environment.

- In Spain 1 per cent of the State Administration budget must be used to assist the historic heritage – support can be provided for maintenance, preservation and rehabilitation work. Income tax deductions can be provided for work on protected assets and for donations to defined beneficiaries (for example, the state, the church authority and national foundations). Other forms of fiscal relief are provided with respect to corporation tax and VAT, as well as relief from local taxes. The autonomous regions also provide some assistance.

- In the United Kingdom support is mainly provided through grant aid. Individually important assets are usually supported (grade I and II* listed buildings) (generally 25–40 per cent, but higher amounts can be permitted) and some other listed buildings may receive assistance particularly if they are 'at risk' or located within a conservation area. There has been a reorganization of assistance programmes in recent years particularly due to the creation of the Heritage Lottery Fund which distributes funds from the National Lottery for Townscape Heritage Schemes and good causes. Grants can also be provided via Heritage Economic Regeneration Schemes and via Urban Development Corporations, and other regeneration budgets. There are limited possibilities for tax relief via inheritance tax and relief from VAT for alterations (but not repairs) which has been the subject of critical debate recently. The Architectural Heritage Fund can provide low interest loans to assist building preservation trusts.

There is also a further consideration in relation to the archaeological heritage in terms of who should pay for rescue and preventative archaeology. Increasingly developers and landowners are being asked to contribute to the safeguarding of ancient assets as progress in the form of new activities threatens to cause irreversible damage to this area of the immovable heritage. By example, this approach has operated in Ireland, the United Kingdom and France, but for the latter difficulties with the practice has led to new provisions to tax developers in order to pay for necessary work. Otherwise archaeological investigation is generally paid for by state funds either directly or through agencies.

The role of agencies and specialist organizations

While the protection of the cultural heritage is a matter of national government policy and control, other public agencies may be involved with the management of this activity – either within government departments and ministries or as independent state bodies. The *Duchas* in Ireland, the *Soprintendenze* in Italy, the *National Forest and Nature Agency* in Denmark and state services in the Czech Republic and Latvia are examples of specialized services. In countries where there are federal regions and states, such as Belgium and Germany, the service is based regionally, although in Spain the autonomous regions have a separate function to that of the state role in administering heritage protection.

Specialist organizations of a public or quasi-public nature can have a statutory function such as English Heritage, the Heritage Council in Ireland, the various consultative or advisory institutions in Spain, the *King Baudouin Foundation* (Belgium), the Academies of Science (Georgia, the Czech Republic) and museum authorities in Denmark and Malta.

In Thüringia (Germany) consideration was given to the idea of allowing non-governmental organizations (NGOs) a statutory right to participate, but the idea was not approved when the protection law was passed in 1992. But the six national amenity organizations in England have a statutory right to be consulted on applications proposing the demolition of listed buildings.

Religious authorities and places used for worship may be given specialized consideration in terms of management and control in Belgium, Denmark, Germany and the United Kingdom (in the latter through subscribing to a code of practice that allows some exemptions from normal control procedures). In Georgia consideration is being given to this issue.

Associations of owners and organizations to assist owners are evident in England (Historic Houses Association) and in Denmark and France such organizations play an active role in assisting owners in claiming tax relief (BYFO and VMF). Foundations and sponsorship bodies play an active role in France, Denmark, Germany, Spain and in the United Kingdom charitable bodies can be set up to support heritage assets (for example the National Trust and the many building preservation trusts). For Georgia, the Fund for the Preservation of the Cultural Heritage of Georgia has played an important role with the assistance of the World Bank and new legislation is being proposed to find ways of financially supporting the heritage through charities and sponsorship.

Independent technical support organizations operate in some countries such as *Monumentenwacht* operating in Belgium and The Netherlands (which may be linked to financial assistance programmes) or elsewhere by NGOs which offer technical advice, such as SPAB in the United Kingdom, the Walloon Heritage Institute, and the Irish Georgian Society.

NGOs may also have a significant role to play in promotion and in acting as an independent (and often influential) lobby on heritage matters such as Save Britain's Heritage and the Civic Trust (United Kingdom), Club for Old

Prague and Prague Society (Czech Republic), *Italia Nostra* (Italy). The importance of voluntary and NGO organizations in promoting, lobbying and providing technical and financial support is well recognized in some countries. Further consideration of the role that such organizations can play is to be examined in a conference organized by the Council of Europe and the Norwegian government in Oslo in September 2000. This may help to promote the development of such organizations, particularly in the countries of central and eastern Europe where there is a relative paucity of activity in this context (for example, in Georgia and Latvia).

Education and training

The need to increase the availability of professional and craft education and training is advocated by the Granada and Malta Conventions. It should be endorsed as a sustainable activity – part of the process of sustaining the heritage for future generations. Awareness raising at the earliest level can also help to raise community interest in the protection of the cultural heritage. A community involvement can help to ensure that heritage management involves a democratic process by which the public can have a sense of ownership of their heritage.

It is essential for those involved in the management process to have relevant professional qualifications – especially for architects, archaeologists and other recognized professional disciplines in conservation matters. Likewise, craft skills, particularly for the architectural heritage are equally important. The development of modern technology and new materials has had a dramatic impact on buildings of the cultural heritage over the last century. Many important skills have been lost, particularly in the countries of central and eastern Europe where mass concrete housing reduced the need for specialist craft skills during the period of the totalitarian regime. In all areas of Europe it is now recognized that these skills should be revived.

A brief summary of education and training provision can be provided as follows.

- In Belgium the need to expand specialist training has been recognized particularly in relation to craft skills. The *King Baudouin Foundation*, the Euro-regional Centre for Heritage Crafts and the *Paix-Dieu Centre* managed by the Walloon Heritage Institute have been active in promoting education and training and ensuring high standards.
- There is a well-developed system of education in the Czech Republic at university level (history of art, conservation techniques, philosophy and archaeology) and also in technical schools but not in general education (which is considered a weakness).
- Traditional craft skills have been maintained in Denmark largely through the *Raadvad Centre* and, at a professional level, architects are trained in all aspects of the built environment. The specialist skills of experienced restoration architects are often demanded by the building preservation authorities.

- In France there is a National Heritage School (established in 1990 by the Ministry of Culture). Some architectural schools provide training in conservation but there is one specialist school (the *Chaillot* school, established 1887) which trains qualified architects wishing to work on the architectural and urban heritage. Training is also provided for trade guild members and craft-workers both within the building trades and the *Avignon* school (established in 1983) which was set up to re-master the knowledge and skills needed to work on old buildings. There are also associations of architects specializing in heritage and a National Association of historical monument restoration enterprises (established in 1959).
- In Georgia there is currently a shortage of specialist skills in the field of cultural heritage but technical assistance rendered by other countries and international organizations is helping to develop education and training. There are also a number of state and non-state institutions that have assisted in developing specialist training.
- In Germany there is a relatively good coverage of training institutions including a Centre for Craftsmanship in Conservation, technical colleges and universities – which tend to deal with professional training at post-graduate level. Permission to work on monuments may be dependent upon those overseeing the work having specialist qualifications.
- Training in archaeology is covered at three higher educational institutions in Ireland but there is a shortfall in specialist skills in conservation work for buildings. In 1998 the government implemented action to improve research and development skills and to raise the standard of conservation practice amongst owners, trades and professions including the facilitation of training agencies. Within the construction industry the establishment of specialist conservation contractors is being considered.
- In Italy training at a professional level in conservation and restoration forms a small part of courses in schools of architecture. These are some specialist courses offered at PhD level and in conservation of architectural and environment assets in Venice.
- Latvia has various institutions for training in the field of cultural heritage including a Society of Restorers, Crafts Chamber and the Cultural Academy and university provision, but there remains a distinct shortage heritage of specialists. At school level, heritage issues are taught to raise awareness.
- Specialist training in conservation work in Malta is organized by private institutes in co-operation with the government to provide technical courses. At school level, awareness-raising is pursued through adopting a historic building for educational study.
- Since 1991 there has been an expansion of education provisions at all levels in Spain. Specialist courses are designed for architects (but are not obligatory) and there is encouragement for training in craft skills and the Ministries of Labour and the autonomous regions have set up training courses in heritage skills for unemployed young people.

- At a professional level, architects, surveyors and planners have some training in conservation work in the United Kingdom. There has been an expansion in university level courses in recent years and the various professional bodies for the built environment have been widening their interests in conservation matters. The Conference on Training in Architectural Conservation has been active in promoting training particularly at the craft level. The Institute of Historic Building Conservation (established in 1998) has provided clearer identification of necessary skills in relation to all aspects of the historic built environment (a branch of the Institute was opened in Ireland in 1999). The Historic Building Contractors Group (an association of specialist firms) has also been established. Specialist qualifications to work on conservation projects are not necessary except in the case of churches.

Conclusions

This study has provided a remarkable insight into the different legislative and policy provisions for the protection of the cultural built (or immovable) heritage. Whether or not the Granada and Malta Conventions have been signed or ratified, there are clear indications in this sample of countries of a movement towards the principles that have been set down. Apart from the Czech Republic, Georgia and Latvia, there are many other countries in central and eastern Europe which are in the process of reforming procedures and policies which will take some time to implement. Furthermore, in western Europe there is evidence that similar actions are taking place as evidenced by the *Belvedere* policy in The Netherlands and the recent reform of legislation in Ireland and Italy. A major review of policies relating to the 'historic environment ' will also take also place in the United Kingdom in 2000.

The debate on the protection of the cultural heritage is now moving forward. There will soon be a need to re-examine the articles of the existing conventions particularly due to the fact that policies on sustainable development are now being advocated. The debate on sustainability suggests that a wider analysis of issues than is currently advocated under the concept of integrated conservation is required. Moreover, a draft European Landscape Convention, which aims to address aspects of both the natural and cultural heritage, has been formulated (and may be ready for signature by the end of 2000).

At the present time there remains a need to monitor compliance with the existing conventions and to assist national governments in developing procedures that satisfy their articles. This process should be aided by the Council of Europe's *Herein Project* (the European Information Network on Heritage Policies: http://www.european-heritage.net) which is currently being developed and aims to provide information on heritage policies throughout Europe. The Legislative Support Task Force (operating from the Cultural Heritage Department of the Council of Europe) has also been working in association with the governments and heritage services in Albania, Belarus, Georgia, Latvia, Macedonia, Malta and Slovenia, and has developed guidance in the field of legislative and administrative reform (Council of Europe, 2000). Other international organizations, such as UNESCO and ICOMOS, also have an important role to play in this process.

References

Bell, D. (1997): *Guide To International Conservation Charters*, Technical Advice Note 8, Technical Conservation, Research and Education Division, Historic Scotland.

Council of Europe (1975): *Amsterdam Declaration*: Congress on the European Architectural Heritage, 21–25 October 1975.

Council of Europe (1995): *Core Data Index to Historic Buildings and Monuments of the Architectural Heritage.*

Council of Europe (1999): *Core Data Standard for Archaeological Monuments and Sites.*

Council of Europe (1999a): *Report on the Situation of Urban Archaeology in Europe.*

Council of Europe (2000): *Guidance on the Development of Legislation and Administration Systems in the Field of Cultural Heritage*, Legislative Support Task Force, Technical Co-operation and Consultancy Programme, Cultural Heritage Department.

Council of Europe (2000a): *Archaeology and the Urban Project: A European code of good practice.*

Getty Information Institute/Council of Europe (1998): *Documenting the Cultural Heritage.*

ICOMOS (1964): *International Charter for the Conservation and Restoration of Monuments and Sites* (the Venice Charter).

Morris, W. (1877): *Manifesto* (Society for the Protection of Ancient Buildings), Athenaeum, June 1877.

Pickard, R. D. (ed.) (2001): *Management of Historic Centres*, Conservation of the European Built Heritage Series, Spon Press, London.

Ruskin, J. (1849): *The Seven Lamps of Memory*, 'The Lamp of Memory', XVIII.

Voillet-le-Duc, E. (1866): *Dictionnaire raissonné de l'architecture française,* Vol. VIII, Paris.

Index

1300